# Public Finance in a Democratic Society

## Collected Papers Volume II

By the same author

*The Theory of Public Finance* (McGraw-Hill, 1958)
*Classics in the Theory of Public Finance* (with A.T. Peacock)
(Macmillan, 1958)
*Fiscal Systems* (Yale University Press, 1969)
*Fiscal Reform in Colombia* (with M. Gillis) (Harvard University Press,
1971)
*Public Finance in Theory and Practice* (with P. Musgrave)
(McGraw-Hill, 1973)

# Public Finance in a Democratic Society

## Volume II: Fiscal Doctrine, Growth and Institutions

Collected Papers of
**RICHARD A. MUSGRAVE**
*H. H. Burbank Professor of Political Economy, Emeritus
Harvard University*

**NEW YORK UNIVERSITY PRESS**
Washington Square, New York

First published in 1986 in the U.S.A. by
NEW YORK UNIVERSITY PRESS
Washington Square,
New York, N.Y. 10003

**Library of Congress Cataloging-in-Publication Data**

Musgrave, Richard Abel, 1910–
  Public finance in a democratic society.

  Includes bibliographies and indexes.
  Contents: v. 1. Social goods, taxation, and fiscal
policy — v. 2. Fiscal doctrine, growth, and institutions.
  1. Finance, Public. I. Title.
HJ141.M796     1986      336      85–32053
ISBN 0–8147–5428–7 (v. 1)
ISBN 0–8147–5429–5 (v. 2)

Typeset in Times Roman, 10 point
Printed in Great Britain

# Contents

# Part I
# Fiscal Federalism

# 1  Multi-level Finance<sup>*</sup>
1958

This chapter considers briefly the complications that arise in a federal system where any given individual is a citizen of more than one level of government. The solution depends on what view of federalism we wish to take.

## PURE FEDERALISM

Let us begin with a case where state governments (a term here used for regional units) possess full autonomy. They differ from the central government only in area covered. Whereas the central government covers the entire area of the federation, each state government covers only its respective region.

### Allocation Branch
Each state has a budget serving its allocation branch, as does the central government. To simplify matters, let us assume for the time being that all services are of such a type that they benefit either individuals in all states or individuals in one state only. The central government will then provide services whose benefits accrue to individuals in all states alike; and each state government will cover those services that benefit only the individuals within its particular boundaries.

Now let us assume further that preferences regarding the satisfaction of social wants are similar among all people with the same incomes. Taxpayers with a given income may then be expected to pay the same central tax in whatever state they live. The principle of equal treatment of equals applies to central taxation on a nationwide basis. At the same time, taxpayers with the same income may pay different state taxes, depending on the state in which they live. Not only may average incomes differ between states, but the citizens of different states may choose to provide for different levels or patterns of public services. The principle of equal

---

* From R.A. Musgrave (1958), *The Theory of Public Finance* (New York, McGraw-Hill), pp. 132–3, 179–83.

treatment applies to state taxes among equals within any one state, but it does not apply on a nationwide level. By the same token, the principle of equal treatment of equals does not apply to total (state plus central) taxes on a nationwide level. This is nothing to object to. Indeed, it is as it should be. The very purpose of fiscal federalism, according to this approach, is to permit different groups living in various states to express different preferences for public services; and this, inevitably, leads to differences in the levels of taxation and public services, a feature which is noted further below. The resulting differentiation in tax levels may interfere with the most efficient allocation of resources and location of industries for the region as a whole; but such is the cost of political subdivision, be it on an intranational or international level.

While the general principle is clear, some specific points remain to be noted. First, there is the question of how income that originates in one state and accrues to someone residing in another should be divided between the states. The answer differs for the finance of final and intermediate expenditures of government. Where the finance of final expenditures is concerned, income is properly imputed to the recipient in his state of residence, whether it originates from the outside or not. Where the finance of intermediate expenditures is concerned, income is properly taxable in the state where it originates, since it is here that the benefit is derived. This principle is relatively simple if taxes are assumed to stay put, but it becomes exceedingly complicated once the possibility of tax shifting between the residents of various states is introduced.

Next, there is the question of how any one government should treat taxes paid to another government. In the perfect system, no deduction of taxes from taxable income should be permitted. In the ideal solution to the problem of the allocation branch, taxes must be considered uses of income aimed at the satisfaction of social wants; thus they would be similar in principle to other uses of income for the satisfaction of private wants. There is no more reason, in principle, for deducting taxes than for deducting private outlays. At the same time, it must be recognised that taxes of the allocation branch are determined by voting rules that may leave the minority dissatisfied. Failure to allow deduction of taxes paid to other governments may compound the hardships imposed on minorities and may lead to rates of tax in excess of 100 per cent. In view of this, some allowance may have to be made for taxes paid. The question remains whether the allowance should be at the state or central level, or whether it should be on a mutual basis. For reasons of fiscal discipline at the state level, a good case can be made for limiting deduction to central taxes in computing taxable income for purposes of state taxation; but this is a consideration in fiscal politics rather than in principle. Mutual deduction, moreover, complicates the entire process of budget determination, even though the problem remains determinate at a theoretical level.

Finally, let us drop the assumption that all public services can be divided between those which benefit all citizens of the federation independent of the state in which they live, and those which benefit the citizens of one state only. Allowance must be made for services whose benefits accrue to citizens of states A and B alike but not to citizens of state C; and for services whose benefits accrue in different degrees to citizens of states A, B and C. The former case might be handled by establishing a structure of federations, including combinations between A and B, B and C, and A and C; the latter case may be dealt with in the framework of the overall federation. Even if we retain the assumption that people with equal incomes have similar preferences regarding public wants, this system leads to unequal treatment of equals in the central tax structure, since the quantity of services received becomes a function of the state where the taxpayer resides. For any particular service, the greater the differential in benefit levels among residents of various states, the more the service becomes one that is more properly supplied at the state level.

## Distribution Branch

So much for the problem of the allocation branch. The situation differs for the budgeting of the distribution branch. Let us begin with a system where the distribution branches of the various state budgets apply their distributional adjustments first, and where the central adjustment is applied after the state adjustments have been made. In this case, the central adjustment will be applied to incomes adjusted by the states. As a result, the final distribution will conform with what is considered proper at the central level. The preceding adjustments at the state level will have a bearing on the required patterns of central taxes and transfers, but they will not affect the final result. The opposite holds if we assume that the central adjustment comes first and that state adjustments follow. A situation in which both the state and central governments insist upon their particular patterns of proper distribution as the final result is not feasible: it would lead to a continuous set of adjustments and readjustments without a final equilibrium being reached.

Since one or the other level of government must be given priority, there is much to be said, in the federal system, for permitting this adjustment to be made at the central level. Unless this is done, distributional adjustments at the state level may come to be nullified by interstate movement, and serious barriers to an optimal location of economic activity may be imposed.

## Stabilisation Branch

The function of the stabilisation branch, finally, must be performed largely at the central level. While some degree of coordination may be attained between the levels, the compensatory function must be coordinated for the nation as a whole, and this requires central action. The heart of fiscal federalism thus lies in the proposition that the policies of the allocation branch should be permitted to differ between states, depending on the preferences of their citizens. The objectives of the distribution and stabilisation branches, however, require primary responsibility at the central level.

## Location Effects

There remains to be noted a special problem posed by local finance. It arises where the individual has an option to leave one fiscal community and move to another rather than submit to the majority decision of any particular place. To simplify matters, let us suppose that there are no transportation costs that enter into the choice of location. Let us now assume a situation where all people are in a similar position with regard to income, but some value social wants higher, relative to private wants, than others. In this situation it will be advantageous for people to join up with others who have similar preferences. Where social wants are concerned, a person stands to gain from having a preference pattern similar to that of others. For private wants, the opposite tends to be the case: a person who prefers Florida vacations in August has an advantage over someone else who likes them in January.

Next, let us consider a situation where all people have similar preference for social wants but differ in income. In this case, it will be advantageous for people with high incomes to associate with others with high incomes, while excluding people with low incomes. At the same time, it will be desirable for people with low incomes to enter a community with as high an average income as possible. This principle is reflected in the history of the Poor Laws as well as in the sociology of suburbia. It applies if taxes are proportional and more so if they are progressive.

The choice is less obvious if differences in income are combined with differences in preferences. Moreover, transportation costs and other factors enter into location, and fiscal considerations may be more or less minor. Nevertheless, the possibility of moving to other communities establishes something equivalent to a market mechanism in local finance. The determination of social wants within any one community remains a problem in social wants, but that of choosing among communities becomes a market problem. Thereby a more homogeneous pattern of preferences tends to be established within any one community, and the task of finding a satisfactory solution is simplified.

## QUALIFIED FEDERALISM

We now turn to a qualified and less consistent application of the principle of federalism.

### Horizontal Equity for Total Taxes

It might be held desirable, as a matter of efficiency or equity, to apply the principle of horizontal equity with regard to the total tax bill, including all levels of government. Thus, people in equal positions should pay the same total tax bill in whatever state they live. To accomplish this, the federal tax for a taxpayer living in state A and receiving income Y must consist of a standard amount *minus* that amount by which the state A's tax on income Y exceeds (or *plus* that amount by which state A's tax on income Y falls short of) the average of the state taxes imposed on income Y.

Such a formula would enable a state to vote additional services while assuming only a fraction of the increased cost, since increased state taxes would be offset largely by reduced federal taxes. Fiscal irresponsibility would result. Indeed, this is the case to some degree whenever state taxes may be offset against income subject to central tax. This difficulty is avoided if the principle of equal tax treatment of equals is replaced by a new rule, according to which people with equal incomes should experience the same *fiscal residue* or *net* benefit derived from budget operations [1]. This principle requires that benefits from public services must be imputed to individuals in order to measure the fiscal residue; let us assume that this can be done. Thus the equalising function of the central budget does not induce fiscal irresponsibility. The citizens of different states may provide for varying levels of state services at their cost. If financed by taxes in accordance with benefits, such an arrangement will not affect the fiscal residue that various taxpayers enjoy. Under these conditions, the plan would be more or less similar to that of permitting differentials in the tax structures of the allocation branches for the various states while concentrating distributional adjustments at the federal level.

## Assurance of a Minimum Level of Public Services

The preceding views of fiscal federalism were based on the proposition that the function of the central government allocation branch should be limited to services whose benefits are nationwide; while the state government allocation branch should supply services whose benefits are limited to citizens of the state, which citizens should be free to determine the level of public services. This philosophy of fiscal federalism was essentially one of independent units joined only to accomplish overlapping objectives.

We now turn to an entirely different view, according to which it is the obligation of the federation to see to it that the citizens of each state can enjoy a given minimum level of public services. If any one state is too poor to provide this minimum level, even though a required minimum degree of tax effort is made, the federation steps in. It calls for a transfer from wealthy states where the minimum level of public services is provided while tax rates are below the stipulated minimum level. If, however, the citizens of any one state fall short of the required tax effort, no claim for support can be established. Thus the citizens of wealthy states are assured that transfers will be made only where justified by the basic criteria of fiscal deficiency.

This approach contains an element of regional equalisation of income, since transfers are made from wealthy to poor regions; and it contains an element of provision for the satisfaction of merit wants, since the equalisation refers to minimum standards of social rather than private wants. In as much as the concern is with a minimum level of social wants in general, the appropriate transfer to state budgets is made in a general cash grant.

If the considerations of the two preceding paragraphs are combined, redistributional elements may be attached to a specified grant, as is the case if the matching ratio is rendered a function of state need and fiscal ability.

The problems of fiscal federalism are complicated further if the levels of government are expanded beyond two, if overflows of public services from one state to another are allowed for, and if the possibility of mutual taxation (domestic tariff) is considered. The choice between the various suggested approaches, as well as other patterns, is not a matter of fiscal analysis only. It is basically a matter of how to interpret the nature of the federation, thus involving political no less than economic considerations.

An alternative view of this approach is an interpretation of fiscal federalism as an assurance to each citizen of the federation that specific social wants, such as elementary education, will be provided for adequately in all states. The social wants covered by this proviso may include those on the borderline between nationwide and regional benefit. Or they may include social wants belonging to the state level but recognised as merit wants at the national level. Here we have the rationale for earmarked grants and for matching grants from the central to the state level.

# REFERENCES

[1] Buchanan, J. (1950) 'Federalism and fiscal equity', *American Economic Review*, 40.

# 2 Approaches to A Fiscal Theory of Political Federalism* 1961

The fiscal structure of a federation may be seen as determined by considerations of economic efficiency [Tiebout, 10]. These considerations demanded central provision for services the benefits of which accrue equally throughout the federation, while leaving the supply of other services to various regional units of government. This study is concerned with a quite different approach, where the role of the central fisc is not limited to considerations of efficiency, but set by the very objectives of political federalism. When independent states join in a federation, they may do so to develop a common foreign defence, or establish a customs union, or they may wish to pursue certain objectives which require central government interference in the finances of the member states.[1] It is this interference which is the subject of this chapter.

Central interference in state finances may be based on various objectives. One set of objectives relates the central fisc to the *groups of individuals* comprising the various states. Here the central fisc respects the determination of fiscal policies at the state level, and leaves the individual citizen of the federation at the fiscal mercy of the political process in which he partakes as a citizen of his particular state. However, the central fisc may influence the terms at which public services are provided at the state level. Thus, it may choose to equalise the fiscal operations of the various states, where equalisation may be defined in a number of ways. Or the objective might be to provide incentives to states to raise their service levels. Finally, central policy may wish to assure a minimum level of state services, independent of self-finance by the states.

Another set of objectives relates the central fisc to the *individual citizens* of the federation, whatever the particular state to which they belong. Here the central fisc may try to equalise differentials in the position of federal citizens which arise from their respective citizenships in particular states. Thereby the central fisc attempts to isolate federal citizens from the fiscal consequences of their respective state citizenships. As such, this approach is less federalist and more centralist in spirit than the preceding view, wherein the central fisc deals with the states as political entities.

* *Public Finances: Needs, Sources, and Utilization* (1961) National Bureau of Economic Research, Princeton, N. J., Princeton University Press.

The final choice among these approaches, and among various forms of each, is a matter of political philosophy rather than economics. However, the various plans differ in their economic consequences. My purpose is to explore these differences, especially as they apply to various interpretations of the first approach. The second approach will be considered but briefly.

## PLANS RELATING CENTRAL FISC TO MEMBER STATES OF FEDERATION

Plans involving relationships between the central fisc and the political units of the various states will be considered first. Here it is the purpose of the central fisc to influence the fiscal performance of the various states. The objective may be to bring about various forms of equalisation, be it in actual performance, in fiscal capacity, or in fiscal potential; or the objective may be to induce the states as a group to raise their service levels.

The various plans will be examined as to their distributional results and their incentive or disincentive effects on state services. To make this a meaningful investigation, each case must allow for such central taxes or transfers as may be needed to finance the plan and to clear the central budget. This budget equation appears to have been overlooked in most discussions of such plans and is the crux of our analysis. The following symbols will be used:

$n$ = number of states

$T_i$ = taxes collected by the $i^{th}$ state, in dollars

$S_i$ = subsidy (+ or −) received by the $i^{th}$ state, in dollars

$A_i$ = total dollar outlay by the $i^{th}$ state

$P_i$ = level of performance in the $i^{th}$ state

$N_i$ = index of need in the $i^{th}$ state

$t_i$ = tax rate in the $i^{th}$ state

$t_c$ = tax (+) or subsidy (−) rate of central government, required to clear the central budget

$t_s$ = standard rate

$B_i$ = tax base of $i^{th}$ state

$m$ = minimum outlay per unit of need

$k$ = rate of matching grant

$K$ = lump-sum grant, in dollars

Use of bars indicates averages.

To simplify matters, these rather heroic assumptions are made:

1. There is only one type of state service.
2. Taxes collected by any one state are in fact borne by the citizens of that state. This rules out the possibility of exporting tax burden, or shifting taxes to the citizens of other states.
3. Benefits from expenditures in any one state are limited to citizens of that state. This rules out spillover of benefits.

4. All state expenditures are tax financed. This rules out borrowing.
5. A full-employment income prevails. This rules out problems which arise from cyclical fluctuations.
6. Changes in policy of any one state will not lead to retaliatory measures by other states. This rules out strategy.

These assumptions will be reconsidered briefly later on.

## Pure equalisation plans

*Equalisation of Actual Outlay or Performance*
Plan 1. A first and rather primitive approach to equalisation is one where the central government equalises actual per capita dollar outlays on state services in all states. In other words, it taxes away the above-average revenue from high-revenue states, and pays transfers to meet the deficiency in low-revenue states.

The definitional equation is:

$$A_i = T_i + S_i \qquad\qquad i = 1,2,\ldots,n, \qquad\qquad (1.1)$$

one such equation being given for each of the $n$ states. Since it is the object of central government policy to equalise the outlay $A_i$ in all the states, it must meet the condition:

$$A_i = \frac{\Sigma_i A_i}{n} . \qquad\qquad (1.2)$$

Finally, the central budget must be balanced, so that:

$$\Sigma_i S_i = 0. \qquad\qquad (1.3)$$

This leaves $n + (n - 1) + 1 = 2n$ equations. Given the $T_i$s, all $A_i$s and all $S_i$s can be determined.

The $S_i$s represent a subsidy from the central government if they are positive, and a charge if they are negative.
Obviously,

$$S_i > 0 \text{ if } T_i < \frac{\Sigma_i T_i}{n} = \overline{T}; \text{ also}$$

$$S_i = 0 \text{ if } T_i = \overline{T}; \text{ and}$$

$$S_i < 0 \text{ if } T_i > \overline{T}.$$

The plan results in a redistribution from states whose tax yield exceeds the national average to states whose tax yield falls short of the average.

Summing the $n$ equations under (1.1), solving the system for $S_i$ and taking a partial derivative with respect to an autonomous change in taxation by the state $i,$[2] gives the following:

$$\frac{\partial S_i}{\partial T_i} = \frac{1}{n} - 1. \tag{1.4}$$

The partial derivative is negative, so that an increase in the tax yield of any state getting a subsidy reduces that subsidy, part of the yield being drained off to other states.

Effects of changes in the state's tax yield on its total outlays are obtained by solving for $A_i$ and taking the partial derivative with regard to $T_i$. The result is:

$$\frac{\partial A_i}{\partial T_i} = \frac{1}{n}. \tag{1.5}$$

Since $n$ represents the number of states, $1/n$ is always a fraction. The partial derivative falls short of 1, so that the substitution effect imposes a disincentive to state taxation. State $i$ only retains a fraction of its own yield and the own-cost of state services is increased. If the number of states is large, $1/n$ becomes very small and the benefit to any one state from increased taxation approaches zero. Thus, this system has an extreme disincentive effect on state taxation. All states will reduce their own revenue, and the system may tend towards a zero level of taxation.[3]

Plan 2. Quite apart from its extreme disincentive effects, Plan 1 is unsatisfactory because there is no allowance for differences in the needs of various states. Equal dollar outlays may result in great differences in performance levels; and if public policy is to aim at equalisation of actual levels of some sort, it will be more meaningful to equalise performance levels. This is done in Plan 2.

Two sets of definitional equations apply:

$$A_i = T_i + S_i, \qquad\qquad i = 1,2,\dots,n; \tag{2.1}$$

$$P_i = \frac{T_i + S_i}{N_i} \tag{2.2}$$

where $A_i$, $T_i$ and $S_i$ are defined as before. $P_i$ is the performance level of the state $i$ and equals the ratio of outlays in state $i$ to the index of need for state $i$.[4] The index $N_i$ may be standardised so that:

$$\overline{N} = \frac{\Sigma_i N_i}{n} = 1$$

Thus, a state with an index $N_i = 1$ has needs equal to the average for all states in the country. If $N_i > 1$, the state is needier than the average, and if $N_i < 1$, the state is less needy.

As before, it is assumed that the central government pursues a policy such that its proceeds from and disbursements to the states are balanced, or:

$$\Sigma_i S_i = 0. \tag{2.3}$$

The purpose of these central subsidies and taxes is to equalise performance levels in all states, so that:

$$P_i = \frac{\Sigma_i P_i}{n} \tag{2.4}$$

Considering $T_i$s and $N_i$s as given, there are $n + n + 1 + (n - 1) = 3n$ equations. Thus, all $A_i$s, $S_i$s, and $P_i$s can be determined.

As may be seen from equation (2.7);

$$S_i \gtreqless 0 \quad if \quad P_i \cdot N_i - T_i \gtreqless 0.$$

The redistribution now is from low need–high tax yield to high need–low tax yield states. A state which is average in both respects remains unaffected, as are states which combine proper degrees of excess or deficiency on both counts.

As before, the (2.1) equations can be summed, the system solved for $S_i$, and a partial derivative with regard to $T_i$ taken.[5] The result is:

$$\frac{\partial S_i}{\partial T_i} = \frac{N_i - n}{n}. \tag{2.5}$$

Since $\Sigma_i N_i / n = 1$, the derivative is negative. An increase in the tax yield of any one state always reduces its subsidy, the loss being smaller the larger is the state's need.

In order to determine the effects of changes in a state's tax yield on its total outlays, the system is solved for $A_i$, and a partial derivative with regard to $T_i$ taken to obtain:

$$\frac{\partial A_i}{\partial T_i} = \frac{N_i}{n}. \tag{2.6}$$

Since the partial derivative is a fraction, the substitution effect always imposes a disincentive to state taxation. For the average state, where $N_i = 1$, the disincentive is the same as under Plan 1. It is smaller for more needy states and greater for less needy states. As before, the system tends towards a zero level of taxation.[6]

### Pure equalisation plans

*Equalisation of Differentials in Need and Capacity*

Next, the central fisc may wish to equalise differentials in fiscal capacity, rather than in actual outlays or performance.

Plan 3. The yield or performance level which the states themselves choose to provide is now disregarded and attention focused on their ability to provide for a centrally-set level of performance. The two definitional equations are:

$$A_i = T_i + S_i \qquad\qquad i = 1,2,\ldots,n, \qquad\qquad (3.1)$$

$$S_i = m(N_i - \bar{N}) + t_s(\bar{B} - B_i). \qquad\qquad (3.2)$$

Equation (3.2) defines the subsidy to any one state in two parts. The first is the deficiency in yield, obtained by applying a standard rate in state $i$, as compared to what is obtained by applying it in the average state; and the second part is the excess of expenditure required to give a set performance level $m$, as compared to the amount required in the average state. Each part of the subsidy will equal zero for the group as a whole, so that the central budget will balance. Such is the case at whatever levels $t_s$ and $m$ are set, but it is reasonable to assume that:

$$t_s\bar{B} = m\bar{N} \qquad\qquad (3.3)$$

so that the standard rate provides the required revenue for a state of average base and need. Given $m$ and the values of $T_i$, $N_i$, $B_i$, as well as $\bar{N}$ and $\bar{B}$, the system can be solved for the values of $A_i$, $S_i$, and $t_s$.

Setting $\bar{N} = 1$ as before, and substituting, the result is:

$$S_i = t_s(\bar{B}N_i - B_i). \qquad\qquad (3.4)$$

Redistribution is from low need–high base, to high need–low base states.

This approach may also be looked upon as providing for a block grant, adjusted to need so as to assure an equal level of performance, and financed by a proportional central tax $t_c$. Thus in place of (3.2)

$$S_i = mN_i - t_cB_i \text{ and in place of (3.3)} \qquad\qquad (3.2a)$$

$$m\bar{N} = t_c\bar{B} \text{ can be written,} \qquad\qquad (3.3a)$$

from which an expression similar to (3.4) may be obtained.

Written in either form, the essential feature of this plan is that $t_i$, the state's own tax rate, does not appear. Therefore, the plan has no substitution effect. This is a great advantage as compared to Plan 1 or 2, where the disincentive effect was of prohibitive magnitude. However, Plan 3 still retains the disadvantage that no allowance is made for the state's own tax effort. Thus, state X may be forced to contribute to public services in state Y, even though the residents of Y fail to make even a modest effort to meet their own problems. This, the residents of state X will rightly object to.

## Pure equalisation plans
### Equalisation of Potentials for State Finance
This disadvantage can now be removed and a more sophisticated approach considered, where the function of the central fisc is not to equalise actual

levels or capacities in the various states, but to equalise fiscal potentials. Underlying this approach is a philosophy of fiscal federalism which says that the societies of each state should be permitted to determine their own levels of fiscal activity, but that the central government should equalise the fiscal opportunities of the various states, or the potential levels which they might achieve with their own action.

Plan 4. A first variant of this approach is equalisation of fiscal capacities, in the sense of equalising the tax revenue which various states might obtain by imposing any given rate of tax. To simplify, this rate is here defined as the ratio of state revenue to the tax base of the state. The tax base, in turn, may be defined as private income in the state.[7] Differences in need are disregarded for the time being.

In this plan each state will obtain a subsidy or pay a tax equal to the difference between the revenue which would be obtained if its tax rate was applied to the average tax base, and the revenue which *is* obtained by applying its tax to its own base. If the claims of small-base states exceed the contributions of large-base states, a further central tax is needed to clear the budget, and a further central transfer is required if contributions exceed claims. It is assumed that this central tax or transfer is assessed proportional to state income.[8]

Proceeding as before, two sets of definitional equations arise:

$$A_i = B_i t_i + S_i, \qquad\qquad i = 1,2,\ldots,n, \qquad\qquad (4.1)$$

$$S_i = (\bar{B} + B_i)t_i - B_i t_c, \text{ where } \bar{B} = \frac{\Sigma_i B_i}{n}, \qquad\qquad (4.2)$$

and the condition:

$$\Sigma_i S_i = 0. \qquad\qquad (4.3)$$

Equation (4.1) is similar to that in previous plans. The subsidy as defined by equation (4.2) now consists of two parts. The first part equals the state's own tax rate times the excess of the average tax base over its own tax base; and the second part equals the product of central tax (or transfer) rate times the state's tax base. Either part, and hence the total, may be positive or negative. There are now $2n + 1$ equations, and, given the values of $B_i$ and $t_i$ as parameters, they can be solved for all $A_i$s and $S_i$s, and for $t_c$.

Solving for $t_c$:

$$t_c = \frac{\Sigma_i(\bar{B} - B_i)t_i}{n\bar{B}} \qquad\qquad (4.4)$$

is obtained.

Thus, $t_c \gtreqless 0$, depending on whether $\Sigma_i B_i t_i \gtreqless \bar{B}\Sigma_i t_i$. If tax rates in small-base states are high relative to tax rates in large-base states, $t_c$ is positive, and vice versa.

From equation (4.2) the pattern of redistribution can be determined, as shown in Table 2.1, where + indicates gain, − indicates loss, and 0 indicates no change.

Whatever $t_c$ is, there will be a redistribution from states with larger bases to states with smaller bases. If tax rates in small-base states are high relative to those in large-base states ($t_c > 0$), the gaining group will include states with less than average bases only. If tax rates in large-base states are high relative to those in small-base states ($t_c < 0$), the gainers may include some states with above-average bases.

*Table 2.1  Redistribution between states*

| $B_i$ | $t_c$ | | |
|---|---|---|---|
|  | $> 0$ | $0$ | $< 0$ |
| $< \bar{B}$ | + or − | + | + |
| $= \bar{B}$ | − | 0 | + |
| $> \bar{B}$ | − | − | + or − |

Moreover, it follows from equation (4.2) that, for any given value of $t_c$, states with a base below the average base will be better-off (gain more or lose less) if their own tax rate is high; and that states with a base above the average will be better-off if their tax rate is low. Thus redistribution is primarily among high-rate states.

However, equation (4.2) does not tell what happens to a state if it changes its own tax rate, since resulting effects on the central rate must be allowed for. Solving the system for $S_i$ and taking a partial derivative with regard to $t_i$,[10] the following is obtained:

$$\frac{\partial S_i}{\partial t_i} = (\bar{B} - B_i)\left(1 - \frac{B_i}{n\bar{B}}\right). \tag{4.5}$$

Since $n\bar{B} = \Sigma_i B_i$, the expression $(1 - (B_i)/(n\bar{B}))$ is always a positive fraction, and the partial derivative is positive, zero or negative, depending on whether $B_i \lesseqgtr \bar{B}$. Thus, the state with a less than average base always increases its gains or reduces its losses from the central tax-transfer process by raising its own tax rate; and the opposite holds for a state with a more than average base.

Most important will be the effect of the plan on the total outlays of any state, including finance out of its own revenues and by subsidy. The system is now solved for $A_i$ and a partial derivative with regard to $t_i$ taken. The answer is:

$$\frac{\partial A_i}{\partial t_i} = B_i + (\bar{B} - B_i)\left(1 - \frac{B_i}{n\bar{B}}\right). \tag{4.6}$$

The substitution effect is such as to give an incentive to (reduce the cost of) state services if the second term on the right is positive, and to pose a disincentive to (raise the cost of) state services if it is negative.[11] Since the second term equals $\partial S_i/\partial t_i$ the conclusions are the same as in the preceding paragraph. States with a less than average base are subject to an incentive effect, and states with a more than average base suffer a disincentive effect.

Assuming the income elasticity of demand for public services to be unity in all states, and price elasticity to be equal for all states and to exceed zero, tax rates will be higher in small-base states. As shown by equation (4.4) this means $t_c > 0$. This being the case, equation (4.2) reveals that only states with a base below the average will gain. The losers will include states with an average base, and may include states with less than average base.[12] This suggests that there may be a disincentive effect for the group as a whole, although no definite conclusions can be drawn without introducing behaviour assumptions and assigning weights to various states.[13]

Plan 5. In the preceding plan, the equalisation objective was stated in terms of revenue capacity. This plan considers equalisation in terms of need. The purpose under this plan is to enable all states to obtain the same performance levels per dollar of their own tax revenue collected. Differences in base are completely disregarded. Again a federal tax or subsidy may be needed to clear the budget.

Proceeding as before, the definitional equations are:

$$A_i = B_i t_i + S_i, \qquad\qquad i = 1,2,\ldots,n; \qquad\qquad (5.1)$$
$$S_i = (N_i - \bar{N})t_i B_i - B_i t_c; \qquad\qquad (5.2)$$

and the usual condition

$$\Sigma_i S_i = 0. \qquad\qquad (5.3)$$

Given the $n$ values of $B_i$, $\bar{B}$, and the parameters $t_i$, the $2n + 1$ equation permits the determination of $n$ values of $A_i$ and $S_i$, as well as $t_c$. Equations (5.1) and (5.3) are the same as before. According to (5.2) the subsidy again consists of two parts. The first part adjusts the state's own tax yield so as to provide average performance per dollar of self-financed outlay; and the second again reflects the state's participation in the central tax or transfer such as may be needed to clear the central budget.

Solving for $t_c$,[14] the following equation is obtained:

$$t_c = \frac{\Sigma_i(N_i - \bar{N})t_i B_i}{n\bar{B}}. \qquad\qquad (5.4)$$

Thus, $t_c \gtreqless 0$, depending on whether $\Sigma_i(N_i - \bar{N})t_i B_i \gtreqless 0$. The central rate, $t_c$, will be positive if the yield of state taxes or $t_i B_i$ is large (be it due to high rates and/or large bases) in high-need states relative to the yield in low-need states, and $t_c$ will be negative if the opposite holds.

*Table 2.2 Redistribution between states*

| $N_i$ | $t_c$ | | |
|---|---|---|---|
| | $> 0$ | $0$ | $< 0$ |
| $< \bar{N}$ | $-$ | $-$ | $+$ or $-$ |
| $= \bar{N}$ | $-$ | $0$ | $+$ |
| $> \bar{N}$ | $+$ or $-$ | $+$ | $+$ |

From equation (5.2) the pattern of redistribution may again be determined, as shown in Table 2.2.

Whatever $t_c$, there will be a distribution to more needy from less needy states. If state tax yields are relatively high in high-need states ($t_c > 0$), the gaining group will include states with more than average need only. If yields are relatively high in low-need states ($t_c < 0$), the gaining group will include some states with less than average need.

Also, it follows from equation (5.2) that, for any given value of $t_c$, states that are subject to a more than average need will be better off if their tax rate is high, while states with less than average need will be better off if their tax rates are low. Redistribution will be again primarily among high rate states.

In order to determine the effects on a state's position which result from changes in its tax rate, resulting changes in $t_c$ must be allowed for. Solving the system for $S_i$ and taking a partial derivative with regard to $t_i$[15] gives this equation:

$$\frac{\partial S_i}{\partial t_i} = (N_i - \bar{N})\left(1 - \frac{B_i}{n\bar{B}}\right)B_i. \tag{5.5}$$

Since $B_i/n\bar{B}$ is always a fraction, the derivative will be positive, zero or negative depending on whether $N_i \gtreqless \bar{N}$. The state with a more than average need always increases its gain (or reduces its loss) by raising its own tax rate, whereas the state with less than average need reduces its loss (or raises its gain) by reducing its tax rate.

Turning again to the effects of changes in a state's tax rate on its total outlays, the system is solved for $A_i$ and a partial derivative taken with regard to $t_i$. The result is:

$$\frac{\partial A_i}{\partial t_i} = B_i + (N_i - \bar{N})\left(1 - \frac{\bar{B}_i}{n\bar{B}}\right)B_i. \tag{5.6}$$

The substitution effect is such as to give an incentive to (or reduce the cost of) state services if the second term on the right side is positive, and to result in disincentive if the term is negative. Since the second term equals

$\partial S_i/\partial t_i$, the conclusions are again similar to those of the preceding paragraph. States with more than average need are subject to an incentive effect, while those with less than average need are subject to a disincentive effect.

In the absence of incentive or disincentive effects, there is reason to expect that tax yields in high-need states will be high relative to those of low-need states.[16] This finding is reinforced by the incentive and disincentive effects of the plan. Therefore, equation (5.4) tells that $t_c$ will tend to be positive, and equation (5.2) permits the conclusion that only states with more than average need will gain. The losers will include states with less than average and states with average need, and may also include some states with more than average need. Again it appears that there may be a disincentive effect for all states as a whole, but it must again be noted that no definite conclusions can be drawn without introducing behavioural assumptions and assigning weights to various states.[17]

Plan 6. While Plan 4 neglected differences in need, Plan 5 neglected differences in fiscal capacity. Plan 6 is a more nearly perfect equalisation scheme where both sets of differences are allowed for. In this plan, performance per effort unit, as measured by the state's own tax rate is equalised. The definitional equations are:

$$A_i = B_i t_i + S_i, \qquad\qquad i = 1,2,\ldots,n; \qquad\qquad (6.1)$$

$$S_i = (\bar{B} - B_i)t_i + (N_i - \bar{N})\bar{B}_{ti} - B_i t_c. \qquad\qquad (6.2)$$

It will be noted that equation (6.2) is similar to (4.2) in the treatment of differences in tax base, but differs from (5.2) in the treatment of differences in need. In the present case, the correction for need is applied to the yield from the equalised base, whereas in Plan 4 (with capacity differences disregarded) it was applied to actual yield. The more refined treatment of (6.2) is in keeping with Plan 6 which is designed to make full allowance for both capacity and need differentials.

As before, the condition of clearance in the central budget is:

$$\Sigma_i S_i = 0. \qquad\qquad (6.3)$$

Given the $n$ values of $B_i$, $N_i$, and the $n$ parameters $t_i$, the $n$ values of $A_i$ and $S_i$, as well as $t_c$, may be determined.

Solving for $t_c$, the following equation results:

$$t_c = \frac{\Sigma_i(\bar{B} - B_i)t_i + \bar{B}\Sigma_i(N_i - \bar{N})t_i}{n\bar{B}} . \qquad\qquad (6.4)$$

Thus, $t_c$ tends to be positive if tax rates are high in small-base and high-need states relative to those in large-base and low-need states; and $t_c$ tends to be negative if the opposite holds. However, it will be noted from

(6.4) that need differentials are now weighted, reflecting application of the need correction to the average tax base in (6.2).

Turning now to the pattern of redistribution, equation (6.2) is considered. The results which may be derived from inspection of that equation are summarised in Table 2.3.

The tendency is for a redistribution from low need–large base states to high need–small base states. For any given level of $t_c$, a high rate of state tax will increase gains for winning states and losses for losing states, provided that low bases are paired with large needs, and vice versa. If these characteristics are crossed, the opposite result may prevail. The earlier conclusion, that redistribution is primarily among high-rate states, need not apply here.

Proceeding as before, the system may be solved for $S_i$ and a partial derivative taken with regard to $t_i$. The result:

$$\frac{\partial S_i}{\partial t_i} = \left(1 - \frac{B_i}{n\bar{B}}\right)[(\bar{B} - B_i) + (N_i - \bar{N})\bar{B}].$$ (6.5)

Since $B_i/n\bar{B}$ is a fraction, the sign of the partial derivative now depends on $B_i$ and $N_i$, as given in Table 2.4. An increase in the state's tax rate tends to increase the gain or reduce the loss for the high need–small base states, and to reduce to gain for low need–large base states.

The gain in state outlays to be obtained by raising the state tax is now given by:

$$\frac{\partial A_i}{\partial t_i} = B_i + \left(1 - \frac{B_i}{n\bar{B}}\right)[(\bar{B} - B_i) + (N_i - \bar{N})\bar{B}].$$ (6.6)

The second term on the right equals $\partial S_i/\partial t_i$, so that the results of Table 2.4 will again apply. The substitution effect is such as to provide an incentive to state taxation for small-base, high-need states; and a disincentive for large-base, low-need states. If state tax rates can be expected to be higher in the former group, the central tax rate (as shown by equation (6.4)) will

Table 2.3 *Redistribution between states*

| $N_i$ | $t_c > 0$ | | | $t_c = 0$ | | | $t_c < 0$ | | |
|---|---|---|---|---|---|---|---|---|---|
| | $B_i$ | | | $B_i$ | | | $B_i$ | | |
| | $< \bar{B}$ | $= \bar{B}$ | $> \bar{B}$ | $< \bar{B}$ | $= \bar{B}$ | $> \bar{B}$ | $< \bar{B}$ | $= B$ | $> \bar{B}$ |
| $< \bar{N}$ | + or − | − | − | + or − | − | − | + or − | + or − | + or − |
| $= \bar{N}$ | + or − | − | − | + | 0 | − | + | + | + or − |
| $> \bar{N}$ | + or − | + or − | + or − | + | + | + or − | + | + | + or − |

*Table 2.4 Relation between state tax rate and subsidy*

$$\left(sign\ of\ \frac{\partial S_i}{\partial t_i}\right)$$

| $N_i$ | $B_i$ | | |
|---|---|---|---|
| | $> \bar{B}$ | $= \bar{B}$ | $< \bar{B}$ |
| $< \bar{N}$ | $-$ | $-$ | $+$ or $-$ |
| $= \bar{N}$ | $-$ | $0$ | $+$ |
| $> \bar{N}$ | $+$ or $-$ | $+$ | $+$ |

be positive and the redistribution pattern will be as shown in the left section of Table 2.3. No definite statement can be made regarding the net effect of the plan on aggregate yield of state taxes in all states, but the earlier comments in connection with Plans 4 and 5 suggest that the overall level of service may well be reduced.

Plan 6 is superior to Plan 3 in that the degree of benefit received by low-capacity, high-need states is made to depend on their own tax effort. This removes the serious defect inherent in Plan 3 that receiving states may enjoy a free ride while the contributing states are held responsible for their lack of tax effort. At the same time, is not Plan 6 inferior to Plan 3 in that it reintroduces substitution effects? I do not think so. Since it is the very objective of Plan 6 to equalise the tax effort (rate level) required to obtain any given level of performance, the resulting incentive or disincentive effects are not to be looked upon as undesirable side-effects of the plan, such as is the case with Plan 2. Rather, the resulting changes in the relative cost of public services reflect the central objective of the plan, which is to equalise the relationship between tax effort and performance.

### Pure incentive plans

The preceding plans were concerned primarily with matters of equalisation. While these plans may raise or lower the total level of state outlays in the process, these changes in overall level were incidental by-products of the main objective of equalisation. Here is a different set of plans where the objective is to give an incentive, by way of matching grants, to all states to *raise* their tax and service levels. Such plans may have redistributional results (with regard to fiscal capacity and/or need) but these now become incidental.

Plan 7. A pure incentive plan is illustrated by a system of matching grants, where the central fisc matches all state revenues or outlays at a uniform rate. The system is given by the definitional equations:

$$A_i = B_i t_i + S_i, \qquad\qquad i = 1,2,\ldots,n; \qquad\qquad (7.1)$$

$$S_i = k t_i B_i - t_c B_i; \qquad\qquad (7.2)$$

and the usual condition

$$\Sigma_i S_i = 0. \qquad\qquad (7.3)$$

Given $k$ and $n$ values of $B_i$, as well as the $n$ parameters $t_i$, there are $2n + 1$ equations with which to determine $n$ values of $A_i$ and $S_i$, and the value of $t_c$.

The central tax now equals:

$$t_c = \frac{k\Sigma_i t_i B_i}{n\bar{B}} \qquad\qquad (7.4)$$

which is always positive. As may be seen from equation (7.2),

$$S_i \gtreqqless 0, \text{ depending on whether } t_i \gtreqqless \frac{t_c}{k}.$$

There will be a redistribution from states with low tax rates to states with high tax rates. A large base means a higher gain to the winner and a higher loss to the loser, redistribution now being centred among the large-base states.

Solving the system for $S_i$ and differentiating with respect to $t_i$, the following is obtained:

$$\frac{\partial S_i}{\partial t_i} = kB_i\left(1 - \frac{B_i}{n\bar{B}}\right). \qquad\qquad (7.5)$$

A state may always increase its subsidy by raising its tax rate. The resulting gain will be the greater the larger is the state's tax base, and the smaller is its share in the aggregate base for all states.

Solving for $A_i$, and differentiating with respect to $t_i$, the result is:

$$\frac{\partial A_i}{\partial t_i} = B_i + kB_i\left(1 - \frac{B_i}{n\bar{B}}\right). \qquad\qquad (7.6)$$

Since the second term on the right, equal to $\partial S_i/\partial t_i$, is positive, the substitution effect offers an incentive to all states to increase their tax rates. The cost of state services is reduced for all states, but especially for states with a large base. The plan is likely to raise the aggregate level of state services, but again we cannot be quite sure of the overall result.[18]

**Evaluation**

Additional forms might be developed, combining the characteristics of the various plans. Block grants of the Plan 3 type may be made subject to a minimum-effort requirement. The equalisation of fiscal potential of the Plans 4 to 6 type may be combined with incentive factors of the matching grant type. And the incentive or matching grant approach of Plan 7 may be tempered by allowing for equalisation features.[19] In all cases where a central tax is needed, this tax may be rendered progressive in terms of $B_i$, and so forth. There is no end to possible combinations, but the above sets will suffice to show the nature of the problem.

Final choice among these plans is a matter of political philosophy as well as economics. However, some plans are more sensible in objective than others, and some have less disturbing secondary results. Thus, Plan 2 is more sensible than Plan 1, if equalisation of actual budgets is to be achieved. Both Plans 1 and 2 are untenable, however, as they have violent disincentive effects and tend to a zero level of state services. If there is to be equalisation of actual performance, central finance has to be substituted for state finance. A high degree of absolute equalisation is not compatible with a workable system of fiscal federalism.

Equalisation of capacity to meet a centrally set level of performance, as described in Plan 3, renders any one state's position in the scheme (its own gains or losses) independent of its own tax rate. The disincentive effect on state taxation disappears, but there remains the disadvantage that some states are called upon to contribute to the services of others which, while needy, refuse to make an adequate effort of their own. This remains a serious detriment to the establishment of an orderly system of fiscal federalism.

Equalisation of potentials, as provided by Plans 4 and 6, does not give rise to this objection. A state now receives support only to the extent that it qualifies by its own tax effort; and other states will contribute more if they themselves value public services more highly. Incentive or disincentive effects again result. They differ for various types of states, and the overall level of state services may now be affected in either direction. Substitution effects are less severe than under Plan 2, and they differ in nature. Substitution effects are now an essential part of the approach, designed to equalise the tax effort required to reach various levels of performance. Equalisation of potentials may thus be accomplished within an orderly system of fiscal federalism, and among the various plans here described, Plan 6 is my favourite. It offers the most comprehensive approach to equalisation. By leaving the level of state services to their own determination, it also appears to be most compatible with the spirit of fiscal federalism.

Incentive schemes such as Plan 7 are designed to raise the overall level of state services. The distributional results of the plan are incidental and tend to contradict equalisation objectives as usually conceived. However, these results may be neutralised by rendering the central tax progressive, or, as noted before, equalisation and incentive objectives may be combined.

## Review of assumptions

It remains to review the assumptions listed at the beginning of this discussion.

1. Allowance for various categories of state services complicates matters but does not change the principle involved. A state may now have different indices of need for various services. Equalisation plans may be applied to taxes for (or outlays on) particular services only, or a generalised equalisation plan may be based on a composite index of need. Incentive plans may now involve different matching rates for different types of services, so that the losses or gains for any one state come to depend on its budget pattern.

2. If taxes collected by any state may be shifted to residents of other states, the simplicity of the argument breaks down. However, the case may be salvaged, provided that the fraction of a state's taxes the burden of which actually falls within the state can be determined.[20] Only this fraction can be taken as an index of tax effort within the state. In the absence of a matching spillover of benefits, state taxes which are exported constitute an anarchic element in a system of fiscal federalism.[21]

3. If spillover effects are allowed for, an efficient fiscal system permits the state to tax outside its jurisdiction, be it directly, or by appropriate shifting of tax burdens to outside residents. Where this cannot be handled on the state level, a central tax-transfer system may serve to neutralise spillovers. However, such a system does not provide for redistribution or equalisation. On the contrary, it serves to prevent regional redistribution, and bears no relation to the problems here considered.

4. Introduction of loan finance breaks the equality between tax yield and amount spent, but this does not matter. In the long run at least, there is no reason why the revenue effort might not be measured in terms of 'own' finance, be it in taxes or loans.

5. By assuming full employment and price-level stability the problem of stabilisation policy has been eliminated. Substitution of $B_i^f$ and $\bar{B}^f$ (where superscript $f$ stands for full employment) for $B_i$ and $B$, permits insertion of a stabilisation feature into the discussion; and it may be desirable also, in this context, to substitute a term $t_s$ (statutory tax rate) for our term $t_i$. Lest there remain a mere regional equalisation of cyclical differentials, a spreading of income losses and gains over the cycle, it will be necessary in this case to drop the requirement that the central budget should be cleared and to introduce deficit and surplus finance.

6. Finally, it has been assumed that changes in the tax rate by any one state will not affect tax rates imposed by other states. In reality this may not be the case, and considerations of strategy may become important in the tax policy of large states. This must be allowed for when the stability of the various plans is considered.

## Empirical application

These various equalisation plans, or variants thereof, might be applied to available fiscal data in order to determine the resulting values of $t_c$ and patterns of redistribution between the 50 states in the United States. This may be done either with regard to total state finances, or various segments thereof such as education finance. Time did not permit the undertaking of such applications, but they are quite possible. While the definition of appropriate indices of fiscal capacity and need is troublesome, it can be handled [Mushkin, 7]. Also, the various plans here outlined may be compared with recommendations of the Royal Commission on Dominion–Provincial Relations [8] and with actual practices in such countries as Australia, Germany and Switzerland, where fairly refined methods of fiscal equalisation are used.

As far as such applications are concerned, the preceding models of central interference in state finance are quite operational. However, the discussion left open the question of just how various states would react to changes in their fiscal resources and to changes in the own-cost of public services, and what would happen to the total level of state services as a result. In order to permit conclusions in this respect, the models must be supplemented by behavioural assumptions, but unhappily little empirical data are available on which such assumptions may be based.

## PLANS RELATING CENTRAL FISC TO INDIVIDUAL CITIZENS OF FEDERATION

The philosophy of fiscal federalism underlying the preceding plans was that all states of the federation should be placed in a more or less equal fiscal position, be it in the sense of service levels, capacities or potentials, and that all states should be induced to raise their services. Beyond this, there was no attempt to equalise the gains which *individual* citizens of the federation may derive from state fiscal activities. Rather, the individual is left to the mercy of the political decisions arrived at in their particular states. By its very nature, this approach required transactions between the central and the state fiscs.

There is a second and quite different philosophy of fiscal federalism. Here, the idea is that the central fisc should neutralise the individual citizen of the federation against the fiscal operations of the particular state in which he resides. This requires direct transactions between the central fisc and the individual citizens of the federation. For this reason it seems more centralist in spirit, but this need not render it necessarily inferior or superior. The choice, as noted before, remains one of political philosophy and social preference.

No attempt will be made to explore this second approach in detail, but a brief discussion is needed, if only to place the first approach in its proper perspective. It is necessary to distinguish between (1) objectives relating to problems of 'horizontal equity' or the principal that equals should be treated equally, (2) objectives relating to 'vertical equity' or the requirement of differential treatment of unequals, and (3) efficiency objectives.

## Equity objectives
*Horizontal Equity*

It is assumed that the fiscs for each state meet the requirement of horizontal equity among their own citizens, and that the same holds for the operations of the central fisc in providing federation-wide services. As a result, horizontal equity is assured for citizens of state X in so far as the combined state X and central fiscs are concerned, and the same holds for citizens of state Y and other states. However, the same need not hold as between citizens of states X and Y. While their positions are the same under the central fisc, the position of equals may differ with regard to their respective state fiscs. Hence their positions may differ with regard to the total (combined state and central) fisc.

J. M. Buchanan, in his pioneering paper [1,2], has suggested that it should be the function of the central fisc to eliminate such differences, so that all citizens of the federation who are otherwise equal will be treated equally under the total fisc, no matter what state they live in. Buchanan argues that this objective has a certain claim for priority because: (1) it is more sensible to consider relationships of the central fisc to individuals, rather than to the states 'as such'; (2) as a matter of equity, the requirement of horizontal equity is more meaningful than is that of vertical equity; and (3) the scheme tends to neutralise distorting effects on resource allocation which result from differences in the fiscal activities of states. Leaving (3) for later consideration, I should note that to me neither (1) nor (2) is convincing.[22] However this may be, the matter of priority need not be debated here. For present purposes, it is quite sufficient to recognise Buchanan's interesting case as one among possible objectives.

Suppose first that the requirement of horizontal equity is applied with regard to taxation only. Assuming tax structures in all states to be proportional, an opposite of Plan 1 could be applied, except that the subsidy now would go to each individual citizen rather than to his state. Redistribution is from low-rate to high-rate states, and severe incentive effects result with regard to the level of state taxes. If the tax structures of states are progressive by varying degrees, a more complex pattern of interstate redistribution results. However this may be, there is still a strong disincentive effect.

This difficulty is avoided by Buchanan's proposal to reinterpret the requirement of horizontal equity in terms of equality of fiscal residue, defined as expenditure benefits minus tax payments. Given the crucial assumption that benefits from state expenditures are equal for all citizens of the state, Buchanan can easily compute the fiscal residue for taxpayers at various points in the income scale. In a state which relies only on poll tax finance, the fiscal residue equals zero for all residents, regardless of income. For any tax structure less regressive than a poll tax, the residue falls from a positive to a negative level when moving up the income scale. As states do not use poll tax finance and the tax structures and service levels of various states differ, individuals with equal incomes but living in different states are left with different fiscal residues. A central tax-transfer plan is devised to equalise them.

A comparison may be drawn between state X with a high, and state Y with a low, per capita income. We assume that both pay a proportionate tax. If the rate is the same in both states, an individual with a given income would have a higher fiscal residue if living in X than if living in Y. This follows because he pays the same tax in both cases but receives more benefits if residing in X. Similarly, the residents of X will be better-off than their counterparts in Y if the same total revenue is collected in both states, since now a person with a given income pays less tax if living in X while receiving the same benefits. In both these cases in which the residents in X are better-off, the central equalisation scheme will favour the residents of Y. The same conclusion applies to the in-between cases, where the tax rate in X is lower than in Y while total revenue in X is still higher. No simple rule can be set down, however, for situations where total revenue in X is less than in Y, or where the tax rate in X exceeds that in Y. In these cases the outcome depends on the relative levels of tax rate as well as per capita incomes.

It should be noted that these particular results, as well as Buchanan's illustrations, are based on the assumption that expenditure benefits may be distributed on a per capita basis. If we assume instead that benefits are proportional to income, the result changes. In a state with a proportional tax structure the fiscal residue is now zero at all income levels, and the principle of equal treatment of equals now holds as between the residents of all states which have proportional tax structures, whatever their service levels. While this does not change the formal nature of Buchanan's argument, it indicates that the specific results will depend entirely on one's assumptions regarding the distribution of benefits. While the redefinition of horizontal equity in terms of fiscal residue is an interesting and sensible idea, its implementation is exceedingly difficult.

This leads me to a more basic point. If state taxes, imposed to finance public services, are allocated on a benefit basis, all citizens of the federation will be taxed on a benefit basis by their respective states. In this case, no central equalisation is needed since the requirement of horizontal equity is met by the very condition of universal taxation according to benefits received.[23] Differences in treatment can arise only out of tax-transfer schemes, imposed by states to implement their particular notions as to what constitutes the socially desirable state of distribution.

*Vertical Equity*

The problem, in this case, becomes one of desired central interference into income redistribution policies of the states. Let us suppose that both central and state fiscs have distributional objectives. If the state adjustment is made first (where state taxes and transfers apply to income before central tax) and the central adjustment comes second (where central taxes and transfers apply to income after state taxes), the state adjustment will not affect the end-result, but only determine the particular pattern of federal taxes and transfers. If the central adjustment comes first, the state pattern is the one which finally prevails in each state. If both levels insist on their pattern as the final goal, an unstable situation results.

Since one level must be given priority, there is much to be said for making this adjustment at the central level. Looking at the matter in a normative way, it is clear that state taxes will then be based properly on income minus those central taxes or plus those central transfers which reflect distributional adjustments by the central fisc. Central taxes raised to provide for central services will not be allowed in deducting for purposes of state taxation, as they may be considered use of income. Central taxes in turn would be assessed on total income, without allowance for state taxes to provide state services.

## Efficiency objectives

In the preceding discussion, the Buchanan plan was looked upon as a formula for horizontal equity. Alternatively, it may be considered a design to neutralise distorting effects on location which result from differentials between the fiscal operations of various states.

Let it be assumed that, in the absence of differentials among state fiscs, market forces lead to an optimal location of economic activity in the private sector. Now fiscal differentials are introduced between the states, and the pattern of location changes. Buchanan suggests that such changes could be avoided if fiscal residues were neutralised. Following the preceding argument, it is again concluded that such differences would not arise, and that locational distortions would be avoided, if all state taxes were imposed on a benefit basis, even though at different levels. Differences in net residue would remain only if various states pursued different distribution policies, in which case the appropriate adjustment would be to let the central plan for distribution dominate.

All this is a much too simplified view of the problem. For one thing, there is again the question of just how the benefits are distributed among individual residents. For another, there are a host of difficulties which arise from inter-state commerce and the structure of the corporation. Even if it is assumed that all tax revenue is obtained from personal income tax, benefit taxation or equalisation of net residue at the personal level neutralises the location of firms only if management is identified completely with the owner, which is surely an unrealistic assumption. Moreover, certain benefits accrue to business firms rather than to individuals, and many state and local taxes are (and for benefit purposes must be) levied on the firm rather than the owner. This poses difficult problems of inter-regional shifting of benefits and burdens, all of which complicate benefit taxation by regional units, as well as inter-regional equalisation of net residues. Certain gains in efficiency may be derived by appropriate regional dispersion of the fiscal system. At the same time, the mechanism of decentralisation is apt to be imperfect. It will tend to introduce un-neutralities and, by narrowing the 'common market', add new in-efficiencies. Not only may location of industry be interfered with by differential fiscal policies, but also the threat of capital flight to low-tax (or, rather, high net residue) states may prevent a proper allocation of resources between the satisfaction of public and of private wants.

Apart from all this, there remains the question of how efficiency in location is affected by various plans for equalisation between states, such as were discussed in the first section of this chapter [Buchanan, 3; Scott, 9]. By increasing the economic capacity of poor regions, the outflow of resources is checked, and this may interfere with speedy transition to more efficient location. At the same time, mobility may be limited to begin with, and appropriate plans for regional equalisation may aid rather than hinder efficiency for the country as a whole.


# ADDENDUM*

If I understand Professor Buchanan's comments on this chapter [4] correctly, he now proposes a double standard. As far as *equity considerations* are concerned, he agrees with me that adherence to benefit taxation by states equalises net residues, thus rendering central interference un-necessary. This assumes the usual interpretation of benefit taxation as equating the marginal utility of tax and private outlays for any one taxpayer. However, Professor Buchanan suggests that such a policy would not to the job of neutralising the *allocation effects* of state fiscs. In order to accomplish this, so he argues, there would have to be equalisation of total net benefits (including consumer surplus) as between taxpayers. Thus, equity and efficiency considerations require different standards and are, in fact, incompatible.

Suppose that citizen x obtains a greater total net gain from his transactions with the fisc in X land than does y in Y land, both x and y having equal tastes and incomes. This will be the case where the cost share for x in public services will be smaller if he resides in X land than if he resides in Y land because (1) the tastes of other residents place a higher preference on public services in X land than in Y land or (2) average income is higher in X land than in Y land. Depending on the importance of these factors relative to the weight of other locational considerations, fiscal factors may have a significant effect on x's choice of location. Such will be the case even though the tax structure in both X and Y adheres to benefit taxation in the marginal sense.

However, I am not at all certain that such influences on the location of X should be classified as 'distorting' the regional allocation of resources. Rather it appears that they constitute a given datum for location, just as does the geographical distribution of natural resource deposits. The fact

---

* Rejoinder to comments by James Buchanan.

that the benefit incidence of public services is spatially limited, and that this has a bearing on how people wish to group themselves, is part of the economic map which determines resource allocation. Efficiency is not served by erasing this feature of the map. Indeed, a central policy aimed at nullifying resulting differentials (such as remain with universal benefit taxation) in state finance will interfere with efficiency in the regional structuring of public finances.

## NOTES

1. The terms 'central' and 'state' are used here in a generic sense of reflecting higher and lower levels of government.
2. Summing (1.1) gives $\Sigma_i A_i = \Sigma_i T_i + \Sigma_i S_i$, and substituting from (1.3) gives $\Sigma_i A_i = \Sigma_i T_i$, or $n\bar{A} = \Sigma_i T_i$, or $\bar{A} = \Sigma_i T_i / n$. Since by (1.2) it is known that $A_i = \bar{A}$, this can be substituted in (1.1) to obtain $S_i = \Sigma_i T_i / n - T_i$, from which (1.4) follows.
3. In addition to this substitution effect, gaining states may increase their taxation due to income effect, while losing states may reduce theirs, but these effects will tend to cancel out on balance.
4. If public services are in the form of education, $N$ may be an index of school-age children. In the case of highways it may be an index of traffic needs, e.g. dispersion of population and so forth. Construction of appropriate indices for all services creates difficult though not insurmountable problems.
5. From equation (2.2) comes $P_i N_i = T_i + S_i$. Summing and substituting from (2.3) gives $\Sigma_i P_i N_i = \Sigma_i T_i$, or $P_i = \Sigma_i T_i / n$. Substituting into (2.2), we get $S_i = \Sigma_i T_i N_i / n - T_i$, from which (2.5) follows.
6. With regard to income effects, the same observations apply as to Plan 1.
7. The question whether property as well as income should be allowed for in measuring the tax base is not here entered into. For the present purposes, the simple definition of the tax base in terms of income will do.
8. If allocation is on a progressive basis, the redistributional effects of the plan between small and large base states is accentuated.
9. Equation (4.2) is summed, set equal to zero according to (4.3), and solved for $t_c$.
10. The value of $t_c$ as given in (4.4) is substituted into (4.2) from which (4.5) is obtained.
11. The fraction by which cost is increased (if $-$) or reduced (if $+$) if given by

$$(\bar{B} - B_i) \frac{(n\bar{B} - B_i)}{n\bar{B} B_i}.$$

12. This result is reinforced if income elasticity is less than unity, but need not apply if income elasticity exceeds unity, or if price elasticities differ by states.
13. Also, allowance must again be made for income effects, which go to increase public services where $S_i > 0$, and decrease public services where $S_i < 0$.
14. As before, equation (5.2) is summed and, substituting from (5.3), we obtain (5.4).
15. The value of $t_c$, as determined in (5.4) is substituted into (5.2) from which (5.5) is obtained.
16. It should be recalled that need as here defined is independent of fiscal capacity.

17. As noted in Plan 4, the result will depend further on the operation of the income effect.

18. Suppose there is only one citizen, who consumes units of $X$ and $Y$. Now let the central government impose a lump-sum tax on him, and use the proceeds to subsidise $X$. It may be shown that this will result in increased consumption of $X$ and reduced consumption of $Y$. However, our case is more complex, as a number of states are involved, and each may react differently. Any one state finds the cost of state services reduced, and this is an inducement for higher taxes and outlays on such services. However, due to the action of other states, the residents of any one state also find their income reduced since the central tax $t_c$ must be paid. This will lead them to reduce outlays on state services. In states where the demand for state services is highly elastic with respect to income but inelastic with respect to price, the level of state services may decline, and this may outweigh the resulting increase in other states. However, this does not seem a likely outcome.

19. For instance, the subsidy under Plan 7 may be redefined as:

$$S_i = kt_i\bar{B} + (N_i - \bar{N})kt_i\bar{B} - t_cB_i.$$

Since $\bar{N} = 1$, we have:

$$S_i = kt_i\bar{B}N_i - t_cB_i$$

and:

$$\frac{\partial A_i}{\partial t_i} = B_i + kN_i\left(\bar{B} - \frac{B_i}{n}\right).$$

20. For a discussion of the difficulties involved see Musgrave and Daicoff, [5].

21. Taxation of income by state X, even though such income is received by residents of state Y, should be considered as falling within state X, provided that such income is earned in state X, and the tax is in line with benefits which accrue to such income from expenditures by state X. The same holds for benefit taxation of commuters. On the other hand, it is not part of the tax effort of state X, as defined for purposes of this argument, if X taxes residents of state Y (through use of taxes which are exported or shifted to the outside) who do not benefit from expenditures in state X.

22. With regard to (1), I would not interpret the preceding plans as relating the central fisc to the states 'as such'. Rather, the central fisc takes as given the political process of social preference determination as arrived at by various groups of citizens of various states. This indeed would seem the essence of political federalism.

    With regard to (2), how can it be held that 'equal treatment of equals' as a matter of *equity*, is more important than is the proper differentiating between unequals? If the latter does not matter (because it cannot be determined or otherwise), how can any meaning be imputed to the former, other than that of establishing a rule which avoids malicious differentiation? If so, tax distribution by lottery would do as well.

23. The concepts of horizontal and vertical equity do not fit into a normative system, where public services are supplied on a benefit basis and a tax-transfer mechanism is used to redistribute income. The principle of equality then becomes that everybody is subjected to benefit taxation, and everybody is

made subject to the same scheme of redistribution. On this division of functions see Musgrave (5, chs 1–2).

This leaves open the question whether benefit taxation (and hence the principle of equality) should be defined in terms of equal *marginal* benefits or equal *total* benefits. In the first case, everyone is taxed so that the marginal benefits which *he* derives from his outlays on public services equals the marginal benefit which *he* derives from his private outlay. In the second case, there is an equating of the total benefits which various people derive from their transactions with the fisc. This includes the consumer surplus which Mr X derives because his co-citizens like public services so that the unit cost to him is low, as compared to that derived by Mr Y who lives in a state where his co-citizens do not wish to pay for public services. This difference corresponds to gains which the consumer derives in his private purchases if his preferences are dissimilar from those of rival consumers. Since the latter gains are usually taken as given when defining a 'proper' distribution of income, it seems preferable to apply the same reasoning to the tax case and to define benefit taxation in marginal terms.

# REFERENCES

[1] Buchanan, J. (1950), 'Federalism and fiscal policy', *American Economic Review*, 40.

[2] Buchanan, J. (1951), 'A rejoinder', *Journal of Political Economy*, 59.

[3] Buchanan, J. (1952). 'Federal grants and resource allocation', *Journal of Political Economy*, 60.

[4] Buchanan, J. (1961), Comments, in *Public Finances, Needs, Sources and Utilization*, (Princeton, N. J., Princeton University Press).

[5] Musgrave, R. (1958), *The Theory of Public Finance* (New York, McGraw-Hill). Also see ch. 1 in this volume.

[6] Musgrave, R. and Daicoff, D. (1958), 'Who pays the Michigan taxes?', *Staff Papers*, (Lansing, Mich., Tax Study Committee).

[7] Mushkin, S. and Crowther, B. (1959), *Federal Taxes and the Measurement of State Capacity*, (Washington D. C., US Department of Health, Education and Welfare).

[8] *Report of the Royal Commission on Dominion–Provincial Relations* (1940), Book II (Ottawa).

[9] Scott, A. D., (1952) 'Discussion with Buchanan', *Journal of Political Economy*, June.

[10] Tiebout, C. M., (1961) 'An Economic Theory of Fiscal Decentralization', in *Public Finances, Needs, Sources and Utilization*, (Princeton, N. J., Princeton University Press).

# 3   Economics of Fiscal Federalism*
## 1971

The recent rise of interest in fiscal federalism stems from a variety of sources. At the academic level certain developments in the economics of public finance, in the making over the last two decades, naturally pointed in this direction. The renewed concern of fiscal economists with issues of allocation and expenditures (as against stabilisation and taxation) drew attention to state and local finances as a field of research. It is here, after all, where the provision of social goods primarily occurs. Developments in the theory of social goods, in pushing beyond the polar case where equal benefits are enjoyed by all, pointed to differences in the spatial benefit characteristics of various public services. This, then, led to a normative theory of fiscal structure, based upon spatial considerations. Other features adding to the analytical interest in local finance were: (1) the role of location choices as a mechanism by which preferences for social goods may be revealed, and (2) the operation of inter-community fiscal agreements as a real-world illustration of the small-number case in the theory of social goods.

At the same time interest in fiscal federalism was fanned by other developments. One of these is the increased interest in decentralisation as a way of life. My generation of public-policy oriented economists has been essentially centralist in approach. In part, this was due to our concern with macro problems which by their very nature must be handled at the central level. But it was due also to a political climate in which centralised action stood for positive policy responsibility, while decentralisation stood for minimising public sector activity and public interference. I am not persuaded that this nexus has ceased to hold, but one must take note of the voices for decentralisation which now come from all sides of the political spectrum. 'Let each commune do its own thing' is anticentralist, no less than the states' rights doctrine of old, even though the two may be antithetical in their views of what constitutes the proper size of the public sector at the local level.

* The C. Woody Thompson Memorial Lecture delivered at the opening session of the annual meeting of the Midwest Economics Association, Chicago, 29 April, 1971, and first published, *Nebraska Journal of Economics and Business*, vol. 10, 1971.

Finally, concern with issues of fiscal federalism has been the inescapable result of the fiscal distress in which many jurisdictions—hard-pressed urban centres in particular—find themselves. The situation is one which cannot be met without a transfer of fiscal responsibilities and/or resources. Such a transfer, by its very nature, must be implemented through the federal budget.

Given these various strands of interest in the federalism issue, what can be said about its basic economics, and what policy measures are needed to resolve the current difficulties?


## SPATIAL ASPECTS OF SOCIAL GOODS

To begin with, consider the provision for social goods, leaving distributional aspects for later consideration. Should such goods be provided on a centralised or a decentralised basis? If all social goods were such that the benefits were equally available to all, independent of their location, the problem would be simple. Provision, wherever made, would necessarily be 'central' and should be determined on a nationwide basis. But such is not the case. It is feasible to light one street corner more brightly than another, to have better fire-fighting services in this town than that, to have a better state university in one state than another, and so forth. The spatial incidence of social goods differs. They may thus be arranged depending on whether their benefit incidence is local, state-wide, regional or national. The question arises, therefore, of what goods should be provided where and by whom.

If preference patterns regarding social goods differ between communities, there is everything to be said for permitting them to differ in their provision for social goods, just as individuals should be permitted, in the absence of externalities, to arrange their consumption patterns to their own liking. This suggests a fiscal structure where local goods are provided locally, regional goods are provided regionally, and national goods are provided nationally. In short, the budget should be determined and paid for by the residents of the particular benefit area.

Let me call this the principle of reciprocity. Provision for various services will thus involve varying degrees of centralisation, that is, service areas of various radii of coverage. Differences in fiscal patterns between jurisdictions will reflect differences in effective demand (that is, in preferences and incomes) of the residents. Efficiency will be served, moreover, by permitting people with equal preferences for social goods to live together, since this permits them individually to obtain the desired amount of social goods at a lower price. Whereas in the world of private goods it may be disadvantageous to have atypical tastes, the opposite holds for public goods. Moreover, since political decisions can only approximate individual preferences, similarity of tastes also reduces the risk that individuals will be faced with budget decisions that they consider non-optimal.

This spatial model of fiscal structure has its attraction, but it oversimplifies matters. One difficulty is that benefits from services provided in any one jurisdiction may not be limited to residents of that jurisdiction, but spill over to residents of other jurisdictions. This may be the case because jurisdictions are inefficiently designed, at least from the fiscal point of view; or it may come about because the spatial patterns differ for various types of public services. The reciprocity principle would thus call for different but overlapping jurisdictions for each service. A person residing in any one location would be a member of various 'service clubs', aimed at providing him with different services. For some services, he would join with close neighbours only, while for others the neighbourhood concept would be extended to involve a radius of 10, 100 or 1,000 miles. The system would be exceedingly complex and might not be desirable even if feasible. Complete separation of services would render the decision process more difficult, as the bargaining feature of changing the budget mix would be lost. Moreover, jurisdictions are historically given and not created on the basis of fiscal rationality alone. State or city boundaries do not neatly coincide with benefit areas.

Thus spillovers remain and must be dealt with. They must be made to enter into the calculus of the decision-making unit if service levels are to be set efficiently. Such spillovers are the public sector counterpart of externalities in the provision of private goods where each household is its own jurisdiction. Such jurisdictional externalities may be accounted for by direct bargaining between the units involved. Since numbers are typically small, bargaining may work (if not necessarily optimally), even though it is not operational in the large-number situation which is typical for most social goods problems. Nevertheless, mediation by a higher level government—which, for our purposes means a government whose jurisdiction covers the combined areas—may be called for.

Similar problems arise in the spillover of burdens. The logic of our spatial model rests on the proposition that the provision for social goods be determined (voted upon) and financed by the group of people who will benefit. Reciprocity implies that the taxes used to finance such services should be borne by this group. The burden should not be 'exported' to the outside, so as to obtain public services free of charge or at a reduced cost to the beneficiaries. Just as the spatial incidence of benefits is the key to locating expenditure functions, so should the spatial incidence of tax burdens be the key to determining which tax instruments are used properly at various levels of government. National services are to be paid for by taxes with nationwide incidence, while local services are to be paid for by taxes with a local burden incidence. To some extent, this results automatically from the nature of jurisdictions, since a jurisdiction can tax only within its borders. But burden spill-outs may occur through trade and 'foreign' ownership of capital. Such burden spill-outs are not to be permitted in the ideal system, unless they are charges for intermediate public goods which lower the cost of the exported products and hence should be paid for by 'foreign' consumers. Enforcement of this rule again calls for supervision by a higher level of government, the current efforts for tax coordination among the member states of the European Common Market being an interesting case in point.

Note that in this dream world of fiscal efficiency, location decisions would not be independent of fiscal considerations. Such considerations would be included, not as a distorting element but so as to secure a more efficient solution. Association with others of similar social goods preferences is efficient. For this to be the case, the principle of reciprocity must hold not only between groups of cost-bearers and beneficiaries, but also for each individual. Taxation must be based on benefits secured. The price charged to a beneficiary must be equal at the margin to his benefit derived, and since this condition may be met by more than one pricing rule, the same rule must be used by all jurisdictions. If any one jurisdiction undercharges or overcharges relative to others, location decisions are distorted.

Such, of course, is the case in the real world, where taxes are not imposed on a benefit basis, and burden distributions by income level differ among communities. These inefficiencies would be avoided in a unitary system, where the cost-benefit patterns are the same everywhere, but this would be at the cost of losing the gains from variety which are possible under the multiple system. Which system is better on balance thus cannot be decided on *a priori* grounds. Under optimal arrangements the multiple system is clearly preferable, but in the actual setting a unitary solution may be superior. One would have to examine, for instance, how much less variety there is in local services in centralised countries such as the Netherlands or the United Kingdom than in a decentralised system such the USA.

## DISTRIBUTIONAL CONSIDERATIONS

So far I have assumed that the state of income distribution is given and that individual preferences are to be weighed accordingly. We must now drop this assumption. Fiscal policy is concerned not only with provision for social goods but also with adjustments in the distribution of income. How is fiscal federalism to handle this function, and is there a problem of adjustment not only between poor and rich individuals but also between poor and rich communities?

Policies to adjust the distribution of income among individuals must be conducted on a nationwide basis. Unless such adjustments are very minor, regional differentiation leads to severe locational inefficiencies. Moreover, regional measures are self-defeating, as the rich will leave and the poor will move to the more egalitarian-minded jurisdictions. Progressive income taxation at the upper as well as transfers at the lower end of the scale—if substantial in scope—must be uniform within the entire area over which there is a high degree of capital and labour mobility, which means they have to be a function of the national government. Failure to meet this condition, as we shall note presently, is responsible for much of the fiscal distress with which we are now confronted.

This much is evident, but there remains the puzzling question whether national concern with distribution should go beyond the state of distribution among individuals and include inter-community distribution as well. Does the existence of poor communities call for equalising measures among them, as distinct from that of equalisation among rich and poor individuals? Given an individualistic social welfare function, policy must ultimately be concerned with the welfare of individuals rather than of groups, so that the answer to this question would seem to be in the negative. Such at least is the case in a world of private goods. The question is whether the same holds for a world with social goods.

The distribution issue, basically, relates to the distribution of welfare, and not the distribution of income. Since the former depends on the pricing rule as well as on the distribution of income, the latter (in order to achieve the desired welfare distribution) must be set with reference to the prevailing pricing rule. In a world with private goods only, this rule is given by uniform marginal cost pricing. Now let social goods be introduced and suppose that these are priced (by means of the tax system) so that each person pays in line with his marginal evaluation. With the same amount being 'bought' by all, differential prices will be paid. High-income people will tend to pay a higher unit price than low-income people. This being the case, the same distribution of welfare now calls for a less equal (pre-tax) distribution of income. In a world with public goods, less pre-tax income equalisation is needed to achieve a given state of equality in welfare than in a world with only private goods.[1]

This is all that need be said if social goods are national in scope and centrally provided. But now consider the case of local social goods. For any one person their unit price will be the less, the higher is the income of his co-residents. Under our pricing rule, a person with a given income will be better-off if he resides with rich than with poor neighbours.[2] This much we can conclude, but what follows regarding the overall state of inter-individual distribution, including the residents of both towns? The fact that High Town has a higher average income than Low Town means that local provision of social goods will tend to increase inequality among the total population, including residents of both towns. But this does not answer our problem. The question is whether this result simply calls for a more equal income distribution (as compared with the unitary system) among individuals, or whether it calls for a transfer from the residents (rich and poor) of High Town to those (rich and poor) of Low Town. Only in the latter case will the distinction between poor and rich communities be relevant for policy purposes.

The answer at a normative level at least is the former. If the inter-individual distribution of income were adjusted properly, no redistribution between communities would be needed. The reason is that the proper state of inter-individual distribution would allow (as part of the pricing rule) for the unequalising effect of local public goods on welfare. This allowance in turn would have called for a more equal income distribution, and having provided for this, a second round of adjustment would not be called for.

But however this may be, the distinction becomes vitally important once we discard the unrealistic assumption that the desirable state of inter-individual distribution has been established by national policy. The local fiscal authority must then act as the social conscience of last resort. It must assume responsibility for such redistributional functions as welfare, health care and other public services. These needs rise as average community income and hence fiscal capacities fall. Thus extreme imbalance between fiscal capacities and needs has developed among communities and becomes steadily worse. As higher-income residents of poor jurisdictions are burdened more heavily relative to those of richer jurisdictions, they leave, and the tax base deteriorates further. The result is a downward spiral of deepening fiscal distress.

While the distinction between rich and poor communities does not call for distributional measures in a normative setting in which a 'proper' inter-individual state of distribution is assumed to prevail, it is of crucial importance in our actual setting, where this condition is not met. Policies of fiscal equalisation are needed, involving revenue transfers from jurisdictions with a high ratio of capacity to need to jurisdictions with a low ratio. Fiscal federalism cannot function properly without either a central policy of inter-individual or (second-best) inter-community equalisation.

## MERIT GOODS AND OTHER MATTERS

To complete the picture, I must add a word about the role of public merit goods in the federal system. In a unitary system the merit–good problem is whether government wishes to interfere with individual preferences by encouraging the consumption of particular goods, be they social or private. In the federal system, we have the additional question whether the federal government wishes to interfere with local community decisions and encourage the provision of certain local-type social goods. The central government may do so because of spillover effects to the rest of the nation.[3] Or it may be that for some reason certain local social goods are more highly valued from a national than a local point of view. Local preferences are to be interfered with and federal preferences are to be superimposed. The case is quite analogous to other merit–good situations where certain private goods are to be subsidised or taxed in interference with private preference.

Federal policy may aim at assuring minimum performance levels for such services as health and education, or the purpose may be to encourage local provision by reducing the cost of a particular service to the local community. The appropriate device in the former case is a block grant, earmarked directly for the provision of the particular service; in the second case it is a matching grant, similarly earmarked for the service in question.

The essential point is that certain specific services are to be considered as being of particular merit from the national point of view and hence to be deserving of special support. The appropriate instrument, as just noted, is a categorical grant. To propose a general grant is to argue that, in fact, all local public services should be considered federal merit goods. This I find difficult to accept. While all local public services may be in short supply, this does not suggest to me that there is an equal need to expand all of them. On the contrary, if the deficiency is great, limited means should be directed toward those services which are most in need of expansion.

By the same token, the case is for the matching rather than for the block grant variety. If increased purchases of particular local social goods are to be encouraged, more can be done, with a given budget constraint, by reducing their price to the local community than by making a block grant. The latter may be used for tax reduction, which will increase purchase of private goods, no less than for the increased provision of social goods.

The four major ingredients to my recipe for fiscal federalism may be summarised as follows:

1. *The principle of reciprocity*. Various social goods should be provided for at the local, regional, or national level, depending on the range of their spatial benefit incidence, so as to let provision be decided and the cost be borne by the residents of the particular area in which the benefits accrue.
2. *The principle of centralised redistribution*. Adjustments in the distribution of income should be the responsibility of central policy, since it is only here that such measures can be conducted effectively and without causing severe efficiency losses.
3. *The principle of fiscal equalisation*. In the absence of an adequate inter-individual distribution policy, the central authority must secure some degree of fiscal equalisation among poor and rich communities.
4. *The principle of federal merit goods*. The central government may wish to encourage the supply of certain locally provided social goods, either because these involve spillover of national benefits or because they are considered of special merit from a national point of view, with matching grants the appropriate instrument for this purpose.

## THE PLACE OF REVENUE SHARING

What do these principles of fiscal federalism imply for the current debate over revenue sharing? The administration's proposal (and with but minor differences, the original Heller–Pechman plan and other variants) provides for a block grant of about $5 billion, to be distributed to the states on a per capita basis, with minor allowance for tax effort. Part of the funds are to be passed through to local governments, in line with their past shares in total (state and local) expenditures in their state. While the per capita formula is redistributive, it is but modestly so and even the Javits plan which goes furthest in this respect does not get very far.

The administration's basic case, as that of other advocating similar plans, is that the sharing of federal funds brings badly needed fiscal relief at the state–local level, that this relief should be given in order to leave states and localities free to decide how the funds should be used, and that population is a simple and otherwise acceptable distribution base.

The question is not whether this proposal, taken by itself, is a good thing. To appraise the plan, its merits must be compared with those of alternative uses of these federal funds. The alternative of federal tax reduction would be clearly inferior. Reduced federal tax dollars do not mean increased state–local tax dollars, but a net reduction in overall fiscal resources. This would be unfortunate, as the federal funds are needed for purposes of equalisation and to provide nationally important public services. But to argue that the proposed revenue sharing is preferable to federal tax reduction is damning with faint praise. The point to be made is that better uses of these fiscal resources are available and should be preferred.

I begin with the simple fact that federal fiscal resources are strictly limited. The vision of a substantial fiscal dividend—or budget margin, in the current, less glamorous, lingo—which would be available for all sorts of major new programmes is rapidly vanishing. For two or three years (1972–75) the margin is $3 or $4 billion only, and even by 1976 the prospective excess of full employment revenues over the cost of present programmes is at best $20 billion. (This allows for termination of Vietnam hostilities but not for domestic cutbacks in other defence expenditure.) Moreover, even this margin may well not materialise, since it reflects in large part a surplus in the social security trust funds. Given this restraint, the proposed type of revenue sharing does not rate the high priority which is assigned to it.

As I see it, federal finance of poverty programmes, including welfare, must come first. While the administration's plan for welfare reform points in the right direction, the additional funding is very small and inadequate. Much larger amounts (say, $20–30 billion) will be needed, especially if the expanded programme is to be in the form of a negative income tax. Next, I would favour substantial federal participation in the financing of elementary education, designed in particular to assure adequate minimum standards on a nationwide basis. These objectives, combined with other new requirements, such as environmental programmes, will easily exhaust or exceed the available margin. Yet until they are met, I am not prepared to divert scarce funds into a broadside grant, which in the end will do very little to relieve the fiscal crisis.

Let me note once more that, as long as central finance fails to deal adequately with inter-individual distribution, concern with poor communities remains of paramount importance. As it now stands, there are vast differences in the capabilities of various jurisdictions to meet their fiscal responsibilities. While it is true that poor jurisdictions are frequently located in high-income states—as in the case with the distressed core cities of the eastern seaboard—this gives little reason for comfort. It is fair enough to call on the residents of the suburbs to defray the cost of the inner city for services rendered to them, but it does not follow that they should also be called upon to defray the cost of the inner city's poverty problem. The residents of Westchester County should not be responsible for welfare in New York City any more than should wealthy residents of Hawaii or Alaska. The concentration of poverty in the core cities is a national problem, the cost of which should be defrayed on a national basis.

Given federal assumption of fiscal responsibility for an adequate income maintenance programme and for minimum levels of pre-school and primary education, the problem of 'poor communities' would be largely solved. Under this premise it would also be easier to reconstruct city finances so as to create metropolitan-wide fiscal units. To the extent that a problem of poor jurisdictions still existed, these measures could then be supplemented by a general grant, designed to reduce remaining discrepancies in fiscal capacity and need. But even then, the grant would differ from the present plan for revenue sharing. It would be on a matching basis, rather than a block grant, and more redistributive than is the case with the present per capita arrangement. Matching rates would ideally be related to capacity–need differentials. As it stands, we do not have the data on which the need side of such a formula could be based, but the basic information could, and I hope will, be developed. In the meantime, the obvious first step is the assumption of federal responsibility for financing an adequate income maintenance programme. Generalised revenue-sharing is an attractive idea, but we are just not wealthy enough, fiscally speaking, to indulge in it at this point. Let first things come first.

The design of federalism, as I see it, should permit constructive cooperation among regions within the nation, retaining freedom of local action where it is feasible and providing joint policies where they are called for. Federalism, then, should not be viewed simply as a halfway house or compromise between the extremes of complete centralisation and decentralisation. Rather, it should be a constructive way of doing at each level of government what can be done best at that level. At the same time it is more than a convenient arrangement between independent units, similar to an agreement between foreign powers. The federal structure, after all, is erected within the context of a national union. National responsibilities and rights should encompass all members of the sub-jurisdictions who, while residents of different localities, are nevertheless citizens of the same nation. This at least is the spirit in which my design for fiscal federalism should be read.

## NOTES

1. The term 'pre-tax income' here refers to income before tax payments for public services, but after redistributional (tax-transfer) adjustments.

2. If the tax allocation is by majority decision (rather than a strict benefit rule), this conclusion must be qualified. If the demand for social goods is income-elastic, an individual residing with co-residents of equal income runs less risk of being confronted with a budget vote which deviates from his preferences. This runs counter to the consideration noted in the text so that his tendency to choose richer neighbours will be dampened.
3. It might be argued that correction for spillovers is not really a merit–good problem, since it does not involve an interference with preferences but merely a correction for benefits which are not internalised.

# 4 Inter-Nation Equity*
## 1972

The issue of tax equity in a unitary fiscal setting is relatively simple. Only equity among individuals has to be considered and that in terms of a single tax system. The situation is more complicated in a multiple-unit system, whether composed of member states within a nation or a group of nations. Since the various units are engaged in trade, involving product as well as factor flows, the following question arises: How should such inter-state or international transactions be taxed? This complicates realisation of equity among individuals and creates the additional problem of equity among states and nations.[1] Our concern here is with the inter-nation aspect and its relation to inter-individual equity.

This chapter explores inter-nation equity, as it applies to the taxation of income and profits.[2] Issues of inter-nation equity in this case arise in two situations. One comes about as the result of factor movements and the other where a business transacts in more than one jurisdiction. The former has been primarily the concern of international tax treaties; the latter has been the central issue in the coordination of state corporation taxes in the United States and is also a matter of vital international concern.

## HISTORICAL BACKGROUND AND CURRENT PRACTICE

Beginning with the case of factor movements, our discussion will be largely in terms of capital flows and the taxation of capital income. In recent years, labour movement (especially within the Common Market) has also emerged as an important factor, but capital movement still poses the major and more complex issue. If residents of country A invest in a business incorporated in B and operating in C, who should be permitted to tax the income on such capital and at what rate? Should there be a rule pertaining to this, or should unrestricted multiple taxation apply? Moreover, if there are such rules, should they apply equally at the corporate and individual level of taxation?

* With P.B. Musgrave, in *Modern Fiscal Issues* (1972), ed. R. Bird and J. Head (Toronto, University of Toronto Press).

## Historical background

The search for principles in international revenue and tax-base allocation is nothing new. The allocation of property as a tax base between property situs and owner's domicile was discussed first by the Italian theologians of the thirteenth century.[3] The German Cameralists considered the matter in the sixteenth and seventeenth centuries, while the international treatment of death duties was a topic of much discussion in the eighteenth century. Towards the end of the nineteenth century, the discussion was resumed in terms of income taxation. This is where the emphasis has remained. Throughout, 'double taxation' was considered an evil and attempts were made to avoid it by appropriate tax-base allocation.[4] In the 1870s, both Germany and Switzerland moved to prevent multiple taxation by member states and cantons. Subsequently the matter was discussed extensively within the British empire, leading to recommendations by the Royal Commission on the Income Tax (1919) and subsequent legislation to avoid double taxation of income between the United Kingdom and the Dominions. International tax treaties date back to 1843 and greatly increased in number after World World I.

During the 1920s the problem was considered in several reports sponsored by the League of Nations. In 1920, a Committee of Economic Experts was assembled by the International Chamber of Commerce to propose a general set of principles for tax-burden allocation [Seligman, 8, ch. 6]. The distinguished membership of the committee included Luigi Einaudi, E.R.A. Seligman and Sir Josiah Stamp. The basic approach was to derive an elaborate schema of tax classification and to apply a concept of 'economic allegiance' allowing for (a) the location of production or of source of income, (b) the location at which the final product is used or the income is received, (c) the location of the legal machinery by which property rights are enforced, and (d) the domicile of the property owner. Ideally, different types of taxes would be imposed on the situs of wealth or of source of income as split up among various locations according to each of these four factors. In practice, such a solution was not considered feasible, and it was recommended that property taxes on tangible wealth as well as *in rem* taxes on income derived from such wealth would be allocated according to situs of property and source of income. Taxes on moveable and intangible property, as well as the personal income tax, in turn were to be assigned to the country of domicile. In the latter case, the idea of crediting foreign against domestic taxes by the domicile country was rejected as too favourable to the debtor countries.

These recommendations were submitted subsequently to a Committee of Technical Experts, assembled by the League of Nations [ibid., ch. 7]. Reporting in 1927, the technical experts followed the previous committee in its general recommendations, but went further in retaining the source principle for certain non-personal taxes, including 'schedular' (as distinct from global) taxes on income. In a subsequent report (1929) these principles were reaffirmed, and it was recommended that profits from business enterprises be taxed at the place of permanent establishment.

Thereafter, the continuing work of a permanent fiscal committee of the League of Nations led to the Model Conventions of Mexico (1943) and London (1946), the major provisions of which were similar to those later adopted in the Model Tax Treaty Convention on Income and Capital drawn up by the OECD Fiscal Committee in 1963.

Though not binding, this draft convention is widely regarded as the basic framework for good international manners in this matter and has served as a model for subsequent tax treaties among member countries. Its basic philosophy has much in common with the earlier recommendations of the League of Nations. A schedular approach was again taken, with profits as well as other income and capital gains earned on immovable property assigned to the country of source. The right to tax dividends and interest payments was largely assigned to the residence country with maximum withholding rates of 15 per cent for dividends (5 per cent in the case of intercorporate dividends with ownership connection of at least 25 per cent) and 10 per cent for interest permitted to the country of source. Royalties were to be free of tax in the source country, being entirely assigned to the residence country as were capital gains earned on certain 'moveable' assets. The only (and somewhat circular) justification given for this jurisdictional division seems to have been the 'close economic connection between the source of income and the State of Source' [OECD, 1, p. 78, para.1] said to exist with respect to those primary forms of income arising from productive assets in the country of source.[5]

The above notion is also implicit in the criterion of 'permanent establishment' which plays an important role in the model treaty. The right to tax business profits by the country of source is limited to profits arising from the so-called permanent establishment, a somewhat less than clear-cut concept. The category of permanent establishment excludes certain ancillary service activities which are 'so far antecedent to the actual realisation of profits by the parent body that no profits can properly be allocated to it' [ibid., p. 74, para. 2]. and those which are of an intermittent and casual nature.

**Current practice**
Current practice under both individual and corporation income tax reflects a mixture of two norms, one being the residence and the other the source, or territoriality, principle, henceforth simply referred to as source rule.

The *residence principle*, as applied to the individual income tax, holds that all income earned by an individual—whether at home or abroad—is taxable by his country of residence (and/or citizenship). As in the domestic setting, the tax is applied to investment income only in so far as it is received by the individual and not as it accrues in the form of undistributed corporate profits retained abroad. The corresponding principle for the corporation income tax is that of place of incorporation and/or management. The United States, for instance, taxes global income of US-incorporated companies, while the United Kingdom bases its 'residence' criterion for the corporation on the locus of management. As with the personal income tax, however, domestic corporations are usually not taxed on their share in the undistributed profits of foreign corporations, such tax being deferred to the time of distribution.

The *source of income* rule says that income is taxable in the jurisdiction in which it originates. This 'source rule', as it applies to business profits under the corporation tax, is generally defined in tax treaties to permit the source country to tax the profits of any permanent establishment operating within its borders, but only so as not to discriminate between income accruing to domestic and foreign ownership. These source and non-discrimination rules, however, are applicable in full only to profits taxes. A partial application of the rule pertains to the personal income tax on dividends, rentals, and interest on which withholding taxes are usually imposed by the country of source. Most tax treaties provide for these withholding taxes to be imposed at reciprocally equal rates.

It is in deference to the source country's primary right (or ability) to tax that the country of residence (incorporation) generally modifies its own taxation of foreign-source income either by giving outright exemption, by allowing foreign taxes to be deducted from taxable income or to be credited against the domestic tax. However, where dividends from a foreign subsidiary are paid to a parent company at home before being distributed to the latter's individual shareholders, the foreign withholding tax is not 'passed through' as a credit against the individual income tax.[6]

## SINGLE-SOURCE COUNTRY: TYPES OF EQUITY

In this and the following sections we deal with the claims of the country of residence of owners (country A), the country of source of income (country B), and the country of incorporation (country C). How should these claims be divided, and on which rules of inter-nation equity should the division be based? To simplify, we assume that the entire operation (production and sales) is in B. Thus there is no problem of determining the income source. The problem of determining this source arises where corporations operate across countries ($B_1$, $B_2$, etc.) and will be dealt with in the final section.

### Posing the problem
While the foregoing sketch of past and present practice brings out the complexities involved, past discussion has been in pragmatic and legal terms, and no clear picture emerges as to what the underlying principles should be. In approaching the matter, we distinguish between (a) the problem of inter-nation equity, (b) the problem of inter-individual equity, and (c) the avoidance of distorting effects on international capital flows. The key point is that appropriate solutions to (b) and (c) may be applied while leaving open the issue posed by (a).

## Inter-nation equity

Inter-nation equity deals with the allocation of national gain and loss. Let x, a resident of A, invest in B. Income earned thereon constitutes a national 'gain' to country A. If country B taxes the income earned by x, the gain accruing to country A as a nation is reduced. This is the issue of inter-nation equity. The fact that the gain accrues to B's treasury is not the crucial point. B may pass this gain on to its taxpayers by tax reduction, but it still retains the national gain. Similarly, A has suffered a national loss due to B's tax. This national loss results, whether A gives a credit to x for taxes paid to B, thereby suffering a Treasury loss, or whether the income is taxed again and x is left to bear the burden. National gain or loss may or may not be accompanied by a Treasury gain or loss; the latter is a matter of intra-nation transfer between Treasury and individual and does not affect the existence of national gain or loss. It is thus the national gain or loss (not the Treasury gain or loss) that is the subject of inter-nation equity as defined here.[7]

## View of inter-individual equity

Fairness requires that a taxpayer's liability payable to his country of residence should be the same whether income is derived from foreign or domestic sources.[8] But 'tax liability' may be defined in international or national terms.

If country A takes an *international* view of individual equity, tax liability will be interpreted as total (i.e. domestic plus foreign) liability. Taxes are taxes, and it does not matter to whom they are paid. If x has his primary tax allegiance in country A and earns capital income in B, his total taxes (payable to A and B) should be the same as if his entire income had been earned in A. A's tax law should be controlling, but this does not mean that B cannot tax such income. If the income is taxed only by A, no further problem arises; but if it is taxed by B, individual equity requires that A should grant a credit to x for his taxes paid to B. By granting this credit, horizontal equity between x and other taxpayers of A is established. But, as noted before, the credit does not involve a matter of inter-nation equity since it constitutes a transfer from treasury to taxpayer within A only.

If country A takes a *national* view of individual equity, equal treatment is defined in terms of A's taxes only. In this case, A will consider B's taxes imposed on x as expenses and permit x to deduct them. The tax reduction resulting therefrom is again an intra-A transfer between Treasury and taxpayer and does not involve the issue of inter-nation equity. The latter was settled by B imposing its tax, the choice between credit and deduction on the part of A being an internal matter of individual equity only. An equitable treatment of x by the laws of his country of residence (be it in terms of international or national equity) may thus be achieved whether B is permitted to tax the income or not.

### Relation of the two equity concepts

The issue of inter-nation equity is thus settled by whether and how B will tax. Inter-individual equity (between x and his co-residents in A) in turn depends on A's response to B's tax, which response also determines the tax base available to A's Treasury. It is misleading, therefore, to think of inter-nation equity between the countries of residence and source in terms of a division of treasury gains. Rather, it should be thought of in terms of national gain sharing or revenue participation by B, the country of income source.

### Inter-nation equity vs. efficiency

Efficiency of capital movement, similarly, may be assured independently of how national gains are assigned. Efficiency, as seen from a world point of view, requires that an investor's choice of country in which to invest should not be affected by tax differentials. He should pay the same tax wherever he invests. The most readily implemented method for accomplishing this objective is taxation by B with a credit for the foreign tax granted by A, a practice which is also consistent with the international view of individual equity. Provided that A takes this view, efficiency is assured whether or not the income is taxed by B.

But what if efficiency is viewed more narrowly from the point of view of national interest? Efficiency then requires that foreign investment be carried to the point where the return net of foreign tax equals the domestic return before tax. This may be accomplished by the deduction method, also called for by the national view of individual equity. As before, we find that the efficiency criterion can be met whether or not B is permitted to tax.

### Conclusion

Restating the matter, inter-nation equity involves the question of whether B should be permitted to tax the income which A's investors derive from investment in B. If such a tax is imposed by B, it thereby derives a national gain which, in turn, reduces A's national gain derived from its foreign investment. This may or may not involve a loss for A's Treasury, depending on how A chooses to treat (overlook, deduct, or credit) B's tax. The treatment, however, has a bearing on individual equity and the efficiency of capital flows. These two issues may be dealt with one way or another (as, for instance, via crediting or deduction procedures) whatever is done about B's right to tax.[9]

## SINGLE SOURCE COUNTRY: CRITERIA FOR INTER-NATION EQUITY

Having separated the issues of individual equity and efficiency from that of inter-nation equity, we may now turn to various principles of inter-nation equity.

## Allocation under benefit taxation

One such principle and much the most clear-cut follows under a benefit rule. Under a system of benefit taxation each jurisdiction would charge for services which it has rendered. Income taxes would play a minimal role in such a system. Direct charges would be imposed on the consumer for final public goods provided to him and on the firms for intermediate goods provided to them. Company taxation would thus be imposed largely by the jurisdiction in which the production process occurs and the benefits (intermediate goods) were received. Moreover, the nature of the tax would be quite different from that of a profits tax. If a general proxy were used, this might be furnished best by an *ad valorem* tax on cost payments, assuming intermediate public services to reduce all private costs equally. In a competitive system, this would amount to allocation of the profits tax base according to value added, but not necessarily so in the real world where mark-ups at various stages of production may differ. Inter-nation equity under the benefit principle would be self-implementing.

While such a system would make for a neat solution to our problem, it is unfortunately not a realistic view of the matter. Most taxes are not imposed on a benefit basis, so that inter-nation equity is not secured automatically in this fashion. Another allocation rule must be found to deal with general, non-benefit taxation. At the same time, the benefit idea may be allowed for in allocating gains among nations, i.e. a country should be entitled to charge for the cost of public services which it has rendered to the foreign investor.

## Residency vs. territoriality

Let us return to our example of x, a resident in A, deriving income from an investment in B, and briefly re-state the preceding argument. In the absence of taxes the earnings from this investment accrue to A as a 'national gain'. This will remain the case whether or not A imposes a tax, as such a tax is merely an intra-nation transfer between A's Treasury and x. If B imposes a tax, the situation is changed. A's national gain is reduced and part thereof is transferred to B. The question of inter-nation equity therefore is only whether B should be permitted to tax, and if so, by how much.

What do the legal principles of residency and source imply in this respect? If the 'residency' principle is interpreted simply as saying that country A is entitled to tax x's income because x is a resident of A, it has no bearing on inter-nation equity. Such national gain as country A derives is obtained by it whether A's Treasury imposes a tax or not.[10]

The source principle means that a country is permitted to tax income which results from activities undertaken in its borders. That is to say, B is permitted to tax x's income and thus to appropriate part of A's national gain. This will be the case whether or not A also taxes this income under the residency principle. Thus, we have the asymmetric result that inter-nation equity is affected if the residency principle is supplemented by source, but not if source is supplemented by the residency principle.

If the source rule is to be applied, it should be non-discriminatory. The legal philosophy on which the rule is based is that a sovereign country is entitled to tax all activity which occurs within its borders. Given this view and following the general principle of equality under the law, it follows that all activity within the border should be treated alike. Therefore, B should tax income received by x as if it were received by B's own residents. A rule of non-discrimination should apply.[11]

Emphasis on activity within the jurisdiction explains why the territoriality principle has been associated traditionally with *in rem* taxes, whereas the residency principle has been associated with the individual income tax. There is, however, no compelling reason for this association. The territoriality rule may also be interpreted to mean that B should be permitted to tax the income (*qua* income tax) which x has earned from his operations in B. While the association of income taxation with residency makes sense in the context of inter-individual equity (the net liability payable by x should afford him equal treatment with other residents of A), this does not hold for the quite different issue of inter-nation equity.

## National rental

Both the residency and source rules are essentially legal concepts and do not carry a clear economic content.[12] A more meaningful approach from the economist's point of view may be derived by taking a broader look at the national gain, including gains other than those which accrue via profit-sharing through tax participation. As residents of country A invest in B, A's capital earnings are moved above the level which would be obtained from domestic investment. To be sure, the net gain to country A falls short of its increased capital income because its labour income will be reduced. However, within certain limits of capital export at least, country A will gain. Labour income in B will gain from the capital inflow while its own capital income will fall, but, on balance, B also stands to gain. The question is whether this gain is enough.

If B is capital-poor but rich in other resources, A's gain (over and above the alternative gain from home investment in A) tends to be large. B might, with some justification, argue that it should obtain a rental or royalty share in A's gain over and above the addition to its labour income; and the appropriate way for B to obtain this gain would be to charge a tax.

If this approach is taken, such a charge would be independent of B's own tax structure. As against the 'treat income accruing to foreigners as if accrued to residents' principle of the source rule, the approach now becomes one of charging a rental or royalty on foreign operations, and to do so *outside* the domestic tax system. The tax, in fact, becomes an *in rem* tax on operations by foreigners.

This leaves open the question of how high the rental charge should be. Should it equal B's income loss from its own capital, a fraction of A's national gain from not investing at home, or what other rule should be followed? The matter is complicated further since capital inflow might bring intangible gains such as technical and managerial know-how as well as intangible burdens such as foreign control and slowed down emergence of a native entrepreneurial class. Obviously, there is no precise level at which to fix the rental, but the general notion is not without appeal. Such is the case especially since appropriate crediting or deducting devices may be used by the capital-exporting country to neutralise effects of the national rental on capital flows and individual tax equity. There is nothing in the logic of the national rental approach which suggests that rates on foreigners would be the same as those applicable to the residents of the capital-importing country. Quite possibly, the national rental would be below the capital-importing country's corporation tax.

In addition to the national rental, a country may impose a benefit charge to defray the cost of public services rendered to the operations of foreign-owned capital. As noted before, such a charge may be imposed (as a matter of inter-nation equity) even though domestic taxation is largely on a non-benefit basis. It is not likely, however, that such a supplement to the national rental would be very large since only a small part of public expenditures tends to go into provision of intermediate services for production. Thus, a modest charge might be set internationally,[13] and a higher rate be applied where intermediate services can be shown to be unusually large.

## Distributional considerations

Finally, it might be argued that the taxation of income from foreign-owned capital should be used as an instrument of international redistribution. With a highly unequal distribution of resource endowments and per capita income among countries and in the absence of an adequate method for dealing with the problem, an appropriate pattern of tax-imposed national gains and losses might be used to secure some degree of adjustment.

In the context of a corporation tax in particular, it might be desirable to apply a uniform rate schedule, agreed upon by *international* convention and applicable in all capital-importing countries. To allow for the redistribution norm, such a rate schedule should not be based on reciprocity or equal rates (as is now common for withholding rates) but might be constructed along the lines of Table 4.1. These rates would be substituted for both the corporation and withholding tax now imposed by B on income accruing to A's investors. The applicable rates as shown in the table would be related inversely to per capita income in the capital-importing country and directly to per capita income in the capital-exporting country. This would improve the relative position of low-income countries.

Now it might be objected that the vertical progression reflected in the above-rate schedule would not be beneficial to low-income countries because it would deter capital inflow. This, however, would be the case only if the capital-exporting country failed to maintain individual equity and investment-flow neutrality among its residents by appropriate crediting. General acceptance of such a schedule would avoid the possibility of low-income countries imposing extreme rates which would then have to be recouped by the Treasuries of high-income countries. Also, adoption of a

*Table 4.1*

| | Per capita income of capital-exporting country ($) | | | |
|---|---|---|---|---|
| Per capita income of capital-importing country ($) | < 250 | 250–500 | 500–1000 | 1000 + |
| | Tax rates (per cent) | | | |
| Below 250 | 40 | 50 | 55 | 60 |
| 250–500 | 30 | 40 | 45 | 50 |
| 500–1000 | 20 | 30 | 35 | 40 |
| 1000+ | 10 | 20 | 25 | 30 |

common rate schedule would forestall low-rate competition for foreign capital by low-income countries.[14]

## SINGLE-SOURCE COUNTRY: PROBLEMS OF INCORPORATION

In this section, some additional aspects of the single-source country case are considered. So far, no allowance was made for the fact that investment is usually in corporate form and that income is taxed at both the corporate and the individual level. In fact, the issue of inter-nation equity is largely dealt with in terms of corporate rather than individual income taxation. With the introduction of the corporation into the picture, two further problems arise: (1) the country of incorporation enters as a third potential claimant for tax revenue; and (2) there is the problem of taxing at both the corporation and the shareholder level.

### Residence principle applied to corporation

As long as the source rule is followed, the place of incorporation does not matter. But it does matter if the residence rule is applied to the corporation tax.

This discussion, dealing with the taxation of corporations and their subsidiaries, necessarily views the corporation tax as an 'absolute' tax imposed on the corporation as such. If we consider the position of individual shareholders who are residents in A but derive income from investment in corporations in B, the problem depends on how corporation tax is viewed, i.e. as (1) an individual income tax on the shareholder, or as (2) an absolute tax on the corporation. Under (1) the source principle calls for taxation by B and the residence principle for taxation by A, with (given the international equity view) crediting of B's tax. Under (2), A has no claim and B is entitled to tax under either the source or residence principle. If residence is interpreted as place of incorporation, the distribution of national gain will now depend on where incorporation occurs. This problem is of particular importance for the case where a corporation earns income through its foreign subsidiary: the question arises as to whether residence is in the country of incorporation of the parent corporation or of its subsidiary.

1. Suppose first that a corporation is incorporated in A, has a branch in B, and derives earnings from the operation of that branch in B. Looking at the corporation tax as an 'absolute tax', i.e. imposed on the corporation 'as such' rather than on the shareholder, should A tax the branch income? Under the source rule the answer is clearly no, but what if the residence rule holds? In fact, what does it mean to apply the residence rule under an absolute corporation tax? Presumably the country of incorporation would be the corporation's residence. Thus, only A would be entitled to tax. If B also taxes under the source rule, A may credit B's tax, this being the practice followed under US law. The principle is the same as that developed above.

2. Suppose next that the corporation incorporated in A operates a subsidiary which is incorporated in B and derives income from business in B. Country B is now both the country of source and of incorporation for the subsidiary. Again, there is no problem under the source rule, as B alone is entitled to tax. But interpretation of the residence rule is now difficult. If residence is now defined as being in B, then the residence principle strictly interpreted means that only B is eligible to tax the entire profits of the subsidiary, while A would be eligible only to tax such *part* of the profits as is remitted to the parent corporation in A.

The next question is whether considerations of inter-taxpayer equity (now applied to horizontal equity among corporations) calls for A to credit B's tax. The answer is no, because this would not be compatible with the principle of deferral which is based on the recognition of parent and subsidiary as distinct entities. If A has no right to tax the undistributed profits of the subsidiary, why should it credit its corporation (the parent) for the tax paid by B's corporation (the subsidiary)? The US practice of granting deferral and then crediting is thus inconsistent and one or the other (preferably deferral) should be abolished. This would mean abandoning the country of incorporation qua residence approach while applying a global tax to the parent.[15]

3. Difficulties are compounded in a situation where the subsidiary incorporated in B (and earning income in B) in turn has subsidiaries incorporated in C and earning income in C. This is a so-called two-tier problem in which the issues raised in the preceding section are expanded further. This will not be followed through here beyond noting that it accentuates the inconsistency involved in both giving deferral and allowing an 'indirect' tax credit.

In other words, in the absence of incorporated subsidiaries, the choice is between permitting taxation by B (source rule) or by A only (exclusive residence principle). Given the existence of subsidiaries, there is the additional problem of determining the 'residence' of the subsidiary, be it as its place of incorporation or the place of incorporation of its parent. If the parent incorporated in A has a subsidiary incorporated in C but earning income in B, application of the source rule will determine whether B can tax. Suppose that it can do so and thus derives a national gain at the expense of A or C, depending on where the residence is taken to be. But this is not all. If residence is taken to be in C and C thus is permitted to impose a further tax, A will suffer an additional loss. The national loss to A in this case depends not only on the level of taxation in B, but also in C. Whereas in the absence of subsidiaries the matter of national loss was determined by the application of the source rule only, we now see that the operation of the residence principle enters into the picture.

## Individual tax plus corporation tax

Turning now to the fact that corporation profits are taxed at both the corporate and the shareholder level, should non-discrimination under the source rule be interpreted as permitting B to impose both an individual and a corporation tax on foreign capital, provided it does so on earnings from its domestic capital? We see no reason why this should not be the case. If the source reasoning applies to the one tax, it should also apply to the other. At the same time, it must be admitted that non-discrimination is easier to apply with regard to the corporate than with regard to the individual tax. Short of requiring x to file a return in B, the latter may have to be approximated (as is the case in current practice) by a flat withholding tax imposed by B on dividends flowing to A.[16]

Nevertheless, the role of the withholding tax as an approximation to a properly assessed individual tax makes it clear that the level of a country's withholding rate should be a function of its *own* individual income tax rate schedule, corresponding, say, to the marginal rate paid by its shareholders on the average dividend dollar. It follows from this that the idea of reciprocity in withholding rates is inappropriate in the context of non-discrimination.

## National rental approach

Under the national rental approach, taken in its pure form, the two-tier issue is irrelevant. B imposes its tax on income earned by foreign capital, outside its own tax (individual or corporate) system applicable to B's residents. Or, if the rental charge is collected as a part of B's income and corporation taxes, what now matters (with regard to inter-nation equity) is the combined take of B under both taxes. Separate consideration of the 'proper' charge under either tax is meaningless in this context. Moreover, under the national rental view, C would clearly be disqualified as a claimant for tax revenue since it does not contribute to the economic sources of A's national gain.

# CONCLUSION ON SINGLE-SOURCE CASE

It is difficult to compress the various strands of the preceding discussion into a neat set of conclusions, but the following judgements emerge.

## Inter-nation equity

A solution to inter-nation equity in line with the principle of taxation by residence only would be undesirable. It would be inequitable from the point of view of source countries, especially for the case of low-income countries. Moreover, for the all-important subsidiary case and the corporation tax it would involve the arbitrary decision of where corporate residence is to be recognised.

The principle of taxation by source is preferable. While it raises the difficulty of determining source (see next section), this difficulty can be overcome in line with meaningful economic principles. The appropriate rate at which the source country should tax may be set in line with either the principle of non-discrimination (i.e. taxing profits of foreigners at the same rate as profits of domestic capital) or in line with the national rental principle. Tempered possibly by distributional considerations, a set of rental rates might be agreed upon on an international basis. The latter is our preferred solution.

In the absence of subsidiaries, the above would take care of the problem; but given subsidiaries, an additional problem of inter-nation equity arises with the levels of taxation chosen by the respective countries of residence of the subsidiary corporations. Now it might be argued that the primary concern of inter-nation equity is to distinguish between the claims of the source country and all other countries, and there is something to be said for this view. However, the distribution of claims among the different countries of incorporation (*qua* residence of corporations) is also relevant. A possible solution here is to provide that the country of incorporation is entitled to tax only if it is either the country of source or the country of primary tax allegiance[17] for individual shareholders owning a substantial proportion of the equity.

Whichever principle is recognised, and whatever rate structure is set to achieve what is considered inter-nation equity, efficiency effects may be neutralised by appropriate treatment of foreign taxes within each national tax system.

## Taxpayer equity

Taxpayer equity in the international context is primarily a matter of horizontal equity among corporate taxpayers. Whatever the rate at which the source country taxes, the country of residence may deal with the tax paid in the source country in line with its own choice between viewing inter-taxpayer equity on international or national grounds, i.e. it may credit or deduct.

However, whichever solution is chosen, it should be applied consistently. Thus, if one adopts the international view which underlies the US credit provision, such credit should be given to the US corporation only for such foreign taxes as it pays against *its* profits earned abroad. Since the foreign tax is paid by the subsidiary, this implies that the profits of the subsidiary must also be considered the profits of the parent. If so, there is no justification for deferral of US tax until foreign earnings are repatriated. Alternatively, deferral may be justified by strict application of the residence (country of incorporation) principle. But the crediting of foreign taxes placed on the foreign corporation is then no longer justified.

## Implications for tax treaties

Regarding improvements of tax treaty practices, the following suggestions might be made.

1. Tax-treaty formulation should not be left to purely bilateral agreements. An internationally agreed-upon framework, analogous to the GATT rules for the treatment of commodity taxes, is called for. This is needed in particular if redistributional considerations are to be introduced and if this is to be done without interfering with capital flows to low-income countries and without inviting low-rate competition among them, such as is solicited by the tax-sparing practice.

2. In considering the appropriate arrangement between any two countries, the treatment of withholding tax and corporation tax should be considered jointly, not separately. Thus, attention will be directed at B's total take, which is what matters from the inter-nation equity point of view.

3. The principles of reciprocity, while meaningful as a bargaining device, have little economic justification, nor are they compatible with the non-discrimination requirement of a legal territoriality rule, especially where the source country has an integrated system. Non-discrimination calls for withholding rates tuned to each country's own personal rate structure.

4. The non-discrimination principle, while in line with the territoriality rule, is incompatible with the national rental or redistributional approach. High-income countries should allow for this in tax-treaty arrangements with low-income countries.

5. Separate treatment of certain income sources (e.g. interest, royalties, etc.) are a carryover from a schedular approach to income tax and should give way to a global approach, combining all gains of capital income into one total. This is called for under the logic of either the territoriality or national rental view.

Other suggestions may be added to this list, and those made here may have to be revised after further consideration. The subject-matter, as we recognise, is highly complex, especially if considerations of administrative feasibility (which we have largely overlooked) are added. Nevertheless, it seems evident that the matter needs rethinking, extending the discussion beyond the narrow confines of the legal residence and territoriality rules.

This is called for in the relationships among developed countries, but even more so in their dealings with low-income countries.

## Implications of shifting

Finally, it should be noted that the above argument has been developed on the assumption that the corporation tax falls on profits. The situation changes if we assume that it is shifted to consumers. A profits tax imposed by B is now equivalent to a consumption tax on the consumers of B's product. This is the case whether the capital involved is owned by residents of A or B. Assuming consumption to occur in B, no national gain to B or loss to A results.[18]

Imposition of a profits tax by A on its foreign investment (assuming the tax to be shifted in B) now results in a national loss to B and gain to A. This cannot be defended by any of the rules considered here, whether on benefit, territoriality or national rental grounds. For redistributional reasons, similarly, taxation by A would be inappropriate, since the capital-exporting country will hardly be the low-income country. The residence principle must be rejected in this case. In the all-shifting world, country A should exempt foreign earnings of its residents from its profits tax, for the same reason that under GATT rules exports are exempt from commodity tax.[19]

## EQUITY IN THE MULTI-SOURCE CASE

To isolate the first problem posed by the taxation of income from foreign investment, we have assumed earlier that the capital which residents of A invest in B is invested in a company whose entire operation is in B. We now turn to the second problem, which arises if the operations of a company extend over more than one country. This poses no difficulty under the pure residence principle. But under the other rules which involve the determination of source (source rule, national rental, redistribution), there now arises the further problem of how to divide the income among the participating countries. In terms of our previous illustration, there now exists a set of Bs among whom the tax base must be divided. Assuming that they apply the same rate, the national loss to A will be the same, but the distribution of the national gain among the Bs will differ. If these rates differ, the total loss to A will be affected as well.

## Background

This problem has been the subject of much discussion as it applies to the taxation of corporation profits by individual states in the US. While the taxation of profits from a single-state company is uniformly based on the territoriality (source) principle, the division of the tax base for a company operating across state borders has been handled in a variety of ways.

Among these, the so-called formula apportionment or allocation method is most generally used, with other techniques represented by the separate accounting and special allocation methods [9, ch. 5 f.]. In most cases, the locations of property, payroll and sales are given equal weight. The assumption had been that the inclusion of sales would be helpful to the less industrialised states, but a recent study has shown that the distribution of the tax base among states is not changed greatly if sales are excluded. The reason, of course, is that the more industrialised states also offer the larger markets for sale [ibid., ch. 16]. Because of this and since the sales component is most difficult to administer, it has been recommended recently that the sales factor be dropped and a uniform property–payroll formula be adopted [ibid., ch. 39]. Assuming no shifting, this may be a reasonable solution, but to the extent that shifting occurs, inter-nation equity would suggest that the sales component in the formula be retained and given increased weight.

As noted before, at the international level, a different approach has been taken. Primary reliance under the model treaty is on the concept of 'permanent establishment'. Under this approach, each permanent establishment operating in one country as an affiliate to a parent company in another is to be treated for tax purposes as a separate entity and profits must be assigned to it using arm's-length accounting. The latter then becomes a crucial factor in the model treaty approach to apportionment of profits. The underlying rationale appears to be more or less similar to that of the separate accounting approach at the US level and the same difficulties apply. Division of profits among those earned by operations within various jurisdictions would be a meaningful approach if it could be accomplished, but the difficulties of separate accounting are considerable, and the concept of 'permanent establishment' itself is rather vague. Certain activities are considered as being conducted by a permanent establishment while others such as sales activities are often largely excluded.

### Determination of source

Neither the discussion of base allocation among the US states nor the literature on international agreements is very enlightening in explaining what the underlying principle should be.[20] Presumably, the objective is to divide up the tax base in line with the territorial origin of profits. Given this principle, the problem becomes one of economic imputation.

This problem, it must again be noted, is quite different from that which arises under benefit taxation. There, the issue is one of determining the situs at which public services were rendered. In the absence of 'itemised billing', a proxy might be furnished by the situs of cost incurred, assuming the provision for intermediate public goods to be a constant matching factor in relation to other on-site costs incurred (i.e. value added less profits). As noted before, the logic of the approach would point to an *ad valorem* charge on such costs. Under competitive assumptions this would be similar to allocation by value added, but it would have nothing to do with a profits tax. The US-type apportionment formula is in line with this in so far as value added by payroll is concerned, but not with regard to the capital and sales factors. The capital factor (in the benefit context) should enter by depreciation rather than by value of capital and the sales factor should enter by sales margin rather than gross sales. By overweighting capital and sales, the formula greatly underweighs the labour component.

Our concern, however, is not with a benefit tax but with a tax on the earnings of capital and with tracing the source of these earnings. The first and obvious question is why this should not be identified with the location at which the actual operation of the capital occurs. Thus, profits would be imputed according to the location of capital use, including fixed capital as well as working capital. Payroll would enter the formula via average working capital needed for wage payments, and sales would enter via investment in sales establishments. Payroll and sales would thus be accounted for, but their weight would be much less than in the apportion-ment formula of the US type, while the weight of capital would be much greater.

Such an allocation would be in line with the source concept, calling for the taxation of capital earnings where the capital operates. But it involves the assumption that the return to capital is the same in all locations. This would be the case in a competitive equilibrium where the return to capital is equalised at the margin and intra-marginal profits are assigned as rents to other factors. However, these are hardly realistic assumptions to make. Suppose first that the product market is competitive, but that the particular location of production permits production at lower cost, the gains of which accrue (at least in part) to capital. In this case, capital operating in that particular location should be assigned a higher share in profits. The problem, in principle, would have to be solved by 'separate accounting' for the firm's operation in each country, with the arm's-length rule being used to divide costs and receipts among the component units operating in various countries.[21]

As a compromise, the location of capital approach (broadly defined) might be used as the rule, with special allowance being made for excess returns in certain situations, such as involve the use of raw materials and low labour costs, where such an adjustment is clearly appropriate. This may be looked upon as but another way of expressing the excess earnings feature of the national rental norm. Assignment of a larger share in the base is essentially the same as permitting the charging of a high tax rate on profits from an unweighted capital base.

Another complication arises where the product market is non-competitive. Suppose the firm has a monopolistic position and is able to sell at differentiated prices in various markets. In maximising profits from total sales, the average return per unit of sale will differ among markets. This being the case, is there justification for differential treatment of the sales factor, giving more favourable treatment to the country in which a larger share of the monopoly profits originate? In principle, it is difficult to deny that there is some justification for such an allowance, but it would be difficult to implement. The determination of price differentials (after allowing for differences in selling costs) would hardly be a feasible procedure. The national rental idea, it appears, is both more feasible and meaningful on the production than on the sales side of the picture.

## Conclusion

The conclusion with regard to base allocation is straightforward for the benefit setting. Allocation should be on a cost-incurred basis. For the case of general revenue, the problem does not arise if the pure residence principle is used. Under source rules, location of capital offers the most reasonable first approximation. This should be tempered, however, by allowance for excess returns where they clearly occur.

Applied to the allocation of tax bases among US states, it appears that the three-factor formula, with more or less equal weights given to capital, payroll and sales, meets neither requirement. For benefit purposes it grossly underweights payroll, while for general revenue, capital is under-weighted. A reasonable solution might be to divide the tax bill into two parts, including (1) a benefit charge based on costs incurred, and (2) a profits tax based largely on capital location. Presumably the latter would command the larger part of the yield.

Applied to the international setting, which involves the finance of central government expenditure, the benefit component tends to be less important. The permanent establishment approach is hardly satisfactory. Implementation of a *bona fide* separate accounting approach is exceedingly difficult and the dividing-line between what does and what does not constitute a separate establishment is arbitrary. Use of a complex apportionment formula, on the other hand, requires multiple returns and is hardly feasible in the absence of international administration. Ultimately, the only satisfactory solution (in line with the conclusions of the preceding section) would be the taxation of such income on an international basis with subsequent allocation of proceeds on an apportionment basis among the participating countries, making allowance for distributional considerations. This is especially called for in view of the rapid growth of the multinational corporation.

In conclusion, it should be noted that the problems dealt with above cannot be wholly separated. The issue of source allocation is clearly linked to that of charging differential rates under the national rental approach. Assigning a larger share of the source to a particular jurisdiction at a uniform rate of tax is equivalent to assigning it a smaller share but permitting a higher rate. On the whole, it would seem desirable to implement redistributional objectives through rate differentiation while attempting to divide the source in line with 'true' economic imputation.

# NOTES

1. Another aspect of inter-nation equity with which we are not concerned here arises in the case of benefit spillovers or of joint ventures such as the St Lawrence Seaway or NATO, where the cost has to be allocated between jurisdictions.

2. Analogous problems arise with product taxation, but are not dealt with here. Thus efficiency considerations favour use of the destination principle but the resulting distribution of national gain may not be acceptable. Net exporters of taxed products (or of products taxed at higher rates) will do better under the origin principle while net importers will gain from destination. It appears that the Common Market plans to use inter-governmental transfers to adjust for this and to obtain a result more nearly in line with inter-nation equity, while otherwise adhering to the origin principle.

3. For a brief history of the subject, see Seligman [8, ch. 2].

4. The term 'double taxation' is ambiguous in the international setting (taxation of a given activity by more than one government) no less than in the domestic setting (multiple taxation of a given activity by a single government). In both cases, what matters is the combined tax burden and its relation to the tax burden borne by other activities. In the domestic setting, multiple taxes may simply be an administrative device to obtain a desired total burden, in which case it is entirely unobjectionable. In the international setting, taxation of a given activity by various governments is similarly unobjectionable provided that such taxes are coordinated to give an appropriate total burden.

5. The principle of source taxation was also endorsed by the Fiscal and Financial Committee of the EEC in the 'Neumark Report' on the grounds (a) that it is more efficient for the country where the activity takes place to administer the tax, and (b) that it is politically desirable for the foreigner to be taxed where he earns his income. [10, para. 3458.25].

6. A proposal to pass through to the individual shareholder foreign withholding taxes on dividends paid to a parent company at home was made in a recent Canadian report on tax reform [7, vol. 4, p. 516].

7. This concept of inter-nation equity might be extended further to include not only the division of income from any given unit of foreign capital but also any allocation effects of taxation on the capital itself. This aspect leads to the concept of the 'optimum tax' analogous to that of the 'optimum tariff'. See [2;3;4, chs. 13, 14].

8. It is assumed for purposes of this discussion that the country of 'primary tax allegiance' is the country of residence, rather than domicile or nationality.

9. For fuller analysis of the matters discussed in this section, see [5; 6, ch. 10].

10. Using a more far-reaching interpretation, the residence principle may be taken to mean that *only* the country of residence is permitted to tax income. In this case the rule would define inter-nation equity. The country of source would be barred from taxing (and deriving a national gain from) foreign investment income. Application of the source principle would be ruled out.

11. The interpretation of this rule if applied to the individual income tax raises a question whether B, in determining the marginal rate at which x's income is to be taxed, should consider his income earned in B only, or his total income including that earned in A. B's share will be larger if the latter view is taken, since a higher marginal rate will apply. This procedure, while correct in principle, is difficult in practice as it would require the filing of multiple returns.

12. It is interesting, therefore, to note that economists have tended to use the term 'taxation by country of income source' rather than 'territoriality'. This may only be a difference in words since in both cases B is entitled to tax and the territoriality rule is also a source rule. At the same time the legal philosophy of the territoriality rule, combined with equal treatment under the law, suggests non-discrimination, whereas the economists' notion of source carries no such connotation.

13. As discussed at other points in this chapter, there remains the objection that profits are not the appropriate base for benefit taxation.

14. In this connection, see also n.7 above.

15. Actually, the problem is complicated because B applies not only its corporation tax to the subsidiary, but also a withholding tax to dividends paid to the parent. An argument may be made that it is consistent for A to credit this withholding tax while granting deferment, the reason being that the withholding tax may be considered as being imposed on the parent directly. Current US practice is to permit both a 'direct' credit for withholding tax but also (and not properly so, since there is deferral) an 'indirect' credit for B's corporation tax.

  It may also be noted that in the case of portfolio investment the proper procedure of giving the direct credit only is followed.

16. Note also that if B has an integrated tax, non-discrimination by B will leave x in the same position as residents of B only if A passes B's tax on to him as a credit against his individual income tax. If at the same time A has an *absolute* tax, this will not be compatible with individual equity in A, and crediting against A's corporation tax is called for. The essence of non-discrimination rests on equal treatment of x by B. It does not require that after A's tax treatment is allowed for the final position of x must be the same as it would if he were a resident of B. Rather, horizontal equity for A is determined by equal treatment with other residents of A under the law of A.

17. We leave open the question of whether this should be defined in terms of residence or citizenship or by other criteria.

18. The reader will recall that in the present discussion we assume the entire product of the firm to be sold in B. If export occurs, B may achieve a national gain. But such national loss to A as may result will be *qua* importer of products, rather than exporter of capital.

19. Complications which arise if the tax is shifted in one country but not in the other, or shifted in varying degrees, cannot be dealt with here.

20. Unfortunately, the extensive analysis of the problem in the Report of the House Judiciary Committee [9] contains little discussion of this aspect.

21. This solution, which more or less resembles actual international practice, does, however, suffer from a number of complications. One of these is that not all foreign business is done through permanent establishments. Yet foreign activity conducted outside permanent establishments cannot be accounted for by separate accounting. Apart from this the concept of arm's length pricing is frequently difficult in application if not in principle. For this reason, treatment of the firm as a unit with apportionment according to location of activity may be preferable. See P.B. Musgrave, 'International division of tax base and the less developed countries', a paper prepared for the UN Division of Public Finance and Fiscal Institutions (1970).

# REFERENCES

[1] *Draft Double Taxation Convention on Income and Capital*, Report of the OECD Fiscal Committee (1963).
[2] Koichi Hamada, 'Strategic aspects of taxation on foreign investment income', *Quarterly Journal of Economics* LXXX, August 1966.
[3] Ronald W. Jones, International capital movements and the theory of tariffs and trade', *Quarterly Journal of Economics* LXXXI, February 1967.
[4] Murray C. Kemp, *The Pure Theory of International Trade* (Englewood Cliffs, N.J., 1964).
[5] Peggy B. Musgrave, *United States Taxation of Foreign Investment Income* (Cambridge, Mass. 1969).
[6] Richard A. Musgrave, *Fiscal Systems* (New Haven, Conn. 1969).
[7] *Report of the Royal Commission on Taxation*, 6 vols., Ottawa 1967.
[8] Edwin R.A. Seligman, *Double Taxation and International Fiscal Cooperation* (New York, 1928).
[9] *State Taxation of Interstate Commerce*, Report of the Special Subcommittee on State Taxation of Interstate Commerce, Committee of the Judiciary (House of Representatives, Washington, 1964).
[10] *Tax Harmonization in the Common Market* (Commerce Clearing House, 1963).

# Part II
## Social Security

# 5 The Role of Social Insurance in an Overall Programme for Social Welfare* 1967

To discuss the role of social insurance in an overall programme for social welfare is no small undertaking. It invites a look back at the evolution of social insurance (with its changing function), at its role in the current scene of affluence ridden with pockets of dire poverty, and at its place in the society of the future, when the economic problem may have become one of the lesser social issues.

My time being short, I shall say very little in the historical vein. At its beginnings, as in Bismarck's path-breaking legislation of the 1880s, social insurance was a means of giving support to the poor, focusing on those conditions (sickness, unemployment, old age) under which the poor suffered the greatest distress. Since then, the western world has enjoyed a vast rise in per capita income, but the need for supporting the poor has not disappeared. Rising incomes have been more than matched by a growing sense of social responsibility toward the underprivileged; and the distribution of income has shown little change, leaving the lowest groups approximately as low, relative to the mean, as they had been before.

But though the relief of poverty remains an important part of social insurance, it is no longer the core issue. Increasingly, social insurance has become a budgeting aid for the middle class and a device to protect the more prudent members of society against those less given to provide for future needs. The modern social insurance model, Swedish-style, operates in a quite different setting and meets a quite different function from that performed by the early systems.

These changes offer an interesting perspective on social history, but we shall not pursue them here. Instead, let us take the analytical tack, and inquire how an 'efficient' society would make use of the social insurance technique in its overall programme for social welfare. By efficient society, we mean a society which is not tied to traditional arrangements and which need not rely on inferior techniques as a political device to secure desired goods, i.e. a society which will apply the most expeditious means in implementing given ends. Having gained some insights on this basis, we

* The Princeton Symposium on The American System of Social Insurance (1967), ed. W. Bowen et al., (New York, McGraw-Hill).

shall then move on to a brief appraisal of the US policy setting, and sketch what the future role of social insurance should be.

## THE RATIONALE OF SOCIAL INSURANCE

Social insurance is not a goal in itself but a technique of securing social welfare. We must begin, therefore, by identifying the objectives of welfare policy and defining what is meant by social insurance.

### Objectives and Definitions

For our purposes two objectives need be distinguished. One, to which we refer as the *humanitarian* objective, demands that no one should suffer economic distress, and accordingly calls for the assurance of minimum incomes.[1] The other, referred to as the *egalitarian* objective, demands that the coefficient of inequality should not exceed a certain level, and calls for general measures of redistribution.

The two objectives, of course, are not unrelated. Egalitarian policies, if carried sufficiently far, will take care of minimum levels; and providing for minimum levels is itself an equalising measure. Yet, two distinct philosophies are involved. Being a humanitarian does not imply being an egalitarian; and while the humanitarian objective is a more or less accepted feature in the mores of our society, the egalitarian goal remains controversial, with its ups and downs.

Turning now to social insurance as a technique for securing social welfare, we define the term rather narrowly so as to distinguish it from other policies of income transfer or social security at large. 'Social insurance' in *our* sense means *mandatory* provision for economic contingencies, financed out of *contributions* on a *quid pro quo* basis. Thus, all those subject to certain contingencies must contribute and the actuarial value of each person's benefits must match the cost of his contribution. Welfare payments drawn from general budgetary finance are not societal insurance in this functional sense, nor are privately organised schemes on an individual or group (company) basis. Social insurance as here defined is thus a much narrower concept than social security or social welfare at large and strictly distinguishable from redistributive transfers. We are aware, of course, that the term 'social insurance' is frequently used in a much broader sense and that actual systems of social insurance contain mixed features. Our narrow concept is not advanced as a terminological point but to permit us to separate issues and to assess the functional role of the insurance technique.[2] Whether the scheme is publicly operated, as is usually the case, or makes use of regulated private insurance carriers is not crucial to our argument.

### The Humanitarian View

Consider first a society which accepts the humanitarian goal, but is not egalitarian. While it is held necessary to transfer income from those above the minimum to those below, the prevailing distribution of income is otherwise accepted as proper and not subject to correction. The scope of required transfers will then depend on the lower tail of the distribution and on how minimum income is set. If defined in terms of biological need (calories required), the transfer share in national income will decline as per capita income rises provided that the lower tail (say decile) of the income distribution continues to receive at least the same percentage of total income. If defined in relative terms (percentage of mean income) such will not be the case. The needed transfer share remains unchanged unless distribution at the lower end becomes more equal.

At first glance it would seem that there is no role for social insurance under these conditions. To implement the humanitarian principle of minimum income, transfers from those above the minimum to those below (in effect a zero yield of positive–negative income tax) will be called for. Beyond this, why should social insurance be needed? If people wish to insure as a matter of household budgeting let them do so on a voluntary basis. This seems convincing, but at closer consideration proves incorrect. It overlooks the fact that the goodwill of the humanitarian is not boundless. While he agrees to income transfers when the need arises, he also demands measures which will minimise this need. This is the key consideration which underlies much of the following argument.

Economic distress (which requires relief) may arise because (a) lifetime earnings are too low, (b) the time distribution of need differs from that of income, and (c) contingencies occur which have not been provided for in advance. Cause (a) poses no problem of abuse. It neither calls for nor can it be met by a social insurance approach. Outright transfers are needed, making the humanitarian objective a special case of the egalitarian, e.g. redistribution toward the lower tail financed by proportional taxes above.[3] Let us suppose that such transfers are made, leaving individuals with a lifetime income which with prudent management is adequate to meet contingencies. This still leaves causes (b) and (c), and these are the ones which may be countered or minimised by social insurance.

Beginning with (b), suppose that everyone is certain to die at age 90, while income ceases at age 65. Thus 25 years of minimum income must be provided for. Now let Calvin and Homer, who are prudent, provide for their old age, while Jack lives it up and does not. Calvin and Homer, knowing that they will have to provide for the aged Jack, will call for a social insurance plan which will force Jack himself to make his own provision and thus relieve them of the burden. Note that the role of social insurance in this case is not technically an insurance function at all. Having assumed perfect certainty as to the length of retirement, we are not dealing with a situation where there is a probable risk which may be provided for more cheaply by group action, on an actuarial basis. The objective is not one of spreading risk but of forestalling the need for transfers from the prudent to the feckless. The essential function of social insurance, in this case, is compulsory saving.

But in case (c) an insurable situation does arise, Calvin, Homer and Jack all face the contingency of illness, or uncertain length of retirement life, or of the needs of their dependants in case of death. For this reason they will find it cheaper to join in insurance than to provide individually. This mere fact (that there is an economic case for spreading risks via insurance) in itself does not establish the need for social insurance. Insurance could be purchased privately but becomes a matter of public concern only because Jack will not do so, while Homer and Calvin will. Given their humanitarian premise Calvin and Homer must bail out Jack should the contingency arise. They will require therefore that Jack should insure. Social insurance is now insurance in the technical sense, but its basic function (and especially the rationale for making it mandatory) is again to avoid burdening the prudent. This is the basic point, and not the fact that we are dealing with uncertainty and a technically insurable situation.

Now it might be argued that Calvin and Homer, instead of forcing everyone to insure, have the alternative of joining Jack in not insuring and relying on budgetary support (assistance payments from general revenue) should the contingency strike them. If we assume that the contingency (e.g. illness) is equally probable for all three, universal non-insurance with budgetary compensation to the damaged (financed by head tax) is equivalent to universal insurance. Hence why require social insurance? The answer is that the equivalence holds only if everyone receives the same budgetary support if the contingency strikes. But in a non-egalitarian world this is not the case since the humanitarian premise calls for damages only if income falls below the minimum. Suppose Calvin is 'rich' and has sufficient reserves to meet his needs if the contingency strikes, while Homer and Jack are 'poor' and without reserves. The budgetary alternative to social insurance will then be acceptable (and indeed preferable) to the Homers as well as the Jacks, but not to the Calvins. The Calvins will call for social insurance not only to avoid discrimination against the prudent (in which they are joined by the Homers) but also to minimise the extent to which the rich will be called upon to finance the poor (i.e. Homers and Jacks).

Indeed, the case for social insurance is even stronger than the preceding argument suggests. The very guarantee that minimum income payments will be received when needed gives an incentive (under the budgetary system) not to provide for old age and not to insure. Even Homer, though potentially prudent, will try to maximise his consumption over time by creating situations of need. Putting it differently, minimum income becomes a social good which may be substituted for private provision. This substitution, to be sure, will not be complete since the publicly required minimum will seem inadequate to many people who, therefore, will make additional provision. Nevertheless, unqualified application of the humanitarian principle creates a disincentive to provide, which calls for a social insurance approach.

We thus arrive at the conclusion that the functional role of social insurance, far from being a means of helping the careless and the poor, is a device to protect the prudent and the rich. Such at least is the case in our assumed setting, where the humanitarian objective of minimum income must be met with or without a responsibility test. Lest this seem too startling a view, let me add that these considerations apply to the functional role of social insurance in our hypothetical and efficient system. They are not offered as a theory of history or of social insurance development. The rise of social insurance, as it actually occurred, involved extensive reliance on non-contributory finance, thus combining humanitarian and egalitarian objectives. Indeed, social insurance was the redistributive wedge driven into a social structure hesitant to accept either the humanitarian or the egalitarian objective. But even as such, it was more acceptable, because of its inherently conservative nature, than an outright assault on redistribution. It was, after all, Otto von Bismarck who first introduced social insurance, and not David Lloyd-George or Franklin D. Roosevelt.

## The Egalitarian View

Foregoing the temptations of fiscal sociology, we return to our 'efficient' model and now introduce the egalitarian objective. Suppose the goal is to move all incomes by a given fraction towards the mean. To accomplish this, we need a progressive tax-transfer scheme, i.e. a positive–negative income tax with a zero rate at the minimum income. There is no need in this case for social insurance. If Calvin and Homer wish to insure, they may do so; but since there is no humanitarian (minimum-income) commitment, they have no reason for requiring Jack to do the same. If he fails to insure and is caught without income, this will be his problem only. The rationale of social insurance relates to the humanitarian, not the egalitarian, objective.

## Combined Objectives

We may now combine the two objectives. In the limiting case, redistribution may be so extensive and/or the mean income so high relative to the humanitarian threshold that all individuals have sufficient reserves so that no one will suffer distress, whatever contingency may fall upon him. But short of this golden age, income may still fall below the minimum, and our earlier rationale for social insurance still applies; and even in the golden age voluntary private insurance (which reduces the cost of meeting contingencies) remains efficient.

But for the foreseeable future social insurance will remain necessary. This is the case especially since the time dimensions of the humanitarian and egalitarian objectives differ. The provision for minimum income, designed to assure that no one should suffer economic distress, must by its very nature be related to current needs. It is not enough for the humanitarian to assure adequate lifetime income. The aged but penniless Jack has to be supported even though his earlier income would have been sufficient to provide for his old age. Distress must be relieved even when due to negligence, and this is precisely why social insurance is needed. The case differs for the egalitarian objective. Here, redistribution is ideally in terms of lifetime income,[4] leaving it to the individual to arrange his time pattern of consumption. This is but an extension of the familiar principle that there should be averaging under the progressive income tax. But if egalitarian redistribution is to be on a lifetime basis, it will be relatively ineffective in removing the need for social insurance. Jack may call for support, even though he should have been able to provide for himself, and Homer and Calvin will want to be protected.

Since social insurance is a means of reducing the humanitarians' burden nothing essentially new is added by combining it with the egalitarian goal. We are now concerned with two sets of payments involving (1) redistribution from high to low incomes, and (2) a contributory insurance scheme. The former as noted before requires a progressive positive–negative income tax. The latter requires equal per capita contributions,[5] and payments to those below the minimum. It may then be convenient as a matter of administrative simplification to add insurance premiums to and deduct benefit payments from the positive–negative income tax. The result would be a net schedule which is less progressive at the upper and more progressive at the lower end of the scale than the redistribution tax by itself.[6] But though the combination of both sets of payments would give the appearance of budgetary finance, it would only involve a netting process still containing the core of a contributory system.

## Further Considerations

Before leaving the theoretical discussion, we may note certain additional considerations which have been passed over so far.

### *Regressivity of Contributory Tax*

Viewed as a contributory system, the true distributional effect (benefits minus contributions) of social insurance is neither progressive, proportional nor regressive, but cancels out to zero. While the introduction of social insurance changes the size distribution of annual income for the group (rendering it less equal at the upper and more equal at the lower end), it does not affect the individual's lifetime income or the distribution of lifetime incomes for the group.

Looking at social insurance as a contributory system, it thus makes no sense to talk about the 'regressivity' of a truly contributory tax. One might as well talk about the regressivity of food prices. (A loaf of bread costs more, as a percent of income, if the buyer's income is low.) In either case, the benefit side must be considered as well, and benefits (by definition of a contributory system) are as progressive (relative to lifetime income) as contributions are regressive. What is net-regressive, however, is the extent to which income is subject to compulsory use, be it in the saving or insurance context. This regressivity of compulsion follows from the humanitarian objective, which assures a minimum income only, i.e. an amount that constitutes a larger part of the low lifetime income.

The perspective is changed, of course, if we step outside our 'efficient' system, with its separation of social insurance and redistribution, and consider social insurance a means of redistribution. In this case, benefits are part of the transfer side, and contributions are part of the tax side of the general redistribution scheme. It then becomes inconsistent to combine a crudely regressive payroll tax with a progressive income tax in one and the same overall revenue system.

## Intergeneration Equity

The problem of inter-generation equity, which has bedevilled the OAS-DHI discussion since its inception, is peculiar to the problem of old age insurance. It does not arise with other contingencies, such as health and disability, where the volume of claims is level from the outset, and a mature system can be started almost *de novo*. In the case of retirement needs, contributions exceed benefits for a long time, unless the initially old are given benefits without having contributed accordingly.

Now it might be said that this poses no problem in the context of our model. Social insurance is imposed in order to protect the prudent, given the humanitarian premise that a minimum income must be provided. This being the case, nothing is lost if at the outset of the humanitarian regime it is decided to pay benefits to the present old. If these were not paid *qua* social insurance, they would have to be paid *qua* budgetary provision. Thus, it is merely a formality under which heading the present old are to be included.

Moreover, it might be argued that the cost of 'giving' benefits to the initial generation of the old is not borne by those currently of working age, but by the last (doomsday) generation. To simplify matters, suppose that population and per capita income are constant. Each generation, A, B ... J, lives 2 'years', one during which it works and contributes, and another during which it is retired and receives benefits. We begin in year 1 when A is retired and B works. B's contributions then support A's benefits. But in year 2, B is retired and C works. Now B's benefits are financed by C's contributions, and so forth. If the world were to end in year n, the then-working would have contributed to the then-old without compensation thereafter, so that in this sense the cost of supporting A would fall upon them. As long as the world continues (and since this is a hypothetical discussion we may expect it to do so) the cost of supporting A is postponed indefinitely.[7]

Looked at this way, the system is on a pay-as-you-go basis from the outset, even though the contributory principle applies except at the very beginning or end of the process. A need for reserve accumulation arises only if the initially aged are excluded, and the financing of relief paid to them is treated as unrelated to the insurance system. However, we have assumed that population and per capita income remain constant. If population increases, each generation is subsidised by the succeeding generation, unless reserves are built up; and the same holds if per capita income rises and the minimum income (i.e. benefit level) rises with it.[8] Thus, pay-as-you-go (meaning equality of total current contributions and total current benefits and thus absence of reserves) is compatible with the contributory principle (meaning equality of present value costs and benefits for each individual) only under very simplified assumptions. Whether reserve accumulation is compatible, in the context of macro-economic considerations, with an effective stabilisation policy is a different matter, which cannot be considered here.[9]

### Goods–Leisure Preference

Nothing has been said so far about the effects of our policies on the choice between goods and leisure. These enter the argument in two ways.

We have argued that the humanitarian, though willing to provide minimum income, also wishes to protect himself against abuse. In particular, we have noted that the 'prudent' will wish to protect themselves against having to bail out others less given to providing for the future. A similar problem arises regarding the choice between goods and leisure. The humanitarian's objective of providing for 'income' ideally aims at providing a minimum level of welfare, or bundles of goods and leisure. If the rate of substitution between leisure and goods were uniform, the provision could be made in terms of goods only. But with preferences differing, income provision in terms of goods may lead to transfer from those who value goods highly relative to leisure, to others who value leisure highly relative to goods. This presumably is not part of the humanitarian objective. An additional reason for protection against abuse arises.

Looking at any one individual, the optimal solution would be to provide him with such subsidy as would lift him to whatever indifference curve is considered to constitute his welfare minimum, leaving it to him to choose between the goods–leisure allocation.[10] But this is not an operational approach, since his utility levels are unknown, not to speak of the interpersonal comparisons involved in applying the minimum among the group of individuals. A more feasible approach may be to use a wage rate subsidy such that $(w + s)h = Y_m$ and $s = M - hw/h$, where $w$ is the worker's wage rate, $h$ is the 'standard' number of hours worked per week, and $Y_m$ is the minimum weekly income. By postulating $h$ in this fashion a social goods–leisure preference is introduced, and the solution will be short of optimal; but it will be preferable on both equity and efficiency grounds to paying $L = Y_m - Y$, where $L$ is a lump-sum subsidy and $Y$ is the income actually received.[11]

### New Contingencies

It is only reasonable to expect that the types of contingencies which should be subject to social insurance will change with changing technology and social practices.

Automobile insurance is of particular interest in this connection. Injury caused by A to B, be it his person or his property, establishes B's right to compensation from A, and vice versa. Suppose B is prudent and covers himself by liability insurance while A does not. Also, suppose that A's property is insufficient to compensate B in the case of injury to B. The Bs will therefore require that everyone be insured so that the possible victims can be compensated. This makes the situation one of social insurance. The difference from preceding cases is but minor; in both situations the measure is essentially designed to protect the prudent party whether against abuse of his humanitarian commitment as above or in support of his right to compensation as in the case of automobile insurance.[12]

## THE US SETTING: APPRAISAL AND OUTLOOK

Let us now leave the normative level and step down (or up) to the concrete problems of welfare policy in the US. Looking at the 1960s scene, what is to be said about the scope of social insurance and its future role in a balanced policy for social welfare? Raising this question is to begin a new paper, but I must not leave the formal approach without placing it at least briefly in the perspective of our policy problem. My view in a nutshell is that social insurance needs to be strengthened, but that it is not the aspect of welfare policy which, in the decade to come, is most in need of attention. Emphasis should be above all on the poverty issue, and this is not primarily a matter of social insurance.

The US structure of income maintenance payments (i.e. social welfare programmes providing for cash support) is shown in Table 5.1. For 1965 it included $21 billion of social insurance and $4 billion of assistance payments. The former is very largely old age and survivors' insurance. The

*Table 5.1 Income maintenance payments in the US, 1965 (in billions $)[1]*

| | | | |
|---|---|---|---|
| 1. | Social insurance | | |
| | OASDHI | | 18.3 |
| | unemployment | | 2.4 |
| | temporary disability | | 0.4 |
| | | Total | 21.1 |
| 2. | Public assistance | | |
| | old age | | 1.6 |
| | dependent children | | 1.7 |
| | aid to the blind | | 0.1 |
| | aid to the disabled | | 0.4 |
| | general assistance | | 0.3 |
| | | Total | 4.1[2] |
| 3. | Total | | 25.2[3] |

*Notes:*
1 Social Security Bulletin (June 1967).
2 Vendor payments are excluded.
3 Excludes military pensions, veterans payments, government pensions and railroad retirement. The grand total of government transfers to persons, as reported for 1965, is $37.1 billion. See Survey of Current Business (July 1966), p. 23.

latter includes miscellaneous assistance programmes paid to eligible groups on a need basis. It is these programmes which have increasingly become the subject of criticism and which are most in need of reconsideration.

### Insurance and Contingencies

But let us begin with the insurance programmes. Unnecessary to say, these programmes are not 'social insurance' in the strict sense in which the term has been used in the preceding discussion. While they are compulsory and financed by special contributions, they involve a considerable degree of redistribution among covered individuals, and are thus not contributory in our strict sense of the term. Also, and most important, the insurance system operates not on the basis of a 'proper' distribution of income which has been established by other means. Thus a person may not have enough income to buy his social insurance and the social insurance system becomes part of the equalisation mechanism.

Nevertheless, OASDHI contains a sufficient social insurance content to be discussed under this heading. The continued need for OASDHI is without question. We shall hardly be sufficiently wealthy, in the foreseeable future, to remove the state of the aged and their dependants from public concern. The question rather is how the system can be strengthened and how it should be financed. Coverage now approaches a state of being fairly complete but some still remain outside and should be included. Benefit levels should be raised to the proposed $70–100 minimum a month; even this remains well below the required minimum for acceptable existence. Apart from this, it is surely appropriate to adjust benefits for inflation as this merely expresses the contributory approach in real terms.[13]

More controversial is the question of whether the system should continue on the basis of payroll tax finance, or whether a budgetary contribution should be included. I am aware that the *quid pro quo* principle is not implemented in any strict sense by the present set of contribution and benefit formulae, but that there exists a complex (and, I gather, largely accidental and even unknown) set of redistribution patterns.[14] I am also aware that the very nature of the tax (with its employer and employee side) does not quite fit the contributory approach. Yet I am hesitant to proceed to the conclusion that therefore budgetary finance should be used primarily to deal with the poverty problem. Even though the aged are a sizeable part of this problem (some 35 per cent of the heads of poor families, using the Council of Economic Advisor's (CEA) definition, are over 65) only 60 per cent of the OASDHI benefits go to the poor, or families which otherwise would be poor.[15] Moreover, such redistributional patterns as exist within OASDHI are not primarily pro-poor, if seen in terms of lifetime income. Budgetary finance of OASDHI, therefore, is only a second- or third-best approach to the poverty problem. This being the case, I prefer to see the latter tackled directly, while permitting OASDHI to play what should be its proper (as previously outlined) role in a high-income society.

Similar considerations apply regarding health insurance. Our first timid step in this direction, providing health insurance for the aged, is to be welcomed, and extension to the rest of the people is to be hoped for. The case for it seems so obvious that even the organised medical profession should, in due course, find it an acceptable proposition. It is the kind of contingency which, *par excellence*, requires social insurance (i.e. mandatory provision) for the very reasons which have been outlined above.[16] Moreover, I should be happy in *this* case to go beyond the contributory idea and provide for budgetary help. Basic health, like education, is of such importance to the nation (the externalities involved are so strong) that public support is called for. Moreover, mandatory provision for health insurance is justified in that health may well be considered a 'merit want' which the individual should be forced to meet.

Unemployment insurance, finally, should have a successful and relatively tranquil future. My reason for saying so is the optimistic but, I hope, not wholly unjustified assumption that stabilisation policy will be successful in the future to avoid severe periods of unemployment. By creating a sustained level of high employment, it will also create the environment in which unemployment insurance, operating *qua* insurance, can play a meaningful role. Indeed, thought may be given, in this new setting, to reorienting the system away from cyclical and toward seasonal structural unemployment, thus aiding in the adaptation of the labour force to the changing needs (technological and regional) of the economy. This also places experience rating in a new perspective [Lester, 3]. Whereas it made little sense to hold particular industries responsible for cyclical unemployment, it may well be desirable (on grounds of efficient allocation) to have them bear the cost of seasonal unemployment and of certain types of structural unemployment.

## Redistribution and Poverty

This much for social insurance: while it has played a great role in the past and is essential to a secure future, it is not our main problem. Social insurance is, and properly will become, increasingly a budgetary aid for those who basically are financially solvent. The main, and most urgent, problem ahead is to deal with the abysmal pockets of poverty which disgrace our otherwise affluent social scene. As estimated for 1964 poverty (defined by the CEA as familial income below $3000) involved 33 million people, leaving a 'poverty income gap' of $11 billion. Such is the case, notwithstanding a $21 billion level of social insurance, and $4 billion of assistance programmes of various kinds.[17] Income maintenance payments in all comprise some 40 per cent of the income of the poor,[18] but they fall far short of the job which is needed. The 'war on poverty' as well has been a rather half-hearted affair and a new look is urgently called for.

It goes without saying that the solution not only involves a revised and expanded system of income payments, but also (and perhaps primarily) more direct measures to integrate the poor into a constructive society, including education, retraining, resettlement, and so forth. Also, there is no question that high employment and an expanding economy are pre-requisites to meeting this task. Unless there are jobs for newly-trained workers, training them but leads to increased frustration; and unless employment is kept high, the first to lose their jobs will be those who barely escaped the poverty trap.

These aspects are vital, but I must set them aside and concentrate on the income maintenance problem which is more closely a part of my topic. We begin with a limited budget or budget constraint and then see how best to meet the problem. Two basic policy issues are involved. First, there is the question whether payments should be related to income and family size only, or whether other need factors should be considered as well. Second, there is the question of how payments should be related to income so as to minimise interference with incentives.

With regard to the first, it is obvious that the greatest relief of distress can be obtained if limited funds are distributed according to need, allowing for income differentials as well as other characteristics of the family unit such as size, age of children and parents, state of health, assets, housing, and so forth. This is the means test approach. While most efficient in the budgeting sense it has the disadvantage that its application may be humiliating to the recipient. Such is the case especially if absurd conditions (i.e. absence of male head of family) apply which are detrimental to family life. The question is how and whether the valuable core of the approach, that benefits from limited payments are maximised if they are directed to the *most* needy recipients, can be retained while eliminating the most objectionable features. This, I take it, is the crux of current thinking about revision of the welfare programme. The alternative is to replace the tailored welfare approach by a formula under which payments are related to total income and family size only, without allowance for other family characteristics. This obviates the means test, but leaves us with a less effective distribution of payments.[19] The larger the available budget, the less serious will be this disadvantage.

With regard to the more general approach it is evident that a payment formula which uses the available funds to raise substandard incomes toward the standard (thus setting a floor below which no family unit income can fall) is most effective in meeting need. But it also means that a family finds its subsidy reduced, dollar for dollar, as its earnings rise.

The poor are thus made subject to a marginal tax of 100 per cent, and might as well retain their leisure. This is objectionable to those who finance the support by working (see above), and is harmful to the recipient because useful work is needed to integrate him into society and to break the poverty cycle. Within the context of income equalisation the problem is basically insoluble. Income equalisation, be it by financing general budget benefits through progressive taxation or by redistributing to the poor, involves marginal rates in excess of average rates and has an adverse substitution effect on effort. Rate structures may be developed which will moderate the severity of this effect but they will not eliminate the problem.

If a negative–positive income tax is applied, the transfer rate (transfer as a per cent of income) may be permitted to decline gradually toward zero, and no sudden cut-off is needed. This has the advantage that the filling-in of income at the lower end of the scale can be accomplished with a much lower marginal rate (say, 30 per cent, as in Professor Tobin's proposal), thus avoiding the extreme effect of a 100 per cent rate. But it is accomplished at the cost of spreading the transfers over a much broader income range, i.e. being less effective (for any given total budget involved) in relieving low-income distress.[20] Again, this cost is more acceptable if the available budget is larger.

In conclusion, the solution depends on the size of the available budget. If the budget is small relative to needs, the welfare approach is needed, and detrimental effects have to be accepted. If the budget is large, a generalised income formula can be used together with a pattern of payments which involves lower marginal rates. Whichever approach is taken, and most likely a mixture of both is needed, it is imperative to spread the cost of financing the relief of poverty over a nationwide revenue base. The concentration of poverty in a particular city or region is typically the result of national, not local, economic development; and local needs to combat poverty are typically associated with lack of fiscal resources to meet them. For both reasons, relief of poverty is not a function which can be met adequately by local finance. By its very nature it must be met at the national level. The implications of this for the relationship of federal to state and local finance are evident. While in the past the federal contribution to welfare policy has been primarily through social insurance, the future role of federal finance will have to be on a much broader basis.

## NOTES

1. As noted below in connection with rescue cost the same principle may be extended to non-economic distress.
2. If the reader wishes to include a broader range of welfare policies under the term 'social insurance' he may do so. This paper then deals with that *part* of social insurance which involves contributory and mandatory provision.
3. The taxes are assumed to be proportional because we assume absence of egalitarian objectives.
4. While the principle is clear, implementation of redistribution on a lifetime basis is difficult. The annual tax (plus or minus) would have to be reassessed at, say, five-year intervals on an averaging basis, and it may be necessary to consider changes in presumptive future income as well as in actual past income.
5. This assumes that everybody is equally risk-prone, and thus pays the same premium to insure for receiving the same (minimum income) amount.
6. This follows because the equal per capita contribution is regressive, while the benefits go to low-income brackets (people subject to the contingency will earn little or not at all) and are thus progressive.
7. This way of putting the matter somewhat overstates the case. Actually, B (and each following generation) loses the interest which it would have earned if its

savings could have been invested rather than used to support the consumption of the then-aged. The A generation, in fact, receives an interest-free loan which is extended indefinitely, and even the capital obligation comes to be forgiven by the doomsday generation.

8. Under pay-as-you-go each working generation pays for its contemporary retirement generation. Given a constant level of per capita income, the latter receives more, if numbers rise, than it has contributed. Similarly, if numbers are constant but per capita income rises and contributions rise with it, each retirement generation will receive more than it has contributed.

9. Compatibility exists in a 'classical' system, where investment matches *ex ante* saving. But where this is not the case and stabilising policy is needed, the necessary rate of saving in the economy (including private and budgetary) is determined by the requirements of stabilisation. Thus, if social insurance saves more, the required surplus (deficit) in the remainder of the budget will be correspondingly less (larger). Similar conflicts arise even in the classical setting if the growth rate becomes a further policy target.

10. The subsidy may be given to him either as a wage rate subsidy or as a lump-sum payment. The individual will be indifferent between the two, but in the former case he will work more and demand a larger payment.

11. This discussion is merely to indicate the lines along which this argument could be extended, without trying to do so here.

12. Other situations in which 'social insurance' is in order may be thought of readily. Amateur sailors or mountain-climbers should be required to insure for the cost of rescue. Obviously some such situations are more important than others and not equally in need of legislative consideration.

13. Productivity gains will be reflected automatically in rising benefits (on the contributory basis) provided that contributions remain a constant percent of rising earnings. As a result, the absolute difference between the benefits of the retired and the earnings of the working generation will rise, but the ratio will remain constant.

14. The major redistribution is among individuals who have participated for different lengths of time and are subject to changing contribution rates or levels. I have not been able to find estimates of what the redistribution pattern would be if present contribution and benefit rates were to apply for a full working life. For a discussion of redistribution effects see Aaron [1] and [2].

15. See *Economic Report for 1967*, p. 139.

16. We recall that the principle of social insurance leaves open the question whether the insurance carrier should be public or private or how (apart from assuring that the mandatory buyer be given his money's worth) health services should be rendered.

17. *Economic Report for 1964*, p. 68.

18. The actual amount is larger as related programmes not involving cost disbursements are not included.

19. How much less effective it will be depends on the extent to which the needs of families of equal size and income differ. A study of this question would be most helpful in permitting a choice between the various income maintenance problems.

20. The importance of incentive effects in choosing between the strategy of matching the difference between actual and minimum income (allowing for family size but not for other need characteristics), and the strategy of using a transfer-tax formula (which lets the transfer rate decline and become negative

as the minimum income is approached from below and passed), depends on the extent to which the poor are indeed potential members of the labour force. It was recently reported that of the 5.3 million people on the welfare rolls, only about 50,000 fathers are potential supporters of their families. The biggest single group of recipients (and the most important for avoiding the proliferation of poverty) are the 3.5 million children of poor families not yet in the labour force.

# REFERENCES

[1] Aaron, H. (1967), 'Benefits under the American Social Security System', in Eckstein, O. ed., *Studies in the Economics of Income Maintenance*, (Washington, DC, The Brookings Institution).
[2] Deran, E. (1966), 'Income Redistribution under the Social Security System', *National Tax Journal*, XIX, 3.
[3] Lester, R. (1967), 'The Uses of Unemployment Insurance', in Brown, D. ed., *The American System of Social Insurance*, (New York, McGraw-Hill).

# 6 Cost-Effectiveness of Alternative Income Maintenance Schemes* 1970

The traditional approach to welfare has come under increasing criticism. The major objections are (1) that benefit payments are inadequate, (2) that they differ sharply among states, (3) that work incentives are reduced by a high marginal tax rate implicit in the formula, (4) that incentives are given to break up families, and (5) that detailed regulations interfere with the privacy of the welfare recipients.

Objection (1) calls for a larger budget, while (2) calls for replacement of state plans by a federal scheme. To eliminate adverse substitution effects of income payments, it would be necessary to make grants to all family units independent of income status or family structure, and equal in amount to the average poverty-line income. Such a scheme would involve astronomical costs. Paying an average of, say, $2500 to 70 million households would cost $175 billion as compared to a poverty gap of below $10 billion. The incremental cost would be enormous, even if savings on present programmes are allowed for. Given the infeasibility of this type of plan, the lesson is that income maintenance must be approached within a realistic budget constraint; and once this is done, not all the criticisms of the traditional system can be met equally well and at the same time.

Rather, there has to be a trade-off between closing the poverty gap and other objectives such as non-interference with work incentives, family structure and privacy. Recent proposals recognise this and attempt to compromise between objectives. The administration proposal of August 1969 may be viewed as a negative income tax with a minimum income of $1600 for a family of four and a dual tax rate of 0 for the first $720 of annual earnings, and 50 per cent thereafter. In addition, certain categories of recipients are required to register for work to be eligible. The additional cost of the revised programme (i.e. the amount by which costs will exceed those of the present assistance programme) is estimated at $2.5 billion for fiscal 1971 [7]. The proposed benefit level is substantially above that of the low-welfare states, but it is below the 1969 state average of $2252. The overall increase in benefits is thus slight, and limited to the low-welfare states. The proposal of the Income Maintenance Commission is for a

* With P. Heller and G. Peterson, *National Tax Journal*, vol. XXIII, 2 (1970).

negative income tax with a minimum of $2400 for a family of four, and a tax rate of 50 per cent. The plan is to be substituted for present welfare payments at an additional cost of $5.9 billion for 1971 [6]. Both proposals thus choose the negative income tax route and for most of the range use the same 50 per cent of tax rate. Both plans are modest in scope. While the Income Maintenance Commission's proposal goes somewhat further in closing the poverty gap, even its benefit levels remain one-third below the poverty-line.

The practical problem, therefore, is to choose the most efficient scheme available within a tight budget constraint. This calls for examining how alternative schemes perform under changing budget constraints, and in terms of specified criteria, especially the trade-off among gap-closing and maintenance of work incentives. The recent availability of the Survey of Economic Opportunity data has made such calculations possible, and the results are presented here.[1]

While our results are of considerable interest, a warning is in order. Our findings apply to a static setting, in which effects on work effort are disregarded. The level of earnings which is to be supplemented is assumed the same under all plans. This is a serious shortcoming, but no reliable information on work responses is as yet available. In the meantime, this type of analysis offers a first step towards a more complete investigation.

## POVERTY AND PUBLIC ASSISTANCE PAYMENTS, THE PRESENT STATUS

Table 6.1 summarises the composition of poor households and the impact of the public assistance system for 1966, the year of the SEO survey.[2] The survey covers a sample of some 26,000 households and presents comprehensive information on the income sources and structure of the sample families. Though not without problems, the sample provides the most complete information now available.[3]

Horizontally, Table 6.1 classifies households by type of family head. Vertically, lines 1–6 group households by income brackets, where bracket limits relate to income as a per cent of the SSA poverty-lines for 1966.[4] In carrying out the classification, the poverty-line appropriate for each household is used. Lines 7 and 8 show total households and total number of persons in poverty, while line 9 shows the total poverty gap in billion dollars. Finally, for each household category, the distributions are shown with reference to income positions before public assistance payments and federal income tax, after assistance but before tax, and after assistance and tax.

The total number of households in poverty after assistance and income tax was 11.1 million, as against 11.5 million before assistance and income tax. The net effect of assistance payments in removing people from poverty was thus very small, although the reduction in the number of families

*Table 6.1 Effect of present public assistance transfers and federal income tax on distribution of household income**

| Item | Households headed by males < 65 | | | Families headed by females < 65 | | | Unrelated females < 65 | | | Households headed by persons > 65 | | | All households | | |
|---|---|---|---|---|---|---|---|---|---|---|---|---|---|---|---|
| | B.A. B.T. | A.A. B.T. | A.A. A.T. | B.A. B.T. | A.A. B.T. | A.A. A.T. | B.A. B.T. | A.A. B.T. | A.A. A.T. | B.A. B.T. | A.A. B.T. | A.A. A.T. | B.A. B.T. | A.A. B.T. | A.A. A.A. |
| *Income as per cent of poverty line* | | | | | | | *Number of households in poverty (millions)* | | | | | | | | |
| 1. 0 to 0.25 | 0.8 | 0.6 | 0.6 | 0.7 | 0.25 | 0.25 | 0.4 | 0.3 | 0.3 | 0.9 | 0.3 | 0.3 | 2.8 | 1.5 | 1.5 |
| 2. 0.25 to 0.50 | 0.8 | 0.8 | 0.8 | 0.4 | 0.4 | 0.4 | 0.3 | 0.2 | 0.2 | 0.9 | 0.8 | 0.8 | 2.4 | 2.2 | 2.2 |
| 3. 0.50 to 0.75 | 1.1 | 1.2 | 1.2 | 0.3 | 0.5 | 0.5 | 0.3 | 0.4 | 0.4 | 1.3 | 1.3 | 1.3 | 3.0 | 3.4 | 3.4 |
| 4. 0.75 to 1.00 | 1.4 | 1.4 | 1.5 | 0.3 | 0.45 | 0.45 | 0.4 | 0.3 | 0.3 | 1.3 | 1.7 | 1.7 | 3.4 | 3.8 | 3.9 |
| 5. 1.00 to 1.25 | 2.1 | 2.1 | 2.5 | 0.25 | 0.3 | 0.3 | 0.2 | 0.3 | 0.4 | 1.2 | 1.2 | 1.2 | 3.8 | 3.9 | 4.4 |
| 6. 1.25 to 1.50 | 2.3 | 2.3 | 3.0 | 0.3 | 0.3 | 0.4 | 0.2 | 0.3 | 0.3 | 1.1 | 1.3 | 1.3 | 3.9 | 4.2 | 5.0 |
| 7. Total, (line 1–4) | 4.1 | 4.0 | 4.1 | 1.7 | 1.6 | 1.6 | 1.4 | 1.2 | 1.2 | 4.4 | 4.1 | 4.1 | 11.6 | 10.9 | 11.0 |
| | | | | | | | *Number of persons in poverty (millions)* | | | | | | | | |
| 8. Total | 17.0 | 16.3 | 16.4 | 7.5 | 6.9 | 6.9 | 1.5 | 1.4 | 1.4 | 7.2 | 6.9 | 6.9 | 33.2 | 31.5 | 31.6 |
| | | | | | | | *Poverty gap (billions)* | | | | | | | | |
| 9. Total | 5.9 | 5.3 | 5.3 | 3.5 | 2.3 | 2.3 | 1.3 | 1.1 | 1.1 | 3.8 | 2.7 | 2.7 | 14.5 | 11.4 | 11.4 |

* Numbers have been rounded.
B.A. = before public assistance; B.T. = before tax; A.A. = after public assistance; A.T. = after tax.

falling within the lowest quarter of our distribution was substantial.[5] The size of the poverty gap before welfare was $14.5 billion as against $11.4 billion after welfare.[6] Thus, the net effect of welfare payments was to reduce the gap by 21 per cent.

Finally, it is of interest to compare the effects of welfare payments on household groupings by characteristic of family head. It will be seen that the extent of poverty gap closing differs sharply among these groups. Thus, the poverty gap for families with female heads under 65 was reduced by 34 per cent, that for all families with heads over 65 by 30 per cent, and that for households headed by unrelated females and males under 65 was reduced by only 15 and 10 per cent, respectively. These differences reflect the heavy emphasis of the programme on aid to families with dependent children and the tendency to exclude from welfare eligibility families with male heads under 65. Such differences provide an incentive to potential assistance recipients to break up (or appear to break up) their families in order to increase receipts, provided that the welfare gains are not offset by additional living costs.

## CRITERIA AND TECHNIQUES

Our first step is to define the criteria to be used for evaluating various schemes, and the choice of techniques to be examined.

### Criteria
In evaluating the performance of various programmes, the following criteria are used:

1. Number of families or persons moved out of poverty.
2. Dollar amount of gap closed.
3. Per cent of cost reflected in gap reduction.
4. Per cent of weighted gap closed.
5. Tax rate payable by family of four at poverty-line.

Measures (1) to (4) relate to the reduction in poverty. Measure (1), though most frequently used, is least significant since improvements in the position of families at the upper end of the gap only are considered, while giving zero weight to improvements further down. Measures (2) and (3) are more significant, with (3) especially useful for comparing cost-effectiveness of various schemes under different budget constraints.

Referring to the familiar negative income tax diagram of Figure 6.1, OA is the guaranteed minimum income, OB is the poverty income and OG = OC is the break-even income. The vertical distance between the total income line AD, and the earnings line OD is the net subsidy paid at various earnings levels. Weighing each earnings level by the numbers involved, the area ODA reflects total net payments or the cost of the plan, i.e. the amount which has to be financed from other sources.[7] Area OEFA

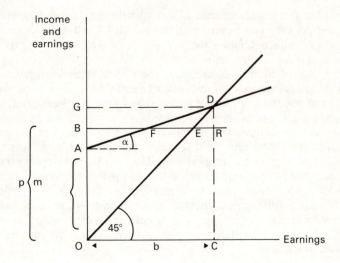

*Figure 6.1: Negative income tax*

reflects that part of net payments which goes to recipients below the poverty-line, while EDF reflects the 'wasted' part which goes to families above that level. The ratio of OEFA to ODA is the per cent of cost which goes to close the gap.

The fourth measure finally assigns weights to dollars of gap-closing, giving more weight to gains which are received by families whose earnings are lower relative to their poverty income. The weights used are six for payments which go to bring families up to 25 per cent of their poverty-line, five for payments in the 25–50 per cent bracket and so forth, down to one for payments of 125–150 per cent of a family's poverty line. Zero weights are given to payments above that line. While these particular weights are arbitrary, the falling scale allows for the reasonable hypothesis that the social utility of raising income declines as income rises relative to the poverty-line. Also, a modest weight is assigned to income gains up to 50 per cent above the poverty income since this income is set at a low level.

The final criterion is the level of tax rates, reflecting the possible disincentive effects on work effort. Under most income maintenance schemes a constant marginal tax rate is used. In terms of Figure 6.1 the slope of the total income line AD or tan $\alpha$ is equal to $1 - t$, where t is the marginal rate. Under the welfare approach the marginal tax rate prior to the reforms of 1967 and 1969 was 100 per cent, making for a horizontal total income line. At present, states may not reduce AFDC payments by more than two-thirds of family earnings, and a minimum portion of earnings is disregarded entirely. Under various negative income tax schemes the NIT rates range from 25 per cent to 75 per cent, with 50 per cent the usual level.[8] In some instances, a tax-free earnings minimum is allowed.

As will be seen from Figure 6.1, four variables are involved, i.e. minimum income, the break-even income, the tax rate and the cost. For any given income distribution and net cost, only one among the three other variables may be chosen and the two others follow from this.[9] Our procedure has been to set the tax rate while letting minimum income and break-even income adjust accordingly. It will be seen from Figure 6.1 that an increase in t or reduction in the slope of the total income line must be accompanied by an increase in the minimum income and a decline in break-even income if cost is to remain unchanged. Since this reduces the 'wasted area' EDF, greater effectiveness in gap closing must be purchased at the cost of a higher tax rate and potentially greater work disincentive.[10]

## Techniques

The logic of Figure 6.1, and the constraints which it imposes, apply to all income maintenance plans, even though they may differ substantially in their outward appearance. The techniques to be considered here include various forms of negative income tax, demogrants and a scheme under which net disbursements would be such as to fill the gap from the bottom. Also we consider the implications of a cut in tax rates and increase in exemptions.

Under the negative income tax (NIT) approach, a family in effect receives a payment equal to the stipulated minimum income and pays a tax at rate t on its earnings. Below the break-even point, it receives a net payment equal to the excess of minimum income over negative income tax liability. Above the break-even point, it pays a net tax equal to the excess of tax over minimum income. The family switches from the negative income tax programme to the regular income tax at that earnings level (called the tax break-even point) at which the net tax under NIT exceeds its liability under the regular income tax. Thus, no family's liability under the NIT can exceed that imposed under the regular income tax. This may be seen from Figure 6.2. The horizontal axis measures earnings as in Figure 6.1, and OC is again the break-even level of earnings. The vertical axis now measures net benefits or taxes under the NIT plan, with OH equal to the minimum income OA in Figure 6.1. Up to the break-even point C, HK reflects net receipts and above C, net tax payments under the NIT plan. LM shows liabilities under the regular income tax. For earnings in the C–N range, the family pays tax under the NIT plan because its net liability is less, but beyond N the regular income tax liability is less and the family switches to regular income tax payments. The combined negative–positive tax path follows HJM. Earners between C and N benefit from the NIT plan in the form of tax reduction, even though their earnings are above the break-even point, as defined by Figure 6.1.[11]

Under a demo-grant plan, payments are made independently of income level but depend on family size. In our version, relative payments per adult and child have been set such that under any budget constraint payments to a family of four represent the same per cent of poverty income as do payments to a married couple without children. The demo-grant is thus

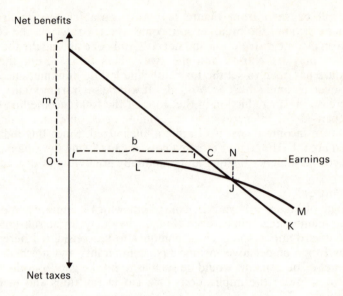

*Figure 6.2: Relation to regular income tax*

similar to a children's allowance scheme supplemented by an allowance per adult. Payments received under the demo-grant are taxable at the regular income tax rate. Because the demo-grant obviates the need for personal exemptions under the income tax, its application is combined with a repeal of exemptions. Under Plan A the increase in income tax liabilities from repeal of exemptions is limited in such a way that there can be no net loss to a family. Under Plan B the repeal of exemptions applies throughout, so that higher income families lose more in additional tax liabilities than they gain from demo-grant receipts.

The scheme which provides for gap filling from the bottom (GfB), finally, involves payments such that no family will be left with less than a certain per cent of its poverty income. This is equivalent in approach to a negative income tax with a tax rate of 100 per cent. It is also similar to the traditional assistance programme, except that the latter is limited to certain groups, largely families with dependent children.

## Budget Constraints

The performance of the various plans is examined within the context of three budget constraints, i.e. $3.6 billion, $14.5 billion and $25 billion. The first corresponds to the level of assistance payments accounted for in our sample,[12] the second corresponds to the before assistance poverty gap recorded in the sample, and the third is chosen to reflect a more ambitious scope of income maintenance. In each case, the plan is imposed in lieu of the prevailing $3.6 of public assistance thus involving additional costs of zero, $10.9 billion, and $21.4 billion, respectively. Our middle cost level is somewhat below that called for by the Income Maintenance Commission's plan, but substantially above that of the administration's plan.[13]

## Measuring Cost of Plans

The budgetary cost (i.e. $3.6 billion, $14.5 billion and $25 billion) equals the excess of payments over collections under the scheme. This excess must be provided for from other sources, presumably from taxpayers with earnings above the poverty line. Referring back to Figure 6.2, the full net cost under NIT may now be defined. Applying weights according to number of families at each earnings level, net cost equals area OHC or payments to net benefit recipients under the negative income tax plan (where OHC = OAD in Figure 6.1) minus CNJ or collections from net taxpayers under the plan, plus LNJ or the loss of revenue under the regular income tax.[14] In computing liability under the NIT tax rate, the computation was related to total earnings, thus bypassing the question of how taxable earnings should be defined for purposes of the negative income tax.[15] Under this procedure, a family's tax change-over point differs, depending on its relation of total to net income.

Under the demo-grants the cost equals benefit payments minus increased income tax revenue due to inclusion of benefit payments in the tax base and repeal of exemptions. As noted before, the repeal of exemptions is limited for demogrant A but unlimited for B. Demogrant B, therefore, is not quite comparable with the other plans on cost grounds, since it benefits from revenue gained through loss of exemptions in the higher brackets. Under the GfB plan, finally, the procedure is the same as under NIT, since the plan is equivalent to an NIT with a tax rate of 100 per cent.

## RESULTS

We may now compare the performance of the various schemes under alternative budget constraints, and of alternative plans at the $14.5 billion level.

### Performance with Changing Cost Levels

The results of the various plans for changing budget constraints are recorded in Table 6.2. For the $3.6 billion level, the results of the actual assistance programme, as tabulated from our sample are also recorded. In measuring the performance of the NIT, we use a 50 per cent tax rate throughout. The minimum income at each cost level is determined so as to give the same per cent of the poverty-line income for all family sizes. This per cent equals 0.34, 0.67 and 0.85 for the three cost levels, respectively.[16]

Under demo-grant A, grants per adult equal $152, $262 and $364 and grants per child are $66, $131 and $172 for three cost levels. Under demo-grant B the corresponding figures are $197, $266 and $344 per adult, with $94, $133 and $172 per child.

*Table 6.2 Performance with rising budget cost**

| | Budget constraint ($ billion) | | |
|---|---|---|---|
| | 3.6 | 14.5 | 25.0 |
| *Number of households moved out (thousands)* | | | |
| 1. Closing gap from bottom | 0 | 11,600 | 11,600 |
| 2. Assistance | 700 | – | – |
| 3. Negative Income Tax[1] | 0 | 4,500 | 8,500 |
| 4. Demo-grant A[2] | 800 | 2,000 | 3,100 |
| 5. Demo-grant B[3] | 1200 | 2,100 | 3,100 |
| | | | |
| *Number of persons moved out (thousands)* | | | |
| 1. Closing gap from bottom | 0 | 33,200 | 33,200 |
| 2. Assistance | 1700 | – | – |
| 3. Negative Income Tax | 0 | 13,600 | 24,000 |
| 4. Demo-grant A | 1900 | 6,200 | 9,100 |
| 5. Demo-grant B | 3400 | 6,400 | 9,100 |
| | | | |
| *Gap closed ($ billion)* | | | |
| 1. Closing gap from bottom | 3600 | 14,500 | 14,500 |
| 2. Assistance | 3100 | – | – |
| 3. Negative Income Tax | 3600 | 11,400 | 13,700 |
| 4. Demo-grant A | 2600 | 4,700 | 6,200 |
| 5. Demo-grant B | 3100 | 4,800 | 6,200 |
| | | | |
| *Gap-closing as per cent of cost* | | | |
| 1. Closing gap from bottom | 100 | 100 | 58 |
| 2. Assistance | 86 | – | – |
| 3. Negative Income Tax | 100 | 79 | 55 |
| 4. Demo-grant A | 72 | 32 | 25 |
| 5. Demo-grant B | 86 | 33 | 25 |
| | | | |
| *Per cent of weighted gap closed* | | | |
| 1. Closing gap from bottom | 22 | 64 | 87 |
| 2. Assistance | 17 | – | – |
| 3. Negative Income Tax | 21 | 61 | 80 |
| 4. Demo-grant A | 16 | 30 | 38 |
| 5. Demo-grant B | 19 | 30 | 38 |
| | | | |
| *Marginal tax rate at poverty line (per cent)[4]* | | | |
| 1. Gap closing from bottom | 100 | 100 | 100 |
| 2. Assistance | 67 | – | – |
| 3. Negative Income Tax | 14 | 50 | 50 |
| 4. Demo-grant A | 16 | 15 | 15 |
| 5. Demo-grant B | 15 | 15 | 15 |

*Notes to Table 6.2*

* All comparisons are with the situation existing before assistance payments but after federal income tax. This original situation involves 11.6 million households and 33.2 million persons in poverty, and a poverty gap of $14.5 billion.

[1] The negative income tax rate is set at 50 per cent throughout. The minimum income as per cent of poverty line equals 34, 67 and 85 per cent, respectively. The $14.5 billion case equals plan d, Table 6.3.

[2] Grants per adult are $152, $262 and $364 for the three cases, respectively, with grants per child of $76, $131, $172, respectively. Personal exemptions are disallowed, subject to condition that increase in liability must not exceed benefit from negative income tax plan for any one taxpayer. The $14.5 billion case equals plan j, Table 6.3.

[3] Grants per adult are $192, $266, and $344 for the three cases, respectively, with grants per child of $94, $133 and $172, respectively. Personal exemptions are disallowed throughout. The $14.5 case equals plan k, Table 6.3.

[4] Family of four, marginal rate applicable to families with poverty-line earnings. In the case of demo-grants, the tax rate shown is that applicable to such earnings plus grants received.

Beginning with the $3.6 billion level, the demo-grants score best in terms of numbers moved out of poverty, while NIT and GfB score poorly; but, as noted before, this is not a very useful measure. In terms of dollar amount of gaps closed, the order is reversed. The negative income tax scores as well as GfB, but demo-grant A is not too far behind and demo-grant B does almost as well as the other plans. Considering the per cent of weighted gap closed, GfB does best with NIT a second and the demogrants coming last. Even demo-grant B remains substantially behind NIT in per cent of weighted gap closed. In terms of tax rates, the demo-grants do much the best while GfB does much the poorest, the respective rates in the two cases being 16 and 100 per cent.

As higher levels of budgetary cost are considered, the gap closing effectiveness of GfB and NIT becomes vastly superior to that of the demo-grants[17] and the difference between the two grants disappears. All this is brought out clearly in Figure 6.3, where the per cent of gap closed is shown on the left and the per cent of weighted gap closed is shown on the right. We note on the left that NIT and GfB do not differ greatly for the $3.5 billion budget, with the NIT falling behind at the middle level but catching up partly for the high budget. This reflects the fact that for the lowest budget, the break-even point for NIT is below the poverty-line but rises above it as the budget is increased. Thus, NIT drops below GfB in our performance measure. As the budget increases further, the difference in performance eventually diminishes since GfB can do no more than close the gap fully. As may be expected, Figure 6.3 also shows the performance difference to be greater for the weighted than for the absolute gap measure. GfB now maintains its advantage also for the large budget.

In all, the gap-closing pay-off from moving to larger budgets is much greater for NIT than for the demo-grant approach. While this advantage is obtained at the cost of a 50 as against a 16–18 per cent marginal tax rate, the demo-grants are clearly disqualified if a closing of the gap is to be even approximated.

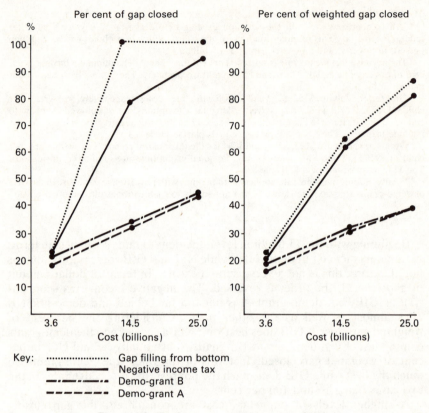

*Figure 6.3: Performance at various cost levels*

At the same time, comparison of the negative income tax and GfB techniques shows that the former does nearly as well as the latter. According to these results, the additional amount of gap closing obtained under GfB appears slight, relative to the disadvantage of moving from a 50 to a 100 per cent tax rate.

### Trade-offs around $14.5 billion Level

The performance of alternative schemes at the $14.5 billion level of budget cost is examined in Table 6.3.

This level is of particular interest because it corresponds to the size of the poverty gap. Plans (a) – (g) are negative income tax variants with constant tax rates and values of t ranging from 25 to 100 per cent. The 100 per cent tax rate case (plan (g)) is equivalent to the GfB approach. Given the constant budget constraint, the minimum income (recorded in Table 6.3 as a per cent of the poverty-line) rises with the tax rate. As before, the minimum income is the same per cent of the poverty-line income for all family sizes.[18] Cases (h) and (i) are further variants of the negative income tax. In both cases payments differentiate between adults and children, with (i) making further allowance for tax free earnings up to $720. Plan (h) is thus similar in approach to the scheme proposed by the Commission on Income Maintenance, although the support levels of plan (h) are somewhat lower.[19] Plan (i) adopts the dual tax rate characteristic of the administration proposal. Plans (j) and (k) repeat the preceding demo-grants, while (l) offers a conventional income tax reduction approach.

*Gap Closing vs. Tax Rate*
Moving from NIT plan (a) to (g), we compare the performance in terms of various measures of gap closing while the marginal tax rate rises. This relationship is shown in Figure 6.4 where the retention rate or $1 - t$ is plotted on the vertical axis while the per cent of gap closed is measured horizontally. In the upper part this per cent refers to gap closing measured in dollar terms, while in the lower it refers to reduction in the weighted gap. The resulting curve reflects an opportunity locus giving the choice between two desirable objectives, i.e. maximum gap closing and as high a retention rate (or as low a disincentive) as possible.

Moving down the line in the upper part of Figure 6.4 we note that successive increases in the tax rate (or reductions in the retention rate) buy successively smaller amounts of gap closing. Whereas raising the tax rate from 25 to 50 per cent permits $4.1 billion in gap-closing or nearly 60 per cent improvement in performance, a further increase in the tax rate to 70 per cent secures an additional gap closing of only $1.6 billion. The reason for the declining rate of pay-off may be seen by referring back to Figure 6.1.[20] As t is increased, the slope of AD falls. For cost to remain constant, its intercept (the minimum income) must rise and its intersection with the 45° line (the break-even income) decline. 'Wasted' payments as measured by FED decline. This decline tapers off and reaches zero when the total income line goes through E. In the present case, where the cost is set to equal the poverty gap, this comes about where the total income line is horizontal and $t = 100$ per cent.

The same general pattern is shown in the lower part of Figure 6.4 where the percentage reduction in weighted gap is recorded. The curve lies to the left of that for the unweighted gap and the decline in pay-off for successive rate increases occurs more rapidly. Note that even with a 100 per cent rate the gap is not fully closed. Such is the case because the poverty line for weighted gap is in effect set at 150 per cent of that for the unweighted case, some weight being given for the first two quartiles above the poverty lines.

As will be seen from Figure 6.4, plans (h) and (i) are inferior to (a)–(g) as they lie inside the opportunity locus. Such at least is the case in terms of the criteria on which Figure 6.3 is based. Under plan (h), the substitution of a payment scale less sensitive to changes in the poverty-line due to differences in family size results in a somewhat less satisfactory performance than is the case for the otherwise similar plan (d). A large fraction of the payment is 'wasted' or goes to households whose income deficiency is

*Table 6.3 Variants with $14.5 billion budget cost*

| Negative income tax | | | | | | | | |
|---|---|---|---|---|---|---|---|---|
| Plan | t | Minimum income as per cent of poverty-line | Households removed from poverty (millions) | Persons removed from poverty (millions) | Gap closed (billion dollars) | Gap closed as per cent of cost | Per cent of weighted gap closed | Marginal tax rate at poverty line |
| (a) | 0.25 | 0.385 | 2.7 | 8.1 | 7.3 | 50 | 42.8 | 0.25 |
| (b) | 0.33 | 0.50 | 3.5 | 10.7 | 9.2 | 63 | 52.0 | 0.33 |
| (c) | 0.40 | 0.575 | 4.0 | 12.2 | 10.3 | 71 | 56.4 | 0.40 |
| (d) | 0.50 | 0.67 | 4.5 | 13.6 | 11.4 | 79 | 60.7 | 0.50 |
| (e) | 0.60 | 0.75 | 5.0 | 14.9 | 12.2 | 84 | 61.9 | 0.60 |
| (f) | 0.70 | 0.825 | 5.4 | 15.9 | 13.0 | 90 | 62.9 | 0.70 |
| (g) | 1.0 | 1.0 | 11.6 | 33.2 | 14.5 | 100 | 64.5 | 1.00 |

| | | | | | | |
|---|---|---|---|---|---|---|
| *Negative income tax variants* | | | | | | |
| (h) t = 0.5. Minimum income of $700 per adult and $420 per child | 3.6 | 16.0 | 9.8 | 68 | 56.0 | 0.50 |
| (i) t = 0 on first $720 with 0.5 thereafter. Minimum income of $574 per adult and $344 per child | 4.0 | 15.1 | 10.6 | 73 | 57.8 | 0.50 |
| *Demo-grants* | | | | | | |
| (j) Plan A: $262 per adult $131 per child limited repeal of exemptions[1] | 2.0 | 6.2 | 4.7 | 32 | 29.6 | 0.15[2] |
| *Tax cut* | | | | | | |
| (k) Plan B: $266 per adult $133 per child total repeat of exemptions | 2.1 | 6.4 | 4.8 | 33 | 30.0 | 0.15[2] |
| (l) 7 per cent cut in rates, exemption raised to $1000 | 0.05 | 0.15 | 0.2 | 1 | 1.0 | 0.00[2] |

[1] The increase in tax liabilities, due to repeal in exemptions is limited to the amount of net benefits, so that no net burden is imposed by the plan.
[2] Family of four.

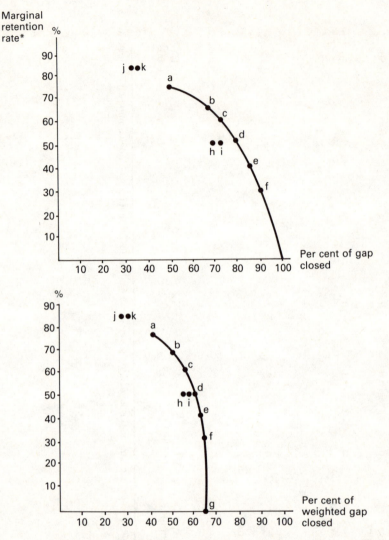

*Family of four, earnings equal to poverty income.

*Figure 6.4: Performance at $14.5 billion cost*

less.[21] Under plan (i), this feature of (h) is retained and the exemption of an initial amount of earnings from the NIT tax is added. This raises the gap-closing efficiency of this plan over that of (h) but not sufficiently to catch up with plan (d).[22] Of the two adjustments here considered, the use of flat minimum income amounts thus reduces efficiency while the use of a tax-free minimum income tends to raise it.

Two additional points should be made, however, in favour of plans (h) and (i) to secure a fair comparison. The flat allowance approach of plan (h) is superior in administrative feasibility to (d), where the minimum income varies with family size and composition. The case for plan (i) similarly may be stronger than Figure 6.4 suggests. There, the retention rate has been recorded at 50 per cent, which does not allow for the zero tax rate below $720. A weighted average of marginal rates (weighted by hours worked below and above $720 of earnings) would give a much higher retention rate and might move point i up and outside the opportunity locus. Moreover, the significance to be assigned to marginal rates applicable to various income ranges depends on differences in work-effort response.

The demo-grants (plans (j) and (k)) are roughly in line with the upper end of the opportunity locus. They are more or less similar to NIT plans with zero tax rates. Plans (j) and (k) come out very similarly, the gain obtained from unlimited removal of exemptions under (k) being quite small. The tax reduction approach, finally, is also in line with the opportunity locus, but it does practically nothing to close the poverty gap, the result being much inferior even to that of the assistance approach under the $3.6 billion budget. Income tax reduction, as has been noted before does not help the poor because they pay little or no income tax. As recorded by our sample, total federal income tax payments by families in poverty were below $50 million.

Given these alternatives, the policy choice depends on the values to be assigned to a high degree of gap closing on the one side, and the maintenance of a high marginal retention rate on the other. Intuitively, a negative income tax with a t of between 0.5 and 0.75 would seem an attractive choice. Such at least seems the case in the static setting. If tax rate effects on work incentives could be allowed for, the picture might differ. A plan which is superior if effects on the size of the initial gap are disregarded, may be inferior if such effects are allowed for. Allowance for changes in earnings may be expected to shift the pattern in favour of low tax rate plans. If the work response were known, this could be incorporated into the estimation of gap-closing and the schemes could be compared in terms of this single criterion. But, as noted before, no reliable basis for such estimation is, as yet, available.[23] However, a rough view of the magnitudes suggests that the picture would not be changed greatly, at least not in the short run, if such effects were allowed for. On the basis of 1966 data, the feasible degree of gap-closing due to increased earnings of poverty families then unemployed could hardly have exceeded 15 per cent of the gap. Thus one would not expect substantial differences in earnings levels to result from varying the tax rate somewhat around the 50 per cent level. This merely reflects the familiar facts that heads of poverty households who are most likely to be employed are already employed; and that the bulk of unemployed poverty households have heads over 65 or are headed by females with children who are not readily drawn into the labour force. The full impact of incentive effects is thus limited to a relatively small sector of the poverty population.[24]

*Impact by Type of Family*

Evaluation of the various plans in terms of their overall performance is important, but differences in their impact upon particular family types may be equally significant. In Table 6.4 net gains for various types of families are compared under plans (d), (h) and (i). Under plan (i), initial earnings up to $720 do not reduce benefits, making this plan preferable for families with such earnings. Plan (d) proves superior for single persons because the other plans assign a smaller allowance to such persons than follows from the 'equal per cent of poverty income' rule. Plan (h), finally, is preferable for households with a large number of children, because allowance per child does not decline with number of children as follows from the 'equal per cent of poverty income' rule of plan (d). Differences such as these are important and reflect the particular amounts stipulated in the various plans as well as the differences in technique. If enough complication is admitted, almost any inter-family pattern can be obtained.

*Table 6.4 Impact of various plans by family structure\**

|  | Plan(d) | Plan(h) Net gains per family | Plan(i) |
|---|---|---|---|
| Female, under 65 |  |  |  |
| Earnings of $– | 1084 | 700 | 574 |
| $1000 | 584 | 200 | 434 |
| $2000 | 84 | – | – |
| Female, supporting households |  |  |  |
| Earnings of $– | 1650 | 2100 | 1722 |
| $1000 | 1150 | 1600 | 1582 |
| $2000 | 650 | 1100 | 1082 |
| Married couple and 2 children |  |  |  |
| Earnings of $– | 2204 | 2240 | 1836 |
| $1000 | 1704 | 1790 | 1696 |
| $2000 | 1204 | 1240 | 1196 |
| Married couple and 4 children |  |  |  |
| Earnings of $– | 2902 | 3080 | 2524 |
| $1000 | 2402 | 2580 | 2380 |
| $2000 | 1902 | 2080 | 1880 |
|  | Percentage reduction in poverty gap | | |
| All family heads under 65 | 79 | 62 | 74 |
| Female heads under 65 | 75 | 65 | 61 |
| Male heads under 65 | 81 | 74 | 75 |

\* For description of plans see Table 6.3.

*Effects on Family Structure*

This also suggests that it might be desirable to apply a lower tax rate to those family units who are likely to be more responsive to work incentives (i.e. families with male heads and singles under 65) than to families which are less likely to enter the labour force (i.e. families with female heads and the aged). This, however, would reintroduce distorting effects on family structure. An additional trade-off problem arises, as desire to avoid distorting effects on family structure limits the potential usability of rate differentiation. Differentiation by age is less objectionable on these grounds, but may not recommend itself on others.

Some difference in impact upon family structure may be observed also under plans (d) and (h). Assuming no earnings, plan (d) gives a family of four an income of $2215, while the combined incomes after separation of the male would provide them with an income of $2905, leaving a split-up incentive of $690. Under plan (h) the incomes would be $2256 in both cases, with no split-up incentive. This may be considered an advantage of plan (h). This advantage, however, declines rapidly if some earnings exist. If we assume the male head to have earnings of $3000 the split-up incentive of (d) is $1013 while that of (h) is $795. Moreover, it might be argued that the $690 difference in the absence of earnings does not reflect a real gain, since it offsets differences in living costs (provided the division of households is real rather than apparent) under the poverty standard. However, this may be, the difference in impact upon family structure is not major and the trade-off between (d) and (h) should be viewed primarily in terms of gap-closing effectiveness and administrative ease.

## NOTES

1. For a somewhat similar attempt based on 1959–1960 data, see David and Leuthold [2]. Also Brazer [1].
2. The category of public assistance payments is defined to include the following programmes: Aid to Families with Dependent Children, Aid to the Blind or Totally Disabled and Old Age Assistance. The term 'household' as used in this chapter is defined s.v. 'interview unit' in the SEO survey underlying this analysis.
3. 38,044 households were included in the sample, and interviews were carried out for 26,473 households. The sample was divided into two parts; a national sample, with 15,900 households interviewed, representative of the national population, and a supplementation in non-white areas, based on 10,573 interviews, designed to provide a firmer basis for statistics regarding non-whites and poor. All families then were weighted so that the weighted frequency of the household type in the sample is the same as its frequency in the general population. The weighted households sum to the national total, and our analysis was carried out on the weighted totals.
4. To illustrate, the poverty-line incomes for 1966 were $1758 for a single male under 65; $2198 for a family of 2 adults; $3306 for a family of 2 adults and 2 children; $4354 for a family of 2 adults and 4 children, and so forth.

5. As shown in Table 6.1 the number of households below the poverty-line is the same before and after income tax, except in the case of male-headed families, where the imposition of the income tax increases the number of poor by 0.1 million.

6. The 1966 total gap of $14.5 billion or after-welfare gap of $11.2 billion compares with an after-welfare gap of $11.0 billion as estimated by Orshansky for 1965. The number of persons estimated to be in poverty in 1966 was 29.7 million, as against our figure of 31.4 million. See Orshansky [5].

7. Simplifying matters, Figure 6.1 disregards effects on liabilities and revenue under the regular income tax. For a fuller definition of cost see Figure 6.2 and note 14 below.

8. These rates typically exclude other taxes paid, such as employee contributions to social security.

9. Disregarding effects on income tax revenue and writing m for minimum income, b for break-even and p for poverty income, we have $t = 1 - \tan \alpha$ and hence $t = b$.

The cost c according to Figure 6.1 is defined as

$$c = \sum_{i=o}^{i=b} n_i (m - it)$$

where the i s are the earnings levels from o to b and $n_i$ is the given number at the i s earnings level. We thus have two equations with four unknowns, so that given any two (such as c and t) the others (m and b) follow.

Substituting, we have

$$c = \sum_{i=o}^{i=b} n_i t (b - i)$$

so that with a constant c, b must fall as t rises, and as shown by (1), a rising t and a falling b calls for a rising m.

10. The above argument, similar to Figure 6.1, oversimplifies because it disregards effects of the NIT plan on revenues under the regular income tax. If such effects are allowed for, there remains a strong presumption that a rising t involves a fall in break-even point, but the conclusion *need not* follow. See note 20 below.

11. For expositions of the negative income tax technique, see Green [3]; Tobin [10]; and Pechman and Mieszkowski [6].

12. It appears that the sample understates welfare payments as the actual amount of assistance payments for 1966 was $4.3 billion.

13. The previously noted Commission estimate of additional cost is $5.9 billion for 1971. Adding, say, $6.3 billion for 1971 cost of the present assistance programme ($4.3 billion for 1966 plus $2 billion increase), we obtain a total 1971 cost of $12.2 billion, as against our figure of $14.5 billion. Since the 1971 gap is substantially below the 1966 gap, a larger cost is involved to secure the same degree of gap closing in 1966, thus calling for an increase in the $12.2 billion figure to permit comparison. As shown below (see note 19), the benefits of the commission plan, applied to our sample, show a 1966 cost of $17.2 billion. Thus, the Commission plan involves a somewhat higher cost than implied in our middle budget.

14. The cost equation in note 9 should be adjusted accordingly by adding on the right side a term for the loss of income tax revenue from families which substitute the negative income tax. However, except for high-cost programmes with a low marginal tax rate, this cost component is not of great practical importance, since few families over the relevant income range are subject to federal income tax.

15. The host of issues which arise in defining taxable income occur under both the regular and negative income tax. The treatment of work-connected expenses becomes of special importance, as may imputed rent. In dealing with the former, it has been suggested that a fixed per cent of earnings may be deducted for purposes of negative income tax. For a discussion of these issues see Pechman and Mieszkowski [6] and Projector and Weiss [9, p. 14].

16. The resulting ratios depend upon the underlying income distribution and are arrived at by iterative procedures.

17. For a similar conclusion with regard to children's allowances, see Brazer [1].

18. See note 16.

19. The commission plan, as noted above, provides payments of $750 per adult and $450 per child with a marginal tax rate of 50 per cent. Based on our data, the total cost at 1966 income levels would have been $17.3 billion as against our cost of $14.5 billion for plan (h).

20. As noted before, Figure 6.1 disregards effects on regular income tax revenue. As t rises, the intercept of the HK line in Figure 6.2 moves down and point J, the intersection with LM moves to the left. The tax break-even point N falls as does the loss of income tax revenue. This permits increased benefit payments within the given benefit constraint. However, this gain declines for successive increases in the tax rate. The number of families involved decreases as we move down the earnings scale, as does the tax loss per family. The declining slope of the opportunity locus is thus accentuated.

21. This is not to say that our rule of determining minimum incomes as constant per cent of poverty-line income for all family sizes makes for the best gap-closing performance. Gap-closing might be improved, especially if the unweighted gap is used, by using different ratios for different family sizes. But determining minimum income levels for each family type so as to maximize gap-closing would not seem desirable on equity grounds.

22. The improvement arises because tax exemption accrues largely to earners below the poverty line, while the reduction in minimum income necessitated thereby results in reduced net benefits reaching above the poverty-line. Introduction of the exemption into (d), while retaining the (d)-type minimum income provision would raise the degree of gap-closing.

23. Preliminary results of the New Jersey experiment suggest that detrimental effects of a negative income tax plan will not be substantial. See OEO [4].

24. According to our data for 1966, out of 11.6 million poverty households, 7.3 million had heads under 65. Of these, 3.2 were families with male heads, 1.6 families with female heads and 2.5 were unrelated individuals. Suppose that employment in the three groups was two-thirds, one-third and one-half. This gives about 3.5 million households with unemployed heads. Assuming further that 1.5 of these could be drawn into employment (allowing for the fact that female heads would be available for employment only to a limited degree) and assuming that earnings would reach 25 per cent of poverty income, the potential gain in earnings would be about $1.2 billion or below 10 per cent of the poverty group.

25. It must be kept in mind, however, that the higher tax rate under NIT also applies to taxpayers above the poverty line but below the changeover point. Moreover, one must also consider possible disincentive effects which may result from tax increases at higher levels of income needed to finance the schemes.

# REFERENCES

[1] Brazer, H. (1969), 'The federal income tax and the poor', *California Law Review*, 57.
[2] David, M. and Leuthold, J. (1968), 'Formulae for income maintenance: their distributional impact', *National Tax Journal* 21.
[3] Green, G. (1967), 'Negative taxes and the poverty problem', *Yale Law Journal*, 77.
[4] *Preliminary Report for the Graduated Work Incentives Experiment* (1970), US Department of Health, Education and Welfare (Washington, D.C.).
[5] Oshanski, M. (1968), 'The shape of poverty in 1966', *Social Security Bulletin*, 31.
[6] Pechman, J. and Mieszkowski (1967), *Yale Law Review*, 77.
[7] *Poverty Amid Plenty* (1969), Report of the President's Commission on Income Maintenance Programs (Washington D.C., US Government Printing Office), p. 151.
[8] *The President's Proposals for Welfare Reform and Social Security Amendments* (1969), Committee on Ways and Means, (US Government Printing Office), p. 105.
[9] Projector, D. and Weiss, G. (1969), 'Income-net worth measures of economic welfare', *Social Security Bulletin*, 32.

# 7  A Reappraisal of Financing Social Security* 1981

Discussion of social security finance has been conducted against the background of rising concern over the soundness of the system. Will contributions be adequate to meet obligations in the near future, or will the reserve fund be depleted and require outside support? How should this support be rendered? Taking the longer view, will unfavourable economic and demographic trends impose excessive burdens as productivity growth slows and the ratio of retirees to contributors increases? How will this affect the viability of the system? Should we replace the payroll tax with other sources of finance or integrate the social security system into the overall budget? Does the system retard economic growth by reducing saving, and does this call for accumulation of a reserve fund? All these questions give occasion to rethink some of the basic principles underlying the system.[1]

## SOLVENCY, VIABILITY AND THE NATURE OF THE RETIREMENT CONTRACT

Under the present OASI structure the system is said to be in actuarial balance if future payroll tax rates scheduled under current law equal future benefits as a percentage of covered wages. The system is said to be in 'close actuarial balance' if the average of the scheduled tax rates over a 75-year period is within 5 per cent of the benefit ratio. But because it is extremely difficult, if not impossible, to predict economic and demographic variables so far into the future, frequent upward adjustments of tax rates have been needed in the past and cuts in benefits may be needed in the future. This lends a sense of instability to the system. The concept of actuarial balance is thus precarious. Moreover, it rests on a wholly pragmatic basis, telling us little about what is being balanced and why. The situation is worsened by interpreting pay-as-you-go so as to call for a very minimal level of trust fund accumulation only, leading to current cash-flow crises. The system

* *Social Security Financing* (1981), ed. Felicity Skidmore (Cambridge, Mass., MIT Press).

thus remains in a continuing state of disequilibrium, which tends to discredit its reliability.

## Alternative Contracts

It is important therefore to clarify the nature of the social contract upon which the retirement system may be designed to rest and to consider its implications for the concept of system viability. In the absence of a full-fledged reserve approach, the concept of solvency or actuarial balance as now understood is not very helpful. Tax rates can always be adjusted. What matters is the credibility and long-run political viability of the scheme; it must continue to be accepted as fair by both working population and retirees. For purposes of this discussion, I shall distinguish between these approaches.

A. Each generation finances its own retirement, without claims against subsequent or obligations toward preceding generations.
B. Each working generation assumes the responsibility of supporting its retirees while being assured of similar treatment by the next working generation. This inter-generation contract may assume various forms:

1. *Ad hoc* provision: The agreement may be a very loose one, allowing the voters of each period to decide the level of support.
2. *Fixed replacement rate (FRR)*: The retirees are entitled to receive a given fraction of their earnings in the form of benefits. With the replacement rate thus fixed, the working generation must adjust its contribution rate accordingly. The tax rate is the dependent variable in the system.
3. *Fixed contribution rate (FCR)*: The working population is required to contribute a given fraction of its earnings for the support of the retirees. With the contribution rate thus fixed, the replacement rate becomes the independent variable.
4. *Fixed replacement rate, adjusted (FRRA)*: The replacement rate is fixed as under FRR, but the earning base of retirees to which this rate is applied is adjusted upward to allow for the productivity gains and higher wage rates enjoyed by the subsequent working population.
5. *Fixed relative position (FRP)*: Contributions and benefits are set so as to hold constant the ratio of per capita earnings of those in the working generation (net of contribution) to the per capita benefits of retirees.

The initial version of the social security system was in terms of inter-generation neutrality and plan A, but it quickly gave way to pay-as-you-go, for two reasons. First, it seemed unacceptable to exclude the then old generation from benefits, the more so since their plight was accentuated by the Great Depression. And second, the 1937 recession, which followed rapidly upon the introduction of the system, rendered a substantial system surplus undesirable on grounds of stabilisation policy. Thus the system shifted from the type A pattern to an inter-generation context, but it was never considered explicitly what type of agreement was to be adopted. Initially, the approach was in the spirit of FRR, but the introduction of wage indexing in 1974 shifted it toward FRRA.[2]

## Reserve vs. Pay-as-you-go

My major concern here is with alternative formulations of firm contractual arrangements under forms 2–5 of plan B and the resulting distribution of risks between the working population and retirees.[3] But before turning to this, some controversies relating to a comparison of the A and B approaches may be noted. Plan A involves no inter-generation agreement whatsoever. Each generation is on its own. If followed from the beginning, this means that the initial generation of retirees is left without benefits and the first working generation to enter the system must accumulate a reserve. This reserve, together with earnings from it, will then be drawn upon later to pay for its retirement benefits. During the same period, a reserve is being accumulated by the next generation so that (assuming constant population and constant earnings) the reserve fund matures at a constant level. In the absence of intra-generation redistribution, this approach would be generally similar to requiring individuals to take out private insurance.[4] Under the B-type plans, the first contributing generation pays for its retirees, who receive a gift. By the same token, the doomsday generation (which does not reach retirement) suffers a net loss.

Various objections have been raised against the reserve approach, some more justified than others. The reserve approach, so it has been argued, is a fiction. Once the system is underway, the withdrawal by the older generation comes to be matched by contributions from the younger. This being the case, the system simply involves a transfer from the latter to the former, reducing it to a pay-as-you-go approach. This conclusion is incorrect because it overlooks the fact that the reserve accumulation of the first generation has added to the capital stock, so that its withdrawal will not reduce the level of income enjoyed by the next generation. Assuming constant population and productivity, this initial increase in capital stock is maintained thereafter, as future accumulations and withdrawals balance each other. However, this reasoning assumes the reserve to be invested and be reflected in an addition to the real capital stock. This, in turn, implies the questionable assumption of a continuing full-employment economy, where investment matches available savings and no compensatory fiscal policy is required to maintain a full employment level of demand. Critics of the present system in turn accept this assumption and argue that without accumulation, the social security system is detrimental to saving and hence to the rate of economic growth. The debate is still in full swing, and the outcome is far from decided.[5] Whichever the effects on saving may prove to be, social security finance is not the only and hardly the best policy instrument by which to control the rate of saving. A surplus in the general budget is an obvious alternative.

The choice between a reserve and a pay-as-you-go approach may not only affect the rate of economic growth, but economic growth also affects the rates of return that individuals may obtain under the two systems. The pay-as-you-go system benefits from a setting of expanding population and rapid productivity growth. Under a reserve system, the rate of return equals the rate of interest. Under pay-as-you-go, the rate of return from a constant tax rate equals the rate of population and productivity growth. Therefore if the rates of population and productivity growth exceed the rate of interest, the rate of return obtainable under a pay-as-you-go system will exceed that available from a reserve approach. This observation helps to explain the changing perspective on social security over recent years. In the earlier stages of the system, the outlook was for rapid population and productivity growth, which made the social security plan an attractive prospect. Rising contributions and, hence, benefits would become available, and the contribution rate would be stable. Now that the population trends have changed and productivity prospects have become less promising, what once seemed favourable for the working generation appears to be less so. The spectre of declining economic growth, however, does not require us to abandon social security. It merely calls for a reformulation of the underlying contract.

## Inter-generation Contracts and their Implications for the Distribution of Risks

The *ad hoc* provision of approach 1 of plan B can hardly be called an inter-generation agreement. Rather, it views provision for the aged as a redistribution scheme between the working population and the aged, to be decided on a continuing and *ad hoc* basis. I have little sympathy for this approach. I think it essential to view social security as a contractual arrangement that assures each contributing generation of their own support by the subsequent generation. Because of the inter-generation aspect of the problem, explicit and continuing acceptance of the contractual structure of the system is essential to protect it against the vagaries of political swings. The problem is one of structuring the system so that the implicit contract can be adhered to, a condition that I fear does not hold under present arrangements.

The remaining B plans are based on a firm inter-generation agreement. The essential difference among the four approaches lies in the distribution of risks, pertaining to unforeseen changes in productivity and population growth. To simplify the problem, we assume for the time being that all members of any one generation have the same income. Thereby the further problem of intra-generation equity is distinguished from that of inter-generation equity and may be postponed for later consideration. Any of the B plans is open to combination with any approach to the intragen-eration issue, so that the two problems may be dealt with in succession.

Table 7.1 summarises how changes in productivity and population will affect workers and retirees under the various plans, with a more detailed explanation given in the Appendix to this chapter. To simplify, we assume the population to be divided into two generations: workers and retirees. Productivity growth is defined as a situation where the wage rate of the working population exceeds the past wage rate of retirees, and population

*Table 7.1 Effects of productivity and population changes under various formulae*

| | (1)<br>Tax rate | (2)<br>Benefit per re-tiree and replace-ment rate | (3)<br>Net wage per worker[1] | (4)<br>Ratio of (2):(3) |
|---|---|---|---|---|
| **Plan A** | | | | |
| Increase in productivity | 0 | 0 | + | − |
| Increase in population | 0 | 0 | 0 | 0 |
| **Plan B2: Fixed replacement rate (FRR)** | | | | |
| Increase in productivity | − | 0 | + | −[2] |
| Increase in population | − | 0 | + | −[2] |
| **Plan B3: Fixed contribution rate (FCR)** | | | | |
| Increase in productivity | 0 | + | + | 0 |
| Increase in population | 0 | + | 0 | + |
| **Plan B4: Fixed replacement rate, adjusted (FRRA)** | | | | |
| Increase in productivity | 0 | + | + | 0 |
| Increase in population | − | 0 | + | − |
| **Plan B5: Fixed relative position (FRP)** | | | | |
| Increase in productivity | 0 | +[2] | + | 0 |
| Increase in population | − | +[2] | + | 0 |

*Note*: A (+) indicates increase, a (−) indicates decrease, and a zero indicates no change. For further explanation, see Appendix.
[1] Net wage is defined as earnings net of contribution
[2] In most cases, for detail see Table A.2, below.

growth as one where the ratio of workers to retirees rises.[6] Under FRR, where retirees receive a constant fraction of their earnings or replacement rate, such changes leave benefits and the replacement rate unaffected. However, the tax rate falls with population growth and rising productivity, and it rises as population and productivity decline. Under FCR, where the tax rate is fixed, benefits and the replacement rate rise with rising productivity and population growth and fall as productivity and population decline. FRRA leaves the tax rate invariant to productivity changes but causes it to change inversely to population.[7] Benefits and the replacement rate, in turn, are invariant to population changes but rise and fall with productivity.

In a period of rapid productivity and population growth, those about to retire will prefer FRRA and FCR to FRR, with the preference between FRRA and FCR depending on the relative growth rates of productivity and population. Those entering the labour force will prefer FRR, followed by FRRA and then FCR. Preferences are reversed if the outlook is for economic decline. The initial arrangement of the social security system, which resembled FRR, was attractive to entrants into the labour force, given prospects of productivity growth and rising population. More recently, the odds were moved in favour of retirees by allowing for productivity indexing, thus moving the system toward FRRA. But population growth was still available to hold down the tax rate. The situation changed, however, with declining population growth, where FRRA now calls for a rising tax rate.[8]

While the differing implications of the various approaches may be readily observed, it is difficult to say which offers the most equitable solution. For this purpose, it is important to consider what happens to the relative position of workers and retirees. This is shown in Table 7.1 col. 4, where the ratio of per capita benefits to per capita earnings (net of tax) is given. Now assume that productivity rises, with population constant. By permitting retirees to partake in the benefits of productivity, FRRA and FCR maintain per capita income of retirees as a constant fraction of that of workers, whereas FRR lets the relative position of retirees decline.[9] Similarly FRRA and FCR force retirees to share in the burden of productivity decline, whereas they are sheltered under FRR. Using column 4 or constant relative position as criteria of inter-generation fairness, FCR and FRRR are more appealing.

Under the condition of population growth and constant productivity, FRR or FRRA (which coincide in this case) leaves workers with the benefit of a declining tax rate as population increases, causing the per capita income of retirees to fall relative to that of workers. Under FCR the benefits of a growing tax base are passed on to the retirees, causing their per capita income to rise relative to that of workers. The opposite changes result as population decreases. Under all three systems, relative positions change in response to population, and it is difficult to say which pattern of change is better. (I tend to prefer FCR, which stipulates a constant effort obligation, to FRR and FRRA, which stipulate constant entitlements, but this is a personal matter.) Using the superior criterion of constant relative position, neither formulation is satisfactory.

These differences may not be too important if future changes in population and productivity can be foreseen. If the outlook is certain, such changes might be allowed for in the design of the contract. Thus under FRR, a prospective increase in population might be compensated for by setting the replacement rate at a somewhat higher level. But this is not practical, and uncertainty must be allowed for as a major additional consideration. The question then arises of how the risks of uncertain development should be distributed. This may not pose a serious problem with regard to productivity. Based on past experience, productivity may be expected to rise. By adopting FRRA rather than FRR, workers risk losing a decline in tax rate but at least do not suffer the risk of an increase. Energy and raw material shortages may reverse this picture in the future, but let us disregard this possibility. We cannot, however, disregard a population change. FRR or FRRA imposes a severe risk on the working population whose tax rate stands to rise and whose net income stands to fall with declining population growth. If the decline is sufficiently severe, the required wage rate may become untenable, especially in the FRRA setting where the productivity buffer is removed.

In all, the contingency of declining population growth leaves FRR or FRRA a very uneasy foundation for the social security contract.[10] At least it does so for those who take seriously the notion that the system should be based on a contract that can be kept and not be formulated in a way that contains a built-in potential for collapse. In the early stages of the system, pursuit of the FRR approach seemed natural enough, partly because of its resemblance (with a guaranteed replacement rate) to private insurance and partly because of an optimistic view of productivity gains, population growth, and labour force participation. Now the prospect has changed, and the built-in defect of the approach has become apparent. Indeed it has been made more severe by the indexing of productivity. This threat could be removed by adoption of an FCR-type system, which ensures automatic solvency and does not call for more or less impossible long-term projections. The trouble is that FCR places the entire population risk on retirees, which is unacceptable.

We need not, however, despair of a fair and practicable solution. Such, I suggest, is given by writing the inter-generation contract as calling for maintenance of a fixed ratio of per capita benefits to retirees to per capita earnings (net of social security tax) of workers. Having set this ratio at, say, 0.33, the tax rate would then be adjusted as needed (in response to population and productivity changes) to maintain the contractual ratio. The fixed relative position of the FRP approach has all of the advantages of FCR, in that actuarial projections would no longer be needed to determine tax rates. Tax and benefit rates could be set each year (or, say, be adjusted every five years) as a function of the number of retirees, the number of workers, and the fixed relative position ratio.[11] Resulting changes in benefit rates would be applicable to old as well as new retirees.

Beyond this, FRP also provides for a fair sharing of risks with regard to both population and productivity change. As population increases, the tax rate falls while both per capita benefits and net earnings rise at the same rate. If population declines, the tax rate rises and both parties lose at the same rate. Unlike FRR and FRRA, the burden is shared. Similarly if productivity increases, the tax rate remains unchanged, and both gain at an equal rate. Individuals under FRP would be assured fair treatment and a viable system. They would trade this against nominal assurance of a fixed replacement rate, granted in a system that may not prove viable. Under FRR there would still remain a need for short-run compensatory adjustments in periods of severe unemployment, but these would not affect the long-run solvency of the system. Transition to our fixed-share approach would thus remove social security finance from the crisis atmosphere, which under present arrangements is bound to recur, and it would do so while maintaining a contractual basis, thereby shielding the system against the political vagaries of a general redistribution scheme.

## Inflation Indexing

The FRP approach would take care of inflation adjustment automatically. In the absence of FRP, an explicitly and rigidly adhered to provision for inflation adjustment, such as contained in the present law, is essential to the design of a meaningful inter-generation contract.[12] The contract, by its nature being of a long-term character, becomes meaningless without such an adjustment. Current proposals to reduce the inflation adjustment in the determination of benefits should be rejected because they are destructive to the contractual nature of the social security system.[13]

## Transition

Finally the problem of transition should be noted. It is easy enough to argue that were we to start anew, we should follow a pattern such as FRP rather than FRRA, but it is something else to propose that the present system be replaced by FRP. Claims have been accumulated in good faith under FRRA and cannot be declared void. One possible approach would be to buy off present claims, financed by the imposition of a temporary tax. This would be a neat solution but rather expensive and hardly feasible.[14] Or the new scheme could be phased in, with benefits temporarily computed as an average of claims under the old and new plans, permitting the latter to carry increasing weight and reaching 100 per cent in, say, ten years.

Less satisfactory, an explicit change to a new system might be avoided, but *ad hoc* adjustments in benefits and tax rates might be undertaken from time to time and in line with a standard set by a hypothetical FRP system.[15] The two approaches might amount to much the same, but the *ad hoc* device also carries the risk that such changes might run counter to, rather than comply with, the FRP solution.

## Quantitative Significance

In concluding this discussion of alternative inter-generation contracts, we may consider how the future level of tax rates is likely to differ under alternative arrangements.[16] Beginning with a current rate of 9 per cent, that for the year 2030 under the FRR, FRRA and FRP plans may be estimated at 14.3, 13.5 and 12.9 per cent, respectively. Thus increases in the rate by 5.3, 4.5 and 3.9 per cent would be called for. Given our assumption of slightly declining population growth, substitution of FRP for FRRA would reduce the required increase in the tax rate by 0.6 per cent. This differential may be less than expected but would, of course, be larger with a more rapid decline in the ratio of working population to retirees.

# INTRA-GENERATION REDISTRIBUTION

In focusing on the nature of the inter-generation commitment, we have assumed an equal distribution of income among the members of each generation. Or, what amounts to the same, we have compared workers and retirees, both of whom receive the mean income of their respective groups. We must now allow for the existence of income inequality within each generation and consider how each generation wishes to allocate its total contributions and benefits among its members. Thus considerations of intra-generation equity must be added.

## Role of Redistribution

The intra-generation contract with regard to contributions and benefits might be distributionally neutral, leaving each member with the same rate of return, or it may not. In fact, most social insurance schemes, including the USA's, involve some degree of intra-generation redistribution. However, the redistributional component is the smaller part of total benefit payments, perhaps one-third, the remainder being in the nature of returns that would have been received under a non-distributive scheme. It would be a mistake, therefore, to consider as part of redistribution (or, indeed, to classify as income maintenance) what in fact is largely a retirement scheme. To represent as redistribution what in fact is not is undesirable as a matter of social sensibility. Moreover the acceptability for redistribution measures is limited and should not be pre-empted by what in fact is not a part thereof.

Consider now various rationales for introducing intra-generation redistribution into social security. Suppose first that society views distribution in terms of annual incomes and that there exists a scheme of progressive taxes and pro-poor transfers (a negative income tax), which secures what is considered the proper distribution of annual incomes. Retirees would be the recipients of net benefits because their earnings are low. Given such a system, there would be no need for social insurance. There would be no social contract between generations. The requirement would simply be for the 'rich' to support the 'poor' of whatever generation. Provision for low-income aged would be part of the general redistribution scheme. If the negative income tax scheme fell short of the desired degree of redistribution, it would not be appropriate to supplement it by additional transfers to the aged poor only. Age should not enter into an annual income-based redistribution scheme.

Our view of social security rejects this approach. Provision for retirement should not be seen as part of a general redistribution but as part of an inter-generation agreement by which each generation (and, within each generation, each individual) assumes the obligation to contribute, thereby earning a claim to benefit payments later on. This approach fits into a view of distributional equity that relates to lifetime rather than to annual income. Suppose that society did in fact provide for what it considers a correct distribution of lifetime income. In this case no further redistribution through the social security system would be needed. Individuals with lower lifetime earnings would have lower pensions, but this would simply reflect the underlying distribution. But now allow for the fact that the distribution of lifetime earnings is insufficiently corrected for. Since the average level of benefits under the social security system is set well below average lifetime earnings, the level of benefits for low-income retirees, which would result from a non-redistributive scheme, would fall below an acceptable level. This, then, justifies some degree of supplementary redistribution within the retirement system.

## Techniques of Redistribution

In principle, such redistribution could be accomplished either within a unitary system or through a two-tier system. In the former case, contributions could be made progressive in relation to lifetime income, or the ratio of benefits to income could be made to fall as income rises. Taking a more practical view, adjustment from the contribution side is not feasible. Lifetime earnings are not known during the working life, and contributions that are progressive in relation to annual income may not give the desired pattern in lifetime terms. Lifetime averaging of income would be needed. Implementation from the benefit side is more feasible. The benefit levels corresponding to a flat replacement rate will be indicative of the level of lifetime earnings and, if too low, can be supplemented so as to raise the benefit level to an acceptable minimum. By permitting the adjustment to be *ex post*, correction from the benefit side obviates the need for extensive averaging or for predicting lifetime earnings.

Instead of including a redistributive feature into the general scheme, a two-tier approach might be followed, with one part of the system non-redistributive and the other redistributive. This results in greater clarity and may have direct bearing on the choice of appropriate revenue sources.

## Separability of Intra-generation and Inter-generation Issues

Thus far I have dealt with the problems of inter-generation and intra-generation arrangements as separable and distinct issues, proceeding as if any of the plan B approaches could be combined with any degree of intra-generation redistribution. This is clearly the case under plan FRP for which the intra-generation agreement calls for average per capita benefits to equal a given fraction of average after-tax earnings. The inter-generation agreement says nothing on how the taxes are to be allocated among the members of each working generation or how this generation wishes to divide the benefits when it retires. The latter decision bears on intra-generation distribution only, leaving the ratio of average benefits to average net earnings compatible with various ways of distributive contributions and benefits within the generation.[17]

Indeed it might be argued that the requirement of continuity applies to the inter-generation agreement only. Today's workers can be expected to agree on support of the present retirees only if they have assurance of symmetrical treatment at their own retirement. This renders a stable agreement across successive generations necessary. Yet there is no similar reason for stability on the intra-generation arrangement. Why not let each generation handle this part of the problem as it pleases? Conceptually, there is a good case for such flexibility, but severe problems would arise in implementation. Since generations overlap, changing intra-generation roles would call for workers of different ages to contribute under different tax schedules, and for retirees of different ages to obtain benefits under different formulae. To avoid this, stability in the intra-generation as well as inter-generation agreement is called for.

## Source of Finance

The appropriate type of tax with which to finance benefits (1) should be distinct in its role as a social security contribution; (2) should be paid by all members of the working generation but not by retirees; (3) should be personal and income-related; (4) should be adaptable to a moderately progressive burden-distribution over the lower part of the income range; (5) and should be unitary-elastic with regard to long-term productivity growth but possess cyclical stability.

The first requirement follows from our conception of social security as a participatory retirement system. Even though based on inter-generation contract and allowing for intra-generation redistribution, there should be a distinct awareness of the tax as rendering a contribution and the resulting sense of entitlement to agreed-upon terms at the time of retirement. This identification of the tax as an entitlement-creating contribution calls for a distinct and separate tax rather than a general budgetary contribution.

The second requirement follows from the nature of the social security contract that underlies the system. The contribution is to be made while the worker is in the labour force, and the benefits are to be received upon retirement. This simple rule would be contradicted by collecting contributions from retirees.[18]

The third requirement must be met to secure the desired pattern of intra-generation redistribution. Whether the system is to be neutral or redistributive, the contribution should be in the form of a personal rather than *in rem* tax. Assuming that the distribution issue is viewed in income (rather than consumption) terms, it also follows that the tax should be income-based. This runs counter to the traditional argument that earnings or wage and salary income only should be included in the tax base while capital income should be excluded. The reason given for including earned income only is that wages are the part of income that is lost upon retirement and that therefore is in need of replacement. This reasoning is valid in the context of a private *quid pro quo* system, but it does not follow that it holds in the context of social insurance. If each generation accepts the commitment to support the next, why should not individual contributions to this commitment be made as a function of total income? Moreover if intra-generation equity is viewed in redistributional terms, why should this not be based on total income? Such redistribution is to be viewed in terms of lifetime income for all sources and not wage and salary income only.

The fourth requirement is somewhat inconsistent with our earlier conclusion that if a distributional correction is to be made within the context of the retirement system, this correction can be applied better from the benefit than the tax side of the system, so that the contribution rate should be proportional. However, this principle might be compromised by an allowance for an exemption at the lower end of the scale to avoid hardship to workers with low annual incomes and to make an allowance for family size. Moreover the principle might be qualified with regard to the upper end of the income scale so as to avoid excessive marginal rates since substantial rate progression already applies (or in any case could be implemented better) under the income tax. This correction may be accomplished as is now done under the payroll tax by setting a ceiling on the covered earning base.

Finally, the tax should have a low revenue elasticity over the cycle so as to reduce the need for compensatory assistance in the short run. At the same time, the revenue should increase at the rate of productivity growth (that is, it should exhibit a per capita income elasticity of unity) so as to reduce the scope of rate adjustments needed to maintain the system in a solvent position.

The payroll tax as it now stands meets requirements 1 and 5 and comes close to 2, but badly fails the others. The case for some change is thus evident. Various proposals for alternative sources of finance have been made, including resort to general budgetary financing, payroll tax reform and replacement by other tax alternatives.

It is frequently suggested that the US should follow other countries by drawing part of the revenue (say, one-third) from a general budgetary contribution. This would permit reduction of the payroll tax, thereby improving the quality of the general tax system. Although such an improvement would result, financing through the general budget offends our first two requirements. The spirit of social security as a distinct and essentially contributory system requires a separate and visible form of contribution. This requirement remains even if general budgetary finance could be used without rendering benefit payments subject to political manipulation or even an annual appropriation process. In theory, the budgetary contribution could be made as a fixed annual charge, payable to the trust fund, but in practice it may well become subject to current manipulation. Nor are the implications for burden distribution evident. To assess the outcome, one should not simply compare the burden distribution of the payroll tax with that of the average federal tax dollar (excluding payroll tax) but with that of the additional tax dollars that would be needed to replace the payroll tax. Or comparison should be with the other tax dollars that are not cut because the payroll tax is reduced. Seen in this way, the resulting shift in burden-distribution may become less attractive than appears at first sight.

These objections to general budgetary finance are dampened somewhat if it takes the form of earmarking a share in a particular tax for social security. But even this weakens the identity of the revenue source as a social security contribution. Moreover, it exposes the contribution to changes in the earmarked tax that are made for other reasons. If linked to the income tax, as would presumably be the case, the social security contribution would add to the weight of preferences now granted under that tax.

Resort to financing from the general budget becomes more attractive if a two-tier system were used. Such a system could take two forms. Under one approach, the basic component would take the form of a contribution-financed and non-redistributive scheme, but this would be supplemented by budgetary financing of supplementary payments to raise low benefits to an acceptable minimum. This would be an extension of the supplementary security income (SSI) system, which was created in 1972 and which is financed from the general budget. Such a two-tiered scheme has logical neatness and gives added visibility to what is involved, but it also has a disadvantage of exposing retirees whose lifetime income was low to the onus of being given 'welfare' payments. Moreover supplementary benefits have to be related to the recipient's wealth, thus introducing means test considerations. On balance it may be better to retain a modest degree of intrageneration redistribution within the system. Under another approach, the first tier would involve a budgetary-financed minimum payment to all retirees, with supplementary contribution-financed benefits in line with earnings. Under this approach, the share of budgetary finance would be much larger, leaving the need for a supplementary nonredistributive tier questionable. This system therefore would come close to viewing retirement provision as part of a general redistribution scheme, an approach that is not desirable.[19]

## CONCLUSIONS

This appraisal of the financial prospects of the social security system distinguishes between short- and long-run aspects. In the short run, extending over, say, five years, the system will need outside support. This need does not reflect a basic flaw in the design of the system but a temporary revenue shortfall due to stagflation. Given a pay-as-you-go system with a minimal operating reserve, temporary deficit or surplus positions are unavoidable and can be met readily by the borrowing arrangements proposed by the Advisory Council. The current short-term crisis should not be permitted to dominate the more basic reforms, which may be needed to ensure the soundness of the system in the longer run. I am, however, concerned with the tendency of both the trustee report and the Advisory Council to adopt an overly optimistic economic outlook.

The longer-run projection for the system is disturbing. Given current and future demographic developments, the current approach with a productivity-adjusted earnings base may well become difficult or impossible to adhere to. We should therefore rethink the inter-generation contract that underlies the system so as to make it viable and to obviate the need for unreliable long-run projections. A viable system calls for an inter-generation contract that provides for a fair sharing of the risks caused by uncertain future changes in productivity and population growth. Currently the entire burden due to declining population growth is placed on the working generation, thereby endangering the viability of the system over time. As a solution to this problem I propose that contributions and benefits be adjusted so as to maintain a constant ratio between per-capita earnings (net of contribution) of the working population and per-capita benefits of the retirees. Such a formula results in a fair sharing of risks with regard to uncertain productivity and population changes.

The role of intra-generation redistribution with OASI poses a problem distinct from that of inter-generation contract. The role of intra-generation redistribution should be seen as supplementary to what otherwise would be an inadequate adjustment in the distribution of lifetime incomes rather than as a supplement to corrections in the distribution of annual incomes. It follows from this that the redistributive adjustment should be made primarily on the benefit, rather than the contribution, side of the system.

Viewed as a part of the general revenue system, the payroll tax is inferior to either the income tax (assuming income to be the proper base of taxation) or to a personal expenditure tax (assuming consumption to be the proper base). Viewed as a source of social security finance the payroll tax is less objectionable but by no means optimal. Nor are general budgetary contribution, earmarking of the income tax, or a VAT desirable alternatives. Based on the conclusion that capital as well as labour income should be included, a flat rate charge on a broadly defined income base—such as AGI plus certain items of preference income—is the preferred solution.

The social security system should be seen as an arrangement whereby each generation contributes during its working years to the retirement support of the preceding generation and thereby becomes entitled to support by the subsequent generation. The essential nature of the system is thus one of contribution and entitlement, not of redistribution. Although some intra-generation redistribution occurs, the system should not be viewed as or permitted to become part of a general redistribution scheme. The system should keep its distinct identity, outside the vagaries of political change. Moreover it should be reworked in a manner designed to avoid recurring crises and need for adjustment.

## APPENDIX

This appendix offers a simple illustration of how the tax rate and other variables respond under the different formulae to changes in the rate of population growth as reflected in a changing ratio of working to retired population and to changes in productivity as reflected in a changing ratio of current earnings of workers to past earnings of retirees. The following symbols are used:

$N_w$ = number of workers
$N_r$ = number of retirees

*Table 7A.1 Formulae for variables under various plans*

| | Variables | | | |
|---|---|---|---|---|
| | $b$ | $t$ | $c$ | $d$ |
| 1. Initial period | $\alpha\beta t$ | $t$ | $\alpha t$ | $\dfrac{\alpha t}{1-t}$ |
| 2. Period 2 | $b'$ | $t'$ | $c'$ | $d'$ |
| Plan B2 with $b$ constant | $b$ | $\left(\dfrac{\alpha}{\alpha'}\right)\left(\dfrac{\beta}{\beta'}\right)t$ | $\left(\dfrac{\beta}{\beta'}\right)c$ | $\left(\dfrac{\beta}{\beta'}\right)\left(\dfrac{1-t}{1-\left(\dfrac{\alpha}{\alpha'}\right)\left(\dfrac{\beta}{\beta'}\right)^{t}}\right)d$ |
| Plan B3 with $t$ constant | $\left(\dfrac{\alpha'}{\alpha}\right)\left(\dfrac{\beta'}{\beta}\right)b$ | $t$ | $\left(\dfrac{\alpha'}{\alpha}\right)c$ | $\left(\dfrac{\alpha'}{\alpha}\right)d$ |
| Plan B4 with $c$ constant | $\left(\dfrac{\beta'}{\beta}\right)b$ | $\left(\dfrac{\alpha}{\alpha'}\right)t$ | $c$ | $\left(\dfrac{\alpha'}{\alpha}\right)\left(\dfrac{\alpha-c}{\alpha'-c}\right)d$ |
| Plan B5 with $d$ constant | $\left(\dfrac{\alpha'}{\alpha}\right)\left(\dfrac{\beta'}{\beta}\right)\left(\dfrac{\alpha+d}{\alpha'+d}\right)b$ | $\left(\dfrac{\alpha+d}{\alpha'+d}\right)t$ | $\left(\dfrac{\alpha'}{\alpha}\right)\left(\dfrac{\alpha+d}{\alpha'+d}\right)c$ | $d$ |

*Note:* The formulae for $t$ are derived as follows:

Plan B2: With $b' = t'\alpha'\beta'$ and $b = t\alpha\beta$, as well as the option 2 condition that $b = b'$, we get $t' = (\alpha/\alpha')(\beta/\beta')t$.

Plan B3: With $b' = \beta'\alpha't'$ and $b = \beta\alpha t$, as well as the option 3 condition that $t' = t$, we get $b' = [(\alpha'/\beta')(\alpha/\beta)]b$.

Plan B4: With $c' = t'\alpha'$ and $c = t\alpha$, as well as the option 4 condition that $c' = c$, we get $t' = (\alpha/\alpha')t$.

Plan B5: With $d' = [(t'E'_wN'_w/N'_w)/N'_w]/[(1-t)E'_wN_2]$ we get $t' = d'/(\alpha' + d)$. With $t = d/(\alpha + d)$ and by option 5 assumption that $d = d'$ we obtain $t' = [(\alpha + d)\alpha(\alpha' + d')]t$.

$E_w$ = earnings per worker
$E_r$ = earnings per retiree
$t$  = tax rate
$b$  = replacement rate
$c$  = productivity adjusted replacement rate
$d$  = ratio of per capita benefits of retirees to per capita after-tax earnings of workers
$\alpha$  = $N_w/N_r$
$\beta$  = $E_w/E_r$

Given the values of $\alpha$, $\beta$ and $t$ for an initial period, those for $b$, and $d$ may be determined as shown in line 1 of table A.1. We then assume new values of $\alpha'$ and $\beta'$ for a subsequent period and compute the corresponding values of $t'$, $b'$, $c'$ and $d'$ as a result under the formulae of Table 7.1. This is shown in line 2 of the table for plan B2, where $b$ is held constant so that $b' = b$. The formulae in the following lines give corresponding solutions for the other plans.

Table 7A.2, based on Table 7A.1, shows how $b$, $t$, $c$ and $d$ vary with changes in $\alpha$ and $\beta$ under the various plans. Under plan B2, the value of $t$ rises as $\alpha$ and $\beta$ decline or, more precisely, as $(\alpha/\alpha')$ $(\beta/\beta')$ rises. For plans B4 and B5, however, only changes in $\alpha$ enter the picture.

Table 7A.3 gives an application of these results to a change from representative values for 1980 as given in line 1 to computed values for the year 2030. Throughout we assume $\alpha = 3.0$ for 1980 and $\alpha' = 2.0$ for 2030. Similarly we set $\beta = 1.5$ for 1980 and $\beta' = 1.4$ for 2030. The value of $t$ rises from 0.90 to 0.143 under plan B2, to 0.135 under plan B4 and to 0.129 under plan B5. The last increase of 3.9 per cent thus falls half way between the 5.3 point increase under plan B2 and the 4.5 point increase under plan B4.

*Table 7A.2: Effects of changes in and on policy variables*

|          | $t' \gtreqless t$ if | $c' \gtreqless c$ if | $d' \gtreqless d$ if | $b' \gtreqless b$ if |
|----------|----------------------|----------------------|----------------------|----------------------|
| Plan B2  | $\alpha'\beta' \lesseqgtr \alpha\beta$ | $\beta' \lesseqgtr \beta$ | $\alpha' \lesseqgtr \alpha; \beta' > \beta$ | N.A. |
| Plan B3  | N.A. | $\alpha' \gtreqless \alpha$ | $\alpha' \gtreqless \alpha$ | $\alpha'\beta' \gtreqless \alpha\beta$ |
| Plan B4  | $\alpha' \gtreqless \alpha$ | N.A. | $\alpha' \lesseqgtr \alpha$ | $\beta' \gtreqless \beta$ |
| Plan B5  | $\alpha' \lesseqgtr \alpha$ | $\alpha' \gtreqless \alpha$ | N.A. | $\alpha'>\alpha; \beta'>\beta$* |

* Also holds if $\alpha'>\alpha$ and $\beta'=\beta$, or if $\beta'>\beta$ and $\alpha' = \alpha$.

*Table 7A.3 Application to change from 1980 to 2030*

|  | $\alpha^*$ | $\beta^*$ | $t^*$ | $b^{**}$ | $c^{**}$ | $d^{**}$ |
|---|---|---|---|---|---|---|
| 1980 levels | 3.00 | 1.50 | 0.09 | 0.400 | 0.270 | 0.297 |
| 2030 levels |  |  |  |  |  |  |
| Plan B2 | 2.00 | 1.40 | 0.143 | 0.400 | 0.256 | 0.334 |
| Plan B3 | 2.00 | 1.40 | 0.09 | 0.252 | 0.180 | 0.198 |
| Plan B4 | 2.00 | 1.40 | 0.135 | 0.378 | 0.270 | 0.312 |
| Plan B5 | 2.00 | 1.40 | 0.129 | 0.362 | 0.258 | 0.297 |

\* Assumed for 2030 levels.
\*\* Computed for 2030 levels.

## NOTES

1. A section examining the outlook for the US social security system in the original paper is here omitted.
2. See note 6 below where a difference between current law and FRRA is noted.
3. Other and more subtle forms of inter-generation contract might be added, with objectives that transcend the mere provision for old age. The target of such contracts might be to maximise the present value of future consumption or to equalise the level of consumption across generations, and for such purposes a partial reserve approach might be called for. It might be questioned, however, whether the more immediate objective of provision for old age should be mixed with such broader goals of inter-generation redistribution. In any case, the above plan will do for present purposes.
4. There would still be a case for requiring private insurance. Mandatory insurance remains necessary to protect the prudent who save against having to bail out (by way of old age relief) the spendthrifts who fail to provide for their retirement.
5. A sketch of the problem runs as follows. Suppose we begin with a stationary economy (constant population and productivity) with zero net savings. Now a reserve financed social security retirement system is introduced. The initial generation of retirees gets nothing. The result may be that the first generation of contributors considers its contributions (and the consequent promise of benefits) as a substitute for previously necessary private saving. Reserve fund saving is substituted for private saving, with no net change in total saving. The same happens with subsequent generations. Or the result may be that the initial contributors maintain their private saving while adding their social security saving to it, in which case aggregate saving is increased. Of the two, case 1 seems more likely, but the issue is an empirical one.
   Beginning again with a situation of zero net saving, consider now the introduction of a pay-as-you-go scheme. Suppose again that the first generation of contributors substitutes their contributions for private saving. Contributions are transferred to the retirees who receive a gift. They not only consume their

own saving but also their social security benefits. Aggregate saving is reduced. But this reduction in the capital stock is a once-and-for-all effect. In the next round, the contributors pay for the retirees and the economy is returned to a position of zero net saving. This is all there is to it for a stationary economy. Only if growth occurs, a retarding effect on aggregate saving continues. Taking behaviour assumption 2, there will be no effect on aggregate saving. All that happens is a transfer of consumption from the first contributors to their retired contemporaries.

Finally, consider a situation with an ongoing pay-as-you-go system, which (as some suggest we should) switches to reserve finance. To accomplish this, payroll taxes must be increased so as to accumulate reserves, in addition to paying current benefits. Since the additional contributions do not bring a promise of additional benefits, there is no good reason to expect a substitution for private saving. As disposable income is reduced, part of the loss will be reflected in reduced saving, but total (public plus private) saving will rise. A shift to reserve finance will increase aggregate saving (provided, of course, that the reserve proceeds are not used for public consumption). Assuming constant population and productivity, this will be a once-and-for-all addition to the capital stock, as in the introduction of a reserve system. A continuing increase in saving will result only if population or productivity increase.

Various attempts have been made to derive empirical estimates of the effects of social security on saving. Estimating a lifetime consumption function including permanent income, private wealth and social security wealth as dependent variables, Feldstein [2] concluded that social security reduces personal saving by 50 per cent. These results were widely cited and the underlying series on social security wealth was used in various other studies. Recently, careful research into the original estimation showed that Feldstein's social security wealth series contained an error and that re-estimation of the same model does not support and perhaps even contradicts the earlier conclusion (Leimer and Lesnoy, 1980).

6. The problem is thus stated in terms of absolute change, but similar effects will result from changes in the rate of growth.

7. Under FRRA, wage indexing applies not only up to but also after retirement. This renders the tax rate wholly invariant to productivity change. Under the present system, where wage indexing applies only up to retirement, rising productivity lowers the required tax rate although by less than under plan B2.

8. I have here compared the impact of the various plans on the workers and retirees in a two-period model. In fact, each person will move through both categories over her or his lifetime. Taking the entire lifetime perspective, a person's position under the various plans will depend on the pattern of productivity and population growth over the entire period, including both the working and retirement phase.

   Our simple two-generation model also overlooks that the earnings of workers are not independent of population change because the latter affects the age composition of the labour force and hence their earnings and that the age composition of retirees, and hence their earning records, differ.

9. Reference to per capita income of employees is to income net of contribution to the system.

10. It may be argued that this overstates the problem because allowance must also be made for the fact that declining population growth not only raises the ratio of retirees to working population but also reduces that of children to working

population. For the period from 1980 to 2055, the ratio of retirees to working population under alternative 2 is estimated to rise from 0.194 to 0.347, while that of youth to working population falls from 0.56 to 0.48. The net dependence ratio, or ratio of retirees and youth to working population, rises from 0.75 to 0.83 only. See Board of Trustees [1] p.57.

The decline in the ratio of youth to working population may be taken to increase the working population's ability to contribute, and it might be argued that the retiree income should be compared with worker income net of child-rearing costs. Possibly so, but reduction in family size has no direct bearing on the incentive effects of rising payroll tax rates. It may, however, reduce the weight of other taxes.

11. The tax rate might be determined annually or, say, every five years. With $B$ 004 total benefits, $E$ = total earnings, $N$ = number of retirees, $N$ = number of workers, $d$ = set ratio of per capita benefits to per capita earnings net of tax, and $t$ = tax rate, we have

$$\frac{B}{N_r} = d\,\frac{(1 - t)\,E}{N_w}$$

and, since $B = tE$

$$t = \frac{d\,N_r}{N_w + d\,N_r}.$$

12. Under present law the inflation adjustment prior to retirement is included (roughly) by wage indexing (which accounts for both price and productivity changes), while after retirement the inflation adjustment is made in line with the consumer price index, thus excluding further productivity adjustment.

13. At the same time, it may be that the use of the consumer price index as now computed results in an overstatement of the actual increase in the cost of living for the aged, thus calling for the use of an appropriately adjusted index.

14. This approach was suggested by James Buchanan in the symposium discussion.

15. As also suggested in the conference discussion, the *ad hoc* adjustment might take the form of letting indexing lag behind actual price rise. Such an adjustment might be feasible, whereas reduction in nominal benefits might not. Yet in the long run, the system will fare better with a set of adjustments in line with a clearly stated and defensible rule.

16. See Appendix, especially Table 7A.1.

17. Obviously this reasoning does not apply to reserve-type *quid pro quo* plans as listed under A in Table 7.1. Such a plan, in line with private insurance, is devoid of either inter-generation or intra-generation contracts. Nor does the reasoning hold for FRR or FRRA if the fixed replacement rate is applied to individual earnings. Aspects of intrageneration redistribution (on the benefit side) are then built into the intergeneration agreement.

18. Although exclusion of retirees is appropriate in a normative system, it may be bad politics in a period when the ratio of retirees to workers rises, thereby increasing the voting strength of the aged to force transfers from the working generation.

19. A section evaluating alternative sources of tax finance included in the original paper is here omitted.

# REFERENCES

[1] Board of Trustees of the Federal Old-Age and Survivors' Insurance and Disability Insurance Trust Funds, *Annual Report* (Washington, D.C., Government Printing Office).

[2] Feldstein, M. (1974), 'Social security, induced retirement and capital accumulation', *Journal of Political Economy*, 82.

[3] Leamer, D. and Lesnoy, S., "Social security and financing private saving", *Working Paper 19*, (Washington, D.C., Social Security Administration, 1980).

# Part III
## Development Finance

# 8   Revenue Requirements for Growth*
1965

To begin with, it is helpful to view the problem in terms of a fully employed economy and to focus on the role of fiscal policy as a means of raising the domestic savings ratio. In making a first approximation to the amount of tax revenue needed to achieve a certain target rate of growth, differences between various sources of tax revenue are disregarded. Suppose that the objective is to achieve a 2 per cent annual rate of growth in income per capita. With, say, a 2 per cent annual growth rate of population, national income must then grow slightly above 4 per cent per year. This target rate of growth requires a certain rate of capital formation, or investment expenditures as a percentage of national income. This ratio $z$ may be crudely estimated by the use of an incremental capital–output ratio, and is defined as follows:

$$z = \frac{\Delta K}{\Delta Y} = \frac{I}{\Delta Y}$$

where $K$ = the capital stock, $I$ = the level of annual investment, and $Y$ = national income. If $g$ is the desired rate of growth:

$$g = \frac{\Delta Y}{Y}$$

the required investment rate $I/Y$ may be obtained by substitution as:

$$\frac{I}{Y} = \frac{\Delta K}{\Delta Y} \cdot \frac{\Delta Y}{Y} = zg$$

Thus, if $z = 3$, and $g = 4$ per cent, $I/Y = 12$ per cent. This investment ratio must be matched by a corresponding saving ratio to assure economic balance. Therefore, the economy must save 12 per cent of national income to grow at the desired rate of 4 per cent. We must have:

$$S_p + S_g = 0.12Y \tag{8.1}$$

* *Revenue Policy for Korea's Economic Development* (1965), Nathan Economic Advisory Group, USOM/Korea (Seoul).

where $S_p$ is private saving and $S_g$ is government saving. The level of private saving is given by:

$$S_p = s(Y - T)$$

or,

$$S_p = s(1 - t)Y \tag{8.2}$$

where $s$ = the propensity to save out of disposable income, $T$ = tax revenue, and $t$ = the tax rate. The level of government savings equals:

$$S_g = tY - aY \tag{8.3}$$

where $a$ = current expenditures of government as a fraction of national income, and government saving thus defined = the surplus in the current budget. Substituting equations 2 and 3 into 1, we obtain:

$$t = \frac{0.12 - s + a}{1 - s} \tag{8.4}$$

or, since the required savings rate equals $zg$:

$$t = \frac{zg - s + a}{1 - s} \tag{8.5}$$

Using a typical value for $s$ of 3 per cent and for $a$ of 10 per cent, we obtain $t$ = 19.6. That is to say, a tax rate of 19.6 per cent is needed to obtain a growth rate of 4 per cent. With government current expenditures equal to 10 per cent of national income, government saving equal to 9.6 per cent of national income may be either used to finance public investment or loaned out to finance additional private investment. Having made this first approximation to its revenue needs, the government must then judge whether such a target is feasible and can be attained under any realistic tax reform programme. This decision will depend on the institutional framework, the capabilities of tax administration, and the political will to make the necessary tax assessments stick. But two points should be noted. First, a very large effort is required to raise the revenue–income ratio by even one percentage point. Second, a development plan which is too ambitious to be implemented and requires more than the tax system can reasonably be expected to produce may be worse than no development plan at all, for it invites the waste of uncompleted projects and the danger of inflation, not to mention the social repercussions arising from unfulfilled expectations.

# 9   The Theory of Fiscal Development*
## 1969

Fiscal affairs play an important role in the functioning of the economy, whether at a relatively low or high level of income. However, there is good reason to expect that this role will change in the course of development, as the budgetary function is adapted to the changing needs of the economy. The purpose of this chapter is to examine this changing role, thereby exploring what might be called a theory of fiscal development.

## EXPENDITURE DEVELOPMENT

The determinants of expenditure development, it must be admitted at the outset, are not only economic. Other forces, referred to here as conditioning and social factors, must be considered as well.

The changing needs of the economy relate to both the allocation and distribution aspects of expenditure policy, but the former is of primary interest in this connection, as it deals with the 'proper' share of public resource use in the course of rising income. More specifically, the problem may be defined as follows. Let us assume that society divides resource use between private and public goods in an efficient pattern. That is to say, the total output of consumer goods is divided between private (internal benefit-intensive) and social (external benefit-intensive) goods, depending on consumer preferences, and the output of capital goods is similarly divided between private and public so as to secure the most productive use. Public goods are provided (paid for) through the budget but, as noted before, this does not involve the question of whether such goods are produced by private or by public firms. The problem now under discussion, therefore, applies equally to both a capitalist and a socialist setting. We now add the heroic assumption that the conditioning and social factors (as noted below) remain constant, and ask ourselves this question. As per capita income rises due to increasing productivity, either because of a rising capital–labour ratio or for other reasons, what will happen to the

---

* From *Fiscal Systems* (New Haven, Yale University Press, 1969) chs. 3 and 5, where this analysis is followed by empirical studies of expenditure and tax structure development.

public goods share in total output? The answer will then depend on the income elasticities of demand for private as against public consumer goods; and on the appropriate mix of the capital stock between private and public investment goods as the stock increases.

Regarding the distribution function of budget policy, a similar question may be asked. As per capita income rises, is there an increasing or decreasing need for distributional measures, depending on (1) changes in the existing distribution of income, and (2) changes in the need to secure a given pattern of distribution? The resulting hypotheses, as we shall see, will differ depending on the stipulated objectives of distribution policy.

Going beyond economic factors as here defined, allowance must be made for certain conditioning factors which will greatly affect the results achieved by the operation of our economic forces. Among these conditioning forces, changes in technology and demographic factors are of primary importance.

Changes in technology will affect the preferred mix of public and private goods, in both the capital and consumer goods sector. New consumer goods, created by technological innovation, may call for either public or private provision, thereby changing the mix of the preferred basket of goods. Similarly, new production techniques may call for a change in the mix of public and private capital goods. Changes in demographic factors also may affect demand patterns and hence the appropriate output mix. Increased demand for education, for instance, is a lagged effect of an increased birth rate, and so forth.

Finally, allowance must be made for the political, cultural and social factors that determine the environment in which budget policy operates and that affect the underlying value judgements or the political weights attached to them. With changing political institutions and attitudes toward the public sector, the resource allocation between public and private uses may come to approximate more closely, or move away from our model of efficient resource use. Political biases and rigidities may enter the picture. Wars may play a major role in determining what are acceptable levels of taxation, and displacement effects may arise as military expenditures decline at the end of a war. Changes in the climate of social philosophy may be reflected in changing distributional objectives and the budgetary functions that are performed in this area.

The dividing-lines between these categories of economic, conditioning, and social forces, to be sure, are not clear-cut, nor are they wholly independent of each other. At the same time, this grouping will provide a framework within which specific hypotheses regarding expenditure development can be formulated and perhaps tested. In particular, they will permit us to isolate the allocation issues which are of primary interest to the economic analyst.

Even if the conceptual distinctions can be drawn, it remains difficult to verify hypotheses regarding the role of our economic factors. If we consider the change in the expenditure share for any one country over, say, the last 100 years, this change may be related to economic development as measured by rising per capita income. But rising per capita income was not the only influence on budget policy during this period. The other factors, including conditioning and social forces, entered as well, and their influence cannot be separated neatly from that of our economic factors.

Nor are we better-off if the comparison is drawn between a cross-section of countries with differing current levels of per capita income. Here all countries are subject to the same general set of contemporary influences broadly defined, but strong political and social differences remain at any point in time. These differences influence the structure of the public sector and blur such differences as result from varying levels of per capita income.

It follows that the relationships between per capita income and fiscal structure that are obtained from the historical view may well differ from those revealed by the cross-section approach. Low-income countries today do not operate under the same technical, political and value conditions as prevailed in the past when now developed countries were at similar low levels of income. Attitudes towards growth, changed communication, the demonstration effect of affluence and welfare measures abroad, the conflict of political ideologies, all make for basic differences in the historical setting. These factors, in both their historical and sectoral dimensions, affect the fiscal structure along with differences in the level of per capita income. Hence a variety of patterns may be expected to emerge, and the verification of hypotheses regarding the role of our economic factors will be difficult. Nevertheless, let us consider the proposition that these factors play an important role—i.e. that the efficient structure of the public sector varies with the stages of economic development as measured by the growth of per capita income—and examine what hypotheses may be established on that basis.

## ECONOMIC FACTORS

Economic factors, which are our primary interest, will be considered first. As previously suggested, a distinction is drawn between the allocation and distribution aspects. The former deals primarily with the share of public purchases of goods and services in GNP, while the latter deals primarily with the role of transfer payments.

### Resource Use
Ever since Adolph Wagner expounded his law of the 'expanding scale of state activity',[1] economists have speculated on its validity and the under-lying causes. These causes may be economic or political, but it is the former that are of primary interest here.

The proposition of expanding scale, obviously, must be interpreted as postulating a rising *share* of the public sector in the economy. An absolute increase in the size of the budget can hardly fail to result as the economy expands. To focus on the economic factors that support the hypothesis of a rising share or ratio of public expenditure to GNP, let me repeat the mental experiment I wish to make. Holding constant conditioning and social forces, I now follow the development of a country from low to high per capita income in the course of capital accumulation. In such a setting, what will happen to the share of income that, assuming efficient resource use, is to be channelled through the public budget?

As Wagner pointed out to begin with, the course of *particular* types of public expenditures must be considered. But his choice of categories—protection, general administration, economic administration, and education—is not entirely suitable here. While the distinction between defence and civilian functions is accepted, civilian expenditures must then be examined by economic categories, i.e. public capital formation, public consumption and transfers. What reason is there to expect that the share of any of these in GNP will vary in some systematic fashion as the level of per capita income rises?

Given the division of total output between consumption and capital formation, the share of public capital formation in total output depends on the appropriate mix of capital goods.[2] Those that are externality-intensive must be supplied publicly, while others (the benefits of which are primarily internal) may be provided for privately.

This question cannot be answered for public expenditures at large. In our model of efficient resource allocation between public and private goods, there is no presumption that alternative public expenditures are more closely substitutable for each other than are public and private outlays. Hence the growth of public expenditures as a whole is not a dependent variable by itself but must be reduced to its components if prediction is to be made. Later on, when I consider the role of social and conditioning factors, attention will be given to the hypothesis that, in fact, *total* public expenditure levels are a function of the acceptable level of *total* tax rates. In this case, public goods as a group become substitutes for private goods as a group and the total level of public expenditures (as distinct from, or in addition to, specific expenditure items) becomes a meaningful dependent variable. This, however, is not the case in my present model, where resource allocation between alternative public and private uses is made on an efficient basis.[3]

The literature on economic development suggests that public capital formation is of particular importance at early stages of development. Transportation facilities must be provided to open up the country and to link natural resources with the market. Road, rail and port facilities are prerequisites for productive capital formation in the private sector. Improved agricultural techniques require irrigation. Use of machinery demands minimal technical skills, and so forth. All these are types of investment the benefits of which are largely external, and which must therefore be provided publicly, either by local or central government. As the economy develops and a larger flow of savings becomes available, the capital stock in private industry and agriculture must be built up. The basic stock of social overhead capital has now been created and additions are made at a slower rate. The structure of social overhead capital, similar to public utilities, becomes a declining share of net capital formation.[4]

The proposition that public goods must be provided for publicly means that they must be financed through the budget, not that they must be publicly produced. Now it should be noted that the facilities for private capital accumulation are limited at early stages of development, as is entrepreneurial talent. For these reasons public production of certain capital goods may be necessary, even if benefits are of the internal type. This in turn may lead to budgetary provision (in the sense of tax rather than price financing) of such goods.[5] At a later stage, the institutions for private capital formation become more developed and provision of such capital goods may be left to the private sector. Considerations of this sort offer a second reason why the share of publicly-provided capital goods may fall.

This hypothesis is reasonable, but it covers only movement along the earlier to middle stages of economic development. There may well be periods, at a later stage, when the public component of net investment is again rising. As per capita income rises, budget patterns are changed. Private goods which demand complementary public investment may come to the fore, and this in turn may raise the share of public investment. Thus the fiscal systems of European countries will be burdened heavily in the next decade by a greatly increased need for highway facilities, due to the fact that the rise of consumer incomes will permit widespread use of automobiles. The development of urban concentration in conjunction with industrialisation calls for municipal programmes involving large public investment. Increased need for skilled labour places higher demands upon education and the need for human investment. In high-income countries such as the United States, the development of urban slums and the migration of higher income population to the suburbs calls for urban redevelopment and expanded commuter facilities, and so forth. At the same time, the changing private consumption patterns also call for complementary private investment, so that the net effect on the public share depends on the particular case.

In short, the ratio of public to total capital formation may be expected to be high at early stages and to decline at least temporarily after the 'take-off' is reached. At the same time, there may well be periods at later stages of development when the ratio of public to total capital formation rises. Much depends on the particular stage of income and its capital requirements, and there is little reason to expect a continuous trend to prevail.

Apart from the composition of capital formation, it should be noted that the ratio of total (public plus private) capital formation to GNP tends to rise with economic development. This will counterbalance a possible tendency for a declining ratio of public to private capital formation and tend to maintain the ratio of public capital formation to GNP.

Turning now to public consumption, the basic question is whether the income elasticity of demand for public consumer goods is in excess of unity.[6] That is to say, will the demand for consumer goods the benefits of which are highly externality intensive, and which therefore are publicly provided, absorb an increasing share of income as per capita income rises?

In line with an expanded Engel's law, the share of consumer outlays going into private expenditures on the basic needs for food, shelter and clothing declines as income rises. But there are also certain public services which meet basic needs such as protection and other rudimentary functions of government. Much the same argument can be made regarding these, so that no simple presumption regarding the changing ratio of private to public outlays emerges on these grounds. Nevertheless, there seems to remain a case for the primacy of private expenditures at very low levels of income when food, shelter and clothing are all that can be provided. As some slack develops, resources may be applied to satisfy secondary needs, and these will call for a larger public goods share, i.e. education, health facilities, safety and other items which fall on the borderline of the division between consumption and capital formation. Considerations such as these suggest a rising public to private consumption ratio over the early stages of economic growth, but the case appears less clear than with regard to capital formation.

Over subsequent stages, prospects for a rising ratio of public to private outlays are again strengthened by the hypothesis that the pattern of private consumption, which develops at rising levels of per capita income, includes an increasing share of goods, utilisation of which requires complementary public services. In the affluent society, a rising share of consumer expenditures flows into 'adult toys' for leisure-time use, such as pleasure cars, motorboats, and other durables serving luxury consumption. These 'toys' are frequently such as to require substantial public outlays to provide the requisite facilities for their use, either the form of public investment in high-speed roads, marinas, parks, and so forth, or in the form of services such as traffic patrols, park services or weather reporting.

Furthermore, the increasing complexity of economic organisation, which goes with economic growth, may generate a new set of basic public services which are of a remedial sort [Musgrave, 16, p. 189]. The emergence of corporations and large enterprises necessitates the services of regulatory agencies such as the Interstate Commerce Commission and the Securities and Exchange Commission, and the anti-trust activities of the Justice Department. Higher population density raises the need for traffic patrols; advancing industrialisation calls for measures to counteract air and water pollution, and so forth. These activities clearly make for an increased absolute level of public activity, but they need not make for a rising public share. The development of remedial activities is not limited to the public sector but has its counterpart in private services. Thus private swimming pools are needed as public beaches become overcrowded. Residences are moved to suburbs as cities deteriorate, and so forth. Thus the rising need for remedial output does not necessarily make for a rising public share, since remedial needs may also call for increased supply of private goods.

The scope of merit goods, a final aspect of the allocation problem, will be examined briefly after considering the distribution function.

## Distribution

Next the changing weight of transfers in the distribution of income is examined. The combination of tax and transfer policies serves to rearrange the distribution of income as determined by factor returns and endowments in the market. Let us suppose, first, that the distribution of factor earnings does not change with the rise of per capita income and that the goal of redistributional policy remains constant.

Much depends in this case on how the goal is defined. If (1) the purpose is to reduce inequality, as measured by, say, a Lorenz coefficient, to a certain level, the transfer share in total income will remain unchanged (and the absolute level of transfers will rise) as per capita income rises. The same holds if redistribution aims at providing each family with a given minimum income but the minimum is defined as a fixed percentage of average income. The case differs if (2) the purpose of distributional adjustments is not the reduction of inequality *per se*, but assurance of an absolute minimum standard of living as determined by an objective criterion such as nutritional requirements. The requisite ratio of transfers to total income (and, indeed, the per capita level of transfers) will now fall as per capita income rises.

It is evident, without further pursuit of this, that the relationship between the transfer share and the level of per capita income depends on the objective of the distributional adjustment; but since assurance of an absolute minimum standard is at least part of the picture, the transfer share may well fall with rising income.

Certain considerations may be added which qualify this expectation. Even though distributional objectives are held constant, the objective need for distributional measures may change with economic development. Thus, the distribution of factor income may become more equal, due to wider distribution of human investment and of property ownership, thereby reducing the need for distributional measures. Or urbanisation and increasing interdependence may raise economic risks, thus increasing the need for social insurance, both with regard to unemployment and old age.

Finally, there are the questions of whether society can 'afford' any desired degree of redistribution, and of how this relates to the level of income. It is frequently said that low-income countries are handicapped in their growth policy by pressures for welfare measures copied from more advanced countries. If the private savings rate is reduced by equalising transfer measures, the growth rate may be retarded. And even if the desired savings rate is restored through public saving, other disincentive effects might result. Redistribution may thus involve a cost in terms of growth. But as per capita income rises, growth becomes less urgent. The social cost of redistribution, therefore, declines and (contrary to our earlier hypotheses) the transfer share may be expected to rise.

There must be added the complicating fact that redistribution need not involve transfer payments. It may take the form of financing general expenditures by progressive taxation which, in principle, is equivalent to a combination of benefit taxation with a progressive tax-transfer scheme [Musgrave, 16, ch. 2]. It may also take the form of subsidies in kind, thus again raising the previously mentioned case of merit wants.

## Merit Wants

There is no evident presumption as to why public expenditures for the satisfaction of such wants should rise or fall, relative to GNP, as per capita income increases. Having provided for the proper state of distribution by tax-transfer measures, why should there be more reason to interfere with consumer choice at low income levels, where the choice may be between better clothing and more adequate food, than at high ones, where the choice may be between a second car and a motorboat?

Posing the question in this way is to answer it in the negative, but this may not be the right way of putting it. In practice, merit wants tend to be associated closely with redistribution. Public expenditures for low-cost housing or free hospitalisation for the needy combine redistributional objectives with the substitution of imposed for free consumer choice. The imposition of public choice typically relates to the consumption of 'necessities', suggesting a basically different view of redistribution. Putting it in extreme form, let us assume a social philosophy which postulates that everybody should consume a certain amount of basic necessities, such as food, clothing and shelter, but that the distribution of income available for discretionary use is of no social concern. This would suggest that such items would be provided to everyone through the budget; but since they are purchased privately by consumers with higher incomes, public provision may be limited to the lower end of the income scale. If the relevant concept of necessities is defined in absolute terms, this reasoning suggests a falling share of merit wants with rising per capita income. However this may be, it is evident that the prevalence of merit-type expenditures complicates the interpretation of expenditure trends, as it extends the operation of distributional objectives beyond the transfer and into the purchase category.

While these speculations yield no unique hypothesis for the development of the total expenditures share, something can be said about each of the major categories. There is reason to expect that the public share in total capital formation will be relatively high at early stages of development, with less predictable fluctuations thereafter, and that the ratio of transfers (including expenditures for low-income-oriented merit goods) will tend to decline with rising income. Also, there may be a tendency for the ratio of public to private consumption to rise with rising income. Intuition does not tell us how these three trends may be expected to compound into changes in the overall public expenditure to GNP ratio. Moreover, these economic forces are not readily verifiable since they operate concurrently with other variables which may be of equal or greater importance. To these we now turn.

## CONDITIONING FACTORS

So far, we have disregarded certain conditioning factors of change which have important bearing on the efficient expenditure share and which operate on both the numerator and denominator of the expenditure ratio. These can readily be incorporated into our economic model.

### Demographic Change

Demographic factors are an important determinant of the level of public expenditures, and the share of public expenditures in total outlay. Both changes in absolute population size and in age structure are relevant.

Beginning with absolute population increase, suppose first that the level of per capita income is not affected. Such an increase will call for absolute expansion of basic public services and an increased level of expenditures thereon. While this would not be the case if public goods were indeed available for joint consumption by the entire group, many of the goods and services in question are available to sub-groups (e.g. residents of particular cities) only, or represent mixed goods and services the cost of which is not independent of the number of consumers served (i.e. fire protection). But though there is a strong presumption that the absolute level of public expenditures rises with population, effects on the public expenditure share are less obvious. Much will depend on the location pattern of the growing population, the bearing of density on service costs, the presence of economies or diseconomies of scale, and so forth. While it seems likely that a more crowded world will need to spend a larger share of its output on public goods than did Robinson Crusoe and his friend Friday, the case is not as clear-cut. Increased density may involve economies as well as diseconomies in the use of public services.

Changes in the growth rate of population also affect the population structure, and changes in age composition call for varying allocations to particular public services. Thus the ratio of school expenditures to GNP, current and especially capital, is closely related to the ratio of schoolage children to population; a high ratio of aged calls for a larger share of retirement assistance, and so forth. Moreover, increased life expectancy raises the return on investment in education and thus justifies larger outlays. Economies of scale are again a factor in determining the effects of such changes on expenditure shares, and may operate as either a strengthening or a dampening factor.

### Technological Change

Next, there is the impact of technological change upon the public expenditure share, a crucial factor especially in the historical approach to expenditure growth. As technology changes, new products become available and the mix of desired goods changes. Depending upon the nature of the technical change, the relative importance of externality-intensive or social goods may change as well. The invention and rise of the automobile provides the most startling illustration. Highway construction in response to the rise of the automobile in the United States was one of the major factors of expansion in state finances during the interwar years, and a similar experience is now in the making in Europe. Similarly, it is not unreasonable to expect that the future share of public expenditures in GNP will be affected greatly by the development of space technology and by the extent to which related needs can be met privately or must be provided for through the public budget. The implications of changing military technology provide another illustration. Thus technical change will result in unpredictable departures from such basic relation between the expenditure to GNP ratio and per capita income as would prevail under constant technology.

Also there is the problem of statistical bias which arises from differential productivity gains. If, as has been suggested, productivity gains have been greater in the production of private than of social goods, use of an undeflated expenditure to GNP ratio will overstate the gain in the public expenditure share. [Andic, 1] This may have been the case at a time when public purchases were highly labour-intensive, while technical change has been capital saving. Over recent decades, the opposite may hold, as defence purchases have become a large share of the budget and defence industries have been subject to the most rapid technical change.

## SOCIAL, CULTURAL AND POLITICAL FACTORS

A quite different set of factors, non-economic in nature, which cannot be readily incorporated into the economic model but nevertheless have important bearing on the expenditure ratio, remain to be considered. Changes in cultural values and social philosophy affect the extent to which distributional adjustments are desired, and may bear also on the degree to which demand is directed at public as against private goods. Changes in political structure, moreover, alter the effective demand (distribution of votes) for public goods, and hence affect expenditure levels. War finance interrupts the steady path of fiscal development and may have profound after-effects.

### Social Change
The growing sense of social responsibility for the welfare of individuals, which characterised the course of political thought during the twentieth century, greatly increased the demand for transfer programmes, and acceptance of a larger role of the state reduced political resistance to the allocation of resources for the provision of public goods. These changes have occurred at different speeds in various countries—witness the quarter-century lag in the US pattern behind that of Europe—but the general trend has been similar throughout. Undoubtedly it deserves major weight in explaining the rising public expenditure share during this century.

Changes in political structure were equally favourable. Transition from authoritarian to representative government strengthened the effective demand for social goods, as did the subsequent democratisation of representative forms of government through the broadening of suffrage. Since redistribution through tax-transfer programmes was more difficult to achieve than through finance of public services by progressive taxation, the expansion of public services served in part as a means of implementing redistributional measures.

But this may not be a continuing process. At a time when the budget to GNP ratio was relatively low, the voting block comprised by the low and lower-middle income groups could readily place the burden of increased outlays upon the high income minority [Wicksell, 28]. The turning point in this process may well have been reached in the post-war period. With a rising budget to GNP ratio, revenue needs come to exceed the tax base available in the high-income brackets, and additional expenditure prog-rammes come to be financed increasingly by drafts on taxpayers in the middle to lower income groups, where the tax base broadens out with the income pyramid. The impact of the marginal tax dollar moves down the income scale as the average budget to GNP ratio rises. The voting constellation changes, and it becomes more difficult to find a majority in favour of expanding budgets.

A final factor in the politics of fiscal expansion relates to the built-in revenue response to economic growth. The faster the economy grows, the greater will be the 'fiscal dividend' or built-in revenue gain with constant rates of tax. Given the asymmetry of political behaviour which shows voters more eager to reduce rates than they are willing to raise them, a rising absolute level of public expenditures becomes permissible as the economy grows. But this need not imply a rising expenditure to GNP *ratio*. Such will be the case only if the income elasticity of tax yield exceeds unity, i.e. if the tax structure is distinctly progressive over the relevant income range, or if the tax base increases as a component of GNP.[7]

## War and Social Disturbance

It remains to consider the role of war and of major social disturbances such as the great depression of the 1930s. Such events may have a profound effect on the timing of expenditure growth, causing sharp temporary departure from underlying trends; beyond this, they may have a lasting effect on the trend line itself.

Figure 9.1 shows three possible patterns of influence. We assume throughout that during a war the displacement required by the increase in war expenditures is spread between public and civilian uses. Thus, total public expenditures rise sharply, but the increase is below that of war expenditures. This is more realistic than to assume that the entire replacement is in civilian public or in private expenditures.[8]

Our primary interest is in the post-war development, and here the three models differ. In case *a* we assume that civilian public expenditures resume their old growth path after the war. In case *b* we assume that the wartime trend of total public expenditure increase is maintained, with a post-war upward shift in the level of civilian public expenditures. In case *c* we

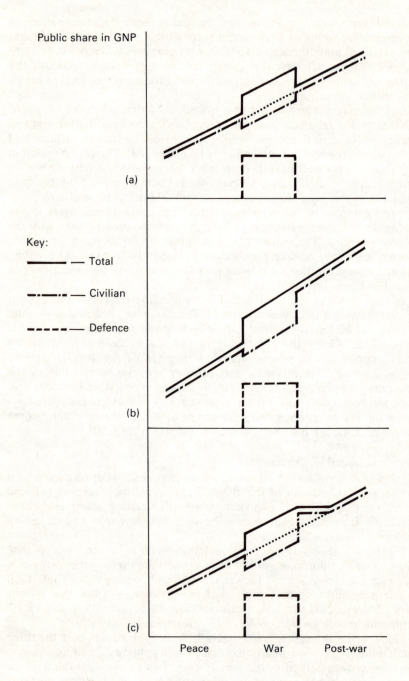

*Figure 9.1: Public expenditure patterns war and post-war*

assume a temporary post-war rise in civilian public expenditures which, however, continues only until the old trend line is reached. The long-run effects are thus similar to case *a*, leaving the level of civilian and total public expenditure as it would have been in the absence of war. There is no permanent displacement effect. Such effect only arises in case *b*, where there has been a permanent displacement of private by civilian public expenditures.

Which of these patterns (or combinations thereof) applies depends on public attitudes toward tax and expenditure policies. Our earlier model of efficient expenditure determination would suggest pattern *a*. The temporary displacement of resources for peacetime use would be spread between both civilian and public peacetime uses, and the longer run pattern would not be changed. Pattern *c* may be considered a qualified version of pattern *a*, as the filling of backlog needs results in a temporary increase in the public service level.

Pattern *b* requires a different explanation. Political behaviour may be such that the voting public (or the ruling group) is unwilling or hesitant to accept an increase in tax rates. There is a bias against public and in favour of private goods. As noted before, this is not in line with our efficient behaviour model, but it may nevertheless reflect the actual situation. Now a war comes along and, considering the urgency of the need for defence outlays, a threshold effect results. The resistance to higher taxes is overcome, and once overcome, the threshold of resistance is moved to a higher level. Thus, civilian public expenditures fill the gap after the war, and the public expenditure share is permanently raised.

In addition, it may be that wars or other major events in the history of a nation, such as the Great Depression, lead to a reassessment of social values or change in the power balance of political groups. This may result in a changed pattern of preferences for public and private wants and may lead to an increase in the public expenditure share. Discontinuous changes in preference pattern, associated with wars and other social disturbances, may thus have been a major factor in the cultural–political environment which determines expenditure choice.

Both these factors—the threshold effect and the change in preferences—help to explain case *b* and both are noted by Peacock and Wiseman [21] in explaining their displacement effect, to which they ascribe a central role in determining expenditure increase. Following case *b*, these forces are said to have a lasting effect on expenditure levels. Without a national crisis, the tax rate threshold would not have been broken, and the change in philosophy would not have occurred. This does not exclude the temporary operation of such forces, in line with pattern *c*, where a temporary shift in tax threshold may explain the willingness to meet backlog needs. But the more important point, made by these authors, is that pattern *b* may explain a lasting rise in expenditure levels.

## TAX STRUCTURE DEVELOPMENT

I now turn to the development of the tax structure, beginning again with speculative observations and proceeding to empirical evidence in both historical and cross-section terms. As in the case of expenditures, I distinguish between economic factors and the broader forces of social and political change, which also shape tax structure development. The in-between category of conditioning factors, noted in the analysis of expenditure development, is here assimilated with the economic factors.

## ECONOMIC FACTORS

Economic factors bear on tax structure development in two ways. As the structure of the economy changes with economic development, the nature of the tax base changes as well, and with it the 'handles' to which the revenue system may be attached. Moreover, the economic objectives of tax policy vary with the stages of economic development, as do the economic criteria by which a good tax structure is to be judged. On both counts, the effects of development upon the tax structure are more a function of institutional change and less in the nature of an inherently economic matter, as was the case with regard to expenditure change.

The economic structure of low-income countries imposes severe limitations on the structure of the tax system.[9] The predominance of agriculture and the difficulty of reaching it through income taxation makes land taxes vitally important. Presumptive methods of assessment and even taxes in kind are called for. Subject to periodic review, the physical output from particular parcels of land can be determined on a presumptive basis by land surveys; and translation into value terms can be linked annually to changes in the prices of agricultural products [Wald 28; OAS, 20, ch. IV; Bird and Oldman, 2, Part V]. Moreover, it has also been suggested that an effective system of self-assessment might be established by requiring the owner to sell at the declared price [Harberger, 9].

Outside agriculture, the organisation of early manufacturing in small-scale establishments limits the effective base for manufacturing excises to certain major products which are produced in larger establishments. The fluid and atomistic structure of retail outlets bars effective retail sales taxation, not to mention the application of turnover or multiple-stage sales tax systems [Due, 4; Goode, 6; Naharro, 18; Desser, 3]. More feasible is the use of pricing policies of public enterprises as a revenue source. This is the case especially where the sale or manufacture of liquor and tobacco products is publicly operated, but it frequently extends over a wider area, including transportation, public utilities and some phases of manufacturing.

Personal income tax, to the extent that it can be applied at all, has to proceed on a highly schedular, non-global basis. The tax is assessed separately on distinct sources of income and not as a personal tax on total income received. As a result, progression is largely ineffective. Wage income is assessed more readily than business income, but the large share of self-employment in total employment renders broad application unworkable. Effective taxation is typically limited to the wage income of civil servants and employees of large firms. Determination of business income is exceedingly difficult. In the absence of adequate accounting practices, income has to be determined on a presumptive basis, e.g. by applying stipulated margins to estimated sales. The tax payable by the individual firm is thus a function of its sales. This suggests that the income tax is in effect a sales tax, with *ad valorem* rates varying with the average margin of the industry. But even this approach is troublesome, because the sales basis cannot be readily established, and further presumptive rules (e.g. square frontage of establishment or number of workers) are needed [Bird and Oldman, 2, Part III; OAS, 20, ch. 6]. Similar limitations apply to corporation taxes, where effective taxation is again limited typically to a few large, and frequently foreign-owned, firms. Since upper incomes are largely from capital sources, failure effectively to assess capital income becomes a severe flaw in the equity of the tax structure.[10]

It is possible, to be sure, to design a system of theoretically interlocking taxes—including levies on income, expenditures, and net worth—which would induce taxpayer compliance [Higgins, 11; OAS, ch. 3]. Thus assuming income to be known, under-reporting for expenditure tax purposes raises liability under a net worth tax, and vice versa. Given the true base for any two of the three taxes, the true base for the third can be determined, and so forth. Ironically, however, such self-checking systems include highly complex taxes, and the very lack of administrative skills that renders the checks so essential also renders such schemes unrealistic. While existence of a net worth tax will strengthen the administration of an income tax with regard to capital income, a country with a highly inefficient income tax will hardly do much better in administering a net worth tax, and so forth. This is the case especially since taxpayer compliance is only half the problem. Tax collector compliance tends to be equally weak, the more so the more complex the tax system. It is advisable, therefore, not to place excessive demands on administrative skills and to minimise opportunities for discretion and collusion.

Finally, it is essential to construct a system that will enforce fines for under-reporting and prosecute offences, rather than accept them as a normal and inevitable feature of the social scene. Without this, effective tax administration is impossible. Indeed, one wonders whether income taxation in high-compliance western countries could survive if courts were as unwilling to support enforcement as is typically the case in low-income countries. Of all the so-called cultural factors, this is surely the most important.

Given these difficulties, the strategy of tax structure development should be adjusted accordingly. Recognising the limitations in book-keeping, administration and judicial support, the task is to strengthen such revenue sources as (1) permit direct (voluntary) assessment, or the application of clear-cut presumptive standards; and (2) lend themselves to administrative devices that minimise the opportunities for evasion by the taxpayer and collusion stemming from discretion by the tax collector. This involves more extensive reliance on commodity taxes than is ideal, and also calls for administrative devices that seem clumsy compared with those of efficiently-administered tax structures in advanced countries.[11] But this is not the relevant comparison. The results of such taxes will be more equitable and efficient in the low-income setting than those obtained from premature application of tax technologies transferred from advanced countries. A system of commodity taxes on luxury items (defined relative to living standards) in particular may prove a more effective means of progressive taxation, and one more in line with the objectives of development, than an ineffective attempt at progressive income taxation.

One bright spot in the search for identifiable tax bases is in the foreign trade sector. Most imports and exports are visible and readily identified, especially where the movement of goods converges on a few major ports, so that smuggling is limited to a minor role. Compliance requirements are reduced to a minimum, and there is relatively little scope for discretion by the official. Moreover, imported consumer goods in low-income countries are frequently luxury or semi-luxury items, since manufactured articles are largely obtained through imports while basic food and shelter requirements are met at home. Thus commodity taxes based on imports tend to be acceptable or even desirable on equity grounds. Exports, similarly, afford a convenient handle for the taxation of domestic production [Goode, 7]. Export taxes, or profits from state export monopolies offer a convenient and politically effective way of imposing a gross receipts tax on the domestic producer, especially in the agricultural sector. The rice export monopoly in Burma, which in fact appropriated the profit formerly made by British exporters as public revenue, is a good illustration of this.

As economic organisation develops, production and sales establishments become larger and more permanent and the scope of indirect taxation may be broadened. Concentration of employment in larger establishments and decline of the rural relative to the industrial sector render personal income taxation more manageable. As the operation of private firms is rationalised and accounting practices improve, effective taxation of business income becomes feasible. The administration of income tax as a globalised personal tax on income becomes possible. Thus there is good reason to expect that economic development will bring with it an increase in the share of direct taxes.

As the system advances into that of a highly developed, pecuniary economy, a much wider range of tax bases becomes available. The great bulk of income and output now moves through the market, and transactions are valued in money terms. Income and expenditure flows may be tapped at almost any point, and revenue be diverted to the Treasury. The tax imposition may be on firms or households, on expenditures or receipts, on products or factor inputs, on flows or on stocks, and so forth.

There remain, to be sure, differences in the ease with which various taxes can be administered, and various components of the tax base can be reached. But these limitations are minor compared with the severe restrictions that prevail in low-income countries. A wide range of possible tax bases is now available. The choice among them is open, and the incantation of 'administrative difficulties', especially in effective taxation of capital gains, is more often a pretext for avoiding comprehensive taxation than a justified cause for rejecting tax reform.

It must not be concluded from this, however, that tax policy and administration have become a bed of roses. The development of the modern economy, while creating a wealth of feasible tax bases, also generates an enormous complexity of legal and institutional forms in which income is received or outlays are made. This complicates the task of securing equal treatment of taxpayers in essentially equal positions but engaging in different types of economic activity and subject to different legal forms. The rise of the widely-held public corporation becomes a central factor in the tax structure. The problem of depreciation, the importance of capital gains, the complexity of estate and gift arrangements, need only be noted to illustrate the host of technical problems that must be met. Where the tax official of old may have worried about how to assess an elusive herd of cows, the tax collector of today's developed economies worries about how to assess a no less elusive flow of capital gains, or how to check tax evasion devices such as holding companies or trust arrangements. Tax planners in the advanced economy do not lack tax bases, but they are plagued by the knotty and never-ending task of adapting the tax statutes to the changing subtleties of the economic structure, and of competing with the inventiveness of the taxpayer in creating new forms of tax avoidance.

## POLITICAL AND SOCIAL FACTORS

So much for economic factors underlying tax structure development. As in the case of expenditure policy, political and social forces must be considered as well. History testifies to a close interaction between changes in political setting and in tax structure [Schumpeter, 24]; and standards of tax equity, closely linked with the social philosophy of the time, have always been a major factor in the choice of appropriate tax instruments. The rise of egalitarian philosophy, in particular, has been the driving force behind the rise of progressive taxation.[12]

Tax structure development over the modern period has been dominated by the rise of direct, and especially income, taxation. With the transition from feudal to capitalist patterns of social stratification, income emerged as a welcome substitute for property as a tax base, and subsequently it became accepted increasingly as the most representative index of economic or social status and of fiscal capacity. At the same time, income offered the most feasible base on which to construct 'personal' taxes and to which to apply progressive rates. Consumption taxes, imposed on manufacturing, on wholesale or retail sales, did not permit adjustment to family size, nor could they be an effective instrument of progressive taxation. While progression could have been achieved by limiting the tax base to a relatively small set of luxury items, this would have limited greatly the revenue-raising ability of consumption taxes. If, on the other hand, a large tax base was retained by taxing more or less all consumer goods, the resulting burden distribution would be regressive. Thus the search for progression had to be met by the income tax.

The historical association between income and progressive taxation, as against consumption and regressive taxation, has been a basic factor in tax structure development, but it is not inevitable in principle. Theoretically at least, a personal tax on spending may be imposed with personal exemptions and progressive rates, and thus assume many of the features of the individual income tax [Kaldor, 13]. This, however, requires a high level of administrative sophistication, which was hardly available at the earlier stages of income tax development.

Just as the historical image of consumption taxes as regressive is not inevitable, so there has been a basic change in the progressive nature of income taxation. The income tax traditionally has been in the nature of a class tax, imposed on a relatively small number of high income taxpayers only. In the United States of 1939, for instance, the income tax exemption (married taxpayer) was over four times per capita income, and only 5 per cent of the total population was covered by taxable returns. But World War II brought a transformation of the income tax into a mass tax, paid by practically all income recipients. Exemptions were cut to less than one-half of per capita income, and 73 per cent of the population came to be included in the base.[13] This change was especially dramatic in the United States, but to a lesser extent it occurred also in most other industrialised countries. Thus the effective significance of income tax progression was broadened out, or, indeed, moved from the upper to the middle and middle-lower end of the income scale. Originally an instrument of penalising extreme wealth and redistributing income away from the upper end of the income scale, it later became a means of securing a broad revenue base. As the lower to middle income range had to be drawn upon to meet revenue needs (this being, after all, where most of the tax base lies), the income tax became a means of avoiding regressive and applying progressive taxation over this income range.

This very change in the nature of income tax also suggests a political realignment in the direct versus indirect tax debate. Not only does the middle and lower income voter become more hesitant to vote new programmes as the marginal tax dollar shifts downward, but he also grows weaker in his allegiance to income and his opposition to consumption taxes as the nature of the income tax changes. This is but another aspect of the change in fiscal politics which emerges as the overall tax to GNP ratio rises and which should provide the basis for a long-overdue reappraisal of the sociology of fiscal politics in the Wicksell–Goldscheid–Schumpeter tradition [Goldscheid, 5; Wicksell, 29].

Finally, the implications of increasing fiscal centralisation must be noted. Whereas this aspect has no simple bearing on expenditure ratios, it is of immediate and obvious importance for the tax structure. The progressive income tax by its very nature is better suited for national administration. Distributional adjustments through progressive taxation cannot readily be applied on a regional basis but require national coverage. Capital income is derived from various parts of the nation and must be collected in a single return for global assessment. Decentralised taxation would thus involve all the difficulties encountered in the tax treatment of foreign source investment income, not to speak of the distortion in regional capital allocation due to differential rates. For these and other reasons, progressive income taxation has to be applied largely at the national level, with regional income taxes limited to relatively low flat rates. Property and sales taxation, on the other hand, are handled more readily at the local level. Thus the use of income taxation has been associated with the movement toward decentralisation of public finances, and income taxes provide a larger revenue source in the more centralised countries.

The shift from indirect to direct taxation that has characterised modern tax structure development is, however, only the latest phase in a much longer development. Seen over the longer course of history, tax structure development began with direct rather than with indirect taxes [Hinrichs, 12, ch. 5]. The ancient world (Athens and Rome) relied on direct taxes imposed primarily on subjugated groups and mostly regressive in character. Medieval Europe relied on direct taxes in the gross product of land, and the same pattern is found in Asia and the Near East. The use of indirect taxation arose only with the dissolution of traditional society. The development of nation states, the rise of industry, and the expansion of trade led to the growth of internal indirect taxes, strengthened by the continued growth of taxes on external trade. The older forms of direct taxation, such as the land tax, thus declined in importance, and indirect taxes became the mainstay of the revenue structure. Only with the beginning of this century or the close of the last was there a renewed shift to direct taxation in the form of income tax, based on the increasingly pecuniary nature of economic life and the new alignment of social forces, making for changes in the balance of power and calling for progressive taxation.[14]

The time trend of social and political forces has been of paramount importance in the development of modern taxation and may be expected to have profound effects on the historical course of tax structure change. At the same time, the results of our cross-section approach may be expected to differ from the historical pattern. The social and political environment in which low income countries of today operate differs greatly from that which prevailed when today's high-income countries were at correspondingly low levels. The demonstration effect is applicable to tax policy as well as to consumption patterns, and current ideas of equity have popular appeal at low as well as high levels of per capita income. Modern forms of direct taxation may thus be associated with lower levels of income in the cross-section rather than in the time-series approach. At the same time, the relationship between per capita income and the availability of tax handles will have changed little, thus making for a general similarity of pattern under the two approaches. It remains to be seen which of these forces was the decisive factor.

## NOTES

1. See Wagner [26, vol. 1, p. 63; 27, 892–906]; also Timm [25, p. 26]. While there is no explicit statement in Wagner that the law of expanding scale relates to the share rather than the absolute level of public expenditures, occasional reference to 'quotas' suggests the former. It is evident, however, that Wagner is concerned not only with the scope of public expenditures for the provision of social goods and redistribution but that his law includes the expansion of public enterprise as well. Indeed, much of his emphasis is on the latter aspect. The operation of more and more industries is seen to involve social considerations. Public control being too difficult, public operation becomes necessary. This blurs the issue, since the determinants of resource allocation to the satisfaction of social wants are quite different from those that involve the choice between public and private production management.

   Recognising various expenditure functions, Wagner distinguishes between expenditures for protection and expenditures for social and welfare purposes. The latter in turn are broken down into general administration, economic administration, and education. The major element of expansion is foreseen in education and in the general area of legal administration and protection.
2. This argument relates to public capital formation in a mixed rather than a socialist economy. In the latter, capital formation is by definition public, although investment planning must continue to distinguish between internality- and externality-intensive types of capital assets.
3. To avoid misunderstanding, I restate the point more fully. In the model, here referred to as following a hypothesis of 'efficient' consumer behaviour, choices are made between outlays on public goods $G_1 \ldots G_J$, and private goods $P_1 \ldots P_J$, so as to maximise welfare from both. In such a world, utility is defined as $U = U(G_1 \ldots G_J, P_1 \ldots P_J)$ and resource allocation to public goods as a whole can be determined only as the sum of specific allocations to $G_1 \ldots, G_J$.

   In an alternative model, here referred to as following a 'political' behaviour hypothesis, it is assumed that people dislike a high tax rate, so that the utility function assumes an additional term. Utility is now defined as:

   $$U = U\left(G_1 \ldots G_J, P_1 \ldots P_J, \frac{\Sigma G_1 \ldots G_J}{\Sigma P_1 \ldots P_J}\right)$$

   where the last term is negative. This we take to be the basic formulation underlying the 'tax resistance' aspect of the Peacock–Wiseman model, as discussed below.
4. For support of this thesis, see Nurkse [19, pp. 58–67]; Lewis [14, p. 211]; Rosenstein-Rodan [23].
5. The reader might rightly feel that allowance for this factor is not compatible with the spirit of our 'efficient' model and that it should be reclassified as a conditioning or political factor.

6. Price-elasticity of demand will enter as well if the relative prices of public and private goods change as per capita income rises. Since there is no reason to expect a systematic relationship of this sort, the problem is primarily one of income-elasticity.

7. In West Germany in the 1950s, for instance, yield elasticity of the personal income tax was very high because a rising share of personal income moved above the initially relatively high exemption level. Given a low exemption level, such as in the United States, the GNP elasticity of income tax yield is but slightly above 1, and that of the total tax structure will be close to 1 if viewed in the secular context.

8. By marketing the vertical axis as public expenditure share in GNP but relating the argument to tax rates, we assume that tax and expenditure rates will move together. This is proper for the trend line, which is our major concern. During the war, the rate of debt finance is likely to increase, which may reduce dampening effects on civilian public outlays.

9. For general discussion of taxation and economic development in low-income countries, see Hicks [10]; Higgins [11]; Lewis [14]; Prest [22a]; OAS [26], Peacock [22]; Bird and Oldman [2] where an extensive bibliography is given; and Hinrichs [12].

10. Difficulties of securing an appropriate coverage of capital income is indeed the main theme of the discussion in OAS [20, p. 402].

11. The literature on taxation and economic development does not offer an abundance of helpful suggestions in this respect, and hence is of limited use to the practitioner.

12. It is interesting in this connection to note the hope, expressed in the *Communist Manifesto* some 140 years ago, that progressive taxation (along with public education) would lead to the destruction of capitalism! Marx and Engels [15]. In fact, both developments have done much to strengthen the structure of modern capitalist society.

13. See Goode [8, pp. 224, 320]. The percentage refers to numbers of taxpayers and depandants covered by taxable return as a per cent of population.

14. For a sweeping model of tax structure development, centred on the changing shares of direct and indirect taxes, see ch. 6 and Appendix. Though highly stimulating as a first approach to the problem, it seems doubtful whether the dichotomy of direct and indirect is the best basis for historical analysis. The difficulty of proper classification, substantial even within today's tax structure, is greatly compounded in the case of historical comparisons ranging over long periods of time.

# REFERENCES

[1] Andic, S. and Veverko, J. (1964), 'The growth of government expenditures in Germany since the unification', *Finanzarchiv*, NF 23, p. 178.

[2] Bird, R. and Oldman, O. (1965), *Readings in Taxation in Developing Countries*, (Baltimore, Johns Hopkins University Press).

[3] Dosser, D. (1969), 'Individual Taxation and economic development', in [22].

[4] Due, J. (1963), *Taxation and Economic Development in Africa* (Cambridge, Mass., MIT Press).

[5] Goldscheid, R. (1917), *Staatssozialismus und Staatskapitalismus* (Vienna).

[6] Goode, R. (1964), *The Individual Income Tax* (Washington, D.C., The Brookings Institution).

[7] Goode, R. (1965), 'Taxation of saving and consumption in underdeveloped countries', in [2].

[8] Goode, R. (1966), 'Role of export taxes in developing countries', *Staff Papers, International Monetary Fund*, 13.

[9] Harberger, A. (1965), 'Issues of Tax Reform in Latin American Countries', in [20].

[10] Hicks, U. (1961), *Development from Below: Local Government and Finance in Developing Countries of the Commonwealth* (London, Oxford University Press).

[11] Higgins, B. (1959), *Economic Development, Principles, Problems and Policies* (New York, Norton).

[12] Hinrichs, H. (1966), *General Theory of Tax Structure Change* (Cambridge, Mass., Harvard Law School).

[13] Kaldor, N. (1955), *An Expenditure Tax* (London, Allen & Unwin).

[14] Lewis, A. (1955), *The Theory of Economic Growth* (Homewood, Ill., Irwin), p. 211.

[15] Marx, K. and Engels, F. (1848), *The Communist Manifesto*, in *Handbook of Marxism* (New York, International Publishers), p. 46.

[16] Musgrave, R. (1958), *The Theory of Public Finance* (New York, McGraw-Hill).

[17] Musgrave, R. and Peacock, A. (1958), *Classics in the Theory of Public Finance* (New York, Macmillan), p. 95.

[18] Naharro, J. (1965), 'Production and consumption taxes and economic development', in [20].

[19] Nurkse (1958), *Problems of Capital Formation of Underdeveloped Countries*, pp. 58–67.

[20] Organisation of American States (1965), *Fiscal Policy for Economic Growth in Latin America* (Baltimore, Johns Hopkins University Press).

[21] Peacock, A. and Wiseman, J. (1961), *The Growth of Public Expenditures in the United Kingdom* (Princeton, N.J., Princeton University Press), p. 24.

[22] Peacock, A. and Hauser, G. (eds) (1969), *Government Finance and Economic Development* (Paris, OECD).

[22a] Prest, A. (1962), *Public Finance in Underdeveloped Countries* (London, Weidenfeld & Nicolson).

[23] Rosenstein, D. (1943), 'Problems of industrialization of Eastern and South-Eastern Europe', *Economic Journal*, 53.

[24] Schumpeter, J. (1954), 'The crisis of the tax state', *International Economic Papers*, 4.

[25] Timm, H. (1961), 'Das Gesetz der Wachsenden Staatsausgabe', *Finanzarchiv*, NF 21.

[26] Wagner, A. (1883), *Finanzwissenschaft*, 3rd edn (Leipzig), Winter, vol. 1, p. 63; also see [17].

[27] Wagner, A. (1892), *Grundlegung der Politischen Oekonomie*, 3rd edn, pp. 892–906.

[28] Wald, H. (1959), *Taxation of Agricultural Land in Underdeveloped Countries* (Cambridge, Mass., Harvard University Press).

[29] Wicksell, K. (1896), *Finanzwissenschaftliche Untersuchungen* (Jena, Fischer); also see [17].

# 10 Objectives: Report of Colombia Tax Mission* 1971

Taxation and public expenditure form the process by which resources are transferred to public use. The tax structure should accomplish its part in this process in an equitable and efficient fashion. But taxation also has important bearing on other aspects of economic policy, such as stability, growth and the distribution of income and wealth. In view of this broader role, the first section comprises a review of the economic setting and the objectives governing tax reform; the second then sets out the reforms of particular taxes which are appropriate in the light of these objectives; and the third examines fiscal reform at the national, departmental and municipal levels.

We begin with the relation of tax reform to the broader objectives of economic policy and then turn to the matter of revenue targets.

## GROWTH

Generally speaking, the purpose of economic development is to improve the welfare of the populace by raising the material standard of living. Such improvement means growth not only in total national income but also in per capita income. Although the gross national product (GNP) of Colombia has grown (in real terms) at an average rate of 4.5 per cent during the years 1961–1967, thereby meeting the target set by the United Nations for the 'development decade', the growth rate of GNP has fluctuated considerably. Some years have shown little if any growth, and with population growth of over 3 per cent per year, the average annual rate of growth of per capita product has been much lower. At a yearly rate of 1.3 per cent, the growth of per capita income in Colombia has also been low relative to that in other developing countries and much below the rate needed to lift significantly the standard of living of most of its people. Raising per capita income must, therefore, be the paramount goal of Colombia's economic policy; and, by the same token, it must be given central emphasis in the formulation of tax reform.

* R. A. Musgrave and M. Gillis (1971). Reprinted with permission from *Fiscal Reform for Colombia*. Final Report and Staff Papers of the Columbian Comission on Tax Reform (Cambridge, Mass.: Harvard Law School International Tax Program, 1971; Copyright 1971 by the President and Fellows of Harvard College), pp. 1–16.

Although there is no simple way to set forth the relationship between tax policy and growth, certain factors basic to this relationship may be noted. To begin with, economic growth may be achieved by greater use of resources, including labour, land and capital. This gain, though important, is a once-and-for-all gain only. In the long run, growth requires increases in productivity, which, in turn, require capital formation, whether in plant and equipment, in the creation of infrastructure such as roads, or in 'human investment' such as education and health. Capital formation may take place in the private or the public sector, but saving is required to finance it in either case.

The needed rate of capital formation, and hence of saving, depends upon the target rate of income growth to be achieved. With an average population growth of nearly 3.5 per cent a year, rates of growth of GNP (in real terms) of 5 per cent and 6 per cent correspond to rates of growth of per capita income of only 1.5 per cent and 2.4 per cent. The former figure matches approximately the growth rate of the 1960s, while the latter approximates the target rate used in discussions by the National Planning Department. Such an increase in the growth rate would represent a substantial improvement in the performance of the Colombian economy, but it would still be behind the record of the more successful Latin American countries, which have reached rates of development of well above 3 per cent.

Next, the chosen target rate of growth must be translated into a required rate of capital formation. This procedure involves the complex production relationships of the economy and the so-called marginal capital–output ratio. If we assume a ratio of 2.5 and a 1971 GNP of P 140 billion, a net investment level of about P 21 billion would be needed to sustain a 6 per cent rate of growth in GNP. This level would be 15 per cent of GNP, whereas the rate has averaged about 10 per cent during recent years. Although the increase would be substantial, it would again be far below the 20 per cent to 25 per cent rate that many students of economic development consider necessary to generate a breakthrough into sustained growth.

Finally, before we discuss the appropriate revenue target, we must determine the share of public sector investment. This share depends on what kind of investment is needed most at the present stage of Colombia's development. If the primary need is for investment in infrastructure or in human resources such as education and health, the public share will be relatively large. This view is reflected in the National Planning Department's projected investment mix for 1968–71, which calls for considerable increase in the share of public sector investment. In fact, public investment in physical capital is expected to nearly double, from P 3.6 billion in 1968 to P 6.9 billion in 1971, with heavy emphasis upon investment in transportation, agriculture and electrification. Although not included in the Department's projections, the revenue targets to be considered here will make allowance for increased investment in human capital in the form of an expanded programme in education, especially at the primary level.

Although this expansion will largely involve increases in so-called current expenditures, it should nevertheless be considered investment. Although it does not lead to plant and equipment, the resulting human investment still constitutes capital formation, for it raises productivity and hence contributes to rising per capita income. Indeed, recent studies have shown that Colombia's rate of return on such investment will be very high.

As the rate of public investment rises, public saving—the excess of public receipts over public consumption—must rise as well. Similarly, if there is to be an increase in private investment, private saving must increase to finance it. Unless measures can be taken to raise private saving or to increase foreign saving (capital inflow) accordingly, private investment will come to exceed private saving. To maintain stability, this excess has to be matched by a budget surplus, that is, by substituting increased public for lacking private saving. The transfer of such saving from the public to the private sector may occur through public lending or by expanding the amount of credit available to the private sector. However this transfer takes place, a higher level of taxation would be needed to provide the public saving. Thus, it is not at all evident that the need for taxation is correspondingly reduced as investment is transferred from the public to the private sector. Moreover, increasing private saving may be no less difficult than raising taxes.

In any case, the tax reform must provide a revenue structure compatible with the financing of an adequate rate of growth. As the target rate of growth increases, so must the necessary level of finance. At the same time, the problem is not one of total revenue only. The way in which a given revenue total is obtained may influence the savings rate. Certain tax measures, such as taxes on luxury consumption, are more conducive to private savings than others, such as high marginal rates under the income tax. This is one reason that the reform favours heavier reliance upon luxury taxation rather than upon high marginal income tax rates. Similarly, the level and structure of taxes on business income may affect the rate of business saving, a factor that the Commission has considered in designing its proposals in this area.

Finally, we note that taxation may affect not only the rate of private saving but also the rate and pattern of private investment. Although rates of return on investment in Colombia are high and the willingness to invest available funds is not lacking, the pattern of private investment has become distorted seriously by tax factors. This distortion has arisen because of arbitrary tax advantages that result from operating in a particular legal form as well as from special incentive provisions. With the exception of export incentives, these provisions have lacked well-defined objectives and have been arbitrary in operation. The tax reform is designed to remove such distorting effects by limiting future use of incentives to situations where they are clearly desirable to correct prevailing deficiencies in the structure of investment. This point is of obvious importance in an economy that cannot afford to squander the growth potential of future investment, where investment is constrained seriously by the availability of imports, and where the market cost of labour relative to capital is higher than it would be if true scarcities were reflected in relative prices.

More generally, the reform must aim at minimising the economic burden resulting from the transfer of resources to the public sector. The tax structure should support but not interfere with the efficient operation of the private sector. Distorting effects upon production techniques and relative prices should be avoided. The proposed tax reform therefore gives particular attention to the coordination of internal indirect taxes and custom duties, which would accomplish the distinct objectives of protection and luxury taxation without unintended and distorting effects upon relative prices and upon the efficiency of resource use. At the same time, neutrality must not be given absolute priority. Tax policy may be non-neutral where non-neutrality will achieve specific objectives, as in the case of export incentives; and some degree of non-neutrality may be required where objectives other than efficiency, such as interpersonal or inter-regional redistribution, are considered of overriding importance.

## STABILITY

In addition to securing adequate growth and, indeed, as a necessary condition of so doing, public policy must maintain economic stability, both internal and external. In both cases, tax policy plays an important role.

### Internal Stability
The objective of internal stability, as usually interpreted, involves the maintenance of (1) a high level of employment, and (2) a reasonable degree of price stability. Both depend to a considerable degree upon the level of aggregate demand, and aggregate demand is in turn influenced by the level of public expenditures and receipts. Fiscal policy is therefore an important factor in stabilisation.

Aggregate demand—that is, total expenditures, public plus private—should be held at a level that is sufficient to buy the product of a fully-employed economy, and it should be permitted to expand in line with economic growth. If demand is deficient, output will fall short of its potential, and resources will be wasted. On the other hand, excessive demand, under which shortages will occur and prices will rise, leads to the distortions and inequities of inflation.

It follows that revenue requirements will depend upon the level of public expenditures, as such expenditures are an important component of total demand. But the level of public expenditures is not the only factor to be considered. If the economy is slack, it may be desirable to let receipts fall short of public expenditures; and if demand is excessive, it may be desirable to let revenues exceed expenditures. This principle of 'compensatory finance' has become generally accepted in developed economies, but it is also applicable in developing countries such as Colombia.

With regard to unemployment and the potential need for expansionary measures to eliminate it, some economists argue that the nature of unemployment (or underemployment) in developing economies is such that it does not lend itself to remedy by demand expansion. It is to be explained by structural factors, rigidities, lack of capital, and productivity that is generally low relative to labour costs. There is considerable truth in this argument, but it goes too far by excluding demand considerations. A brisk level of demand helps to unfreeze structural rigidities, and situations may arise where unemployment is more readily subject to reduction by demand measures. As agricultural population migrates to the cities, pockets of unemployed labour may develop. Thus unemployment rates of well over 10 per cent have been recorded in Cali and Bogotá. Such unemployment may often be reduced by a higher level of demand, provided that the injection of purchasing power can be localised and the supply of labour is sufficiently elastic. In this connection, public expenditures on highly labour-intensive projects may be helpful. Careful economic analysis is therefore needed to determine whether the current policy of fiscal surplus is appropriate under prevailing conditions.

With regard to inflation, Colombia's record [in the 1960s] has been better than that of most Latin American countries. With the exception of 1963, 1964 and 1966, the inflation rate has been below 10 per cent. Although there are certain built-in pressures for inflation, resulting from such factors as a rising population with limited food supplies and cyclical adjustments to balance-of-payments deficits, overall policy has been relatively successful in restraining price rise. In Colombia, as in most developing countries, there has been, however, a tendency to think largely, if not exclusively, in monetary terms. Although the important and perhaps primary role of monetary policy is unquestionable, it must be pointed out that fiscal measures may also play a significant part in combating inflation. The monetary implications of financing deficits or disposing of surplus receipts establish an obvious link between fiscal and monetary measures; and, apart from this fact, changing levels of tax receipts or expenditures directly affect the level of demand.

Although the function of the Commission is not to deal with these problems in detail, we wish to point out the need for closer coordination of fiscal and monetary policies, and for more explicit consideration of fiscal policy as a stabilisation tool. Moreover, efforts to dovetail fiscal and monetary policies for stabilisation purposes should be made within a framework of macro-economic thinking, built around the design of a national economic budget, and should be related to both the short-term objective of stabilisation and the long-term objective of economic growth. The absence of such a framework has made it difficult for the Commission to determine the appropriate revenue target and to decide on certain structural aspects of tax policy.

Here it need be mentioned that the fiscal structure should be flexible enough to meet the needs of a dynamic economy, in which conditions are subject to more or less continuous change. The tax structure should be such that rate adjustments can be accomplished fairly promptly when the economic need arises. This aim will be served by broadly-based income and sales taxes, two objectives that are basic to the Commission's tax recommendations. Furthermore, the reform should provide for a tax structure such that revenue responds promptly and automatically to changes in the level of economic activity, especially in the price level. Particularly important in this connection are measures that will place income taxation (personal and corporate) on a current basis and allow property valuation to be adjusted currently to changes in price levels.

Colombia has a large foreign trade sector, with exports constituting over 10 per cent of GNP and imports being of crucial importance to capital formation and development. For this reason, a high premium must be placed on the promotion of external stability, which requires the maintenance of balance between exchange receipts (mainly from exports and loans) and expenditures (mainly on imports and debt service).

Tax policy affects external stability through its effects on internal stability. If tax revenue is deficient (with a given expenditure and monetary policy) and inflationary price rise results, imports will rise and exports will fall, with a resulting loss of foreign exchange and pressure on the exchange rate. Devaluation in turn may temporarily restore balance, but probably at the cost of worsened terms of trade and reduced availability of foreign capital. Although the exchange position has been strong at times, this has not been the past pattern. Six out of the eight years since 1960 involved payments deficits, and the peso was subjected to frequent depreciation.

In addition, tax policy may have various structural effects on trade. If imported goods are taxed more heavily than domestic products, imports may be discouraged; and if exports are subsidised or taxed less heavily than domestic sales, exports may be encouraged. Although the Commission recognises these possibilities, we feel that the role of restricting imports should be assigned to import duties only and that excise and sales taxes should apply equally to imported and domestic products. At the same time, certain tax preferences should be granted to exports which are not applicable to domestic sales. Tax policy can thus contribute to enlarging the size of the trade sector. Moreover, by giving encouragement to new export products, dependence on coffee exports can be reduced, exports can be diversified, and foreign exchange proceeds can be stabilised. As noted before, this effect is of crucial importance to the development of the Colombian economy, since the import of capital goods is a strategic factor in raising productivity.

## DISTRIBUTION OF INCOME

Growth and stability are important objectives of economic policy, but distributional goals must be considered as well.

### Distribution Among Families
In Colombia, as in other developing countries, the distribution of income is highly unequal compared to that of developed countries: over one-half of

total income is estimated to accrue to the top 10 per cent of all income recipients. It is important, therefore, to consider (1) what gains may be made through redistributional measures at prevailing levels of national income, and (2) what public policies that may be chosen will contribute to a broad-based distribution of the gains of growth. In particular, policy should endeavour to improve the position of those sectors of the population which have lagged behind and whose standards of living have remained very low. Fiscal policy must play a strategic role in accomplishing these objectives, and both the revenue and the expenditure sides of the budget operation are involved.

On the revenue side, the tax reform should endeavour to secure an improved distribution of the tax burden, that is, a distribution that will reduce the share borne by the poorer part of the population. Estimates suggest that the present tax structure is more or less proportional and does little to adjust the distribution of income. Such adjustments must be subject to the constraint, however, that they must take into account the detrimental effects on incentives and growth which might arise from them. This consideration points again to emphasis on the taxation of luxury consumption and on measures to reduce income tax avoidance or evasion. Realistic appraisal suggests, however, that the scope for redistributional measures through tax policy is limited.

More can be done on the expenditure side. Transfer programmes may serve to improve the position of the poor, as may the rendering of public services that are of particular importance to this group. Moreover, expenditures on human investment—such as education and health—may serve to increase the earning power of the poor, thereby effecting a more constructive and permanent solution. Since higher expenditure of this sort calls for higher tax receipts, taxation (even though a substantial degree of progression may be difficult to achieve) is related once more to the distributional objectives of public policy.

## Regional Distribution

Colombia, by history and geography, is composed of a set of highly differentiated regions. Average income levels differ sharply between departments, as do prospects for economic development. From a purely economic point of view, this diversity is not necessarily a reason for concern. The basic issue of distribution should be regarded in terms of families, not of regions; and total economic development may be served by encouraging migration from poor and stagnant to richer and developing regions.

But this view may be too simple. Labour mobility may be limited, and non-economic goals of national policy may call for special efforts to secure faster development in the poorer regions. If such a pattern of development is to be achieved, tax incentives may be useful to attract economic activity into such regions. The various measures and incentive devices that will be most efficient for this purpose must then be considered.

## ALLOCATION OF FUNCTIONS BY LAYERS OF GOVERNMENT

The objectives listed so far generally require a growth in the centralisation of government. For example, lower layers of government may have no direct interest in or power to carry out measures that will promote economic stability. Nevertheless, it is natural for citizens to wish to participate in the affairs of government, particularly in those matters which directly concern them in the area in which they live. Present feeling in Colombia appears to favour strengthening departmental and municipal government, and the Commission places this objective alongside others that influence the design of fiscal reform. It may also be argued that, far from hampering the pursuit of other objectives, decentralisation of government that allows citizens to be directly concerned with the development of policy may be an important precondition for popular support of fiscal measures.

The distribution of revenues among layers of government and among particular governments within the same layer is not, however, readily adjustable to fiscal needs. The distribution among layers is determined in part by existing and anticipated constitutional provisions, and reform must allow for the distribution of administrative capabilities and viable political institutions. Also, the technical characteristics of each tax determine the layer at which it may be applied most efficiently. Moreover, the same tax levied at the same rate yields different revenue, depending upon the wealth and hence the tax base in the particular department or municipality. No wonder, ther, that the fiscal capacity of the poorer areas in Colombia is clearly not sufficient to carry out widely accepted programmes in the fields of health and education. Consequently, although lower layers of government in many parts of Colombia may be left to carry out these programmes, grants from the national government are necessary to equalise fiscal capacity, as is the case in many other countries. Inevitably, such a grant system means the growth of control by the national government of departmental and municipal finance in some important fields.

## ADMINISTRATIVE IMPROVEMENTS

Taxes, no matter how well-meaning the statutes enacting them, are no better than the quality of their administration. Improved administration is, therefore, an important aspect of tax reform. Improvement in administration involves simplification wherever feasible, but it sometimes requires more complex procedures in order to secure even enforcement. In both cases, the aim is to eliminate unnecessary administrative burdens on the taxpayer or the official and to secure a more equitable and effective application of the tax. Thereby, the morale and cooperation of the taxpayer as well as of the tax official will be improved and a better revenue structure obtained. An increase in the resources devoted to administration should also be contemplated.

Although we have kept these needs in mind, our primary assignment is not to devise and recommend administrative improvements, but rather to develop structural tax reform and to reconsider the fiscal arrangements that prevail among the levels and units of government. Nevertheless, administrative improvements are recommended in certain important areas. For example, the introduction of a minimum standard deduction would greatly simplify income tax administration. Also, the administration of income tax would be improved, and the tax would apply more evenly, if the recommendations for imposing a presumptive income tax on agriculture and for allowing the government to use presumptive rules in assessing tax on certain hard-to-tax groups outside the agricultural sector were adopted. Similarly, municipal tax administration would be simplified by the substitution of the retail sales tax for the industry and commerce tax.

## CONCLUSION

Tax reform cannot be adapted to a single objective, such as adequate revenue, simplicity or equity. All these must be kept in mind, as must the broader objectives of economic development, stability, and a fair sharing of tax burdens and the fruits of growth. The Colombian tax system, as it stands, contains elements of strength which are in line with these objectives, as well as serious deficiencies, which are not. The purpose of this reform will be to build on the former while correcting the latter. Reform will therefore require recommendations to strengthen the revenue potential, to remove certain inequities, to eliminate ineffective incentive measures, to correct negative non-neutralities, and so forth. In addition, reform will involve a realignment of certain fiscal resources and responsibilities among layers of government. These recommendations, we believe, will substantially improve the tax structure of Colombia, but we do not wish to suggest that this is to be a once-and-for-all reform to solve all problems. Tax reform is a continuous and sensitive process, which, at its best, fosters the orderly development of tax laws responsive to changing economic and social conditions and to the changing balance among and emphasis on public policy objectives.

# 11 Expenditure Policy for Development* 1974

Having worked mainly on the revenue side of development finance, I thought this a welcome opportunity to take a look at the other side of the coin. Tax experts, after all, operate on an act of faith: while taxes may be imposed in a more or less equitable fashion, and with more or less desirable effects, their *raison d'être* is to finance public services. If the tax reformer exhorts developing countries to increase their tax effort, as he is wont to do, this is done on the presumption that resources to be withdrawn from the private sector will be used more effectively on the public side.

What, then, is the validity of this presumption? In exploring this question, one is struck by the dearth of material on the role of public expenditures in economic development. While there are numerous studies dealing with the role of taxation and the properties of a good tax structure, there is little comparable material on the expenditure side. The reason perhaps is that the expenditure problem is inherently more difficult. Where the tax doctor can fall back on a few standard rules, no similar prescriptions are available for expenditure policy. As to taxes, we all agree that the burden should be distributed in an equitable fashion, that disturbing effects should be minimised, that certain corrective or incentive effects on the private sector may be generated, and that allowance should be made for the effects of alternative taxes on saving, investment and the balance of payments. Granting that ideas about an equitable burden distribution differ and that the techniques of generating incentive effects remain controversial, these rules nevertheless go far in suggesting measures which can be considered an improvement of the tax structure.

On the expenditure side, there are no corresponding principles. The proper questions may be asked, but the answers are hard to come by. The two basic questions are (a) what the proper level of public expenditures should be at various stages of economic development? and (b) what constitutes an optimal expenditure composition at each stage? These two issues are largely interdependent, since the overall expenditure level must be derived from the need for particular items. Yet the constraint imposed by the country's taxable capacity is a further variable which acts directly

---

*In *Fiscal Policy for Industrialization and Development in Latin America* (1974), ed. D.T. Geithman, (Gainesville, University of Florida Press).

158

upon the overall expenditure level. Unfortunately, it is not evident on what basis the need for particular services is to be judged. Is it to be thought of in terms of consumer preferences between social and private goods, or is it to be related to an overriding objective of economic growth or indus- trialisation? Moreover, what emphasis should be given to the distributional implications of fiscal measures? These and related questions must be answered before conclusions on an optimal expenditure structure can be drawn.


## THE OVERALL LEVEL OF EXPENDITURES

Beginning with the appropriate overall share of public expenditures, let us see first what the facts have been. This may be viewed in terms of a worldwide pattern or for Latin American countries only.

### Worldwide Sample

Various studies have shown that the ratio of public expenditures (or tax revenue) to GNP rises with rising per capita income. This seems to hold true on both a time-series and a cross-section basis. If we trace the expenditure to GNP ratio historically over the last 75 years, we find that this ratio has exhibited a more or less steady upward trend in most developed countries, such as the United Kingdom, United States, Ger- many, and so forth. Since this was also a period of sustained rise in per capita income, there is a suggestion (though not proof) that the former had been a function of the latter.

A similar result is obtained from a cross-section comparison among countries with different per capita incomes but for the same period. Regressing the size of the public sector (as measured by the expenditure or, with essentially similar results, the tax to GNP ratio) with per capita income for a worldwide sample of some 40 countries, we find a strongly positive relationship. Thus, predicted revenue as per cent of GNP rises from 16 at a per capita income of about $250 to 24 at an income of $1000, and 34 at $2000.[1] The evidence is similar if we use an index of industrialisa- tion in lieu of per capita income. This is as may be expected, since the share of GNP originating in industry is correlated positively with per capita income. Similarly, a negative coefficient is obtained if income originating in agriculture is the independent variable.

In all, it appears that both historical and cross-section approaches sustain the proposition that the share of the public sector increases with per capita income. The cross-section evidence is, however, subject to an important qualification. While a reasonably good regression fit is obtained for the sample as a whole, including low- as well as high-income countries, the fit is much poorer if the sample is divided between low- and high-income countries. While Wagner's law holds if we compare the average low- income country (with per capita income of, say, $500 or less) with the average high-income country (with per capita income of, say, $1200 or more) there is little evidence for its operation within each sub-group. Thus, no significant relationship prevails if one limits the sample to countries with incomes below, say, $400. Since the crucial problem of development is in this range, it is difficult to generalise on expenditure behaviour.

Turning to the place of Latin American countries in the worldwide picture, it is interesting to note that their performance typically shows a less than average tax to GNP ratio. This holds for our sample of 40 countries, as well as for a large sample of 82 countries, using data for the mid-1960s.[2] It appears from the latter that tax revenue as a per cent of GNP for Latin American countries was below the predicted value for 11 countries, while only 8 countries showed a per cent in excess of the predicted value. The shortfall was highest for Mexico, Colombia and El Salvador, while the excess was largest for Brazil and Chile.

## Latin American Sample

If the comparison is limited to Latin American countries, and we use per capita income, industrialisation and openness as explanatory variables, the results given in Table 11.1 are obtained.[3] The relation to per capita income is shown in Figure 11.1.

While the overall fit is less good than for the worldwide sample, this reflects the previously noted phenomenon of clustering, and the fact that the Latin American sample consists of relatively low-income countries. Nevertheless, there remains some positive relationship between per capita income and the tax to GNP ratio. Also, it is interesting to note that adding the degree of industrialisation as an explanatory variable improves the fit, raising the $R^2$ from 0.38 to 0.41. Industrialisation facilitates taxation and/or higher expenditures facilitate industrialisation. Openness enters with a negative sign and is not a significant factor in explaining the revenue to GNP ratio. There is little relationship between openness and per capita income (except for Venezuela and Uruguay), the tax handle aspects of trade (easier collectability of customs) not being a significant factor in generating a higher revenue ratio.

The performance of various countries may again be assessed by comparing the actual with the predicted ratios. The results are shown in column 6 of Table 11.2.[4] As before, we find Brazil to be greatly in excess of the predicted value, followed at some distance by Chile and Argentina, the Dominican Republic, Ecuador and Peru. Uruguay, Panama, Trinidad and Jamaica are also above the line. At the other extreme we have Mexico, which falls greatly below, followed at some distance by Colombia, Guatemala, El Salvador, Venezuela and Honduras. Costa Rica and Nicaragua are also below the line.[5]

## Implications

These facts are interesting, but what do they imply for policy purposes? Should coincidence of predicted and actual behaviour be interpreted as a

*Table 11.1 Determinants of public sector share in Latin America**

---

Variables
  $x_1$ = revenue as a per cent of GNP
  $x_2$ = per capita income
  $x_3$ = value added by industry as per cent of GNP
  $x_4$ = imports as per cent of GNP

---

I      $x_1 =$      9.37166      +      $0.015266x_2$
                (2.03004)           (0.00489)
                   4.6                 3.1                              $R^2 = 0.3870$

II     $x_1 =$      9.11383      +      $0.012399x_2$      +      $0.06077x_3$      $R^2 = 0.4093$
                (2.06341)           (0.00588)              (0.06809)
                   4.4                 2.1                     0.89

III    $x_1 =$      9.68569      +      $0.015403x_2$      −      $0.0100087x_4$      $R^2 = 0.3794$
                (2.68264)           (0.00510)              (0.05343)
                   (3.6)               3.0                    −0.19

IV     $x_1 =$      9.16476      +      $0.01244x_2$       +      $0.060397x_3$      −      $(0.015272x_4$
                (2.77865)           (0.0062399)            (0.071691)                (0.054882)
                   3.3                 2.0                     0.84                      −0.29
                                                                                     $R^2 = 0.4094$

---

* Includes sample of 18 Latin American countries, 1966 (see Table 11.2). Brazil is excluded.
Addition of Brazil greatly reduces the fit, with equations I and II reading as follows:

I      $x_1 =$      11.0759      +      $0.01259x_2$                          $R^2 = 0.1858$
                (2.6098)            (0.00689)
                   4.21

II     $x_1 =$      10.4677      +      $0.0077508x_2$      +      $0.10767x_3$      $R^2 = 0.2584$
                (2.61313)           (0.00738)              (0.08607)
                   4.0                 1.0                     1.3

sign of 'correct' fiscal performance, with Brazil and Mexico equally unsatisfactory deviants, if on opposite sides of the regression line? Or should one say that the predicted value, based on average behaviour, indicates a minimum ratio which should be attained, with an excess an additional gain? Posing the question in this form invites the response that no general rules can be laid down, 'because the circumstances of each country differ'. This homily is always true, but it is not where the matter can rest. While differences exist, there are similarities as well.[6] Moreover, certain relevant differences, such as industrialisation, openness and other variables, are accounted for already in the regression analysis.

The fact that several countries at the below $300 per capita income level have revenues well above 15 per cent is evidence that countries at 10 per

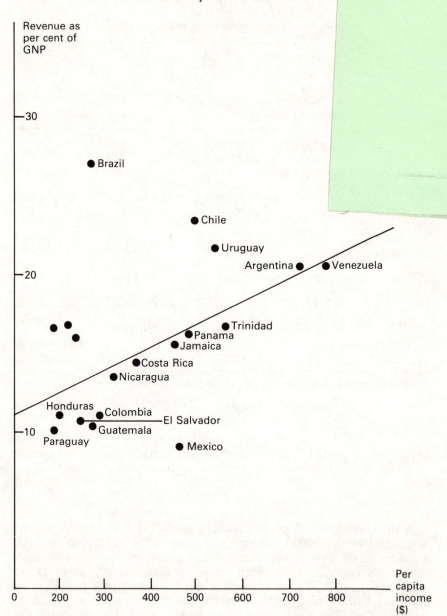

*Figure 11.1: Revenue to GNP ratio and per capita income, 1966\**

\* For data see Table 11.2 columns 1 and 2. The equation for the regression line is given in equation I\*, Table 11.1

cent would have found a higher level within the range of their fiscal capabilities. The more difficult question is whether they *should* have made use of this capability. This poses the question of how much of its resources a country at various levels of income *should* devote to public as against private uses. This depends on preferences, policy objectives and political organisation. Some communities may prefer private goods to social goods and where there are options, such as in education, may choose to provide such services by a private rather than a public route. Others may have the opposite preferences. But granting all this, there are also some basic economic questions to be asked.

## THE ECONOMICS OF EXPENDITURE GROWTH

From the economist's point of view, the central question may be posed as follows. Let us suppose that resources are used efficiently, including the allocation between private and social as well as consumer and capital goods. Private goods, for this purpose, are defined as goods whose benefits are largely internal so that they can be provided for by individual purchase at the market. Social goods, in turn, are goods whose benefits are largely external so that their provision must be determined through the political process and implemented through the budget. This does not mean (or, in any case, need not mean) public production. Budgetary provision for social goods may involve public purchases of privately-produced goods, just as publicly-owned enterprises may produce and sell private goods at the market. Our discussion of the size of the public sector therefore relates to public provision for social goods and not to the scope of public ownership. Defined in terms of social goods share, the size of the public sector thus differs from that defined in terms of public production, a point which is of particular importance for developing countries and mixed political systems.

Our distinction between private and social goods applies to both consumer and capital goods. The question whether, given efficient resource use, the public purchase to GNP ratio should rise with per capita income, may thus be divided into asking: (a) whether the importance of externality-intensive relative to private-type consumer goods rises with per capita income, and (b) whether the importance of externality-type capital goods relative to private-type capital goods increases as per capita income rises. In addition to these allocational considerations, the efficient size of the public sector depends on the further question (c) whether the need for transfer payments should be expected to rise or fall with per capita income.

These three issues, which determine both the appropriate level and the composition of expenditures, will now be considered. I am aware, of course, that the size of the public sector cannot be explained purely on this basis. Historical, political and social factors enter as well. Nevertheless, it is useful, especially in the development context, to pose the problem in these terms.

## Consumer Goods

At the low level of per capita income which prevails in most developing countries, the bulk of consumption goes to furnish the bare necessities, leaving little space for goods of a non-essential kind. This does not mean, however, that there is no need for social goods. Certain basic public services have to be rendered, including municipal outlays for civil adminis-tration, protection, sanitation, and so forth. Such services are no less necessary than the basic items of private consumption. As income rises, part of the gain will generate increasing demand for such services, but it may well be that the demand for an ample supply of private goods (food, clothing, housing) expands more sharply. This will be the case especially in view of the demonstration effects generated by the example of developed countries. Because of this, there is little reason to expect that the income-elasticity of demand for public consumer goods should be in excess of unity over this low per capita income range. Later, as consumption rises into the luxury range, there will be an increasing demand for com-plementary public goods, suggesting an increased share of the latter in expanded consumption. Speculation of this sort suggests a flat and, in any case, hardly rising share of public consumption during the earlier stages of development, with perhaps more rapid expansion in the public share later on.

Two specific points may be added, however, which may change this pattern. First, it should be noted that the consumption pattern at any given average per capita income depends greatly upon the distribution of income. In the growth context, this pattern depends on the distribution of the increment in income or the fruits of economic growth. I would not be surprised to find that an unequally distributed increment will call for a larger share of public consumption expenditures than an equally distri-buted income growth.

Second, the need for increased public services may be affected greatly by the process of urbanisation. If, as tends to be the case, income growth is associated with urbanisation, it is also likely to call for an increased need for public services. This follows because urban living requires more services to be rendered in public form than does rural living, be it because of economies of scale, external costs generated by private provision, or for other reasons. This applies both with regard to current (consumption) and to capital outlays, the latter being especially important during a phase of rapid urban expansion. Growing urban expenditure requirements may well be the decisive factor in the Latin American picture, calling for a more than proportional growth of public services in the present development stage.

## Capital Goods

The investment part of the problem is somewhat easier to handle, at least in conceptual terms. The basic question here is whether the supply of externality-intensive types of investment is of particular importance at early stages of economic development.

This would seem to be the case, because the building-up of an infrastructure dominates investment activity at this stage. The construction of transportation facilities, provision for irrigation, regional development projects—all involve substantial degrees of external benefits which cannot be accounted for properly by private calculus. As industry develops, these needs become less important and a larger share of capital formation comes to be in the form of plant and equipment expenditures which can be undertaken more readily by private firms. Considerations of this sort suggest that public capital expenditures may well occupy a larger share in the earlier development phase (though not the earliest) and then show a relative decline as a higher level of income is reached.

Supposing this pattern to be correct, there is the further question of how large a share of resources is to be allocated to total (public plus private) capital formation. If capital formation is low at lower levels of per capita income, public investment may be a smaller fraction of GNP even though it occupies a relatively large share in total investment. Since economic development implies a rising investment share in GNP, this again suggests that we may expect, initially at least, a rising ratio of public investment.

One crucial factor is the treatment of human investment. While I have been dissatisfied in the context of high-income countries with the preoccupation of US economists with the effects of taxation on earnings, rather than with the role of educational investment as acquisition of a durable consumer good, earnings effects are undoubtedly of major importance for economic development. Industrialisation cannot be carried out without a labour force which possesses the technical know-how needed to operate the equipment. As may be expected, studies have shown the rate of return on investment in education to be very high, higher in many cases than investment in so-called real assets.[7]

It is absurd, therefore, to limit the concept of investment and public capital formation to the latter category. Education as well as bricks and mortar should be counted, with schoolteachers' wages included no less than the structures in which they teach. The concept of public capital formation and saving underlying the model budgetary practices of the United Nations are, I believe, very misleading and should be changed.

Public investment, formally, includes not only externality-intensive investments which must be provided for publicly, but in many instances the government also engages in investment activities which might be undertaken privately. This may be so for lack of entrepreneurial talent in the private sector, or because the necessary amount of capital cannot be assembled privately in the absence of broad capital markets, or because public operation of such enterprises is preferred on social and political grounds. Prestige considerations, such as the presumed value of operating a steel industry (whether profitable or not) may be another factor.

It is interesting, therefore, to see how the size of the public sector (as defined previously in terms of the tax or expenditure ratio to GNP) relates to the importance of public investment activity. As shown in Table 11.2, col. 7, the ratio of investment to GNP varies widely, with five countries in our sample having ratios between 12 and 14 per cent; six, between 14 and

*Table 11.2*

| | $x_1$ T as % of GNP (1) | $x_2$ Y in $ (2) | $x_3$ V as % of GNP (3) | $x_4$ M as % of GNP (4) | $T°$ as % of GNP (5) | (1)–(5) (6) | I as % of GNP (7) | GI as % of I (8) |
|---|---|---|---|---|---|---|---|---|
| Brazil | 26.9 | 269 | 28 | 16.5 | 15.6 | 11.3 | 16.6 | 44.8 |
| Chile | 23.3 | 474 | 26 | 22.5 | 16.9 | 6.4 | 17.9 | 45.3 |
| Uruguay | 21.8 | 531 | 63 | 22.7 | 21.4 | 0.4 | 13.6 | 7.2 |
| Argentina | 20.1 | 705 | 15 | 15.3 | 17.5 | 2.6 | 20.0 | 12.2 |
| Venezuela | 20.1 | 744 | 60 | 60.0 | 22.7 | −2.6 | 21.4 | 39.6 |
| Dominican Republic | 16.9 | 220 | 17 | 34.1 | 14.0 | 2.9 | 12.1 | 23.7 |
| Trinidad | 16.7 | 541 | 13 | 70.3 | 16.1 | 0.6 | n.a. | n.a. |
| Ecuador | 16.5 | 188 | 17 | 27.9 | 13.8 | 2.7 | 14.5 | 26.7 |
| Panama | 16.1 | 451 | 16 | 41.6 | 15.7 | 0.4 | 19.4 | 15.7 |
| Peru | 16.0 | 228 | 18 | 34.7 | 14.2 | 1.8 | 20.7 | 23.4 |
| Jamaica | 15.6 | 427 | 15 | 58.4 | 15.4 | 0.2 | n.a. | n.a. |
| Costa Rica | 14.3 | 362 | 15 | 45.9 | 14.9 | −0.6 | 16.4 | 23.9 |
| Nicaragua | 13.5 | 311 | 13 | 45.4 | 14.3 | −0.8 | 17.0 | 26.6 |
| Colombia | 11.0 | 285 | 22 | 19.2 | 15.0 | −4.0 | 19.7 | 18.6 |
| Honduras | 11.0 | 199 | 15 | 44.6 | 13.6 | −2.6 | 14.3 | 19.6 |
| El Salvador | 10.4 | 240 | 15 | 48.0 | 13.9 | −3.5 | 13.1 | 27.6 |
| Guatemala | 10.3 | 265 | 14 | 28.1 | 14.0 | −3.7 | 12.3 | 18.2 |
| Paraguay | 10.2 | 189 | 15 | 21.3 | 13.5 | −3.3 | 12.9 | 22.8 |
| Mexico | 9.0 | 460 | 29 | 14.4 | 17.2 | −8.2 | 20.0 | 11.9 |

T, revenue; Y, per capita income; V, value added by industry; M, imports; I, total investment; GI, goverment investment; T°/GNP, predicted ratio.

*Sources*: Columns 1, 2, 3, 4, see Sahota. [4, Table 3], based on UN *Statistical Yearbook* (1968) and *Yearbook of National Accounts* (1968); in determining T°/GNP, attempt is made to exclude non-tax revenue but to include all levels of government; data for 1966. Column 5, projected value of T°/GNP based on regresion on Y and V/GNP for 19 countries. Columns 7, 8 see Montrie, Fedor and Davis [1], only central government included.

20 per cent; and four, 20 per cent and above. At the same time (see col. 8), there is no pronounced relation between this ratio and the share of public capital formation in total investment. Some countries with about medium investment to GNP ratios, such as Brazil and Chile, have a very high public share, while others with a higher investment ratio have a low public share. We find, however, some tendency for high tax ratio countries to have a high public investment share. This is the case especially for Brazil and Chile, though not for Uruguay and Argentina. This suggests that the size of

the public sector may be as indicative of differences in organisation as of differences in the division of resources between social and private goods.

## Transfers

It remains to consider the role of transfer payments. Returning to the historical view of developed countries, it is evident that the last 50 years have shown both a rapidly rising per capita income and a rapidly rising share of this income being subject to redistribution through the tax-transfer mechanism. In large part, this reflects the social and political trends toward the welfare state during this period, but it may also suggest that wealthier countries can afford (on incentive or other grounds) to devote a larger share of their income to redistribution. In the developing countries, the level of transfer payments is already substantial, even though per capita income is still very low. Nevertheless, transfer payments are still growing, and frequently in forms which benefit particular groups and contribute to economic rigidities rather than to assuring greater security and a more equal distribution of income for the population as a whole.

Income distribution in most Latin American countries is exceedingly unequal, and I believe that a substantial correction of this situation is prerequisite to orderly social and economic development. The role of expenditure policy in remedying this situation is of vital importance. Where tax policy has been relatively unsuccessful, can expenditure policy be expected to do a better job?

An important contribution can be made on the expenditure side, but transfer payments are not the answer. To be sure, the potential amount of redistribution of consumption is not negligible. As distinct from developed countries, the share of the wealthy in total consumption is quite substantial. Thus, the upper 10 per cent of income recipients typically absorb, say, 45 per cent of total consumption and the upper 5 per cent absorb over 25 per cent. Redistribution of consumption towards the poor could thus be a significant factor in raising their consumption levels. But it is not easily accomplished. The results of highly progressive income taxation may be to reduce saving and to induce capital outflow. Taxation of luxury consumption (be it by excises on luxuries or a progressive spending tax) is more promising. But even then the resulting average level of consumption at the lower-income levels would remain very low. The better approach, therefore, is to divert high incomes now flowing into excess consumption towards capital formation and to assure that the resulting gains from growth are widely shared. This involves not only progressive consumption taxes, but also a proper direction of investment. A substantial share of human investment in particular may be directed so as to upgrade skills of the low-income groups.

Moreover, distributional as well as efficiency objectives will be served by directing investment into more labour-intensive types of technology. Students of economic development are concerned increasingly with the prospect of increasing unemployment as well as lagging income growth. As technology becomes increasingly labour-saving and the growth of capital stock is directed into such channels, the capital–labour ratio rises rapidly and the growth of employment is retarded. This might be the most efficient use of capital if attention is directed at rising per capita income only, but such is too narrow a view. The prospect of rising unemployment is disturbing because it suggests further deterioration of the social situation. To meet the problem, tax measures might be taken to encourage labour-intensive technology; but beyond this, expenditures on research should be helpful in encouraging the development of new technologies, designed to meet the needs of low-income and labour-abundant economies rather than those of high-income and labour-scarce economies.

## INSTRUMENTS OF EXPENDITURE POLICY

I now leave the discussion of expenditure development and turn to some of the instruments for expenditure planning.

### Governmental Organisation

Attention must be paid to the relation (or lack thereof) between finance ministries and planning agencies. While the former typically has the function of budget preparation in a narrow sense, the economic issues of expenditure planning (to the extent that they are dealt with at all) are typically the responsibility of the planning agency. Finance Ministers and heads of planning agencies do not readily cooperate, so that there tends to be little relationship among tax, budget and expenditure policies, and no effective coordination with overall economic policy-making. Expenditure, and especially investment planning, is clearly a basic part of development policy, but so is the tax side of the picture. Neither can be determined intelligently without reference to the maintenance of internal and external balance by monetary and fiscal policies. Given the typical lack of cooperation between Finance Ministers and planning agencies, a coordinating council is badly needed to rationalise policy-making.

Another aspect of governmental organisation which is of major importance for expenditure planning involves the country's vertical fiscal structure. The proper degree of fiscal centralisation or decentralisation in a developing as well as a developed country is a function not only of economic efficiency, but depends in large degree upon historical factors and the strength of regional interests. Nevertheless, in developing as in developed countries, there remains some degree of freedom in securing a more efficient pattern of organisation. A distinction should be drawn between the more highly developed municipalities, usually in the form of metropolitan areas, and the large number of small local units which are frequently incompetent to conduct efficient fiscal administration of either tax or expenditure measures. Governmental reorganisation which grants considerable discretion to selected larger municipal units, while extending central control over the smaller localities, will thus be helpful in improving fiscal performance.

## Cost-Benefit Analysis

I finally turn to the use of cost-benefit analysis as a technique by which expenditure priorities can be set. Much has been written about investment criteria and I shall here only touch on those aspects of this technique which are of special importance in the development context.

Cost-benefit analysis is at its best in the evaluation of specific projects. It is less well suited to designing the general strategies of development policy, such as the relative weights to be assigned to industrial and agricultural development or the choice between regional development patterns. Nevertheless, cost-benefit analysis is useful even in this connection, if only by forcing the consideration of alternatives in more explicit form and by encouraging an attempt to evaluate results.

In one important respect, cost-benefit analysis is more readily usable in the context of developing countries. In developed countries, the projects in question frequently deal with provision of ultimate consumer goods (such as the pleasures of visiting a park or the gain from improved health due to anti-air pollution measures) which by their nature as social goods cannot be evaluated by the market. Yet some evaluation of the final product is needed to measure the present value of the returns. Without an evaluation of benefits, only a cost-effectiveness type of analysis, evaluating alternative methods of providing the same service, can be applied. This difficulty is avoided, or largely so, in development projects such as transportation or irrigation, where the return may be measured by its effects on the cost of outputs which in turn are sold in the market. Development investment is essentially investment in intermediate goods and as such it lends itself more readily to evaluation.

As against this advantage, there are other features of developing economies which render application of cost-benefit analysis more difficult. In order to evaluate a project, its true social costs and gains must be entered. Even where such costs and benefits can be discussed in terms of market prices, these prices may not reflect true social value. Hence, shadow prices which express the proper social cost or benefit must be substituted. In the Latin American setting in particular, this is of importance in connection with the influence of factors such as overvalued exchange rates which understate the true cost of capital equipment and an overvalued cost of labour. Both distortions render capital too cheap relative to labour, and thus contribute to the previously noted problem of labour-saving technology and unemployment. Other price distortions, resulting from market imperfections, lack of mobility, and so forth, pose similar difficulties. In evaluating the benefits of a particular project as well as in determining the opportunity cost of foregoing private projects, prices which allow for these distortions must be used. The design of government projects in particular should allow for these adjustments.

Similar problems arise in the context of dynamic development planning, where the set of prices applicable when the project is planned may be surpassed by a new set which prevails for most of the project's useful life. Similarly, the product prices and costs applicable for any one project in isolation may differ from those which become appropriate if an entire development plan is considered.

Next, there is the need to allow for secondary or indirect effects which are not reflected in the immediate market costs or prices to which the product is directly related. These effects may be of particular importance for development planning. The project may give rise to a complex set of forward and backward linkages which are of major importance to the overall picture of economic development. The conclusion to be drawn from this is that the cost-benefit technique cannot be applied adequately as an isolated project-by-project procedure, but that it must be applied as an integral part of overall development planning.

Matters of distribution, as noted before, are an important aspect of development planning. In recent years there has been an increasing tendency for writers on cost-benefit analysis to include distributional weights in the objective function. While I have been sceptical of this as a general practice for a country such as the United States—where the distributional objectives can and should be met more directly by tax-transfer measures such as a negative income tax or by education program-mes—I feel differently about it in the context of Latin American development planning. Available resources are too limited in many cases to sustain both redistribution and growth policies. The solution, therefore, has to be through a redistribution-oriented growth policy. This is of importance especially with regard to investment in education and health, but it arises also with regard to housing and municipal investment. Going further, it may have important bearing on the promotion of industry vs. agriculture and on the choice of techniques in each case. Nor can the desire for some degree of balance in the rate of development among regions be ruled out of court. The economist's verdict that people should move is all well and good, but historical and political factors cannot be overlooked entirely. There is thus a good case for including distributional considerations (on both the benefit and cost sides) into the cost-benefit calculus for economic development, but it is important that this be done explicitly and uniformly over projects, lest the distributional adjustment be allowed to cover up elements of bias in the planning process.

Determination of the proper discount rate finally remains a major issue for project evaluation in development planning. The literature, delighted with the analytics of the problem, has dealt with this issue at great length. Concern has been with (a) whether the social rate of discount to be used in project analysis should be set below the private rate, and (b) if the latter is used, how it is to be determined. In the context of development planning, much is to be said for the social rate approach. Determination of a private market rate is difficult without a developed capital market and it is complicated further by the presence of inflation. Moreover, private saving is so limited and concentrated in a small sector of the population that the market rate can hardly be taken as a valid measure of the community's time-preference over the asset life. Nor can the level of investment in the private sector be taken as optimal. The private rate of return, therefore, can hardly serve as a measure of the true social return, even if a single private rate could be determined. In addition, there would be reasons in a developing economy for setting the social below the private rate even if these imperfections did not exist.

We can conclude, therefore, that development planning—and project evaluation in particular—must postulate what is to be considered the social discount rate for purposes of public policy. Or, putting it differently and perhaps more realistically, an acceptable minimum consumption path must be postulated and the discount rate derived therefrom. This, of course, must be done within the constraints of available resources and the maintenance of both internal and external balance.

## CONCLUSION

When I first contemplated this paper, I had the vision of ending up with a neat table with rows showing major expenditure categories (such as development, education, health and welfare and social security) and columns showing various levels of per capita income. In each cell, I would then enter a target expenditure to GNP ratio. Such a table would provide a standard against which the expenditure performance of a particular country could be assessed and the structure of its expenditure development could be planned. Unfortunately, we do not have the data (except for the total expenditure to GNP ratios) to do this even in terms of actual figures, not to speak of their normative evaluation. While some data for central governments are available, the expenditures of lower-level governments are not. Yet these must be included to obtain a meaningful picture. Hopefully, researchers will provide such data in the not too distant future.

This spade work must then be followed by the more difficult task of establishing what might be considered optimal expenditure structures. Allowing for the growth contribution of various expenditure categories and for legitimate differences in preference patterns among countries, this is a difficult road to travel; but there is no reason why some progress should not be made. In the meantime, the tax planner will have to continue acting on faith, or else limit himself to dealing with tax structure at whatever overall level of revenue is set for him.

## NOTES

1. See Musgrave [3, p. 112], where a sample based on the mid-1950s was used. The text ratios are based on this equation:

$$T/GNP = 0.1360 \quad + \quad 0.0001076 \, Y_c$$
$$(10.530) \qquad\qquad (6.4360) \qquad R^2 = 0.52.$$

A better fit for the tax to GNP ratio was obtained from a logarithmic function:

$$\text{T/GNP} = e \underset{(-14.90)}{^{-3.6896}} \ Y \underset{(8.1373)}{^{0.3369}} \quad R^2 = 0.64.$$

2. The underlying regression predicts the tax to GNP ratio as a function of per capita income, the degree of industrialisation, and a measure of openness of the economy. See Sahota [4].
3. Based on data from sample by Sahota [4].
4. The predicted values are based on equation II, Table 11.1, with Brazil included.
5. A number of similar and related investigations are available. For the latest study and literature references, see Montrie, Fedor and Davis [13]; and Lotz and Morss [2].
6. It should be noted that defence expenditures are not a major factor in explaining differences in the revenue to GNP ratios among Latin American countries. Such expenditures range from less than 1 to 3 per cent of GNP and mostly absorb less than 10 per cent of revenue. There is no significant relationship between the defence to GNP and revenue to GNP ratios.
7. See Selowsky [5].

# REFERENCES

[1] Montrie, C., Fedor, K. and Davis, H. (1970), Tax performance within the framework of the alliance for progress', *National Tax Journal*.
[2] Morss, E.R. and Lotz, J. (1967), 'Measuring tax effort in developing countries', *IMF Staff Papers*.
[3] Musgrave, R.A. (1969), *Fiscal Systems* (New Haven, Yale University Press).
[4] Sahota, G.S. (1973), 'Empirical standards to appraise the allocation of resources among social goods', unpublished.
[5] Selowsky, M. (1969), 'On the measurement of education's contribution to growth', *The Quarterly Journal of Economics*.

Part IV
Budget Growth and Fiscal Politics

# 12 Theories of Fiscal Crises: An Essay in Fiscal Sociology[*] 1980

Many observers over the past century have theorised that the growth of the fiscal system carries the seeds of its own destruction and that of the capitalist system. This group has included both Marxist and conservative critics of liberal social policies. In this paper, I describe these theories, point out their similarities and differences, and demonstrate that their predictions have been contradicted by events. I also show that the Marxian emphasis on class struggle casts rather little light on the struggle for fiscal influence and power in contemporary America. A pluralistic approach based on income, producer and consumer groups offers a far better insight.

## THE MARXIST TRADITION

Marx's own writings contain only scattered references to fiscal matters. Viewing taxation as an instrument of class struggle [8; 9] he noted its use as a means of exploitation, and pointed to excessive tax burdens as a major cause of social unrest in France. He recommended 'a heavy progressive or graduated income tax' as a means of overcoming the capitalist order [10]. Moreover, he noted the role of public debt in relation to capital accumulation, thus foreshadowing the later emphasis of Marxist writers on state indebtedness as a source of fiscal decline [11].

### Goldscheid and Schumpeter

The first full-fledged effort at analysing the fiscal role of the state in Marxist terms was undertaken by the Austrian socialist, Rudolf Goldscheid. Writing at the close of World War I, and confronted by his country's fiscal collapse, he hoped to develop a science of 'fiscal sociology'. This science was to explain the fiscal crisis by examining the 'social conditioning of the public household, and the fiscal conditioning which it in turn imposes upon society' [6, p. 254]. Placing the fiscal process at the centre of state activity, Goldscheid saw fiscal sociology as the very key to an understanding of

---

[*] In Aaron, H. and Boskin, M. (eds) (1980), *The Economics of Taxation* (Washington, D.C., The Brookings Institution).

social change. The need for financial support of communal activity led to
the creation of state-like organisation. Goldscheid interpreted fiscal history
from the Middle Ages to World World I as the decline of the state from
power and wealth to poverty and debt. Throughout Antiquity and the
Middle Ages the typical state was based on large property holdings of the
lord, who was both proprietor and ruler. His needs were met by sharing in
the produce of his land and in the labour of his serfs. The princes and
monarchs who followed continued to rely on these sources until the rising
claims of war finance and the wasteful maintenance of the royal courts
rendered them inadequate. At the same time, expansion of markets and
the development of trade created new potential sources of revenue.
Taxation replaced income from state property as the principal source of
state revenue.

But whereas the propertied state had been free to use and waste its
resources as it wished, the emerging separation of ownership and state
moved the state into dependency on the private sector. Property holders
resented being burdened by taxation over which they had little control, and
the struggle of the bourgeoisie to control the public purse came to play a
central role in the move toward popular control. Taxation became a prime
issue in the rise of modern democracy.

The new fiscal state, with its reliance on tax revenue, contained a flaw. It
was compelled to preserve the health of the private economy on which it
depended. Taxation, therefore, could not interfere with savings and
investment, a constraint that limited the taxation of profits and the use of
progressive income taxation. At the same time, the revenue requirements
of the state were rising, owing to increasing demands of war finance and a
growing need for social programmes. To meet these needs the state
borrowed increasingly and thereby opened itself to exploitation by its
private creditors. Far from exploiting the private sector, according to
Goldscheid, the state itself came to be exploited [6, p. 266]. Although the
people gained control over the state, they inherited only a debt-ridden and
impoverished state.

Here Goldscheid's story ends. His solution was to return property to the
state through a capital levy sufficient to create a public enterprise sector
that would yield enough income to finance necessary social services. In
proposing state capitalism as a solution, Goldscheid criticised both the
right and the left for rejecting a well-funded state, the former for
considering only the interest of private property and the latter for its
preoccupation with a far-off classless society where no state would be
needed. As he saw it, the root cause of capitalist contradiction was to be
found in the separation of property from the state, rather than in Marx's
separation of property from wage-labour [6, p. 269]. With state property
restored, a mixed economy would exist and social progress would evolve.

Fascinated by Goldscheid's grand design, Joseph Schumpeter undertook
a similar investigation [20]. He again viewed the development of the fiscal
system as a key to understanding the sociology of the state and as an
important indicator and source of social change. A state only comes into

existence, Schumpeter asserted, when the public and the private sectors are distinct. No state in this sense existed in the feudal system, where public and private property were both vested in the rights of the lord, nor will it exist in the communal setting of an advanced socialist society. With the decline of feudalism, distinct public and private sectors emerged. Property once held by the state came to be held by the private sector. With the development of markets, taxation became the dominant form of state revenue and new tax forms emerged with changing patterns of economic institutions and organisation. The rise of the 'tax state' and the rise of capitalism were integral parts of the same process. The emergence of the income tax in particular reflected the increasing use of money and the importance of income as an index of social stratification.

Following Goldscheid, Schumpeter assigned key importance to the resulting dependence of the state on the private sector but his solution to such dependence differed. He argued that because the private sector is interested only in production for private gain, taxation will interfere with economic incentives. When revenue requirements become excessive—and, Schumpeter held, sooner or later they must—this interference will become unsupportable and the tax state will collapse. As economic abundance is reached and 'the circle of social sympathy expands', society outgrows private enterprise and economic development comes to be replaced by other concerns [20, p. 38]. A different form of social organisation will then be needed.

Here the similarity to Goldscheid ends. Capitalism, according to Schumpeter, should be permitted to complete its task of establishing that abundance on the basis of which the new society can be built. This prescription, ironically, parallels Marx's call for the preservation of incentives until the socialist transition to communism has been completed, at which time economic issues lose their importance [12]. While fiscal mismanagement might produce a premature collapse of the tax state, Schumpeter saw no immediate and unavoidable cause for fiscal crisis. The breakdown of Austria's finances after the first world war was not irreparable, and the historical moment for replacing the tax state had not as yet come. Moreover, the public enterprise state would offer no solution since, according to Schumpeter, the taxable capacity of public enterprises would differ little from that of private firms.[1]

## Subsequent Marxist Views

Goldscheid's vision of a public enterprise-financed welfare state, of course, was inconsistent with more orthodox Marxist interpretations of the fiscal crisis. If, as orthodox Marxists held, the basic flaw of the capitalist system was in the institution of wage-labour, a partial transfer of property to the state could hardly correct it; and if, in fact, 'the executive of the modern State is but a committee for managing the common affairs of the whole bourgeoisie', as asserted in the *Manifesto of the Communist Party* [10], state action could hardly be expected to defend the interests of the working class. While Marx conceded that state policies may at times clash with the immediate interests of the propertied classes,[2] apparent social reform will soon turn out merely to strengthen the underlying order of production relations and to sustain capitalist domination [21]. The reformist fiscal state, it is argued, cannot solve the contradictions of capitalist society for the simple (somewhat circular?) reason that it is part thereof.

As suggested by Paul Baran and Paul Sweezy [2], attempts to absorb surplus production through deficit spending can offer a temporary solution only. Expenditures on civilian programmes can only be pushed so far before they run into business opposition based on fears that markets will be pre-empted. Other limitations apply to military expenditures. Due to the increasingly advanced technological nature of military hardware, Baran and Sweezy hold that military expenditures flow into profits and high salaries rather than into wages, and thus add little to demand. Strangely enough, they ignore the alternatives of tax reduction or transfer payments. According to this line of argument the fiscal crisis is a by-product of the capitalist crisis at large. It is a derived phenomenon rather than generated by its own dialectic, as in the Goldscheid–Schumpeter models. The latter and more interesting approach has been resumed in recent neo-Marxist writings.

James O'Connor [17], like Goldscheid, holds that the fiscal crisis occurs because a structural gap has developed between rising expenditure requirements and the limited ability of the state to raise revenue.[3] Both sides of the gap derive from the structure of the capitalist system and the role that the state must play. The state fulfils two conflicting functions according to O'Connor. The first, like the one described by Goldscheid, is to use expenditure policies to preserve profitable accumulation by monopoly capital, a sector that is defined to include not only large-scale industry and finance but also big union labour. The second function is to secure the necessary revenue to finance these outlays without hurting this very sector. The two objectives are incompatible and give rise to the structural gap.

In line with the first function, the state must provide both social investment and social consumption. Social investment, such as outlays on roads and education, is needed to maintain the conditions for profitable accumulation. In Marxist terms such investment increases the productivity of labour by adding to the stock of constant capital. Social consumption, such as outlays on social insurance and public health, adds to the stock of variable capital, thereby reducing the employer's cost of providing for the reproduction of labour. Both forms of social capital tend to increase surplus value and to raise profits. Also in line with the first function, the state must undertake social expenses such as welfare. These expenses do not add to productivity, but they are needed to secure the sufficient social harmony for monopoly capital to function and to legitimise the capitalist system.

The need for all these expenditures expands relative to the gross national product.[4] Social capital formation rises in response to the needs of, or demands by, the monopoly capital sector. Publicly provided investment goods cover more and more of its costs. State expansion, far from displacing monopoly capital, adds to its profits and becomes necessary for its survival. As a rising part of the population becomes proletarianised (moves into the status of wage-labour) and hence alienated, the need for legitimisation and resulting appeasement expenses similarly increases. Miscellaneous private interests accelerate the growth of state expenditures by pushing for a multiplicity of self-serving and frequently contradictory programmes and fighting over them in an administratively incoherent and inefficient budget process.

Although expenditures rise, the revenue base does not. Outlays for social capital, constant and variable, are productive, but the gains accrue to monopoly capital. Recouping them through profit and progressive income taxation is limited because big business and unions will not permit sufficient taxes on profits or income to cover the increased outlays. Hence the state is driven to inflationary finance. Conceivably the state and monopoly capital—an 'industrial–social complex'—could ally to bridge this impasse, but major and unlikely social and political changes would be needed to permit such an alliance. The realistic prospect is fiscal crisis and collapse.

## CRITIQUE AND RESTATEMENT

Marxist fiscal sociology, like Marxist theory, comes in many versions. Depending on which of the traditional tenets of Marxist theory (such as the labour theory of value, wage determination by reproduction cost of labour, surplus production and declining rate of profits) are retained or relaxed, different views of the fiscal state and its sociology emerge. With the orthodox versions of Baran and Sweezy on one extreme, O'Connor's position (with surplus production and reproduction cost-determined wages still a central ingredient) may be placed in the middle, flanked on the other side by the more relaxed and only mildly Marxist positions of such writers as Ian Gough [7] and Duncan Foley [5]. No single critique can cover all, nor would it be helpful to flog what economic history has shown to be dead horses.[5]

Certain propositions run through most of these writings, however, and may be singled out for examination. The first is the assertion that the development of the fiscal system should be interpreted within the framework of overall social, economic and political change. The second is that the class struggle defined as the dichotomy between capital and wage-labour is the key to this interpretation. A third common tenet is the claim that fiscal control is basically (if not in all specific actions) in the hands of the capitalist class. Finally, and most interestingly, it is held that the tax state carries its own seeds of collapse, as rising expenditures outpace lagging revenue capacity.

These propositions lead to the conclusion, happily shared by Marxists and libertarians, that the fiscal system in a mixed economy carries the seeds of its own destruction and is doomed to failure.

## Interaction of Fiscal and Social Change

There is nothing wrong with the Goldscheid–Schumpeter tradition to which Sultan may be added [21], of viewing fiscal development in the context of the broader pattern of social change. It is evident that economic, political and ideological forces all had their impact on the fiscal system.

Goldscheid and Schumpeter showed how economic forces stemming from the decline of feudalism and the rise of capitalism created the tax state with its dependence on the private sector. The revenue structure reflected changing modes of production and the related changes in the structure of industry and financial organisation. Landholding and live-stock, once meaningful measures of ability to pay, gave way to income, and the progressive income tax became the central tool of taxation. With the rise of the corporation, the income concept became more complex and an appropriate measure of taxable capacity became increasingly difficult to implement. Development of representative democracy similarly affected the decision process, creating a new framework for the determination of tax and expenditure policies, the budget system.

Philosophical currents that emerged with the rise of rationalism and of egalitarian ideology also influenced that fiscal development. What Schumpeter called the 'widening circle of social sympathy' (basic as it was to the rise of the welfare state) cannot be explained solely as the grudging concessions of an increasingly beleaguered capitalist class. Ideologies respond to economic circumstances, but they also have their own dynamics and in turn affect the economic setting. Indeed, the most important impact of Marxism in the western world, and certainly its lasting appeal to the young, has been its call for social justice; and this appeal has existed despite Marx's scathing treatment of this very concept [24]. Surely these forces must be taken into consideration when explaining the rise of the progressive income tax, defective though it may have turned out to be.

The fiscal system in turn also influenced events beyond its immediate sphere. Fiscal change contributed to the decline of the feudal system and later to the consolidation of dukedoms into national states. Resentment against taxation without representation, first on the part of vassals and then by the middle classes, contributed to the decline of absolute power and thus aided the subsequent rise of democracy and the private economic sector. Moreover, the tax system had its effect on forms of financial and business organisation, just as public purchase patterns affected the structure of markets.

These interactions, which were of major importance in the past, will continue to operate. In the process the institutions of the tax state will change. But the pattern of this change is not predetermined, just as there is no fixed pattern governing the development of the private sector. At the same time, some likely trends may be detected. With increasing international trade and investment, the international aspects of taxation will gain in importance, both for the taxpayer who becomes subject to several jurisdictions and for the taxing jurisdictions that must divide up common bases of revenue. As capital and labour become increasingly mobile, the widening gap between high- and low-income countries will become increasingly unacceptable, thus adding an international dimension to fiscal redistribution.

## Fiscal Interest Groups

There is much to be said for the Marxist tradition of emphasising the importance of social groups, rather than isolated individuals, as forces that determine fiscal change. But it is incorrect and misleading to formulate the issue in terms of a two-class capital–labour model. While it is not surprising that this dichotomy dominates Marxist fiscal sociology, the outcome is unfortunate because the two-class model, whatever its strength or weakness for general social analysis, is inappropriate for interpreting fiscal conflict. Closer consideration of the fiscal process, especially in its modern setting, shows that many groupings must be considered and that most of them cut across the Marxist class division. Moreover, the groupings interact, so that few problems can be understood correctly as bilateral conflicts.

Stratification by *income level* is central to fiscal analysis, yet it is not adequately allowed for by the distinction between capital and labour income. Although the distribution of capital income is less equal than that of wage and salary income (the top 20 per cent receives about 70 per cent of the former and 40 per cent of the latter), most inequality stems from inequality in the distribution of earned income. The inequality of earnings dominates simply because earnings account for over 75 per cent of total income.

On the tax side of the fiscal equation, grouping by income level (independent of source) is of most obvious importance under the global income tax. Exemptions, standard deductions, and the rate schedule are all related to total income. To be sure, various income sources pose different problems in income tax treatment, so that interest groups form by type of income. For instance, issues of income definition differ between earners of capital gains and wage income. Nevertheless, the battle lines are essentially by income level. Capital income forms a larger share of the total of high incomes, and the higher the income, the greater the potential benefit to be derived (under a progressive rate schedule) from the preferential treatment of capital gains.

Income level once more affects attitudes toward taxes on products. High-income households tend to share the same tastes, regardless of whether their income is received from wages or capital. High-income *rentiers*, executives and professionals alike will join to oppose the taxation of luxury products, while low-income groups find it in their interest to oppose the taxation of necessities. It is appropriate, therefore, that the study of the distribution of the tax burden, pioneered by Pechman, focuses on the distribution of income among income-size groups rather than between capital and labour.

Much the same holds for the expenditure side of budget policy. Programme benefits are frequently aimed specifically at low-income or high-income households but seldom specifically at recipients of capital income or wage income. Welfare programmes and low-cost housing projects favour low incomes; commuter services to suburbs, such as San Francisco's rapid transit system, benefit higher-income groups. The focus is on level of income, not on whether it derives from labour or capital sources.

Stratification by *taste* is also relevant to fiscal alignment. While the budget patterns of households at any one income level share common characteristics, the patterns are not uniform. Taste differences remain that cut across income groups and are independent of income source. Thus smokers with both high and low wage and capital income join in opposing tobacco taxes, and fanciers of big cars oppose gasoline taxes. On the expenditure side conservationists (regardless of income source or income level) combine in supporting national parks; and devoted motorists (regardless of income source or income level) join in favouring highway expenditures.

After income level, the most important grouping is by the source of income. But contrary to the Marxist mould, the strategic distinction is not between capital and labour but between the *industries* from which the income (be it wages or profits) is derived. On the tax side capital and labour in the automotive industry both oppose automotive taxes; both restaurant employees and owners oppose tightening expense accounts. And on the expenditure side capital as well as labour in the automotive and construction industries support highway programmes. Grouping by industry is clearly a dominant factor in the politics of expenditure decisions. In even starker contrast to the Marxist model, US labour and foreign capital have a common interest in opposing tax benefits to capital outflow (that is, deferral of taxes on foreign profits), and US capital and foreign labour share an interest in their support.

Next, consider the role of interest groups based on *age*. Expenditures on education benefit the young and draw support from their families. Such expenditures are of less immediate concern to the elderly and the unmarried, a factor of major importance in considerations of municipal finance. Old age benefits draw support from the retired and those soon to retire, a factor of increasing significance as the ratio of retired population to working population increases. As the influence of parent–teacher associations declines, that of Grey Panther-type organisations increases.

Finally, there are interest groupings based on *region*. Because some industries are geographically concentrated, some product taxes fall disproportionately on particular regions or states. Similarly, public purchases of private output support the economies of particular regions. Because members of Congress represent particular states or districts, regional interests are a major factor in the way they determine fiscal policy. Washington state representatives are preoccupied with defence outlays, Texas representatives attend carefully to the tax treatment of oil, New York representatives pay close attention to urban programmes. Only the President can transcend these interests.

This catalogue of relevant interest groups may be readily extended to include other groups—the healthy versus the sick (of major importance in the debate over national health insurance) and male versus female (for example, child care programmes or the financing of abortions). Such extension may be passed over, however, as by now the multidimensional structure of fiscal interest grouping should be clear. The labour–capital dichotomy is only one, and hardly the most important. In fact, each household belongs to a set of interest groups involving (1) its sources, as well as its level, of earnings; (2) its pattern, as well as its level, of expenditures; and (3) its preferences for, and hence benefits derived from, public services. To understand the sociology of fiscal politics all these fiscally relevant groupings must be considered. They must be allowed for in predicting the voting behaviour of constituents and their representatives. In short, the fiscal game is vastly more complex than the capital–labour dichotomy suggests.

**The Fiscal State**

Not all Marxist theory sees the state as a pure instrument of capitalist domination. Allowance may be made for its operation in the context of balancing political powers, with some independence of state action [3]. Contemporary Marxist writers even recognise the existence of a state based on popular vote and reflecting the public interest. But this view is conditional only, as capital will tolerate such a state only because the image of 'public interest' is needed to dampen alienation and to legitimise capitalist institutions [13; 18]. In the end it is essential for Marxist theory to contend that the state must serve the interest of the capitalist class.

In fact, the contest for fiscal control is an open game with many players. Capital has no exclusive control over the outcome, which (*à la* Schumpeter) may well be to its disadvantage. Moreover, the fiscal process is not a zero–sum game marked only by conflict. It also involves cooperation and mutual gain. By the very nature of social goods, the freerider problem renders their private provision unfeasible. Hence collective action is needed to provide them, and all or most gain from such cooperation. How then do the major fiscal actors—the public, elected representatives, and appointed officials—share in the fiscal powers of the state?

Final voting power rests with the public. In most cases this power is not exercised in a town meeting, where individual voters directly make decisions, but by elected representatives who cannot depart too far from voter preferences if they wish to stay in office. But politicians do more than merely reflect the views of their constituents; they also try to shape these views, either from self-interest (for example, re-election even if on false positions, or power, or pocket book) or to project their own conception of the public interest. They may risk defeat because of commitment to a public-minded programme. Balancing popular approval and likelihood of winning against his or her perceived value of proposed programmes, the candidate engages in risk-taking, much as the investor does when choosing among alternative assets. While it is naive to hold that all politicians are altruistic, it is equally mistaken to hold that all seek power for its own sake.

Once more it is important to allow for the role of interest groups, as distinct from that of individual voters, both in the election of representatives and the positions they espouse thereafter. Such powerful interest groups as corporations, unions, realtors or the Sierra Club enter into the decision-making process by public education, advertising, campaign contributions, or other lobbying devices. As some groups are better organised and more affluent than others, the outcome will not be a finely balanced reflection of voter position. But periodic elections provide a check, so that state policies cannot wander too far from the wishes of the voting majority. While consumers as an interest group have been under-represented, recent developments (both inside and outside the government) suggest that this pattern is changing.

Governmental staff also have an independent influence on public policy. Some officials come close to the Weberian image of the public servant [23]. Acting as technical expert, such staffs present decision-makers with the consequences of alternative measures; acting as administrator, they implement programmes as decided upon by the legislator. At the other end of the scale are the self-serving bureaucrats concerned mainly with enlarging their bureaux and perpetuating their programme functions, thereby enhancing their own salary, status and power. They will push policies that serve their purpose; but even dedicated staff, be they technicians or administrators, cannot avoid introducing their own judgement.

As Emanuel A. Goldenweiser observed to me when I first came to Washington in 1938, it is difficult to give technical advice in a neutral fashion, nor should the professional suppress his own view. The very scale chosen in a chart will determine its visual impact, and the choice of econometric model affects the outcome. Moreover, time never permits all issues to be examined, and the very process of selection involves the 'technician' in a judgement as to what matters.

Much the same holds for the staff involved in administration. Legislation is bound to be general; regulations and guidelines, and their daily interpretation, reflect the exercise of important judgements. Thus public employees (I am using this neutral expression to avoid the value-laden terms 'civil servant' and 'bureaucrat') are policy-makers. They cannot avoid inserting their own choices, choices that may reflect financial or status position, or which may serve what they consider to be the public interest.

Control over the fiscal structure thus does not rest in the hands of any particular agent or group. The interests of capital and labour enter, but so do others. In the end the fiscal process reflects the interaction of pluralistic interests and interest groups. This plurality renders fiscal decision-making complex and difficult to predict, which is unfortunate; but it is hardly a reason for adopting an over-simplified model that gives ready but frequently mistaken answers.

## THE STRUCTURAL GAP RECONSIDERED

My final issue concerns the inevitability of fiscal crisis and collapse. According to Marxist writers, fiscal measures will not only fail to overcome the tendencies toward breakdown inherent in the private sector, but while they are trying to do so, rising expenditures will outrun taxable capacity, leading to the collapse of the tax state itself.

### Wagner's Law—the Marxist Version

The idea that public expenditures inevitably rise is not a new one. A century ago Adolph Wagner argued that the public expenditure share must rise because social progress requires expanding social services and because interdependence of economic activity requires increasing public sector involvement. 'Wagner's law' has been discussed ever since, and the Marxist diagnosis is a variant. However, the specifics of causation differ. The ratio of public expenditure to gross national product, according to the Marxist view, must rise to absorb over-production by the private sector, to provide 'monopoly capital' with increasing amounts of free inputs, and to dampen rising alienation with increasing attention to social services. It remains to be seen whether or not these hypotheses are supported by the facts.

Table 12.1 shows the pattern of US public expenditure growth during this century; a similar pattern may be observed in other countries. Four main features emerge from this table. First, the overall expenditure ratio rose from 7.7 per cent in 1902 to 11.8 per cent in 1927. It nearly doubled during the Great Depression and continued to climb in each successive decade, reaching 36.5 per cent in the 1970s.

Second, only during the 1940s and 1950s did national defence contribute significantly to the rising overall expenditure ratio; between 1950 and 1960, in fact, the civilian ratio declined. During the 1960s and 1970s the defence ratio declined, while the civilian ratio rose dramatically. Over the century until 1977, defence accounted for less than one-fifth of the increase in the ratio of expenditures to GNP.

Third, the rise in the expenditure ratio from 1940 to 1947 was due mainly to a rise in government purchases and a rise in transfers.

Finally, before 1950 the three functional civilian expenditure categories (general government, economic development and human resources) broadly shared in the causes of expenditure growth. Thereafter, more than half of the increase in the civilian ratio was from increased expenditures on human resources, with social insurance and welfare accounting for the largest part. In contrast, the proportion of GNP devoted to economic development as well as that spent on general government shows only a slight gain.

The evidence reveals overall expenditure growth, but it is important to note that this increase has been decelerating.[7] While the ratio of expenditure to GNP need not rise at an increasing rate to generate a crisis (a simple

*Table 12.1 Public expenditures by type and function, selected years, 1902–77*

| Item | Per cent of gross national product | | | | | | | Percentage point change | | | |
| --- | --- | --- | --- | --- | --- | --- | --- | --- | --- | --- | --- |
| | 1902 | 1927 | 1940* | 1950* | 1960 | 1970 | 1977 | 1902–40 | 1940–50 | 1950–77 | 1902–77 |
| Total | 7.7 | 11.8 | 20.4 | 24.6 | 28.2 | 34.2 | 36.5 | 12.7 | 4.2 | 11.9 | 28.8 |
| Defence[b] | 1.4 | 1.3 | 2.1 | 5.4 | 10.2 | 8.9 | 6.5 | 0.7 | 3.3 | 1.1 | 5.1 |
| Civilian | 6.3 | 10.6 | 18.4 | 19.2 | 18.1 | 25.4 | 30.0 | 12.1 | 0.8 | 10.8 | 23.7 |
| Total by type | 7.7 | 11.8 | 19.3 | 22.1 | 28.2 | 34.2 | 36.5 | 11.6 | 2.8 | 14.4 | 28.8 |
| Purchases | n.a. | n.a. | 14.2 | 13.5 | 19.8 | 22.3 | 20.9 | n.a. | −0.7 | 7.4 | n.a. |
| Defence | n.a. | n.a. | 2.2 | 4.9 | 9.1 | 7.8 | 5.3 | n.a. | 2.7 | 0.4 | n.a. |
| Civilian | n.a. | n.a. | 12.0 | 8.6 | 10.7 | 14.5 | 15.6 | n.a. | −3.4 | 7.0 | n.a. |
| Net interest | n.a. | n.a. | 1.2 | 1.5 | 1.4 | 1.2 | 1.2 | n.a. | 0.3 | −0.3 | n.a. |
| Transfers | n.a. | n.a. | 2.7 | 6.3 | 5.7 | 7.9 | 10.7 | n.a. | 3.6 | 4.4 | n.a. |
| Other[6] | n.a. | n.a. | 1.2 | 1.0 | 1.4 | 2.8 | 3.7 | n.a. | −0.2 | 2.7 | n.a. |
| Civilian by function | 6.3 | 10.6 | 18.4 | 19.2 | 18.1 | 25.4 | 30.0 | 12.1 | 0.8 | 10.8 | 23.7 |
| General government[4] | 2.4 | 2.6 | 3.7 | 4.9 | 3.0 | 3.9 | 4.7 | 1.3 | 1.2 | −0.2 | 2.3 |
| Net interest | 0.4 | 1.4 | 1.6 | 1.7 | 1.4 | 1.2 | 1.2 | 1.2 | 0.1 | −0.5 | 0.8 |

| | | | | | | | | | | | |
|---|---|---|---|---|---|---|---|---|---|---|---|
| Economic development | 1.7 | 3.4 | 7.2 | 4.9 | 4.8 | 5.5 | 6.0[e] | 5.5 | -2.3 | 1.1 | 4.3 |
| Transportation | 0.9 | 2.2 | 2.6 | 1.6 | 2.7 | 2.7 | 2.2 | 1.7 | -1.0 | 0.6 | 1.3 |
| Other | 0.8 | 1.2 | 4.7 | 3.3 | 2.1 | 2.8 | 3.8 | 3.9 | -1.4 | 0.5 | 3.0 |
| Human resources | 1.7 | 3.1 | 5.8 | 7.8 | 8.9 | 14.7 | 18.1 | 4.1 | 2.0 | 10.3 | 16.4 |
| Education | 1.2 | 2.4 | 2.8 | 3.4 | 3.7 | 5.9 | 6.2 | 1.6 | 0.6 | 2.8 | 5.0 |
| Social insurance[f] | .. | 0.1 | 1.0 | 2.4 | 2.8 | 4.4 | 6.4 | .. | 1.4 | 4.0 | .. |
| Welfare[g] | 0.2 | 0.2 | 1.3 | 1.0 | 1.4 | 2.9 | 3.8 | 1.1 | -0.3 | 2.8 | 3.6 |
| Health and hospitals | 0.3 | 0.5 | 0.7 | 1.0 | 1.0 | 1.5 | 1.7 | 0.4 | 0.3 | 0.7 | 1.4 |

*Sources:* Percentages based on expenditure data and GNP: for 1902, 1927, and for breakdown by function for 1940 and 1950, US Census Bureau, *Historical Statistics of the United States: Colonial Times to 1970*, bicentennial edition, H. Doc. 93–78 (GPO, 1976), pt. 1: series F 1–5, p. 224, and pt. 2: series Y 533–566, pp. 1120–1; for 1960, 1970, and for breakdown by type for 1940 and 1950, US Department of Commerce, Bureau of Economic Analysis, *The National Income and Product accounts of the United States*, 1929–74, Statistical Tables, supplement to the *Survey of Current Business* (GPO, 1977), Tables 1.1, 3.2, 3.4, 3.14, pp. 2–3, 96, 108, 135, 142, 324, 340–1; for 1977, *Survey of Current Business*, July 1978, Tables 1, 3.14, pp. 1, 44. Figures are rounded.

n.a. Not available

a. Breakdown on type for 1940 and 1950 does not correspond to other categories for those years owing to different source using different accounting procedure.

b. Includes national defence, foreign military aid, and veterans' services.

c. Federal grants in aid to state and local governments, and subsidies.

d. Central administration and management, international affairs, civilian safety, and postal services.

e. Includes $8.3 billion in general revenue-sharing.

f. Old age, survivors', and disability insurance, medical and unemployment insurance.

g. Public assistance, relief and other welfare services.

increase is all that is needed), the declining rate nevertheless suggests an abatement of the crisis potential. More important, the pattern of growth hardly supports the Marxist prognosis. To begin with, defence expenditures have clearly not been the driving force. From the beginning of the century to date, defence contributed only 5.1 percentage points to the rising overall ratio, whereas civilian outlays have contributed 23.7 points. From 1960 on, the defence ratio has in fact declined. These data lend no support to the hypothesis that capitalist societies must spend ever-increasing shares on defence to absorb surplus output. [19]. If war finance has been a major factor, it has been by raising the threshold of acceptable taxation, thus permitting a step-up in post-war civilian outlays. Table 12.1 also shows that interest payments caused by debt finance have not absorbed an increasing share of GNP. Interest on the public debt has never been a significant factor in the overall picture, and the ratio of interest to GNP now stands about where it was in 1940. Unanticipated inflation has served as a built-in mechanism of debt repudiation.

But what of the rising ratio for civilian expenditures? While O'Connor recognises that it is not always possible to assign a particular expenditure item neatly to one or another category, he suggests an interesting formulation of expenditure theory in Marxist terms by distinguishing between the contribution to expenditure growth made by (1) social investment, (2) social consumption, and (3) social expenses. As noted before, the first two are needed for the productivity of private accumulation and add to surplus value, while the third is needed for social harmony. Taking (1) to be reflected in expenditures on economic development, it is seen that the corresponding ratio rose up to 1940 but declined during the 1940s and by 1977 was still below its 1940 level (see Table 12.1). This pattern hardly supports the hypothesis that monopoly capital has exacted increasing subsidies, based on free inputs by the state. Nor does it seem reasonable to interpret the rise of all development expenditure in these terms. The growth of highway expenditures reflects technological change in transportation, which would have occurred as well under alternative forms of social organisation. The fact that such programmes benefit the automobile and construction industries is evident, but it does not follow that they should be viewed as subsidies to these groups. [8] Outlays on environmental and energy resource programmes and on housing and agriculture ('other' economic development, Table 12.1) have risen over the past decade, but once more they may be viewed as subsidies to the consumers of polluting outputs rather than as subsidies to producers.

In O'Connor's category of social consumption one may include programmes in education, social insurance, welfare and health. It is difficult to hold that the sharp increase in the ratio of education expenditures to GNP between 1960 and 1970 constitutes increased subsidies to monopoly capital. Even if education serves to socialise the young to conform with the capitalist system (a questionable proposition, given the educational experience of the 1960s), most of this increase reflects expanded enrolment in the wake of the post-war baby boom and rising teacher salaries brought on partly by increased union pressure. Indeed, support for rising education budgets has come primarily from the political left rather than the right, with emphasis on democratising the educational process rather than serving the interests of monopoly capital.

Next, consider the rising ratio of social insurance outlays. As shown in Table 12.1, this trend has been the dominant factor in the post-war rise of public expenditures. Can one plausibly argue that this trend has decreased the reproduction cost of labour, thereby increasing surplus value and permitting capital to reap a larger profit share? Putting it differently, can it be maintained that in the absence of social insurance, wages would have been correspondingly higher and profits lower? This reasoning is difficult to follow under either neoclassical or Marxist theory. Under the former the employee's portion of the payroll tax used to finance social security leaves wages unaffected unless labour supply changes. Under traditional Marxist theory wages are determined by subsistence needs, needs that set a wage floor that cannot be reduced by payroll taxes. As social security benefits reduce the need for private saving, the share of the worker's wage previously needed for that purpose is replaced by his or her payroll tax contribution. Thus social insurance cannot be expected to reduce the necessary wage or to raise profits. On the contrary, the objective of social security is to improve incomes of the aged while possibly raising the labour cost of industry. The social and political pressures for extension of social insurance, like those for education, are to be found on the left rather than on the right of the political centre.

Turning finally to O'Connor's 'expenses' needed to provide social peace and to legitimise capitalism, it is surprising to find that this category (welfare in Table 12.1) until recently contributed negligibly to total expenditure growth. While part of social security might be included under 'consumption' rather than 'human capital', the picture hardly supports the notion that mounting bribes have been needed to secure popular acquiescence of capitalism. Notwithstanding decreasing self-employment (rising wage-labour), the drastic increase in living standards has provided middle-class status rather than proletarianisation for the bulk of the labour force. While some severe poverty persists, much of it is now segregated in urban and rural slums, thus (unfortunately) reducing its effectiveness as a social force. As a consequence, increases in legitimisation 'expenses' have accounted for little of the budget expansion.

In short, Table 12.1 lends little support to the proposition that the capitalist system, by internal logic, necessitates an ever-rising ratio of public expenditure to GNP. The application of Marxist expenditure categories to the public sector, while an intriguing experiment, proves of little explanatory value.

## Expenditure Growth: An Alternative View

An alternative explanation, which I consider more useful, is based on a distinction between allocational and distributional causes, with the former economic and technical while the latter are political and social.

Beginning with the allocational causes, the efficient mix of output at a given place and time depends on income, technology and demography. This holds for both capital and consumer goods. The type of capital goods required in the early stages of development, especially those needed to develop infrastructure, typically yield benefits that, in considerable part, are external and therefore require public investment. Later on, with the rise of manufacturing and the development of urban centres, the requisite form of capital formation is of the private type, and the share of private investment rises. Still later, environmental problems, urban slums and other contingencies may arise, calling for new forms of public investment. The desired mix of consumer goods similarly changes with rising income. When income is low such necessities as food, clothing and shelter absorb most of the household budget. As income rises, social goods tend to become increasingly important, being demanded directly or as complementary to the consumption of private goods.

The efficient share of social goods is affected also by changes in technology. The invention of the automobile increased demand for highways and dominated the expansion of state budgets for long periods. Progress with space exploration may come to be a major factor in federal finances of the future, as weapon technology has increased the cost of defence and medical technology the cost of health services in past budgets. Technical change thus affects the appropriate share of GNP that is provided through the budget.

Finally, demographic changes have important bearing on the size of the public sector. Increased school enrolment was a major factor of rising budgets in the 1960s, and the growing aged population will demand growing retirement benefits in the coming decades.

These examples show that expenditure growth may be explained in considerable part by factors largely independent of the social system and that prevail in a socialist as well as a capitalist setting. The future directions of these influences are hard to forecast, but more likely than not they will cause a rising public expenditure share. But although this growth of these public outlays may be determined primarily by technical factors, it nevertheless will have significant implications for the political and social structure. Marxist analysis misses this point, as it pays little attention to the inherent nature of public or social (as distinct from private) goods. By assigning a minor role to consumption patterns, Marxist theory fails to explore the social relations of consumption, notwithstanding the central role that materialistic determinism assigns to the social relations of production.

The social relations of consumption of private goods differ from that for social goods. The former are consumed individually, they may be distributed equally or unequally, and their provision may be related to productive contribution. The terms on which goods become available to individual consumers may be considered a matter of entitlement or they may be used as instruments of social power and discipline. Depending on the nature of the social system, the housing space available to a person may hinge on his or her income, standing in a political party, or political views. In contrast, social goods must be consumed jointly, and their benefits tend to be available more or less freely. Such goods tend to be distributed equally, their provision cannot be used to give economic incentives, and they cannot be withheld for purposes of social discipline. All this has immediate and important bearing on the social system, capitalist or socialist. Increased provision of social goods may be favoured or fought as a means of equalisation, and the very fact that their provision calls for social cooperation (that is, a political as distinct from a market process) introduces a new form of social relationship.

Different considerations arise from the growth of transfers. Here redistributional considerations are of major importance. Although welfare and relief programmes account for only a small proportion of the increase in the ratio of overall expenditures to GNP, other transfers, such as social security benefits, play a redistributional role. Moreover, a significant share of public services directly benefits lower-income groups. In all, more redistribution is accomplished by expenditures than by taxes.[9] This growth of redistribution is in line with the Marxist hypothesis if interpreted as increased power of the majority to force transfers from a reluctant minority or as increased willingness of the better-off to appease the masses through transfers. However, it may also reflect an increased willingness to reduce inequality based on a changing sense of social justice, and thereby an adaptability of the system to social needs. Clearly all three factors have been present, but there is no evident way to determine their respective weights.

## Limited Revenue Capacity?

I finally turn to the revenue side of the structural change hypothesis. Taxable capacity in the Marxist model is constrained for two reasons. First, taxation of wage income is limited or impossible because wages are at subsistence. Second, there are limits to the taxation of capital income. In Goldscheid's version the state is reluctant to tax capital income because such taxes interfere with private investment and thereby destroy the state's own revenue base. In O'Connor's version monopoly capital benefits from social investment but refuses to return these gains to the state through taxation. Since the monopoly capital sector includes both capital and labour employed in it, a large share of national income is preempted from taxation. Neither limit is realistic. Most wages are not at subsistence and the middle-income group (including most employees of monopoly capital) carries a substantial and perhaps disproportionate share of the tax burden. Capital, notwithstanding its strong voice in the deliberations of congressional tax committees, also falls far short of complete success in escaping taxation.

What then determines the limits of taxable capacity? Economists answer this question in terms of the impact of taxes on the supply of labour, savings and the willingness to invest.[10] Taxation, and especially the use of high marginal rates, induces the choice of tax-preferred options, thereby imposing an 'excess burden'. Such burdens may arise especially in a capitalist system, where decisions about saving, investment and work are made largely in the private sector. They are of more limited importance in a socialist setting, where decisions on investment and saving, and to some extent those on work, are made by the state.

But taxable capacity is not only a matter of economics. Not only may taxpayers respond individually to such taxes as have been imposed on them; they many also act in consort with others to determine what the tax structure should be. This outer limit on taxable capacity is a matter of political power and may be related only indirectly to individual responses and the economics of excess burden. Such is the case especially with regard to the taxation of capital income. Investors can threaten to penalise government by reducing investment and the threat is effective if politicians react. Their reason for reacting, however, is not that revenue will be lost, as Goldscheid thought, but that unemployment will result leading to loss of votes. Unless the state is willing to substitute public for private investment or to reduce the growth of productive capacity, the taxation of capital income has to remain acceptable to the investment community. Continued deductibility of three-Martini luncheons may become the price of economic recovery and reelection. Labour does not have so potent a threat. While the individual worker may fight increased taxes by working less, the immediate impact of such responses on the economy is less visible. Nor have unions taken to calling strikes to protest what they consider hostile tax legislation. More generally, tax legislation is not a matter of collective bargaining in the United States, although in line with current tax-rebate proposals such considerations might become imbedded in an incomes policy.

The strategic position of capital is stronger in a setting where much emphasis is laid on economic growth as a policy objective. Tax incentives for growth, by their very nature, provide tax relief for capital income, and direct benefits accrue largely to high-income taxpayers. While labour will share eventually in the gains from growth, it suffers a short-run loss as revenue is redirected. This lends validity to the Marxist emphasis on capital–labour conflict in the fiscal scene, especially since little has been done to design growth policies with a less regressive impact.[11]

At the same time, far more voters derive most of their income from labour than from capital, a fact that should be expected to tip the scales in the other direction. Income tax loopholes exist, but so do other taxes. Income from capital is also subject to the corporation profits and property taxes, while labour also pays the payroll tax. In all, it is unclear which source is taxed most heavily. Such is the case especially if actual (as distinct from statutory) incidence is considered and the complexities of tax-shifting in an imperfectly competitive economy are allowed for.

Tax distortions are primarily a function of marginal rather than of average tax rates, yet redistribution through the tax system is not possible without permitting marginal rates to rise ahead of the average. Whether or not a crisis of the tax state materialises, therefore, depends more on the pattern than the overall level of taxation. This pattern in turn reflects social attitudes and the level of income. As income rises, society may find redistribution less necessary. Much depends on the depth of concern about poverty, on whether poverty is seen in absolute or relative terms, and on whether the goal is to achieve some given degree of overall distributional equality. As re-distributive programmes expand, however, the dividing-line between those who gain and those who lose from redistribution moves down the income scale. This makes it harder to secure a majority for further redistribution. For this reason, one may expect successful additions to the tax burden to be distributed less and less progressively.

Tables 12.2 and 3 report on a rather crude attempt to test this hypothesis for the increase in US tax burdens from 1910 to 1975. Based on alternative incidence assumptions, the tables show the estimated distribution, by decade, of the increase in revenue borne by various quintiles. As shown by the more progressive estimates in Table 12.2 trends in federal revenues clearly support my hypothesis. The estimated share of incremental federal revenue collected from the top quintile reached 68 per cent in the 1940s and then declined to 46 per cent in 1970–75 as the shares of the third and fourth quintiles rose. A similar pattern prevails if payroll taxes are excluded; the absorption by the top quintile in 1940–50 exceeded 70 per cent, with a subsequent drop to 53 per cent. The state–local level, on the other hand, does not display this pattern. Under less progressive assumptions regarding incidence the hypothesis is supported less strikingly (see Table 3), but the declining share of the top quintile over recent decades remains apparent.

Given the shape of the income pyramid and the level of tax rates already reached, the fraction of voters supporting higher taxes and more redistribution is likely to decline. This trend, joined to the investors' veto over excessive taxation of capital income, suggests that tax increases will become increasingly difficult to enact. As a result, fiscal expansion may well slow and increased fiscal redistribution may draw to an end. The so-called crisis of the tax state may prove self-terminating. But it does not follow that a happy equilibrium must result. The blocking of the fiscal crisis may simply transfer the crisis into another and less manageable sphere of the socioeconomic system.

## CONCLUSION

Four hypotheses regarding possible sources of fiscal crisis may be distinguished.

First, under the *Marxist* hypothesis the root of the fiscal crisis lies in the tendency for increasing socialisation of costs and rising expenditures to legitimise capitalism, without any corresponding socialisation of the resulting gains to monopoly capital. As a result, the government can no longer pay for needed outlays through taxes. The result is either rising inflation or

*Table 12.2 Estimated distribution of increase in tax burden, by income class, under most progressive incidence assumption, 1910–75[a] (per cent)*

| Income class[b] | 1910–20 | 1920–30 | 1930–40 | 1940–50 | 1950–60 | 1960–70 | 1970–75 |
|---|---|---|---|---|---|---|---|
| | | | *Federal taxes* | | | | |
| Lowest fifth | 4 | −30 | 3 | 2 | 2 | 2 | 3 |
| Second fifth | 9 | −60 | 12 | 6 | 8 | 8 | 10 |
| Middle fifth | 12 | −60 | 20 | 9 | 14 | 16 | 17 |
| Fourth fifth | 16 | −40 | 25 | 15 | 26 | 22 | 23 |
| Highest fifth | 59 | 290 | 40 | 68 | 56 | 52 | 46 |
| | | | *Federal taxes, excluding payroll* | | | | |
| Lowest fifth | 4 | −30 | 3 | 2 | 2 | 2 | 3 |
| Second fifth | 9 | −60 | 10 | 6 | 7 | 6 | 9 |
| Middle fifth | 12 | −60 | 13 | 8 | 12 | 13 | 14 |
| Fourth fifth | 16 | −40 | 19 | 13 | 18 | 19 | 20 |
| Highest fifth | 59 | 290 | 53 | 71 | 62 | 60 | 53 |
| | | | *State and local taxes* | | | | |
| Lowest fifth | 4 | 4 | 5 | 5 | 4 | 4 | 4 |
| Second fifth | 8 | 9 | 13 | 10 | 10 | 10 | 10 |
| Middle fifth | 10 | 13 | 20 | 15 | 14 | 15 | 15 |
| Fourth fifth | 14 | 17 | 26 | 20 | 19 | 19 | 20 |
| Highest fifth | 64 | 57 | 37 | 52 | 52 | 52 | 52 |
| | | | *All taxes[c]* | | | | |
| Lowest fifth | 4 | 3 | 4 | 2 | 3 | 3 | 3 |
| Second fifth | 8 | 6 | 12 | 7 | 8 | 9 | 10 |
| Middle fifth | 12 | 10 | 20 | 10 | 15 | 15 | 17 |
| Fourth fifth | 15 | 13 | 26 | 14 | 20 | 23 | 22 |
| Highest fifth | 61 | 68 | 37 | 64 | 55 | 52 | 49 |

*Source*: Author's calculations based on Joseph A. Pechman and Benjamin A. Okner (1974), *Who Bears the Tax Burden?* (Washington, D.C. Brookings Institution). The analysis is based on the assumption that the distribution of the burden for various taxes by quintiles is as shown in the Pechman–Okner results. An exception is made only of pre-1940 income tax, for which 1920 and 1930 patterns were estimated by the author. The procedure was (1) to determine the revenue increments from various taxes decade by decade, (2) to allocate the increment for each tax in line with the noted pattern, (3) to add the incremental burdens from various taxes, and (4) to determine the percentage distribution of the incremental burden among quintiles. This procedure was then followed on a decade-to-decade basis. Since the quintile distribution of income has remained fairly constant, it may not be unreasonable to assume that the distribution of the tax burden resulting from various taxes has also followed a constant pattern.

a. The most progressive incidence assumption is that of variant 1c, Pechman and Okner, *Who Bears the Tax Burden?* Tables 4–9, 4–10.

b. Households ranked by adjusted family income (family income as derived from the national income accounts plus indirect business taxes).

c. Includes payroll taxes.

Table 12.3 *Estimated distribution of increase in tax burden, by income class, under least progressive incidence assumption, 1910–75[a] (per cent)*

| Income class[b] | 1910–20 | 1920–30 | 1930–40 | 1940–50 | 1950–60 | 1960–70 | 1970–75 |
|---|---|---|---|---|---|---|---|
| *Federal taxes* | | | | | | | |
| Lowest fifth | 6 | . . . | 4 | 3 | 3 | 3 | 3 |
| Second fifth | 9 | . . . | 12 | 8 | 9 | 9 | 10 |
| Middle fifth | 15 | −80 | 19 | 11 | 15 | 16 | 17 |
| Fourth fifth | 18 | −40 | 24 | 17 | 22 | 23 | 23 |
| Highest fifth | 52 | 226 | 41 | 61 | 51 | 49 | 45 |
| *Federal taxes, excluding payroll* | | | | | | | |
| Lowest fifth | 6 | . . . | . . . | 3 | 2 | 2 | 3 |
| Second fifth | 9 | . . . | 11 | 7 | 8 | 7 | 9 |
| Middle fifth | 15 | −80 | 11 | 10 | 14 | 14 | 16 |
| Fourth fifth | 18 | −40 | 25 | 16 | 21 | 21 | 22 |
| Highest fifth | 52 | 220 | 52 | 63 | 55 | 57 | 51 |
| *State and local taxes* | | | | | | | |
| Lowest fifth | 4 | 5 | 4 | 6 | 6 | 5 | 5 |
| Second fifth | 12 | 14 | 13 | 13 | 13 | 12 | 12 |
| Middle fifth | 17 | 18 | 21 | 17 | 18 | 17 | 17 |
| Fourth fifth | 21 | 24 | 25 | 23 | 23 | 23 | 23 |
| Highest fifth | 46 | 40 | 38 | 42 | 41 | 43 | 43 |
| *All taxes[c]* | | | | | | | |
| Lowest fifth | 5 | 5 | 4 | 3 | 4 | 4 | 4 |
| Second fifth | 11 | 14 | 12 | 8 | 11 | 10 | 11 |
| Middle fifth | 16 | 16 | 20 | 11 | 17 | 17 | 18 |
| Fourth fifth | 19 | 21 | 24 | 21 | 18 | 23 | 24 |
| Highest fifth | 49 | 50 | 40 | 54 | 50 | 47 | 45 |

*Source*: See Table 12.2.

  a. The least progressive incidence assumption is that of variant 3b. Pechman and Okner, *Who Bears the Tax Burden?* Tables 4–9, 4–10.

  b. Households ranked by adjusted family income.

  c. Includes payroll taxes.

reduced outlays, or both, leading to deepening class conflict and eventual collapse of the system.

History does not support this diagnosis. There is little evidence of a continuously rising public expenditure share to subsidise private firms through cost reduction, nor have expenses directed at appeasing social unrest continuously increased. The rising real income of most voters, rather than increasing immiserisation of the proleteriat, has been the dominant influence on the social climate. The facts do not support the hypothesis of fiscal collapse in a redistribution-oriented class struggle. If anything, the median voter rebellion indicates the opposite.

Second, under the *structural change* hypothesis, the root of the fiscal crisis lies in certain objective forces of change that require more output to be devoted to social goods to promote economic efficiency. These changes may be technological, as illustrated by the coming of the automobile and the resulting need for highways. Or they may be demographic, such as increased demand for education with rising population growth or for old age pensions as population growth declines. Finally, there may be structural changes in consumer demand with rising per capita income. The income-elasticity of demand for public services may exceed unity.

These forces singly and in combination may cause the budget share and taxes to increase, but higher taxes may distort incentives and reduce economic efficiency. The conflict may be resolved by limiting the size of the public sector or by reducing the weight of efficiency costs. Such costs in considerable part are an institutional phenomenon and may be modified also by institutional change. Distortions in investment and savings decisions, and to a smaller degree decisions between work and leisure, can be reduced by adopting other forms of economic organisation. Suppose that rising income and changing technology produce an increasing demand for social relative to private goods. An efficiency-oriented economist might then have to conclude that a change in economic organisation rather than interference with consumer preferences is the proper answer. A theory of capitalist breakdown might then be derived from neoclassical premises.

The thought is interesting, but the events of recent decades hardly support it. While the structural forces here noted will continue to influence the size of the budget, there are no compelling reasons that the ratio of public expenditure to GNP need rise. For example, declining needs for education may well offset rising needs for retirement pensions, and emission charges rather than expenditures may be used to deal with environmental issues.

A third source of fiscal crisis might emerge from a growing support for *egalitarianism*. But as voters support egalitarian policies through transfers and public services, rising taxes may once more undercut economic efficiency and may call for changes in economic organisation. Under a socialist system investment and savings decisions are transferred to the state.[12] Such a system avoids the unequalising effects of the distribution of private capital income and is less vulnerable to distorting effects on saving and investment incentives. This, I take it, is the meaning of Schumpeter's prognosis of social change, based on a 'widening circle of social sympathy'. But again, this does not seem to be where history is pointed. Rather, it appears that redistribution is a self-terminating activity. The egalitarian philosophy hits a median voter barrier, and future redistribution, for the time being at least, comes to a halt.

Finally, consider the *Santa Claus* hypothesis, which asserts that voters increasingly try to get public services for nothing. This deterioration of the democratic process could again lead to fiscal and economic crisis. But again, such a trend is improbable. For one thing, a learning process should set in, followed by remedial action. For another, the median taxpayer should call a halt. The budget reform of 1974 illustrates the point as does the sweep of Proposition 13-type measures.[13].

In all, the case for fiscal crisis is unconvincing. The Marxist diagnosis, though interesting, is not supported by economic and social history. The allocative roots of fiscal crisis, though conceivable, do not seem likely to expand in the foreseeable future. Nor does the egalitarian trend in social attitudes seem on the upturn, nor does fiscal irrationality go unchecked. Changes there will be, but as Mark Twain said of rumours that he had died, reports of the demise of the tax state are much exaggerated.

## NOTES

1. Schumpeter argues that the proceeds from public enterprises would not be a larger source of finance for public services than the taxation of private firms. This is an interesting observation but overlooks the fact that public and private enterprises differ in their need for 'investment incentives'. [20, 24]
2. See Marx's discussion of legislation to limit the length of the working day in [11, vol. 1, ch. 10, s.6].
3. O'Connor, [17], in particular p. 221. In a note [p. 11] I am cited as a prime example of a fiscal theorist who places excessive faith in the manipulative omnipotence of the state, while disregarding the social structure that determines actual behaviour. Having contributed to an early translation of Goldscheid and Schumpeter, I plead not guilty. Moreover, in my view, the state (while not omnipotent) can contribute to a resolution of social and economic problems, and the economist, through the conduct of normative analysis, can be helpful in this task.
4. While O'Connor does not talk explicitly about a *rising share*, I assume this to be the intent.
5. For an orthodox critique of Gough, see Fine and Harris, [4]. pp. 97–112.
6. For a recent discussion see Wagner and Weber [22, pp 59–68]. The authors find that the 'law' does not apply uniformly, but their conclusions are based on only about a 20-year period of observation. For a longer perspective see Musgrave and Musgrave, [15, ch. 6].
7. This conclusion is strengthened by a more detailed analysis allowing for the fact that the prices of public services have risen more rapidly than prices in the private sector so that the ratio of public services in real terms (using the respective deflators) has risen less rapidly than that in money terms.
8. This is not to deny that industry and consumer pressures have resulted in excessive highway expenditures, thus subsidising the providers and users of automotive services at the cost of taxpayers.
9. See Musgrave *et al.* [15, pp. 259–311]. While the transfer structure is clearly more pro-poor than the tax structure is anti-rich, it may be argued that equal provision of general public services bestows a greater benefit in money terms on high-income recipients, since they are willing to pay more. [1, pp. 907–20].
10. Economic theory in dealing with tax effects on investment has proven surprisingly fickle. A decade or two ago it was shown that taxation with loss offset need not reduce risk-taking and may increase it. Currently this feature has come to be totally disregarded in the design of investment functions, it being assumed as a matter of course that profit taxation will reduce investment.

11. For an early plea to consider the equity aspects of growth policy see Musgrave, [16].
12. It is hardly necessary to add in a paper of this sort that the final choice among economic systems involves more than considerations of economic efficiency and income distribution. Other aspects, such as effects on freedom, must also be allowed for.
13. Congressional Budget and Impoundment Control Act 1974, P.L. 93–344. Also see 'Leviathan Cometh—or Does He?' Ch. 13 below.

# REFERENCES

[1] Aaron, H. and McGuire, M. (1970), 'Public goods and income distribution', *Econometrica*, 38.
[2] Baran, P. and Sweezy, P. (1960), *Monopoly Capital: An Essay on the American Social Order*, (New York, Monthly Review Press), Ch. 6.
[3] Engels, F. (1884) 'The Origin of the Family, Private Property and the State' in Fener W.(ed) (1959) *Marx and Engels*, (New York, Doubleday), 392–94.
[4] Fine, B. and Harris, L. (1981), 'State expenditures in advanced capitalism', *New Left Review*, 98.
[5] Foley, D. (1978), 'State expenditures from a Marxist perspective', *Journal of Public Economics*, 9.
[6] Goldscheid, R. (1925), 'Staat, Offentlicher Haushalt und Gesellschaft' in *Handbuch der Finanzwissenschaft*, ed. Gerloff, W. and Meisel F. (Tübingen) p. 197. reprinted in Hickel, R(ed.), *Goldscheid/Schumpeter, Finanzkrise des Steuerstaates* (Frankfurt, Suhrkamp. For translation of excerpts, see Musgrave, R. and Peacock, A. (1958), *Classics in the Theory of Public Finance* (New York, Macmillan), p. 209.
[7] Gough, I. (1975), 'State expenditures in advanced capitalism', *New Left Review* 92.
[8] Marx, K (1850), 'The class struggle in France, 1848 to 1850' in *Marx and Engels, Basic Writings on Politics and Philosophy*, ed. Feuer, L. (New York, Anchor Books), p. 297.
[9] Marx, K. (1852), 'The Eighteenth Brumaire of Louis Bonaparte', in *Marx and Engels, Basic Writings*, pp. 331, 342.
[10] Marx, K. and Engels, F. (1848), *Manifesto of the Communist Party*, ibid., p. 28.
[11] Marx, K. (1867), *Capital*, vol. 3, (New York, International Publishers), chs. 28 and 29.
[12] Marx, K. (1875), *Critique of the Gotha Programme, Basic Writings, op.cet.*, pp. 104 114–120.
[13] Miliband, R. (1969), *The State in Capitalist Society* (London, Weidenfeld).
[14] Musgrave, R. and Musgrave, P. (1976), *Public Finance in Theory and Practice* (New York, McGraw-Hill), ch. 6.
[15] Musgrave, R., Case, K. and Leonard, H. (1974), 'The distribution of fiscal burdens and benefits', *Public Finance Quarterly*, 2.
[16] Musgrave, R. (1962), 'Growth with Equity', *American Economic Review*, 53.
[17] O'Connor, J. (1973), *The Fiscal Crisis of the State* (New York, St. Martin's Press).

[18] Poulantzas, N. (1973), *Political Power and Social Classes*, (London, New Left Books).

[19] Peacock, A. and Wiseman, J. (1961), *The Growth of Public Expenditures in the United Kingdom*, (Princeton, N. J., Princeton University Press).

[20] Schumpeter, J. (1918), 'The crisis of the tax state', *International Economic Papers* (1954); 4.

[21] Sultan, H. (1952), 'Finanzwissenschaft und Soziologie', in Gerloff, W. and Neumark, F. (eds), see [6] above.

[22] Wagner E. and Weber, W. (1977), 'Wagner's law, fiscal institutions and the growth of government', in *National Tax Journal*, 30.

[23] Weber, W. (1947), *From Max Weber: Essays in Fiscal Sociology*, ed. Gerth, H. and Mills, F (London, Kegan Paul).

[24] Wood, A. (1972), 'The Marxian Critique of Justice', *Philosophy and Public Affairs*, 1.

# 13 Leviathan Cometh—Or Does He?*
   1981

The events of the past decade have brought two striking changes in the intellectual climate. One is a remarkable rise of intellectual conservatism, ranging from those who consider themselves liberals—but hard-nosed liberals—to the minimal-state position of the libertarians. With its advocacy of free markets and capitalist institutions, this new breed challenges what Schumpeter [53] had described as the inherently left-based, anti-capitalist role of the intellectual in society. This change is parallelled by a disenchantment with public controls on the far left, leading to a shift in emphasis from centralised direction to decentralised if communal control. Both these developments, but especially the former, have left their mark on how the role of the public sector is viewed, be it in the press or the more learned journals of the public finance fraternity. Indeed, our fraternity has been a leading force in the process of change. Where the traditional theme since Pigou and then Keynes had been to show how governmental action must correct for market failure, the new thrust is to stress government failure and to view the public sector as an impediment to the market. Central to the new doctrine is the proposition that government has become too large and that constitutional constraints are needed, lest Leviathan (hence my subsequent reference to Leviathan theorists) will swallow the private sector and with it the remainder of our liberties.[1] What is the basis for this proposition?

## 'MARKET FAILURE' AND 'GOVERNMENT FAILURE'

By way of introduction, a word is needed about the implications of the terms 'market failure' and 'government failure'. Market failure may be interpreted to mean (1) that the market, as it actually functions, does not live up to the competitive norm (2) that failure may arise because even a perfectly competitive market cannot secure efficient resource allocation, due to decreasing costs, the presence of externalities, and the provision of social goods. Finally (3), the market cannot provide for what are consi-

---

* In Ladd, H. and Tideman, T. (eds) (1981) *Tax and Expenditure Limitations*. (Washington, D.C. The Urban Institute Press).

dered appropriate corrections in the distribution of income.[2] The latter failures, especially those of type (2), have been the concern of traditional public finance theory and call for remedy by non-market mechanisms.

Can we define a concept of government failure in the provision of social goods parallel to type (1) market failure in providing for private goods? Yes and no. Government may indeed perform below par, because decision-makers may disregard consumer (voter) preferences, taxes may be unduly burdensome, and public services may be delivered in a wasteful fashion. But absence of government failure is not defined as readily as it is for the market provision of private goods. In the latter case, we have the Pareto-efficient outcome achieved in perfectly competitive markets. In the former case we have the efficient solution provided by Samuelson's omniscient referee, such a referee does not exist. With the system of the market inoperative, a political process using a voting mechanism is needed to secure preference revelation. Depending on the institutional arrangements (e.g. voting rules and the role played by the executive and legislative branches of government) the outcome may differ by a smaller or larger margin from the efficient result, but it will hardly reach a Pareto-efficient solution. Notwithstanding interesting recent work in the analysis of voting processes,[3] policy performance will not be perfect. It follows that public sector failure should be defined as failure to reach the best feasible (if second-best) solution, rather than as falling short of truly optimal outcome.

Defining government failure is even more difficult if we consider the distribution function. Assuming that the desired state of distribution or social welfare function has been determined, absence of failure might be defined as efficient implementation of the required pattern of distribution. Since redistribution by lump-sum taxes (that most counterfactual and useless fiction of the economist's imagination) has no operational meaning, the condition of efficient implementation must be interpreted once more in terms of 'as efficiently as possible'.

Extended beyond voluntary giving, redistribution involves efficiency costs which must be considered; and as shown by the literature on optimal taxation, such allowance may be made with the standard tools of economic analysis. But determining the 'proper' target of redistribution policy is a different matter. Some will view entitlements to income or property as rooted in natural law (e.g., Locke and Nozick, who hold that one has the right to the fruits of one's own labour), others begin with the premise that entitlement is only to fairness (e.g., Rawls's choice under the veil of ignorance), and still others (Bentham and the utilitarians) postulate that society should maximise utility, average or total, whatever the resulting distribution. Given the multiplicity of possible rules, it is obvious that government failure in conducting distributional activity cannot be defined without specifying this underlying rule and the social welfare function which derives therefrom. Since the choice of distributive rule (or, one step back, the choice of rules by which to choose this rule) is controversial, we have no ready basis for determining what a 'perfect' government would do, and hence we cannot say in an objective sense whether budgetary redistribution is too large or too small.

## HOW BIG HAS THE BUDGET BECOME?

I now turn to some figures on the growth of the public sector, defined here in budgetary terms. Obviously, this growth cannot be measured meaningfully in absolute dollars but must be related to the expanding size of the economy. The changing ratio of expenditures to GNP, though a crude measure only, will serve the purpose of this brief survey. As shown in Table 13.1, the salient features of more recent developments may be summarised as follows:

1. To begin with, the overall ratio of total expenditures (all levels and types) to GNP rose by 5.6 percentage points during the fifties, 4.9 points during the sixties, and 1.6 points during the seventies. Taking a span from 1940 to 1978, the expenditure-to-GNP ratio rose from .18 to .32, or by 78 per cent. The rise was substantial but it has proceeded at a distinctly declining rate, and during the seventies it slowed down to only a trickle.
2. From 1940 to 1960, the growth in the expenditure-to-GNP ratio was accounted for very largely by national defence. Thereafter, defence declined relative to GNP with the entire expansion in the civilian ratio.
3. From 1940 to 1960 the ratio of federal expenditures (grants included) to GNP rose by 83 per cent, while the state–local ratio remained almost constant. Since then, the latter has risen slightly relative to the federal share, expressing the declining weight of defence and reversing an earlier tendency towards increased centralisation of civilian functions. If grants are included at the recipient's level, the increase in the state–local share is substantially larger. Viewed this way the ratio of federal expenditures to GNP falls from 17.3 per cent in 1960 to 16.8 per cent in 1978, while the state–local ratio rises from 14.6 to 15.7 per cent.
4. Government purchases of goods and services as per cent of GNP rose sharply during the fifties and moderately in the sixties but have declined since then. Almost the entire increase in the overall ratio during the sixties and seventies was thus accounted for by transfers.
5. If both purchases and GNP are expressed in 1972 dollars (adjusting thereby for the more rapid increase in the cost of public services) we find the ratio of purchases to GNP to have risen less rapidly. The move now is from 14 per cent in 1940 to 20 per cent in 1960 and 22 per cent in 1970. Since then, the adjusted ratio declined to 20 per cent in 1978. Considering civilian purchases only, the ratios were 16, 12, 13, 15, and 15 respectively. Both the adjusted purchase ratios now stand at about their pre-World War II level.

Summarising, the overall expenditure ratio rose substantially from 1940 to 1970, but only slightly since then. Both civilian and defence outlays shared in the growth, with civilian expansion largely in the transfer sector. Government purchases of goods and services since 1960 have expanded in line with GNP, not more; and if considered in real terms, the total purchase ratio has fallen and is now substantially below its 1960 level. In all, it appears that the growth of Leviathan, especially in the recent past, is in the eyes of the beholder. Much depends on which aspect is considered.

## PROBLEMS OF MEASUREMENT

There are some obvious and some not so obvious difficulties in measuring public sector growth in these terms.

### Treatment of Social Goods

If the growth of GNP is interpreted as an index of welfare (a rough one, to be sure), the change should be viewed in per capita terms. This is evident for a world of private goods only. If population doubles with output constant, GNP is unchanged while per capita GNP or income, and hence (by rough approximation) welfare, is cut by one half. But the situation is less evident in a world of social goods. If social goods are truly nonrival in consumption (as they are taken to be in textbooks), per capita welfare should be invariant to population growth. Holding the output of social goods constant while population rises, per capita welfare should remain unchanged so that total welfare (defined as per capita time numbers) rises But this is not allowed for in the customary view of GNP under which per capita income falls as population increases, with the entire GNP treated as if in the form of private goods. Does it follow that in a period of rising population (1) the growth of per capita GNP understates welfare growth, and (2) the changing ratio of government purchases to GNP understates the rising share of social goods entering into per capita output?

At closer consideration, this line of reasoning is questionable. The individual consumer should be expected to value his consumption of social goods at his tax price, not at the cost of social goods to the community as a whole. We may thus write GNP $= Q_P P_P + Q_s P_s^c$, where $Q_P$ and $Q$s, are the quantity of private and social goods, $P_p$ is the unit price of private goods and $P_s^c$, where $P_s^t$ is the average tax price of the social good and $N$ is the number of consumers, we also have gNP $= Q_p P_p + Q_s P_s^t N$. Similarly, per capita income equals not

$$\frac{Q_f P_p}{N} + Q_s P_s^c \text{ but } \frac{Q_p P_p}{N} + Q_s P_s^t = \frac{Q_p P_p}{N} + \frac{Q_s P_s^t N}{N} = \frac{\text{GNP}}{N}$$

which is the usual definition. Note, however, that this assumes social goods to be provided in line with consumer evaluation as reflected in the tax price.

### Should One Deflate?

Whether GNP growth is viewed as measuring output performance or as an index of welfare growth, it is necessary to correct for inflation.[5] This would have no effect on the ratio of government purchases to GNP if relative prices did not change, but since public purchases prices rise faster, the ratio

*Table 13.1 Budget trends*

|  | 1940 | 1950 | 1960 | 1970 | 1978 |
|---|---|---|---|---|---|
| *I. Public expenditures as per cent of GNP, current prices* | | | | | |
| 1. Total expenditures | 18.4 | 21.3 | 26.9 | 31.8 | 32.4 |
| 2. National defence | 2.2 | 4.9 | 8.8 | 7.5 | 4.7 |
| 3. Civilian | 16.2 | 16.4 | 18.1 | 24.3 | 27.7 |
| 4. Total expenditures | 18.4 | 21.3 | 26.9 | 31.8 | 32.4 |
| 5. Federal | 10.0 | 14.2 | 18.3 | 20.8 | 20.5 |
| 6. State and local | 8.4 | 7.1 | 8.6 | 11.0 | 9.9 |
| 7. Total expenditures | 18.4 | 21.3 | 26.9 | 31.8 | 32.4 |
| 8. Purchases | 14.2 | 13.4 | 19.8 | 22.3 | 20.6 |
| 9. Transfers | 4.2 | 7.9 | 7.1 | 9.5 | 11.8 |
| 10. Total purchases | 14.2 | 13.4 | 19.8 | 62.3 | 20.6 |
| 11. National defence | 2.2 | 4.9 | 8.8 | 7.5 | 4.7 |
| 12. Civilian | 12.0 | 8.5 | 11.0 | 14.8 | 15.9 |
| *II. Public expenditures as per cent of GNP, 1972 prices* | | | | | |
| 13. Total purchases | 19.0 | 18.3 | 23.5 | 23.2 | 19.9 |
| 14. National defence | 2.8 | 6.5 | 10.3 | 7.9 | 4.7 |
| 15. Civilian | 16.0 | 11.8 | 13.1 | 15.4 | 15.3 |
| *III. Public employment as per cent of total* | | | | | |
| 16. All levels | 13.1 | 13.3 | 15.6 | 17.6 | 18.0 |
| 17. Federal | 3.1 | 4.2 | 4.3 | 3.8 | 3.2 |
| 18. State and local | 10.0 | 9.1 | 11.3 | 13.8 | 14.8 |

*Source*: Economic Report of the President (January 1979), pp. 183, 187, 267.
Line 2:   Includes national defence purchases only.
Line 3:   Line 1 minus Line 2.
Line 6:   Federal grants included at federal level.
Line 9:   Includes interest.
Line 13: Ratio of government purchases at 1972 prices to GNP at 1972 prices.
Line 14: National defence expenditures are deflated by index for federal purchases.
Line 15: Line 13 minus Line 14.
Line 16: Government employment as a per cent of total wage and salary workers in
             non-agricultural establishments. *Economic Report of the President* (January 1979),
             p. 222.

of nominal expenditures to nominal GNP, shown in lines 1–12 of Table
13.1, rises more sharply than do the constant price ratios of lines 13–15.
Therefore, does the pattern of lines 1–12 overstate the growth in the public
share? Clearly, it overstates the increase in the input of physical units into

public relative to private uses. To express changes in the relative weight of such inputs, the adjusted ratios of lines 13–15 should be used. But such is not the case if focus is on the required increase in tax rates, where the increase in nominal rates is relevant. Assuming that the relative prices of social and of private goods reflect consumer preferences, it is the nominal ratios that matter. Similar considerations apply to the secular increase in the relative costs of public services as noted by Baumol[3]. Whether or not deflating is appropriate depends on just what type of change is to be observed.

## IS THE LEVEL OF PUBLIC SERVICES EXCESSIVE?

Even if a meaningful measure of 'share' is agreed on, a finding that the budget is too large (or too small) must be supported by explicit criteria for what size is 'proper'. Without this, we only have the protagonist's own value judgement. To examine such criteria, I make use of my familiar distinction between two objectives of budget policy, i.e. (1) the provision for public goods and services, and (2) the adjustment in the distribution of income [Musgrave, 36, ch. 1]. Of course, the two become intertwined in practice, since proportional taxes may be used to finance 'pro-poor' or 'pro-rich' services, just as progressive or regressive taxes may be used to finance proportional services. However, it is helpful to begin with this distinction.

As noted before, provision for public services may be said to be at its optimal level if a change in the output mix (public and private) cannot improve A's position without hurting B's. Given the previously noted difficulties of implementation, the level of provision is proper if this outcome is approximated as well as possible. Leviathan theorists, therefore, must demonstrate that there is a systematic bias which pushes the budget over its proper or efficient level. There now exists a large body of literature devoted to making this case, and it is growing steadily. Efforts at exploring the fiscal system 'as it really works' are all to the good and I shall welcome the development of a truly positive theory of fiscal behaviour. But I do not see it in the making. The theory of fiscal crisis which emerges from the Marxist literature has the merit of viewing the problem in terms of social structure and the interactions of groups, but it suffers from a too simplistic and one-dimensional (capital vs. labour) view of social conflict, as well as a total neglect of social cooperation [Musgrave, 38]. The theory of government failure which emerges from the Leviathan literature is not one of social structure but one that derives its conclusions (in the tradition of micro and game theory) from behavioural assumptions for the major actors (e.g. voters, officials and politicians) all of whom operate in set institutions. While claiming to offer a positive approach, this literature reflects the consequences (derived neatly and on occasion, gleefully) from a preconceived model of behaviour, designed so that it cannot but result in the demonstration of government failure. As we shall see, many of the arguments employed to show budget excess may, by a change of under-lying assumptions, also be used to predict deficient service levels. It thus remains for careful empirical work to test alternative hypotheses in order to establish the degree and direction of actual bias. While such testing may be difficult, it is essential if the models are to have scientific merit.[6] My purpose here is not to fill this gap but merely to examine the plausibility and implications of certain propositions drawn from the Leviathan model. In the process, reference will be made to important parts of this expanding literature, but my coverage must necessarily fall far short of completeness.[7]

## Voting Bias

The centrepiece of the argument is that majority rule involves an inherent bias towards excessive budget size. The initial presentation, given, I believe, in Tullock's seminal paper [62], examines two situations.[8] In the absence of vote-trading or log-rolling, a majority vote on the size of the budget (assuming well-behaved, single-peaked preferences) reflects the preference of the median voter. This outcome may be excessive or deficient, depending upon the relative intensity of preferences of those who would like more or less, i.e. as compared to the budget size which would result if side payments were permitted and no 'transaction costs' (I use quotes since I consider this to be an ambiguous term of many meanings) intervened in the *tâtonement* process. The agreed budget share will not be optimal, but no presumption on the direction of error can be established. But a presumption for excess arises, so Tullock argues, when log-rolling (in the sense of vote-trading only, but not side payments) is permitted.

Tullock addresses the case of public services (maintenance of access roads to a throughway) which are useful to some members of the community (farmers living on the particular road) but not to others. At the same time, all maintenance costs are distributed by a fixed tax formula (e.g. a head tax) among all farmers, and all repairs are decided upon by majority vote. Consider the case of five farmers, or groups of farmers, A to E, living on five access roads respectively. Farmers A, B and C will form a coalition to vote for maintenance of their roads up to a point where the cost to each (measured by *his* per capita share in the maintenance cost) equals the benefits which he derives from the repair of his own road. Since the two-fifths of the cost borne by D and E are not allowed for, maintenance of roads A, B and C is over-expanded. Similar and overlapping coalitions are formed among other groups (say, D, E and A), providing for repair of their respective access roads, and so forth. In each case the cost share borne by outsiders is neglected and over-expansion occurs. Each farmer, so Tullock argues, maximises his interest but the budget is over-expanded and the overall result is inefficient.[9]

The argument leaves me troubled in several respects. Even if one accepts the underlying modelling of the problem, Tullock's result need not emerge. If farmers A, B and C can coalesce to have their road adopted, so can D, E, F and G join to defeat it. The project may be rejected even at a reduced scale for which A, B and C would have been willing to pay the full cost. The reason is that the opponents must contribute even though to them the road is worthless. The outcome may thus be the rejection of projects which should have been adopted (as measured by the test of a hypothetical case of perfect side payments) as well as the adoption of projects which should have been rejected. To break the symmetry of the argument and to establish an over-expansion bias, it must be shown that the cost of organising a coalition is less relative to the gains for proponents than for opponents of the project. And this is by no means a foregone conclusion.

Next, I feel uneasy with the way in which the problem is formulated. Is it not strange to demonstrate the oversupply of public goods with a model which deals with public provision of what essentially are private goods? Take the extreme case where access to road A is of use to farmer A only, access road B to farmer B only, and so forth. In this situation, what rationale is there at all to provide for road maintenance through the political process? Provision should be left to the market, where quantities can be varied with the preferences of particular consumers. Or suppose that there are a large number of farmers on each road. In this case, what reason is there for submitting the residents of all roads to a central fisc rather than dividing it into 'local fiscs' in which each group of residents can deal with their own problems? The cause of failure thus arises from uniform budgetary provision of private goods, or from too centralised a provision of local social goods, but the fault is not inherent in the voting process as applied to the provision of social goods within the appropriate benefit area. If, on the other extreme, we assume that all roads are equally useful to all farmers, maintenance will be as desired by the median voter, and the outcome, as noted before, may err on either side of the proper level.

Finally, and most important, there is the assumption that cost shares are totally independent of benefit shares. Thereby, Wicksell's key requirement of simultaneous determination is rejected and the stage for public sector failure is set [Wicksell, 70; Musgrave and Peacock, 46]. Nor is there reason for so damning an assumption on empirical grounds. While specific expenditure decisions are made typically without immediate consideration of how the resulting tax cost is to be assigned, in the long run there surely emerges some relationship between how voters feel about their tax bill and about the benefits which they receive from public services. Farmer A, who values road maintenance more highly, will be willing to cooperate with B who values them less and to assume a larger share in total cost; politicians will consider the tax as well as the expenditure wishes of their voters, and so forth. The extent to which the political process is responsive to both sets of voter wishes will depend on legislative and executive institutions. As noted below, public officials who have control over what is to be voted on may limit the choice among tax expenditure bundles so as to keep voters from choosing a preferred solution [MacKay and Weaver, 33]. But this power is surely limited. Governments fall, administrations change, and voter satisfaction (or displeasure) with their tax expenditure packages remains a major determinant of the political process. While only a 51 per cent majority is needed for passage, most major tax and expenditure programmes command a larger support. Moreover, reforms may be undertaken, as shown below, to strengthen the process.

## Bureaucrats

I now turn to the role of the 'bureaucracy', that *bête noire* of the Leviathan syndrome. This role is obviously a key factor in the operation of the public sector and it is appropriate therefore to illustrate it in modelling government behaviour. The question is how?

Here, as in other contexts of social controversy, the choice of terminology is far from harmless. By referring to public officials as 'bureaucrats' and agency heads as 'bureau heads', the Leviathan literature appeals to current US usage in which 'bureaucracy'—as distinct from, say, 'civil service'—has come to be a pejorative term. But it need not be interpreted in that fashion. The classical formulation was given in Max Weber's treatment, where the role of bureaucracy is seen as conducting organisational behaviour (within government or out) in a rational fashion and performing assigned tasks in a strictly hierarchical order (Gerth and Mills, 24, p. 21]. The virtue of bureaucracy thus interpreted is efficient conduct in the performance of assigned tasks. The danger of bureaucracy is an excessive routinisation of life and loss of spontaneous or charismatic leadership and innovation. The Leviathan theorists, in disregard of this twofold connotation, go back to von Mises' dismal view of the bureaucrat as the tyrannical and uncontrolled agent of an all-powerful (Prussian if not Nazi) state [von Mises, 66]. In Niskanen's basic contribution, the official or 'bureau head', far from being the public's servant, becomes the monopolistic supplier of public services [Niskanen, 41; 42]. Acting in analogy to the profit-maximising firm in the private sector, he will do so because his personal interests, be they income or prestige, are linked thereto. For this purpose he will provide services at a level where total benefits equal total cost, this being the highest scale of output which the 'sponsor' may be expected to accept. This scale exceeds the level at which marginal benefits and costs become equal, thus resulting in over-supply. While qualified and extended in various ways by Niskanen and subsequent writers, such is the essential model of bureaucratic behaviour and the premise upon which the discussion proceeds.

Beginning with this characterisation of the 'bureau head', it seems to me mistaken to model his or her behaviour in so close an analogy to that of the profit-maximising business executive. To insist that profit-maximisation is the only mode of behaviour (the 'only game in town' as I have heard it put) extends the market calculus beyond its proper sphere. I have no quarrel, of course, with viewing bureau heads as maximisers, if this is taken merely to reflect purposeful (means and end-oriented) action. Rather, my point is that maximisation may involve targets other than personal economic gain and power (e.g. duty, respect of one's colleagues, realisation of what one considers to be a 'good society', and the satisfaction of having contributed thereto).[10] These motivations may go hand in hand with concern for personal gains (be they in income, power, prestige or security) but they may conflict as well. Libertarians who fail to see this should consult Adam Smith on the complexities of human nature.[11] Human motivation is too many-sided and complex to be captured by the caricature of bureau-grabbing officials which permeates the Leviathan literature.

This critique stands even though Niskanen and others recognise that 'bureau heads' may be nice people who believe in their bureau's function (this being why they are there), and thus their personal fortune and their view of the public interest happily coincide in calling for bureau expansion. In my view, this coincidence frequently does not apply. Responsible public policy requires awareness on the part of department heads (a term which I prefer) of competing needs within an overall budget constraint, and not simply exclusive concern with the function of a single department. My point is not that all 'bureau heads' act exclusively in the public interest but that such motivation plays too significant a part in the typical case to be erased from the model.

The crucial importance of this issue becomes apparent when we compare the roles of bureau and business heads in society. Whereas the profit-maximising behaviour of the businessman may claim social sanction through the (more or less perfect) operation of the invisible hand, bureau-maximising behaviour carries no such sanction. By its very nature the conduct of the bureau head—if performed in the social interest—must be based on an intent to pursue such interest. To deny the possibility of such conduct is to deny the very role of government as a beneficial force, and a governmental model based on such denial cannot but demonstrate the preconceived conclusion of performance failure.

Moreover, Niskanen's model, in my view, makes insufficient allowance for the constraints which the checks and balances of the executive system place on the individual bureau head. This system provides not only a check on efficiency in performance (cost-effectiveness analysis) but also calls for comparative evaluation of alternative projects within a budget constraint (marginal cost-benefit analysis). Operating in such a system, agency heads in search of promotion may well find it to their personal advantage to be efficient in service delivery and to recognise the need for comparative evaluation of alternative projects.[12] To be sure, this mechanism, even at its best, lacks the penalty of bankruptcy which *may* be (note Chrysler) the penalty of inefficiency in the private sector, and civil service rules may reduce the penalties for inefficient performance. Nevertheless, there are budget and examination procedures which play an important role in the executive structure, a role which, though not perfect, must be accounted for in a balanced view of governmental behaviour. The budget requisitions of particular departments serve as inputs into a budget-making process.

The department head, while pressing his particular function, operates in the context of an adversary process (see the budget preparation of OMB) and does not decide single-handedly on how much he should spend. Surely, this budgetary process—involving balancing between functions in the context of a budget constraint—must be given an important role in an unbiased model of governmental operations. In recent decades, the federal budget process has come to be essentially concentrated in what is now called the Office of Management and Budget. Department heads appear before Congress in defence of their programmes as incorporated into the executive budget, and not as advocates of their own decisions. The executive function on budgeting is crucial and I fail to understand why it is largely if not entirely disregarded in much of the Leviathan literature.

Nor can I buy the role of the sponsor or review committee as willing to accept the monopolists' service level (where total benefit equals total cost) without objection. If the sponsor is viewed as an imbecile, no such rationalisation is needed because anything will go. If he is granted the capacity of rational decision-making, why should this rule be appealing to him? Given a sponsor who is concerned only with his particular type of service, he may well wish to go further, since the opportunity cost of reducing other services will be a matter of indifference to him. Given a sponsor who is aware of the need for budgeting and willing to allow for such opportunity costs, the rule of equating total benefits with cost will be rejected as inefficient and marginal criteria will be applied. There may be some merit to Niskanen's hypothesis that review committees are composed of high demanders, but this is not necessarily so. Doves have been known to serve on committees dealing with appropriations to the armed services, legislators hostile to taxation choose to serve on tax committees, and so forth.

Finally, as in the executive branch, allowance must be made for the fact that the legislative budget process involves some degree of apportionment between functions (although not as effectively as it should). If committee A is staffed by high demanders, the same will be true for committee B with which A must compete in the context of an overall budget constraint. Moreover, legislators stand to gain by appeal for expenditure and tax reduction as well by the offer of increased service levels. All this makes for a complex process, the outcome of which (whether for over- or under-expansion) is by no means evident.[13]

## Agenda-Setting

The Niskanen model of bureaucratic behaviour, under which the bureau head is in the position of monopoly supplier, has been extended in the more recent literature to examine the consequences of situations where government is able to determine the agenda of issues on which voters are permitted to vote.[14] Various forms of monopoly practice in agenda-setting are considered. These may range from all-or-nothing offers of single services at fixed prices, to setting discriminatory tax prices to various groups of taxpayers, and to commodity bundling in the group of services that are offered. In posing the problem, it is assumed that the agenda will be set so as to maximise the service level and that the voting public has little if any control over the proposals on which it is permitted to vote. Once more the role of review committees is allowed for, but as in the Niskanen model, they are mostly taken to be dominated by high demanders. Once more, the model cannot but yield over-supply.

While the earlier presentations involved agenda setting by a single bureau [Romer and Rosenthal, 51] later work has come to allow for interaction among multiple bureaux, providing for different services [MacKay and Weaver, 33]. This has made for a richer analysis, since it helps to determine the composition of the total budget. Nevertheless, the composition thus determined remains different from that arrived at by a budgeting process which allocates funds among different services within a given budget constraint, or in a competitive model of costless agenda setting. Interesting and ingenious though these models are, my critique remains essentially similar to that of Niskanen's earlier version. Once more, I question the extreme behavioural assumption underlying budget-maximising agenda-setting, note the neglect of budget-making constraints among bureaux within the executive branch, and doubt that monopoly control over agenda-setting does in fact rest with the executive in general and (even less likely) with particular bureaux.

To be sure, the political process falls short of the perfectly competitive model, but Leviathan theorists, to my mind, undervalue the democratic mechanism by denying all responsiveness of officials and legislators to the agenda-setting wishes of the voters. Surely, elected officials will not be at the mercy of bureaucrats whose action means a loss of votes; surely, legislators must be aware that voters want a say on what is brought to a vote; and surely, voters may reject proposals which in their view result in excessive budgets. Deviations may occur for a while, but sooner or later the public gets what it wants and governments stand to win or lose with fiscal issues. I am not persuaded that monopoly bureaux are a potentially far more serious threat than are private monopolies [MacKay and Weaver, 33, pp. 142, 161] or, for that matter, that power over agenda setting is *the* critical defect in the fiscal process.

## Public Employee Voting

As a further cause of over-expansion, Leviathan theorists point to the voting behaviour of government employees [von Mises, 66; Tullock, 64; Bush and Denzau, 17; Borcherding *et al.*, 8]. The hypothesis is that public employees will be more inclined to support large budgets than are private employees. Thus, as public employment increases, so does the voting power of public employees, generating a snowball effect. As shown in a recent study, this hypothesis may be questioned or at least qualified, even on theoretical grounds [Courant *et al.*, 18]. After all, public employee demands are limited, at least at the local level, by out-migration of private employees, public wage rates for a given budget size must fall as the number of employees increases, and the size of the budget is constrained by voter control. Nevertheless, some such bias may be expected to exist. The question is how important a factor this has been in leading to budgetary expansion.

As shown in Table 13.1, lines 16–18, public employment now accounts for about 18 per cent of the total, with 3 per cent at the federal and 15 per cent at the state and local level. With employed voters accounting for about two-thirds of eligible voters, public employees may be taken to make up 12 per cent of the total.[15] This, however, is a lower limit, since retirees from public employment and members of public employee families need also be accounted for, pushing the public employee voting sector to an upper limit of 18 per cent. Their effective voting impact further depends on (1) their relative voting participation, and (2) the cohesiveness of their vote. Voting participation varies greatly among eligible voters and, although I am not aware of current statistics on voting participation by public as against private employees, one may expect a higher participation among the former.[16] With voting participation of, say, 50 per cent for voters as a whole, suppose that participation among public employees is 80 per cent (the percentage generally applicable to union members), leaving that of other groups at 44 per cent. Public employee votes would then account for 28 per cent of the total. If voting in a block and in favour of budget expansion, this is a sizeable group, which may have a substantial impact on election outcomes, especially at the ·municipal level. But the assumption of perfect block-voting overstates this weight. Employees with seniority may view potential hiring differently from new employees, and family members may not share the public sector bias. Strangely, little empirical work has been done on this interesting and eminently research-able hypothesis.[17]

To demonstrate public employee voting as a cause of public sector expansion in past years, it is not enough, however, to show that there exists such bias. It must also be shown that this is an expanding force. Attention should be given, therefore, to what has happened to the share of public employment over time. As shown in Table 13.1, the rising ratio of expenditures to GNP has in no way been matched by an increase in the ratio of public to total employment. Whereas the ratio of total expenditure to GNP rose by nearly 80 per cent from 1940 to 1978, the employment ratio rose by 46 per cent only. The share of federal expenditures paid as compensation to federal employees fell sharply. Since almost the entire increase in public employment occurred at the state–local level, it can offer no explanation for the rising federal expenditure ratio but runs well ahead of the rising state–local ratio.

**Tax Illusion**

The preceding argument has been that taxpayers are forced to pay for a larger public sector than they want to have. Next it is argued that over-expansion occurs because of fiscal illusion [Schmölders, 52; Downs, 21]. Taxpayers are taken to underestimate the full cost of public services and thus opt for too large a budget.

Taxpayers, so it is argued, fail to perceive their full burden because taxes are hidden in higher prices and lower incomes, or because the tax system is too complex to be understood.[18] I recognise this potential defect and have steadily favoured visible taxes as a precondition of efficient decision-making. I do not feel comfortable with the proposition frequently advanced on the liberal side that hidden taxes are desirable to offset a bias towards deficient budgets which results from imbalance in campaign contributions and other forces. Visibility is one of the main advantages of direct as against indirect taxes. Although withholding has reduced this advantage of income taxes, emphasis on direct taxation in our federal tax system ranks it highly in this respect. But once more there are two sides to the hypothesis. Tax illusion may also work the other way. Apart from visibility, many other factors such as frequency and lumpiness of payment also affect the degree of tax perception. Just as consumers are more aware of the prices of items which absorb a large part of their household budget than they are of items which are purchased in small units, so taxpayers feel more burdened by taxes which come in lumpy instalments as is frequently the case with the property tax. Moreover, the responsiveness to taxes depends on their perceived rather than actual incidence, and while the incidence of some taxes may not be perceived at all, that of others (e.g. the employer contribution to social security) may be perceived more than once. Moreover, people may well perceive declines in disposable income due to taxes as more burdensome than similar losses due to declines in earnings. It hurts more 'to lose what you have', than not 'to get what you don't have'.

However this may be, fiscal illusion is not limited to the tax side only. It is no less plausible to maintain that the benefits of public expenditures are undervalued. The acquisition of private goods which are purchased personally and carried home is evident, and their benefits as valued by the purchase price are highly visible. Publicly provided and jointly consumed goods are not thus personalised. Their benefits are more remote and taken for granted, much like sunshine, and hence may not be given an adequate evaluation.[19]

These potential sources of underestimation of benefits are conveniently disregarded in the Leviathan literature.[20] Instead, the expenditure side is dealt with as a critique of political advertising. Where Galbraith argued that private sector advertising leads to under-valuation of public services and deficient budgets [Galbraith, 23, p. 261], the Leviathan position holds that political advertising leads to overexpansion [Tuerck, 61]. While private advertising is taken to inform consumers, political advertising is said to support the state monopolist and to lead to overexpansion [Wagner, 69]. I find this position questionable. Surely political advertising is directed at urging tax reduction and budget-cutting as well as service expansion, and it would be interesting to investigate the comparative amounts spent in both directions. Moreover, it can hardly be doubted that outlays on advocacy of private services much exceed that spent on advocacy of the public sector. Once more, the Leviathan literature leaves one with an altogether one-sided impression.

Putting the tax and expenditure sides together I can see how various forms of fiscal illusion may distort the outcome but I see no *a priori* reason to expect a net bias towards overexpansion. Empirical analysis is needed to test one or the other proposition.

## Deficit Finance

A further aspect of fiscal illusion stressed in the Leviathan literature arises in the context of deficit finance.[21] Deficit finance of public services, by not calling for taxes, gives the impression that services may be obtained at zero cost and thus encourages over-expansion. There is merit to this argument and I have long been aware of a potential conflict between (1) the need for deficit finance to maintain high employment under depressed conditions, and (2) the desirability of maintaining fiscal discipline by assuring that consumers of public services are aware of the opportunity cost which is involved [Musgrave, 36, p. 38]. To be sure, the conflict may be avoided by relying on tax reduction rather than expenditure increase but, in practice, arguments for expansionary fiscal action are likely to make for programme expansion.

While granting the conflict, I do not think that deficit finance has in fact been *the* or even *a* major cause of US budget expansion. State and local budgets have been essentially in balance with regard to current outlays and even finance of capital expenditures is typically subject to public vote. The conflict between deficit finance and fiscal discipline is thus essentially a federal issue. The question is how much the option of deficit finance has in fact contributed to the increase in federal expenditures. Federal deficits during the 1960s and 1970s ranged from zero to 10 per cent of expenditures with an average of 8 per cent. The potential impact of these deficits on expenditure levels might be viewed in various ways:

1. Suppose expenditure determination operated under a rule permitting 8 per cent of total outlays to be covered by deficit, thus reducing the tax price by 8 per cent. Assuming unit price elasticity of demand for public services, tax-financed expenditures would be unchanged and, adding a matching rate of 8/92, total expenditures would be raised by 8.69 per cent. Taking the initial 1960 expenditure/GNP ratio of 26.9 per cent, this will explain an increase to 29.2 per cent only. This however would be a once-and-for-all increase and could not serve to explain a continuing rise in the expenditure to GNP ratio.
2. Suppose next that the deficit is charged against the marginal expenditure dollar, cutting its tax cost to zero. Assuming the size of deficit to be constant and fixed independent of expenditure level, the resulting expenditure increase would (in analogy to the effects of a lump sum grant) at most reach the size of deficit, i.e. 8 per cent of outlays.
3. A much larger effect on expenditure levels might result if deficit dollars can be created at will and charged against the marginal expenditure dollar, in which case an infinitely large budget level would come to be financed at next to zero tax cost, with the expenditure to GNP ratio approaching 100 per cent.

The latter pattern clearly did not apply, as the deficit to expenditure ratio showed no upward trend. Even during the second half of the 1970s the ratio did not exceed 10 per cent. It appears that 'cost-free' expenditure increases induced by way of deficit finance hardly exceeded the increase in deficit which in fact occurred. With an increase in deficit of about $40 billion from the early 1960s to the late 1970s, and an increase in expenditures of about $300 billion, this calculus suggests that at the most only slightly more than 10 per cent thereof may be imputed to the deficit effect.

But all this is a rather tenuous interpretation. Annual fiscal behaviour shows no evident relationship between expenditure increase and deficit, and it is difficult if not impossible to determine what parts of the annual expenditure changes are imputable to the availability of deficit finance. The reason of course is that changes in deficit do not only reflect discretionary changes in expenditure behaviour but also built-in changes in tax revenue. Indeed, the full employment budget was close to balance throughout the period, with fluctuations in deficit reflecting very largely built-in changes in revenue from their full employment level. Rising deficits due to built-in revenue losses, in fact, might be viewed as retarding expenditure expansion, given a congressional desire to avoid excessive deficit levels. Contrary to the Leviathan message, experience does not suggest that a massive breakdown of fiscal discipline, generated by the impact of Keynesian economics, has been a major cause of expenditure increase.

### Inflation

We have noted that depressed economic conditions calling for an expansionary fiscal policy may generate excess budgets. But once more, objective analysis calls for a further proposition. This is the no less plausible and more timely hypothesis that restrictive policy, called for under the inflationary conditions of the present setting, may depress the budget unduly.

Given a high rate of inflation and the popular if mistaken belief that inflation is to be blamed primarily on excessive public spending, there is strong pressure to fight inflation by curtailing the budget deficit.[22] This might be done by raising taxes but, as in the expansion case, there is likely to be major pressure for the expenditure cuts. Resulting cutbacks or the omission of expansion that would otherwise be undertaken might well exceed what would be called for as a matter of efficient budgeting if no compensatory action was needed, i.e. if resource allocation between social and private goods was in line with consumer preference at a non-inflationary full employment level of income. This is simply the mirror-image of over-spending under pressure for expansion. Given our inflationary age, the bias of stabilisation policy may well be the very opposite of that postulated by the Leviathan doctrine.

I would, however, add another and perhaps more important way in which inflation bears on fiscal discipline. This is through the effects on built-in revenue gains. Nominal increases in income under the progressive income tax generate an increase in effective tax rates at given levels of real income. Assuming the cost of public services to rise in line with the general price level, this permits expansion of public services without requiring the explicit sanction of legislative action to increase tax rates, a factor which may tend to generate a budget in excess of that resulting if such action was required. At the federal level, the tendency towards a built-in increase in the ratio of income tax revenue to personal income was largely offset by repeated legislative action for reducing rates and increasing exemptions or deductions [Pechman and Sunley, 48]. But even this does not entirely neutralise the problem. By gaining approval for tax reduction which in fact tends merely to offset the built-in increase, legislators may avoid pressures for genuine tax reduction or for expenditure cuts that may have resulted otherwise. Moreover, the offsetting tax reductions resulted in substantially shifting the distribution of the income tax burden (from both ends towards the middle) which most likely would not have received legislative approval had there been an explicit adjustment.

The offsetting federal action was not matched with regard to state income taxes, and sales tax revenue as well showed a surprisingly high income elasticity over the inflationary decade of the 1970s. Both these developments enabled the ratio of state expenditures to personal income to rise without matching legislative action to increase rates, permitting some states, such as California, to generate surpluses in state budgets. Much the same development occurred in some instances of local finance, where the property tax base rose faster than the price level. This was the case especially in California where the combination of rather current assessment practices and rapid rise in the value of residential housing resulted in a sharp increase in the ratio of property tax to homeowner's income, a development which goes far towards explaining the Proposition 13 climate and subsequent constitutional amendments.

## Conclusion

Having sketched the main lines along which Leviathan theorists advance the hypotheses of overexpansion, I conclude that there are indeed many reasons why one would expect budget decisions to be imperfect, but on balance no clear bias emerges which tells me that the budget is over- rather than under-expanded. As I see it, the voting bias can go in either direction. The conclusion of bureaucratic over-expansion largely follows from the behavioural assumptions of the model and from its disregard of the checks built into the budgetary process. Public employee voting may be a factor but little effort has been made to provide empirical support for the hypothesis. Fiscal illusion works in both directions, with an uncertain net effect. The bias introduced through deficit finance poses a problem in fiscal discipline, but it has hardly been a major factor in US budget growth. The need for inflationary constraint may well work in the opposite direction. The bias resulting from built-in revenue gains has been a factor at the state and local level, and so forth. In all, there is no simple *a priori* reason to conclude that the net effect of all these factors has been towards excessive expenditure growth.

My contention, to repeat, is not that budget levels are 'just right'. There may or may not have been over-expansion. Rather it is that Leviathan reasoning, although presented as positive theory, has been largely drawn from biased and untested models.[23] Little effort is made to view both sides of the hypotheses and important aspects are omitted, including the role of campaign contributions and of political pressures resulting from supplies of products purchased by government. More generally, the approach suffers from its exclusive reliance on a micro and game theoretical framework, disregarding thereby the broader aspects of social–political interaction which enter in the actual world of fiscal politics and into the shaping of fiscal institutions.[24] All this would not matter if it were simply a question of playing theoretical games. But having created the devil, Leviathan theorists must then proceed to exorcise him or her; and this, as shown in my concluding section, distorts the pattern of proposed fiscal reform.

## IS THE LEVEL OF TRANSFERS EXCESSIVE?

I now turn to the distribution function of budget policy. Since this has been given less emphasis in the Leviathan literature, I shall deal with it more briefly.

As shown in Table 13.1, rising transfers have been responsible for the entire growth in the budget to GNP ratio over the last two decades. While the overall ratio rose from 27 per cent in 1960 to 32 per cent in 1978, that for transfers rose from 7 to 12 per cent. Of this, nearly two-thirds was accounted for by social security and welfare, mostly the former, with the remainder reflecting interest, veterans benefits, and other items. Estimation of the resulting degree of redistribution is difficult, and this is not the place at which to consider the complexities involved. Much depends on how the problem is formulated, which groups are considered, and on whether changes in annual or lifetime incomes are to be determined.[25] However, some conclusions may be ventured. Clearly, the major redistributional impact results from the expenditure side of the budget since the overall tax structure is more or less proportional. Moreover, the major redistributive impact on the expenditure side stems from the transfer system. While low income-oriented service programmes have grown, benefits of many programmes accrue more heavily to middle- and upper-income groups. In all, it appears that the impact of fiscal redistribution on overall measures of inequality such as the Gini coefficient is quite modest, but that the fiscal factor becomes much more important if the share of the bottom decile or quintile is considered, over which range transfer rece are a multiple of earnings.

**Normative Aspects**

Beginning with a normative appraisal of this outcome, I distinguish between two issues. One is whether the implicit policy target 'correctly' reflects the norms of fairness or justice in distribution. The second is whether the policies chosen are efficient means of implementing the target.

As noted before, the usefulness of economic analysis in setting norms for the proper distribution and, hence, redistribution policy is limited. In determining what constitutes legitimate redistribution, various approaches may be taken:

1. The argument may begin with the premise that the given state of distribution is just, so mandatory redistribution is not permissible. This leaves open only a process of voluntary redistribution, where Mrs Rich gives to Mr Poor because she derives satisfaction from his improvement [Hochman and Rogers, 29].
2. The state of equality of inequality may be viewed as a social good, where A prefers a Gini coefficient of 0.5 whereas B prefers one of 0.3. Acting alone, neither can make a significant contribution to bringing about the desired change in the coefficient from its existing level of say, 0.4. The desired state of distribution thus becomes a social good, automatic provision of which is blocked by the freerider problem. Budgetary action and mandatory execution are required to secure the adjustment.[26]
3. Retaining the premise that the distribution of earnings (prior to budgetary adjustments) is just, the initial entitlement may nevertheless be considered subject to change by a voting rule (simple majority or otherwise) aimed at securing whatever state of distribution the majority desires.[27]
4. All these approaches take the existing state of distribution as points of departure—although (1) more absolutely than (2) and (3)—and hence allow for secondary redistribution only. Alternatively, it may be postulated that the given distribution has no basis in entitlements, thus calling for budgetary redistribution as the means of implementing an optimal pattern, be it 'fair' or welfare-maximising [Rawls, 49; Arrow, 2].

Approach (1) may be dealt with as a market problem, subject to the efficiency analysis of economics. No budget is required. Approach (2) requires budgetary action to implement what is essentially a social goods problem. Approach (3) similarly involves a budgetary process. Approach (4) finally poses the basic array of issues involved in establishing norms for a just distribution, be it on the basis of natural law, or some form of social contract. As noted before, this is a range of options among which economics offers no clear choice.

Setting aside the perplexities of determining legitimate redistribution objectives, critical examination *can* be applied to whether policies are in fact designed so as to accomplish the desired objective. For instance, the rural electrification programme which was voted half a century ago to assist small farmers may now go to support well-to-do owners of summer homes. Or, the policy objective may be valid but the policies used may be ineffective in achieving it, or do so at a higher than necessary efficiency cost. Here the economists' contribution becomes essential since cost-effectiveness analysis must be applied to redistributive policies as well as to the delivery of services. Redistribution policies should be designed so as to involve the least efficiency cost, as developed in optimal taxation theory.[28] Beyond this, economic analysis may be helpful in ascertaining the distributive implications of alternative approaches to policy objectives which in themselves are not distribution-oriented. An especially important illustration is given by policies to further economic growth. Much depends on how growth is achieved. While growth ultimately tends to benefit almost all groups, it also involves initial costs and it remains relevant (especially in the shorter run) to consider how these costs are shared. Since investment decisions tend to be made by high-income people, such policies tend to conflict with redistributional goals and little thought has been given to developing growth incentives in which distribution is neutral.[29]

## Positive Aspects

Turning from the normative to the positive side of the problem, it is difficult to ascertain to what extent the actual budget reflects each of the four categories set forth above. Surely, the voluntary giving approach (1) accounts for only a minor part. Treasury matching of charitable contributions at the taxpayers' marginal rate (a tax expenditure which does not appear in our expenditure to GNP ratio) is perhaps the major item, but most such transfers occur outside the budgetary framework. Items (2) to (4) are difficult to distinguish, even on a conceptual level. Moreover, voting on redistribution may reflect not only the implementation of adjustments as legitimated by some prior social contract or constitutional agreement, but also a Hobbesonian free-for-all in the grabbing of income shares. This need not be overt, but voting may reflect responses to the actual or perceived threats to the stability of the system, with potentially more drastic events forestalled if social pressures are appeased [O'Connor, 44].

May one expect redistribution to be of growing importance as the Leviathan framework would suggest? The dynamics of policy change will differ with our four cases. In line with (1), giving will proceed until the marginal gain to the donors matches their loss and then terminate. Under (2) and (3), which combine initial endowments with subsequent budgetary adjustment, the equilibrating process is more complex. Choice by voting in this case cannot be modelled in simple median voter terms, since voters with a median Gini preference may not also be voters with a median income. Moreover, views regarding the desired Gini coefficient (or, say, the desirable share to be received by the lowest quartile) change over time.

However, even here it appears that the redistribution process will proceed at a declining rate. Assume for the extreme case that everyone votes for such redistribution as leaves him or her in a better position. A vote in favour of complete levelling of incomes can carry a majority only as long as the median voter's income is below the average, a condition which in fact is met. But sequential votes in favour of successive levellings from the top down will command majorities only until the levelling reaches down to the median income.[30] The lower the median income relative to the mean, the more levelling will occur.

Tracing the path of redistribution, it may well be that successive redistribution measures (working from the top down) have lowered the level of income up to which voters may expect to gain from further such policies. As this level drops towards the median income, the majority available for further redistribution shrinks and finally disappears. This suggests an outlook rather different from that presented in the Leviathan prognosis. Note, however, that a distinction must be drawn between the median voter and the median income recipient, and allowance must be made for the fact that voting participation tends to increase with income. Future political development may bring about an increased voting participation at the lower end of the scale, a process which would lower the income of the median voter relative to average income, thereby increasing the scope for redistribution by majority vote.[31]

Given these possibilities it seems surprising that in fact so little redistribution has occurred. There are various reasons for this. For one thing, lower-income people may reject levelling as they expect to do better later—witness the fate of Senator McGovern's estate tax proposal in 1972. For another, they may allow for the effects of levelling on their own earnings and the earnings of others available for transfer, be it immediately through labour supply effects or via the longer-run responses through growth effects. Also, redistributive voting may be inhibited by respect for accepted ethics of entitlement to earnings.

A further deterrent to continuing redistribution results from the previously noted shift in political values from centralisation to decentralisation. While there is much to be said for neighbourhood concern in the context of voluntary giving, it is also apparent (although not evident to 'small is beautiful' romantics) that redistribution based on majority vote can function only on a nationwide scale. If concentrated locally, the very effort is aborted by low-income people pursuing those with high incomes, and the latter fleeing those with low incomes, i.e. the familiar urban–suburban patterns. Emphasis on decentralisation therefore provides a further barrier to continuing redistribution.

## Conclusion

In all, it is evident that both normative and positive modelling of budgetary redistribution is exceedingly difficult, but the analytical intractability of the problem is no reason for ruling it out of court. Some writers view consideration of distribution as slightly naughty, upsetting as it were an otherwise harmonious order, and involving jealousy or greed. This view is unacceptable on both normative and positive grounds. Distributive justice, as seen by most people, is not divinely preordained but depends on society's sense of entitlement and fairness; and adjudication of claims to shares in scarce 'goods' is at the heart of the social problem and not limited (as some seem to believe) to poverty settings. Distributional disputes rightly enter into the political process of a democratic society, and it is proper, indeed preferable, that they should find their expression in budgetary rather than other policy tools. There is no universal criterion which tells us that this or that degree of redistribution is too much but there is much to be said for choosing a democratically determined budget process (as distinct from, say, street riots) as the proper arena.

## FISCAL REFORM

There are plenty of reasons why fiscal policies, like other forms of human endeavour, may fall short of efficient performance. Constructive reforms are needed to improve the framework of decision-making. There can be no disagreement about this. Indeed, my early distinction between and separation of the 'three branches' (allocation, distribution, stabilisation) of fiscal action was directed precisely at this purpose [Musgrave, 36, ch. 1]. Where I disagree with the Leviathan theorists is on the content of reform. The objective of institutional adjustment, as I see it, should be to induce more efficient decision-making, be it towards expansion or contraction. It should not be to correct for an unproven hypothesis of over-expansion, or to implement value judgements in favour of small budgets. Moreover, the process of implementation should be by congressional procedure and not by constitutional limitation.

### Brakes on Leviathan

Reform proposals, advanced in the Leviathan literature, include various suggestions, most of which are based on the presumed need to correct for over-expansion. Suggested reforms, designed to restrain Leviathan, include:

1. Overall limitations on the size or rate of growth of the budget;
2. A requirement of two-thirds majority;
3. Increased use of executive veto;
4. Inter-bureau competition in the supply of public services;
5. Competition among review committees;
6. Reducing the monopoly power of agenda-setting;
7. Use of progressive rates of taxation;
8. Avoidance of broad-based taxes.

Among these, item 1 has received most attention, and economists, including Milton Friedman and William Niskanen, have been leaders in the movement. Various states have imposed tax or expenditure limitations, the limit being defined, in most cases, in relation to personal income in the jurisdiction. Similar proposals are being advanced at the federal level. In other instances, the permissible increase in expenditures is limited to the rise in the price level, so as to keep expenditures from rising in real terms. Such limits which fix the public sector share in income, to be sure, are less objectionable than would be the setting of absolute ceilings, but they still place an arbitrary shackle on the fiscal process.[32] Since upper limits tend to be transformed readily into floors, they in fact establish a constant share as a norm. Clearly, this is incompatible with an efficient budgetary system. The income elasticity of demand for public services need not be unity— changes in relative prices may affect the appropriate share, as will changing requirements due to altered demographic, international, and other conditions. All these factors suggest that the efficient expenditure ratio will not be constant, but will call for adjustment to changing conditions.

If it is assumed that simple majority rule leads to over-expansion of the budget, a requirement for a larger majority is, of course, a move in the right direction. If the hypothesis is mistaken, such a move would cause inefficiency.[33] Moreover, even if there is some presumption regarding the direction of error, it remains to be determined whether two-thirds (rather than 60 or 70 per cent) is the proper level. To be sure, budgeting by unanimous agreement would be ideal if there were no difficulty in securing the revelation of preferences. But since such difficulty exists, it in no way follows that increasing the required majority will improve the solution. If each voter were given a veto right, no provision for social goods would result and the efficiency loss to the economy would be enormous. In the absence of a more conclusive demonstration that a higher majority is called for, the proposition that all voters should be given equal weight, and the implicit sanction of simple majority rule, remain appealing.[34] At the same time it appears that adjustment in the required majority level (provided that it could be determined correctly) would be superior to the rigidities introduced by imposition of a ceiling.

The suggestion that increased use be made of executive veto on particular budget items falls outside the Leviathan framework as it emphasises the role of the executive. Nevertheless, it is a useful proposal, which has had broad support for some time. Given the right to such veto, the executive would be enabled to prevent passage of marginal legislation which cannot be checked if attached to essential bills.

Proposals to increase competition among bureaux are in logical response to the hypothesis of over-supply based on bureau monopoly [Niskanen, 42; Mackay, 33]. I find it difficult to visualise just how such competition would function. A multiplication of bureaucratic institutions (imagine, for instance, 10 Departments of Health, Education and Welfare) would seem to be needed and, contrary to consolidation, would add to the bureaucratic apparatus. Integration of bureau claims into an effective budgetary process, increased use of contracting with competing private firms for the delivery of public services, improved bidding procedures, and similar measures seem to me a better approach.

Proposals to facilitate broader participation in agenda-setting, similarly, follow from the hypothesis of agenda monopoly. While widening participation in agenda-setting is attractive, I doubt the overriding importance of agenda monopoly as a source of difficulty. Moreover, I would not like to see such a widening lead to large-scale use of public referenda. While attractive under the rubric of 'grassroots democracy', such procedures induce single-issue voting with its divisive consequences. As I see it, coalition-building, which can operate only in the framework of representative government, is an essential prerequisite for a functioning democracy. Needless to say, commodity bundling to maximise bureau output does not fulfil this same function.

A progressive distribution of tax burdens may be helpful in approximating a system of Lindahl pricing, given the assumption that income elasticities for demand are in excess of price elasticities, as they may well be. However, this argument applies to general social goods only and not to programmes whose benefits are addressed to particular income groups, and it certainly does not hold for transfer programmes. It has also been suggested that the revenue-raising ability of government should be curtailed by excluding part of the potential base from taxation (a recommendation in stunning conflict with the widely accepted notion that broad-based taxes are desirable) and that tax bases should be chosen so as to be complementary to the public service rendered. These latter suggestions spring from so extreme a drawing of the Leviathan monster as to permit exclusion from our consideration [Brennan and Buchanan, 9; 16].

## Alternative Reforms

As I see it, most of these reform proposals mirror the Leviathan image, thereby reflecting an unrealistic reading of the sources of government failure. In my view, reform should address the major needs, for (1) integration of tax and expenditure decisions, (2) integration of decision making so as to combine the components of the budget into a coherent overall programme, and (3) separation of programmes addressing the provision of public goods from others addressing objects of redistribution. I shall note briefly the rationale for these requirements, without however attempting to spell out the detailed institutional arrangements which would be needed to meet them.

The case for integrating tax and expenditure decision is evident. It is clearly impossible for voters to express preferences for programmes unless they know the cost, and preferences will differ depending on how the cost is divided. This is the essence of the Wicksellian message (and not the much emphasised concern with unanimity) which, notwithstanding some attention to earmarking, seems largely neglected in most of the Leviathan modelling of the problem (Buchanan, 12]. In some instances, linkage between the two blades of the scissors is provided, more or less effectively, as in the case of property taxes which specify assignments of revenue shares to particular programme areas. In others, a vague beginning is made, as in the new congressional budget process where the overall size of the budget is related (if only too loosely) to tax legislation, or in the executive budget proposals in which attention is paid to both the tax and expenditure side. There are beginnings, but clearly more need be done. The previously-noted relation of budgetary balance to fiscal discipline is also relevant in this context. The requirement to balance the budget makes sense as an instrument of fiscal discipline, were it not for the conflicting needs of stabilisation policy.[35] Nevertheless, it seems unfortunate that consideration of rules relating to full employment or marginal balance, which were in the centre of attention a decade or two ago, have now been replaced with the cruder techniques of overall expenditure and tax limitation.

Similarly, integration of partial programme decisions into an overall budgeting process is of central importance for achieving an efficient use of public resources. I find it distressing that this central requirement is given so little attention in the Leviathan literature, partly because the role of the executive is disregarded and partly because 'by its nature' government is assumed to be incapable of such constructive action. The budget reforms of 1974 again provide a step in the right direction but once more the task is far from complete. How much better it would be if all of us concerned with fiscal reform were to join in pushing this aspect, rather than advocating limits which stand to impair as much as improve the scope for efficient action. Of course, there can be no detailed and comprehensive review of all programmes each year, but even marginal adjustments are important, supplemented by a more detailed analysis of various parts of the budget on a rotating basis. Various plans for sunset legislation offer a useful approach, as does what appears to be a current shift in budget procedure from detailed analysis of each item to a more comprehensive if less detailed balancing of the merits of alternative programmes.

Separation of policies designed to provide for public services from others to achieve redistributive objectives, is, perhaps, a more controversial issue, but I continue to believe that it is of major importance [Musgrave, 36, ch. 1]. I recognise, of course, that public service programmes may have significant distributional objectives, so that the distribution function is not simply one of transfers. I also recognise that the efficiency cost of redistribution may, in some instances, be less if undertaken through services in kind than through transfers; and that equity considerations, in line with concepts of categorical equity, may indeed call for redistribution in kind [Tobin, 58; Okun, 45]. Yet I think that these are exceptions rather than the rule and that mixing of the two objectives greatly increases the difficulty of efficient political action. In principle, public services should be financed by benefit taxes (which may or may not be progressive depending on income and price elasticities), while redistribution should be implemented through a negative income tax. In theory this calls for two tax systems which, of course, may be integrated in practical administration.

## The Constitutional Issue
In concluding, I offer some comments on whether fiscal reforms should be made through legislative and executive measures, or whether they should be written into the constitution. Emphasis upon constitution-making and

the distinction between constitutional and postconstitutional action plays a major part in the Leviathan literature and should therefore be noted here [Buchanan, 13; Frey, 27].

The basic question is how to draw a dividing line between what does and what does not belong in a constitution. A first purpose of constitution-making is to protect basic rights and liberties, freedoms which are inviolate and cannot be tampered with. These include such matters as freedom of worship and protection against bodily harm. While there is no sharp dividing-line between 'basic' liberties and lesser goods, the case for a fiscal constitution can hardly be made on grounds that not having the expenditure to GNP ratio exceed 33.2 per cent, or not having marginal tax rates rise above 50 per cent are basic rights of this sort.[36] Surely, there are many other issues (e.g. abortion vs. right to life) which are more fundamental and would have prior claim to constitutional prescription. However, it must be admitted that the United States constitution, as an historically arrived-at instrument, is not limited to 'basic' provisions of this sort, and that the literature on constitutional law is painfully short of guidance as to what should or should not be included.[37]

A second case for constitution-making is to determine the rules by which other and lesser issues are to be decided. The generally accepted rule is majority vote with two-thirds required for certain exceptions only. The specific question then is whether fiscal matters belong to the group of issues for which a more demanding majority should be required by constitutional provision. To so conclude, one might argue that entitlements to the acquisition of income are inviolate except by abridgement through two-thirds majority and that, therefore, a special constitutionally guaranteed exception from the simple majority rule is called for. As noted before, I do not find this persuasive. If, instead, it is argued that fiscal issues need special constraints because (due to technical reasons, not applicable to other issues) majority rule gives biased results, it seems to me that the remedy for such a technical fault should be provided for in the more flexible framework of executive or legislative action. Moreover, there are serious difficulties in writing a provision for constitutional limitation so as to (1) maintain sufficient flexibility when exceptions are needed, (2) prevent circumvention by techniques such as tax expenditures, placing programmes outside the budget, or substitution of regulation for public services, and (3) retain sufficient clarity and simplicity to permit judicial interpretation of the constitutional content.

I do not wish to deny of course that the ongoing process of political decision-making has to proceed in the framework of a constitutional rule. It would be too cumbersome and destabilising to remain in permanent constitutional convention.[38] Yet, I find it difficult to conceive of constitution-making as a once-and-for-all, initial act by which basic rules are established for all future. The 'initial state' from which social choices are to be made is not to be viewed as a unique historical event long behind us, but remains present and choices are subject to re-examination. The role of constitution-making as a philosophical issue should thus be seen as a continuing task. Values may change and new issues may arise which will have to be met by new provisions. This does not deny the role of tradition and the wisdom of the founding fathers, but neither does it close the door for reassessment. I realise that this conception of constitution-making as a continuum runs into conflict with the fact that an historically determined constitution must set the rules for its own change, leaving the idea of constitutional process (which is needed for day-to-day operation) in conflict with the idea of continuum of the 'initial condition'. While I cannot resolve this problem (and, unhappily, find little guidance thereto) my instinct tells me to be wary of constitutional constraints which narrow options, especially where the proposed constraints (e.g. budget limitations) may be based on a misreading of the actual defects in the prevailing system.

## NOTES

1. The practice of borrowing the title of Thomas Hobbes' famous treatise [28] may be credited, I believe, to Buchanan [13, p. 147] and since then has been used widely by members of his school. In line with Webster's definition as that 'sea monster, often symbolising evil', the term is well suited to conjure up the dangers which are said to follow from fiscal expansion and the resulting emergence of an all-powerful state. But it would be wrong to claim Hobbes' support for the position taken by Leviathan theorists. The message of Hobbes' *Leviathan*, after all, was that a strong and indeed absolute state 'that mortal God' is needed to permit man to emerge from his natural state in which life 'is solitary, poor, nasty, brutish and short', so that he may enjoy the laws of nature, calling for 'justice, equity, modesty and mercy'. Though awesome in his power, the sovereign as seen by Hobbes was far from evil. This being the case, one wonders why Hobbes chose so ambiguous a title! [Hobbes, 28, pp. 107, 142].
2. Other types of 'market failure', bearing on maintenance of macro stability and the resulting function of stabilisation policy, are omitted from this discussion.
3. See Johansen [30], who argues that the difficulties of the freerider problem are largely overcome under representative government, and Tideman and Tullock [56] for a discussion of voting processes which render it in the voter's interest not to cheat.
4. An earlier increase in the ratio from 7.2 in 1902 to 10.4 in 1927 was almost entirely accounted for by civilian outlays.
5. Peacock and Wiseman [46] consider nominal ratios only, but real ratios have been used in the recent writings of Beck [4] and Durbin [22].
6. Tullock [64], in concluding his presentation of an over-expansion model based on government employee voting, concludes happily that, 'The hypothesis here presented may be difficult to test but this does not mean that it must be wrong'. True enough, but if so, it also means that the hypothesis is of little scientific interest.
7. The spirit of this body of literature is well captured in Borcherding (ed.) [6] and Niskanen [41]. See also the review by Amacher, Tollison and Willett [1]. As is the case with any body of lively literature, there may be many variants of the doctrine, ranging from its most extreme form (see for instance, Brennan

and Buchanan [10]) to more relaxed versions as in Borcherding's imaginative analysis of government growth (Borchering, 6).

 8. Tullock [62]. Thereafter the argument appears and reappears in many places, e.g. Buchanan and Tullock [15, ch. 7]; Buchanan [14, p. 155] and Riker [50].

 9. I here disregard the possibility, noted by Tullock, that all voters may behave as 'Kantians', and agree on the level of maintenance (for all roads) which is desired by the median voter.

10. Becker [5, p. 5] includes such objectives in the preference function upon which the 'economic approach' is based but requires stable preferences and choice through market processes as further characteristics. Since bureaucratic action to implement the public interest is not (or largely not) operative through market processes, an alternative (call it non-economic) mode of behaviour is required. There *is* a need for more than one game in town.

11. Not, of course, the *Wealth of Nations*, but the *Theory of Moral Sentiments* [54], which shows human motivation as highly multidimensional, with 'prudence' but one (and lesser) virtue. I am indebted also to Howard Margolis, whose interesting thoughts on a multidimensional model of motivation are in line with my own thoughts on the matter.

12. As noted by Margolis [34], careers are frequently made by bureau-hopping. Restraint in the conduct of one bureau may lead to a larger position in another.

13. Niskanen [41, ch. 14] in addition to the initial bilateral monopoly case noted above, also offers a more complex model in which action by the review committee becomes subject to acceptance by the legislature. This keeps the review committee (acting in cahoots with the monopoly bureau) from simply reflecting the preferences of the high demanders which it represents, since it cannot ask more than the median voter (in the entire population), and hence the legislature will accept. Thus the level cannot exceed that at which the gain to median voters becomes zero or (if reached earlier) that at which the gain to the high demanders is maximised. In both cases, optimal supply is exceeded. High demanders gain, low demanders lose, and the middle is indifferent.

As Niskanen notes [41, p. 139] the model still excludes the role of the executive, bargaining between the executive and the legislature, as well as bargaining within the legislature, over different issues. Each service is determined by itself, so the essential function of budgeting remains excluded, as is the formation of platforms and coalitions. These factors are of major importance in the real setting, as distinct from the simplified single-issue, median voter model which underlies Niskanen's analysis. Moreover, tax and expenditure decisions remain separated, in itself a defect sufficient to assure budget failure.

14. For a review of this literature, see Mackay and Weaver [33].

15. See *Statistical Abstract of the United States* (1978), p. 520, data for 1974.

16. Bush and Denzau [17] refer to a study by Rosco Martin reporting local public employee participation in local elections in Austin, held in 1933, at 87.6 per cent, as against an overall participation of 58.1 per cent.

17. The papers referred to above only hypothesise on the basis of Martin's 1933 ratio. Also see Greenstein [26] for voting participation of union members.

18. Goetz [25] expands the hypothesis but without empirical evidence, while Wagner [68] makes an attempt at empirical verification. In search of a positive relationship between the complexity of the tax structure and public sector size, Wagner relates city expenditures to (among other variables) a measure of tax concentration (i.e. lack of dispersion among revenue sources) and finds a significant negative relationship. The result is difficult to interpret, however,

since the reader is not given the characteristics of revenue composition which
go with the various degrees of concentration. For instance, if lack of concentration means heavy reliance on the property tax, as it probably does, the result
may simply indicate taxpayer dislike of the property tax as against alternative
revenue sources such as sales or income taxes. A more searching analysis of the
problem is called for.

19. Downs [21] argued precisely this point. Budget size will tend to be deficient
because expenditure benefits seem more remote whereas tax burdens are felt
directly.

20. Goetz [25] and Wagner [68] consider the tax side only.

21. See Buchanan and Wagner [16] for what seems to me a highly alarmist
presentation of the case.

22. I do not share the contention, so popular in an election year, that the federal
deficit has been the main cause of monetary expansion and thereby of inflation.
This contention (1) overlooks inflationary forces on the supply side, including
the dynamics of wage-price escalation and the rising cost of crude oil; (2) errs in
relating demand-side inflation to monetary expansion only; and (3) is mistaken
in viewing the expansion of the federal deficit as the prime cause of money
growth.

My immediate concern is with (3). Here the strategic variable in monetarist
analysis is the growth in high powered money or in the monetary base. What
has been the linkage between its growth and the federal deficit? During the
1960s, the deficit averaged $1.3 billion while the average annual increase in the
monetary base was $2.7 billion. For the first half of the 1970s, the deficit
averaged $14 billion while the average increase in the base was $6 billion. For
the second half of the 1970s the corresponding levels were $42 and $9 billion.
The lack of correspondence between deficit and growth of monetary base is
evident and should not be surprising. Changes in monetary base are a function
of federal reserve policy, mainly open-market operations. This policy is
adjusted to respond to changes in economic conditions, changes which involve
consumers, investors, the foreign sector and (but by no means only) federal
finance.

Following the same development from a somewhat different angle, it is
interesting to note the weight of US debt in the expansion of bank assets. In the
1960s, total loans and investments of commercial banks doubled while their
holdings of US debt declined. During the first half of the 1970s total holdings
rose by 70 per cent with less than 1 per cent thereof accounted for by US debt.
For the second half of the 1970s total holdings rose by 57 per cent with 10 per
cent thereof in US debt. Taking the 1970s as a whole, only 6 per cent of the
increase in total holdings took this form. This picture is qualified by extending
the analysis to savings and loan associations, but the essential finding remains
the same: the main source of expansion of bank assets, and with it of bank
credit, has been the deficit of the household sector, i.e. the issuance of private
debt in the form of consumer credit and mortgages, and not of US obligations.
By the same token, the expansion of the monetary base provided for (rightly or
wrongly) by federal reserve policy was directed very largely at accommodating
the supply of private and not of public debt.

Our focus has been on the relationship of the deficit to monetary expansion,
since this is usually taken to be the key factor in blaming inflation on the federal
budget. But, as was noted under (2), the monetary implications of the deficit
are not all that matters. The effects on aggregate demand of an 'active' deficit

caused by budget expansion will be quite different from those of a 'passive' deficit due to a shrinkage in the tax base, and so forth. There is more to the story than effects on money supply, but to complete the tale would transgress (if I have not already done so) the statutory limitations for the length of footnotes.

23. See, however, Borcherding's study [7]. Reviewing the expenditure growth from 1902 to 1970, Borcherding finds that about one half of the actual growth can be traced to price income and population changes leaving the other half to be accounted for by varying 'political' and presumably distorting forces. It is not possible here to review this analysis with the many assumptions which enter. However, it would seem at the least that separate treatment should be given to (1) defence and civilian outlays in the purchase total and (2) purchases and transfer components in the expenditure total. Nevertheless, this is an interesting and instructive study.

24. For a discussion of fiscal sociology, see Musgrave [38] and Ch. 12 above.

25. For a discussion of the problem, see Musgrave, Case and Leonard [39].

26. See Thurow [57]. Note that the conditional nature of the entitlement to pre-budget earnings is considered subject to amendment by vote only in the context of overall redistribution in which equal treatment is given to people with equal income, thus ruling out changes aimed at individual income recipients.

27. Such a scheme is described though not subscribed to by Buchanan [14].

28. Tullock [63; 65] and Browning [11] note the additional cost of lobbying for redistribution programmes.

29. For an early discussion of this now popular problem, see Musgrave [37].

30. This pattern disregards the possibility of discontinuous redistribution, e.g. transfers from the lower and upper end of the income scale towards the middle. For a discussion along these lines, see Niskanen [41; 42].

31. For a discussion of this point, see Meltzer [35]. It is also interesting to note that a similar argument already appears in de Tocqueville [59]. For a discussion of his view, see Peacock and Wiseman [47].

32. For an analysis of the effect of various types of limitations, see Ladd [31], and Courant and Rubinfeld [19].

33. Niskanen's attempted demonstration [42, p. 181] that a two-thirds rule would be more efficient is based on an ingenious but highly simplified model of the US fiscal system. All the reservations noted in my earlier pages again apply.

34. This concern seems to be shared by Niskanen, who urges prior attention to other measures.

35. I here pass over the distinction between current and capital outlays, and the argument that the latter (on grounds of intergeneration equity) should be debt-financed.

36. Nozick [43] argues in the context of his entitlement theory that taxation in general involves violation of the basic Lockean principle of entitlement. This makes sense if that principle is accepted. Yet, it can hardly be maintained that a rate of 51 per cent is in conflict with such entitlement while one of 50 per cent is not.

37. This includes even so recent and basic a work as that of Tribe [60].

38. For emphasis on institutional arrangements as a device to reduce transaction costs, see Mackay and Weaver [33].

# REFERENCES

[1] Amacher, R., Tollison, R. and Willett, T. (1975), 'A budget size in a democracy: a review of the arguments', *Public Finance Quarterly*, 3:99–120.

[2] Arrow, K. (1973), 'Some ordinalist–utilitarian notes on Rawls' theory of justice', *The Journal of Philosophy*, 70:245–64.

[3] Baumol, W. (1967), 'Macroeconomics of unbalanced growth, the anatomy of urban crisis', *American Economic Review*, 58:415–26.

[4] Beck, M. (1976), 'The expanding public sector: some contrary evidence', *National Tax Journal*, 29:15–22.

[5] Becker, G. [1976], *The Economic Approach to Human Behavior* (Chicago, Ill.: University of Chicago Press).

[6] Borcherding, T.E. (ed.) (1977a), *Budgets and Bureaucrats: The Sources of Public Sector Growth* (Durham, N.C.: Duke University Press).

[7] Borcherding, T. E. (1977b), 'One hundred years of public spending, 1870–1970', in *Budgets and Bureaucrats* [6].

[8] Borcherding, T., Bush, W. and Spann, R. (1977), 'The effects on public spending of the divisibility of public outputs in consumption, bureaucratic power and the size of tax sharing groups', in [6].

[9] Brennan, G. and Buchanan, J. (1977), 'Towards a constitution for Leviathan', Journal of Public Economics, 8:255–73.

[10] Brennan, G. and Buchanan, J. (1978), 'Tax instruments as constraints on the disposition of public revenues', Journal of Public Economics, 9:301–18.

[11] Browning, J. (1974), 'On the welfare cost of transfers', *Kyklos*, 27:374–77.

[12] Buchanan, J. (1963), 'The economics of earmarked taxes', *Journal of Political Economy*.

[13] Buchanan, J. (1974), *The Limits of Liberty* (Chicago, Ill.: University of Chicago Press).

[14] Buchanan, J. (1975), 'The political economy of franchise in the welfare state', in *Capitalism and Freedom: Problems and Prophets*, ed. A. Selden (Charlottesville, Va.: University of Virginia Press), pp. 52–77.

[15] Buchanan, J., and Tullock, G. (1962), *The Calculus of Consent* (Ann Arbor, Mich., University of Michigan Press).

[16] Buchanan, J., and Wagner, R. (1977), *Democracy in Deficit* (New York, N.Y., Academic Press).

[17] Bush, W. and Denzau, A. (1977), 'The voting behavior of bureaucrats and public sector growth', in [6].

[18] Courant, P., Gramlich, E. and Rubinfeld, D. (1979), 'Public employee market power and the level of government spending', *American Economic Review*, 69:806–17.

[19] Courant, P. and Rubinfeld, D. (1979), 'On the welfare effects of tax legislation', unpublished.

[20] Denzau, A., Mackay, R. and Weaver, C. (1979), 'Spending limitations, agenda control and voters' expectations', *National Tax Journal*, supplement 32:189–99.

[21] Downs, A. (1960), 'Why the government budget is too small in a democracy', *World Politics*, 13:541–63.

[22] Durbin, E. (1977), Comment, *National Tax Journal*, 30:97.

[23] Galbraith, K. (1956), *The Affluent Society* (Boston, Mass., Houghton Mifflin).

[24] Gerth, H., and Mills, C. (1970). *From Max Weber: Essays in Sociology* (New York, Oxford University Press).

[25] Goetz, C. (1974), 'Fiscal illusion in state and local finance', in [6].

[26] Greenstein, F. (1970), *The American Party System and the American People* (Englewood Cliffs, N.J., Prentice-Hall).

[27] Frey, B. (1979), 'Economic policy by constitutional constraint', *Kyklos*, 32:307–19.

[28] Hobbes, T. (1651), *Leviathan*, The Library of Liberal Arts, 1958 (Indianapolis, Ind., and New York, Bobbs-Merrill).

[29] Hochman, H. and Rogers, J. (1969), 'Pareto-optimal redistribution', *American Economic Review*, pp. 219–234.

[30] Johansen, L. (1978), 'The theory of public goods: misplaced emphasis?', *Journal of Public Economics*, 7:147–52.

[31] Ladd, H. (1978), 'An economic evaluation of state limitations on local taxing and spending powers', *National Tax Journal*, 31:1–13.

[32] Locke, J. (1690), *Two Treatises of Government*, ed. P. Laslett (Cambridge, Cambridge University Press).

[33] Mackay, R. and Weaver, C. (1978), 'Monopoly bureaux and fiscal outcomes: deductive models and implications for reform', in *Policy Analysis and Deductive Reasoning*, ed. G. Tullock and R. Wagner (Lexington, Mass., D.C. Heath).

[34] Margolis, J. (1975), Comment, *Journal of Law and Economics*, 51:645–59.

[35] Meltzer, A. and Richard, S. (1979), 'Taxes, votes and the distribution of income', unpublished.

[36] Musgrave, R.A. (1958), *The Theory of Public Finance* (New York, McGraw-Hill).

[37] Musgrave, R.A. (1963), 'Growth with equity', *American Economic Review*, Proceedings, 53:323–33.

[38] Musgrave, R.A. (1980), 'Theories of fiscal crisis', in *Essays on Tax Theory and Policy*, ed. H. Aaron and M. Boskin (Washington, D.C., The Brookings Institution).

[39] Musgrave, R.A., Case, K. and Leonard, H. (1974), 'The distribution of fiscal burdens and benefits', *Public Finance Quarterly*, 2:259–311.

[40] Musgrave, R.A. and Peacock, A. (1958). *Classics in the Theory of Public Finance* (London, Macmillan).

[41] Niskanen, W. (1971), *Bureaucracy and Representative Government* (Chicago, Ill.: Aldine).

[42] Niskanen, W. (1975), 'Bureaucrats and politicians', *The Journal of Law and Economics*, pp. 617–59.

[43] Nozick, R. (1974), *Anarchy, State and Utopia* (New York).

[44] O'Connor, J. (1973), *The Fiscal Crisis of the State* (New York, St Martins Press).

[45] Okun, A. (1975), *Equality and Efficiency* (Washington, D.C., The Brookings Institution).

[46] Peacock, A. and Wiseman, J. (1967), *The Growth of Public Expenditures in the United Kingdom* (Princeton, N.J., National Bureau of Economic Research).

[47] Peacock, A. and Wiseman, J. (1979), 'Approaches to the analysis of public expenditure growth', *Public Finance Quarterly*, 7:1–23.

[48] Pechman, J., and Sunley, E. (1977), 'Inflation adjustments for the federal income tax', in *Inflation and the Income Tax*, ed. H. Aaron (Washington, D.C., The Brookings Institution).

[49] Rawls, J. (1971), *A Theory of Justice* (Cambridge, Mass., Harvard University Press).

[50] Riker, W. (1978), 'The cause of public sector growth: resources and minority advantages', unpublished.

[51] Romer, T. and Rosenthal, H. (1978), 'Political resource allocation, controlled agenda, and the status quo', *Public Choice*, 33–4:27–45.

[52] Schmölders, G. (1960), *Das Irrationale in der öffentlichen Finanzwirtschaft: Problem der Finanz Psychologie* (Hamburg, Rowohlt).

[53] Schumpeter, J. (1942), *Capitalism, Socialism and Democracy* (New York, Harper).

[54] Smith, A. (1759), *The Theory of Moral Sentiments* (Indianapolis, Liberty Classics, 1976).

[55] Staff, R. (1978), 'Homo politicus and homo economicus: advertising and information', in *The Political Economy of Advertising*, ed. D. Tuerck (Washington, D.C., American Enterprise Institute for Policy Research).

[56] Tideman, N. and Tullock, G. (1976), 'A new and superior process for making social choices', *Journal of Political Economy*, 84:1145–61.

[57] Thurow, L. (1971), 'Distribution as a social good', *Quarterly Journal of Economics*, 85:327–36.

[58] Tobin, J. (1970), 'On limiting the domain of inequality', *Journal of Law and Economics*, 13:263–79.

[59] Tocqueville, A. de (1835), *Democracy in America*, tr. Henry Reeve (Oxford, World Classics, 1965).

[60] Tribe, L. (1978), *American Constitutional Law* (Mineola, N.Y., Foundation Press).

[61] Tuerck, D. (1978), 'Introduction: the theory of political advertising', in *The Political Economy of Advertising*, ed. D. Tuerck, (Washington, D.C., American Enterprise Institute for Policy Research).

[62] Tullock, G. (1959), 'Problems of majority voting', *Journal of Political Economy*, 67:571–80.

[63] Tullock, G. (1971), 'The cost of transfers', *Kyklos*, 24:629–41.

[64] Tullock, G. (1974a), 'Dynamic hypothesis on bureaucracy', *Public Choice*, 19:127–31.

[65] Tullock,G. (1974b), 'More on the welfare cost of transfers', *Kyklos*, 27:378–81.

[66] von Mises, L. (1944), *Bureaucracy* (New Haven, Conn., Yale University Press).

[67] Wagner, A. (1883), *Finanzwissenschaft*, part 1, 3rd edn. (Leipzig, C.F. Winter). For excerpts therefrom see 'Three extracts on public finance', in [40].

[68] Wagner, R. (1976), 'Revenue structure, fiscal illusion and budgetary choice', *Public Choice*, pp.45–61.

[69] Wagner, R. (1978), 'Advertising and the public economy: some preliminary ruminations', in *The Political Economy of Advertising*, ed. D. Tuerck.

[70] Wicksell, K. (1896), 'A new principle of just taxation', in [40].

# Part V
# Changing Perspectives

# 14    Classics in the Theory of Public Finance[*]
## 1958

Since the Great Depression the theory of public finance has been dominated by the study of the effects of fiscal policy upon the levels of income,
employment and prices. Indeed, the theory of compensatory finance
became the very core around which the new tools of macro theory were
developed. In more recent years, there has been renewed interest in the
classic question of when and where resources should be put to public rather
than private use, and who should bear the cost. The student of public
finance must obviously consider both problems, and it is a moot question as
to which is of greater practical importance, but at the same time, the classic
problem of public resource use remains the central issue in the theory of
public finance.

Beginning with the famous maxims of Adam Smith, writers on public
finance have attempted to establish criteria by which the revenue and
expenditure policies of the government *should* be evaluated; and some
have attempted to explain the principles by which revenue and expenditure
policies *are* in fact determined. Smith considers the type of services which
should be provided for through the public budget, prior to examining
taxation. His approach to the expenditure problem, though less restrictive
than usually assumed, is primarily an historical and institutional one. Some
attempts are made to determine why certain activities lend themselves to
private and others to public finance, but they remain inconclusive. On the
revenue side, a two-pronged approach is taken. Public services which
cannot be financed by fees or direct charges should be paid for by taxes,
allocated in such a way that the citizens contribute 'in proportion to their
respective abilities; that is in proportion to the revenue which they
respectively enjoy under the protection of the state. The expense of
government is like the expense of management to the joint tenants of a
great estate who are all obliged to contribute in proportion to their
respective interests in the estate' (*Wealth of Nations*, Book V, Chapter II).
Thus Smith ingeniously cuts across the ability to pay and the benefit
theories of taxation. In fact, the two are made to coincide, as income

[*] with Allan Peacock, Introduction to *Classics in the Theory of Public Finance* (1958), ed.
R.A. Musgrave and A. Peacock (London, Macmillan).

measures the one no less than the other. Thereafter, a distinct cleavage between the two approaches emerges.

## DISREGARD OF PUBLIC EXPENDITURES: THE ABILITY TO PAY APPROACH

Throughout most of the nineteenth century, writers in the English tradition mainly concentrated on the problem of defining 'ability to pay' more exactly. Viewing the problem of taxation as more or less independent of that of determining public expenditures, their concern was with translating the principle of ability to pay into an actual pattern of tax distribution.

As income came to be accepted widely as the index by which to measure ability to pay, the question became one of deciding whether taxation in accordance with ability to pay should require regressive, proportional, or progressive taxation in relation to income. Reformulated by J. S. Mill, the principle of 'taxation according to ability to pay' became that of 'taxation so as to inflict equal sacrifice'. Moving ahead of his time, Mill suggested that taxation which inflicts equal sacrifice will also lead to that distribution of the tax burden which minimises total sacrifice. Though technically incorrect (as Mill, we may assume, thought in terms of total rather than marginal sacrifice), this foreshadowed the later change in emphasis from an *equitable* distribution by equal sacrifice to an *efficient* distribution by least total sacrifice.

The development of marginal utility analysis in the last quarter of the nineteenth century brought a considerable refinement of the equal sacrifice doctrine. The equal absolute, equal proportional and equal marginal sacrifice concepts were distinguished; and the latter, looked upon as a means of least total sacrifice, was chosen by Edgeworth as the best solution. Proceeding on the assumption of declining marginal income utility, and of an identical utility schedule for all, this called for maximum progression. The principle of equal absolute sacrifice in turn would call for a progressive or regressive rate schedule, depending on whether the elasticity of the marginal income utility schedule fell short of or exceeded unity. It would be proportional for a schedule of unit elasticity as assumed by Bernoulli. Moreover, it was demonstrated by Cohen-Stuart that progression cannot be considered a necessary consequence of the principle of equal proportionate sacrifice, even though a declining marginal income utility schedule is assumed to apply.

Given the principle that the cost of public services should be allocated so as to cause least total sacrifice, it was but a brief step to the dictum that the distribution of income available for private use should be arranged so as to secure maximum total satisfaction. Provided that the expenditure side of the budget is determined independently of the tax side, there is little logic in limiting the sacrifice doctrine to the fraction of income required to sustain total services. Thus Edgeworth visualised the levelling of incomes as the ultimate consequence of the doctrine of equal marginal sacrifice, but he hastened to qualify this conclusion by adding that detrimental effects on output must be considered as well.

A related though different transition from ability to pay to distributional adjustment was made by Adolf Wagner. He proposed to divide the functions of taxation into the purely fiscal and the social welfare function. The former is to supply the means needed to pay for public services, and the required distribution of the tax bill is more or less proportional to income. The latter is to correct deficiencies in the prevailing state of distribution, and calls for a progressive system. This separation of issues, which appeared also in de Viti de Marco's distinction between the economic and political principles of taxation, will be re-encountered presently in the quite different setting of the Wicksellian system.

A final flowering of the least sacrifice doctrine, as it appeared in Pigou's work of the 1920s, added further refinement by including the burden of announcement effects, later referred to as excess burden, into the measure of sacrifice which is to be minimised. Nevertheless, the essential basis of the sacrifice doctrine remained unchanged: this is the assumption of a declining marginal income utility schedule, applicable to all taxpayers alike. Once the assumption of a uniform schedule is dropped, the possibility of drawing general conclusions regarding the proper degree of progression or regression is destroyed. And the subjective foundation of the approach is shattered, if it is argued with the 'new' welfare economics that interpersonal utility comparisons cannot be performed in a meaningful fashion. The 'scientific' foundation of the ability to pay being entirely removed, the institution of progressive taxation must seek its support from philosophical judgements about 'ideal' taxation.

However this may be, the ability to pay approach fell short of providing a full answer to the determination of budget policy, as it dealt with the tax side of the picture only. The determination of public expenditures, in the writings of the typical ability to pay theorist, was considered a 'political' matter, not to be included in economic analysis. Wagner explicitly shifted the determination of public expenditures from public finance to politics and general economics, and the continental texts in public finance tended to become treatises in taxation only. Indeed, it would be rather difficult to explain the support for the ability to pay principle (rather than the benefit approach with its emphasis on individual choice) offered by the Manchester economists, were it not that they assumed that the ideal level of government expenditure was the minimum necessary for the maintenance of law and order. Thus they join forces with the social reformers in support of the ability to pay doctrine, but to promote a very different cause.

Nevertheless, a transition to the expenditure side of the budget was provided by rewriting least total sacrifice in terms of maximum total welfare. The principle of distributing the tax bill so as to equate marginal sacrifices was supplemented by that of allocating expenditures so as to equate marginal benefits; and the formula was completed by determining the total tax expenditure level so as to equate the marginal sacrifice of taxes with the marginal benefit of public expenditures. This formulation, to be found in the later works on public finance of Pigou and Dalton, was foreshadowed earlier, if in less refined form, in Schäffle's law of 'proportionate' satisfaction of public and private wants.

No one can quarrel with the requirement that the budget plan should be designed to maximise welfare, but much needs to be added to give content to this formula. The fundamental question which remains unanswered is just how the benefits from public services are to be valued, and how this valuation depends upon the way in which the tax bill is distributed. Pending an answer to this question, the extension of the sacrifice doctrine to the expenditure side of the budget is a formality; and the ability to pay approach remains an at best incomplete (and, if interpersonal utility comparisons are rejected: subjectively meaningless) answer to the problem.

## SUBJECTIVE INTERPRETATION OF SOCIAL WANTS: THE BENEFIT APPROACH

The benefit strand of Smith's maxim found a more favourable climate among continental writers, notably the French reformers. Several variations of the benefit theory were propounded, and some of the main ones, including the use of the insurance analogy to explain the position of the state in the economy, were discussed in detail by Leroy-Beaulieu. While the link between the determination of expenditure and taxes remained, these writers almost all took it for granted that the sole purpose of government was to provide for defence and law and order, and no real attempt was made to derive the demand for public goods from the tastes and preferences of the beneficiaries.

Such at least was the case up to the closing decade of the nineteenth century. At that time, the theory of value was rephrased in terms of subjective utility, and much attention was paid to the nature of wants. Little wonder then that this new trend of thought should be extended to examine the wants satisfied by government. If expenditures in the market economy were designed to meet subjective wants of individual consumers, could not the same principle be applied to the wants satisfied by government, thus explaining the determination of tax and expenditure policies by the same laws of value which determine market price? Or if the same principle could not be applied, what alternative explanations could be offered, and how far would these imply modifying the laws of value?

These and similar questions were dealt with at length in the literature of the 1880s and 1890s, and Austrian, Italian, Scandinavian and German writers joined in the debate.[1] One of the first attempts at dealing with the determination of the tax expenditure plan as a problem of economic value appears in Pantaleoni's essay of 1883, followed by numerous other contributions, several of which are here included. In 1896 there appeared the important critique by Wicksell, which in a sense terminated this early part of the debate. However, interest in the problem continued, as evidenced in the subsequent contributions by Barone and Wieser. In 1919 there appeared the remarkable doctoral dissertation of Lindahl, written, like Wicksell's work, in German. In it the whole problem was once again reviewed and the voluntary exchange approach to public economy was restated in more rigorous form. There followed a restatement by Sax of his position and Lindahl's rejoinder to various criticisms of his earlier work.

No attempt will be made to discuss in detail each contribution here included, and even less to examine all those other writings which had to be omitted from this collection. However, some of the major issues and positions may be noted. Most important is the initial recognition that the revenue and expenditure sides of the budget are synchronous, and that the determination of both is part and parcel of the same problem. Such must be the case since, in the assumed setting of full employment, the public use of resources involves their diversion from private use. The public budget, so holds Pantaleoni, must be made part of the Walrasian system. This interdependence between the revenue and expenditure problem is the crux of the matter and explains the inherent superiority of the benefit over the ability to pay approach.

Beyond this, the central problem in the debate is the nature of the wants provided for through the budget—referred to variously as social, public or collective wants—and how they may be determined. The peculiar characteristic of these wants, so noted Mazzola at the outset, is their indivisibility. The same amount must be consumed by all. If a single price were set for public services, some consumers would find that this price exceeds the utility which they would derive from the service. Yet, such consumers could not be excluded from the benefit of public services. To avoid this dilemma, each consumer is called upon to pay a price corresponding to the marginal utility which he derives from the service. Thereby, consumer surplus is said to be eliminated in the pricing of public goods, and this is said to constitute the basic difference between public and private pricing. Assuming the satisfaction derived from the public services to be complementary to that derived from the satisfaction of individual wants, Mazzola concluded that total satisfaction is maximised if the consumer equates the marginal utility derived from his outlays, public and private.

While his was a highly subjective approach, Mazzola did not conclude that the prices of public services are in fact set through a market process. Following the earlier work of Pantaleoni, he held that the valuation of social wants is performed by the agencies of government, rather than by all individual members of the group. However, the agency must choose so as to suit their wishes. Equilibrium is disturbed if the budget plan reflects the views of particular interest groups, in which case adjustment is called for. Thus, we meet the idea that a political equilibrium prevails if an economic equilibrium of maximum satisfaction is established. This same thought—an extension, as it were, of the invisible hand into the political sphere—reappears in many subsequent writings, including Edgeworth's doctrine of equality in distribution as agreed upon by reasonable men and Wicksell's principle of approximate unanimity in the determination of the budget plan.

Writing at about the same time as Mazzola, Sax distinguished between collective needs of a sort which permit the determination of specific benefit shares, and others which are purely collective. It is the latter or collective needs proper which constitute the core of the problem. By understanding the community's need for such services, collective needs are identified with the needs of the individual. The level of taxation which the individual is willing to accept must be such as to exclude only private needs which are less important to him than the collective wants which remain unsatisfied. Thus equilibrium is again established in the budget of the individual taxpayer.

Beyond this, Sax held that the total tax bill must be distributed among various taxpayers so that the individual cost shares are subjectively equivalent; that is, each individual must pay what the services are worth to him. If this equivalence is assured, the individual taxpayer is willing to contribute his share of the cost of public services. By the very nature of the system, the level of budget expenditures must be determined together with the distribution of individual taxes.

Shorn of certain complications and confusing distinctions, the systems of Mazzola and Sax already contained the essentials of the later doctrine. Most important, there is the proposition that social wants are to be traced to the preferences of individuals. The distinction between social and private wants arises not so much because they are 'felt' differently, but because public services must be consumed in equal amounts by all, thus precluding single pricing. Since social wants are experienced by the individual, maximisation of satisfaction requires that a balance be established between the marginal gain which individuals derive from these two sets of wants. At the same time, it does not follow that the necessary scheme of multiple pricing can be established through the market. From the outset, we find some awareness that a political process is needed to attain this balance. This recognition is present in the work of Mazzola, and is given much emphasis by such writers as Pantaleoni, Montemartini, Wieser and Barone.

A development of this theme was at the core of Wicksell's contribution made in response to the works by Mazzola and Sax. Contrasting the principles of taxation according to interest and taxation according to ability to pay, he chooses the former as the proper approach. Not only does the benefit principle permit an integration of fiscal with general value theory, but it fits naturally into the modern concept of democratic and parliamentary society. Freedom of the individual is the essential characteristic of this society. Hence it would be unjust if anyone were forced to contribute to the cost of public activities which he does not consider in his interest.

This requirement is met in principle by the systems of Mazzola and Sax, according to which the fiscal equilibrium demands that each individual secure a proportionate satisfaction of his social and private wants. At the same time, Wicksell rejects this equilibrium rule as senseless. Each individual, if left to his own bidding, would choose to contribute nothing to the supply of public goods, simply because the total supply thereof would remain unaffected. The utility which the individual derives from public services does not depend on his own contribution but on that of others. The task of maximising satisfaction, accordingly, cannot be accomplished by the individual taxpayer, but must be solved in modern democratic society by consultation between voters. The crux of the problem then is how this consultation may be arranged so as to obtain maximum utility.

While there are issues on which public policy must be determined by simple majority, Wicksell argues that most matters of budget policy are not of this type. Specific public services should be voted upon in conjunction with specific cost distributions; and their adoption should be subject to the principle of voluntary consent and unanimity. Awed by the consequence of so stern a principle, Wicksell lowers his demand to one of 'approximate unanimity', and proceeds to consider what degrees of majority should be applied to various types of fiscal decisions. Throughout, his concern is to protect the voter who may be unwilling to surrender funds for public purposes.

The principle of approximate unanimity is found to be subject to certain exceptions. One of these relates to the problem of income distribution. Wicksell notes that justice in taxation presupposes justice in the distribution of income. The principle of the veto right of the minority rests on the same premise. At the same time, if the prevailing state of distribution is not just, a correction would hardly be possible if it were to depend on the consent of those who would be hurt thereby. However, Wicksell warns that the greatest care is required in this matter. While he characterises his period as one in which political power is still excessively concentrated in the upper income groups, he foresees the day when a shift in this power may lead to an excessive and harmful degree of redistribution. Thus Wagner's 'social welfare principle' of taxation is recognised as a matter of principle, but Wicksell would be more conservative in its use and is more fearful that it may be abused.

Whatever the desirable degree of redistribution, Wicksell took the important methodological step of separating the problem of just taxation into two parts. On the one side, there is the use of the tax instrument to establish a just state of distribution; on the other, there is the task of distributing the cost of public services in a way which is just in view of this corrected state of distribution.

The concluding and most complete formulation of the doctrine is to be found in the work of Erik Lindahl. Proceeding again from the assumption that a just state of distribution has been established, Lindahl determines the price of public services similar to price determination in the market. Drawing an analogy to the Marshallian case of joint products, the supply schedule of public services for any one taxpayer is a function of the cost of such services and the share of the cost which others are willing to assume for various total supplies. The equilibrium supply of public services and the allocation of its cost are determined by the intersection of such supply and demand schedules. The solution is said to meet the requirements of both the ability to pay and the benefit doctrines. The requirement of ability to pay is complied with because different taxpayers contribute different amounts, depending on their incomes; and that of taxation according to benefit received is met because each contributes an amount based on his personal evaluation of public services.

This is the ultimate answer to be derived from the groundwork laid by the systems of such earlier writers as Mazzola and Sax. It is the ultimate consequence of the benefit principle, or of any system which determines the satisfaction of public wants on the basis of individual preferences. Similarly, the solution is in line with Wicksell's principle of budget determination by unanimous decision. At the same time, the Lindahl solution has lost some of the realism of the earlier views and in particular Wicksell's. Though aware of the fact that the competitive mechanism of price determination may be disturbed by many factors of social and political reality, Lindahl nevertheless holds to what is essentially a voluntary exchange model. Thereby, sight is lost of—or better: emphasis is withdrawn from—the Wicksellian point that the individual, if left to his own devices, will contribute nothing to public services and that therefore the problem is essentially one of compulsion and political process.

It is this fact which in the more recent discussion has led to a distinction between two consequences, which result from the condition of equal consumption of public services.[2] First, and assuming preference patterns to be known, Pareto-efficient satisfaction of such wants involves conditions which differ from those applicable to the satisfaction of private wants. Therefore, the problem becomes basically one of social choice. This difficulty is not evident in Lindahl's system because the satisfaction of public wants is dealt with in a partial equilibrium setting. The second consequence of the condition of equal consumption is that the market as an auction mechanism fails to induce consumers to reveal their preferences with regard to social wants, because all will benefit, whether they pay or not. Hence, there arises the need for a political mechanism, to force or induce consumers into revealing their preferences. Both problems must be solved in the political process of decision-making, and it is here that the newer welfare economics enters the picture.


## SOCIAL MOTIVATION VS. SELF-INTEREST

The trend of thought dealt with in the preceding section firmly rests on the proposition that the valuation of both social and private wants originates with the individual members of the community, all of whom enter into the determination of the budget plan. In both cases we deal with wants subjectively experienced by individuals. Now it is generally held that individual choice in the satisfaction of private wants is based on self-interest rather than altruism; and the tenor of the preceding discussion suggests that much the same applies in the choice of social wants.

Some writers have held that this is incorrect, since the individual's action in matters of public policy is said to be guided by social motivation rather than by self-interest. Formally, this social motivation may be accounted for in deriving individual preference schedules for social wants, but such is considered a somewhat artificial and none too helpful construction. For these reasons, the preceding approach is rejected as too hedonistic.

Be this as it may, we are still left with the need of deriving the budget plan from individual preferences, however determined. Hence, these considerations may be considered a qualification of the preceding approach, rather than a basically different construction.

## COLLECTIVE WANTS AND GROUP NEEDS

A much sharper distinction arises with writers who hold that the public economy must be explained by a quite different set of principles than private economy. Social wants are not merely a set of individual wants, characterised by certain technical features of indivisibility, or minor differences in motivation. They do not originate in the *homo economicus*, but derive from the needs of the group as such. This Hegelian view is evident in much of the German literature, and finds forceful expression in the later work of Ritschl.

Ritschl holds that the basic principle of market economy is that of exchange and self-interest in the satisfaction of private wants; it is to be distinguished from the basic principle of public economy, which is one of social cohesion and the sense of belonging to and serving a community. To be sure, the public economy must economise in the sense of using its resources most efficiently, but beyond this it differs. The rule of *quid pro quo*, which is the crux of the benefit principle, cannot be applied. Nor can the solution given by ability to pay, which is concerned with justice between individuals. The basic principle is that of collective needs. These needs are felt subjectively by the competent public authorities, and by individuals in so far as they think as members of the community. The public economy thus rests on the sacrifice of its members. The individual feels as a member of the community; and where this is not the case, coercion forces him to act as if he felt in this fashion.

There is a clear difference between this approach and the doctrine of the preceding section, according to which the problem is basically one of satisfying individual wants. This difference exists whether it is held that collective wants are experienced by the group as a whole, and revealed in the action of the leader, or whether it is held that some elite (however determined) knows better what is good for the group than do the majority of voters. While the latter interpretation is more palatable to current thought, the essential difference between this and the preceding doctrine of democratic choice remains.

This difference is not one of logic, but of value judgement and social philosophy. Comparison between the various approaches thus emphasises the important fact that the theory of public economy or, for that matter, of any kind of welfare economics must be based on an initial set of value judgements; and that the role of technical considerations—such as that of equal consumption in the satisfaction of public wants—differs, depending on the underlying set of values and institutions to which the theory is to be adapted.

## HISTORICAL VIEWS

It remains to note a further approach to the nature of the public economy, an approach which does not proceed in normative but in historical and sociological terms.

This view is found in Wagner's approach to public expenditures, where prevailing public expenditures are taken to reflect the requirements of a given historical situation, and where changes therein are taken to reflect underlying changes in economic structure and development. Thus, he viewed the justification of public expenditures in terms of objective criteria, such as population growth or transportation needs, rather than in terms of a theory of value. His law of expanding state activity is derived in the same manner.

Stein similarly viewed the development of the fiscal structure in an historical context. As in the later analysis by Schumpeter, the development of taxation as the major source of revenue is related to the rise of the idea that the state should be looked upon as a free association of individuals. Thus the flowering of taxation in the nineteenth century is explained as a by-product of the development of constitutional society. At the same time, stress is laid on the difference in the time perspective applicable to the action of the state and of the individual. Since the life of the state is continuous, its primary concern must be with capital formation and with growth. Taxes, to be efficient, must not impair capital, and budget policy must aim at reproducing the wealth which it consumes.

A quite different framework of historical analysis may be found in Goldscheid. Writing at the close of the first world war, he seeks to explain the development of fiscal institutions in terms of the forces of class struggle. The feudal state, so he argues, was a wealthy state, because it was controlled by the ruling classes. As feudalism broken down and the people gained control over the state, it came to be in the interest of the propertied classes to render the state impotent. As a result, the state became impoverished. If the state is to be rendered a useful instrument in the hands of the people, the lost wealth must be restituted to the state, so that it can meet its welfare functions.

Whatever the validity of Goldscheid's analysis as a theory of fiscal history, his framework of fiscal sociology offers a new and challenging approach to fiscal theory. As distinct from the normative approach of the Mazzola–Lindahl, or even Wicksell variety, his problem is not to determine what would be efficient fiscal action. Rather, it is to develop a framework for explaining why certain fiscal action has occurred. Once developed, such a framework may serve for predicting what action will result under various conditions. Thus a beginning is made towards an econometrics of fiscal politics.

The preceding pages have not been designed to supply a history of thought on fiscal theory.[2] Our intention has been rather to provide a better understanding of the many dimensions inherent in the theory of the public economy by tracing the relationship between the various contributions and between these contributions and the development of economic thought.

## NOTES

1. Extensive discussions of the literature may be found in the works of Wicksell [7]; and Lindahl [1]. Moreover, see Seligman [6]; F.K. Mann [2]; and Myrdal [4, ch. 7].
2. See Samuelson [5], where primary concern is with the first difficulty; and Musgrave [3, chs. 4 and 6], where primary concern is with the second problem.

## REFERENCES

[1] Lindahl, E. (1919), *Die Gerechtigkeit in der Besteuerung* (Lund, Gleerupska).
[2] Mann, F.K. (1937), *Steuerpolitische Ideale, Vergleichende Studie zur Geschichte der Ökonomischen und Politischen Ideen und Ihres Wirkens in der öffentlichen Meinung 1600–1935 (Jena, Fischer)*.
*[3] Musgrave, R.A. (1958), The Theory of Public Finance (New York, McGraw-Hill), chs. 4 and 6.*
[4] Myrdal, G. (1954), *The Political Element in the Development of Economic Doctrine* (Cambridge, Mass., Harvard University Press).
[5] Samuelson, P.A. (1955), 'The pure theory of public expenditures', *Review of Economics and Statistics*, XXXII.
[6] Seligman, E.R. (1908), *Progressive Taxation in Theory and Practice*, 2nd edn, (New York, *American Economic Association Quarterly*).
*[7] Wicksell, K. (1896), Finanztheoretische Untersuchungen und das Steuerwesen Schwedens (Jena, Fischer).*

# 15   Maximin, Uncertainty and the Leisure Trade-Off*
## 1974

The magnificent edifice erected in Rawls' *A Theory of Justice* [10] has been of great interest to economists, partly because a major wing of the structure is assigned to economic issues, but mostly because an economic way of thinking enters into much of its grand design. The economist can feel pleased to see the use of his tools thus extended, but I wonder whether this penetration has not been carried too far. What is sauce for the goose may not be sauce for the gander. The following, therefore, is an economist's view drawn (without union card) from the philosopher's perspective.

## ROLE OF UNCERTAINTY

Next only to the primacy of liberty, the difference principle lays the foundation for Rawls' system of justice. Interpreted in terms of maximin, its application as a rule of optimal distribution has caught the fancy of economists in exploring its implications for redistribution policy. The underlying propositions, namely (1) that decisions in the original state should be made in ignorance of a person's future position, and (2) that choices are determined by risk preference, leave the economist in familiar territory. Given his aversion to interpersonal utility comparison and fascination with risk, a view of the social contract as optimisation under uncertainty offers an appealing approach to the design of a social welfare function.[2] My question is how such emphasis on risk fits into a philosopher's theory of justice.

To separate out the role of various conditions in arriving at maximin, we make three sets of distinctions, including (a) whether or not the risk-aversion of individuals in the original state is in fact total; (b) whether or not they know their earnings capacities; and (c) whether or not they may use such knowledge as they possess. In each case individuals participating in the decision process will vote their self-interest in determining what the state of distribution shall be.[3] The various possibilities and outcomes may then be tabulated as shown in Table 15.1.

---

* *Quarterly Journal of Economics*, vol. LXXXXVIII (1974).

Table 15.1

| Risk aversion | | Earnings capacities | | |
|---|---|---|---|---|
| | | Unknown | Known and unequal | |
| | | | Act as if unknown | Act as if known |
| Infinite | | (1) | (4) | |
| Less | Act accordingly | (2) | (5) | (7) |
| than | Act as if infinite | (3) | (6) | |
| infinite | | | | |

Case (1) supposes that differential capacities are unknown and that risk-aversion is infinite. The Rawlsian rule of maximin is then arrived at by utility maximisation under uncertainty. This outcome is found to be just because it meets moral axioms such as equal worth of individuals and self-esteem and because it translates the accidental fortunes of unequal earnings capacities into a social asset. But given the assumptions of ignorance and infinite risk-aversion, this solution is arrived at without any tension between self-interest narrowly defined and justice. It becomes the outcome of natural harmony. Though still a beautiful thought, this seems hardly the foundation of a contemporary theory of justice, applicable to a world that is above all characterised by conflict.

Now it might be argued that such tension need not prevail in the original position. It might 'precede' this position, with the acceptance of equal worth made a precondition for participation [Dworkin, 4]; or, it might 'follow' when the individual comes to be confronted with the choice between obeying or circumventing the constitution as laid down in that position. Either solution, it seems to me, unduly narrows and sterilises the original position process. The former simply moves the essential problem to an earlier stage. The latter, which is more in Rawls' spirit, seems to rest on too sharp a distinction between constitution making and its application. While it makes sense, as a matter of economy, to avoid reconstructing the social order every time that a trivial decision is made and hence to render such decisions in a constitutional framework, constitutions can be amended, and the process of constitution-making (as, indeed, the original position) becomes a more or less continuing process.

All this was based on the assumption that risk-aversion is indeed infinite. This, however, is unlikely. Even though the stakes are great, people may well wish to trade a reduction in the assured floor against the provision of larger gains. But if risk-aversion is less than infinite, the outcome will not be maximin. A lesser degree of equality will result (case (2)), depending on the spread of risk preferences and on bargaining skills. The outcome will thereby lose its appeal of conforming to the broader axioms of justice that Rawls requires. To derive the maximin result under such conditions, it might be argued that individuals in the original state should act as if their risk aversion was infinite. The result (case (3)) will then be the same as under (1), and our previous concern regarding absence of tension no longer applies. This construction, however, would be rather forced. Since there is no intrinsic good in infinite risk-aversion, the requirement to act as if it applied would be sanctioned only by the result of maximin. It would be simpler therefore, to require directly that maximin be accepted in the initial position, based on the axioms of equal worth and self-esteem from which it derives its sanction. In this case the procedure of optimising under uncertainty becomes redundant, and the solution (case (8)) falls outside the preceding matrix.

Leaving the shape of risk-preference, we now turn to the veil of ignorance. So far we have assumed that this veil does in fact apply, i.e. that people in the original position do not know their capacities and future potential. But this is an unlikely assumption, especially if we think of the state of nature not as an initial historical event, but (as Rawls would have us) as a *Gedankenexperiment* to be made by people who already occupy a real-world position. If instead we postulate that differential earnings capacities are in fact known, we are left with two possibilities. One is to permit self-interested action (case (7)), leading to a result that depends on differentials in earnings capacity and on bargaining skills. Again, varying degrees of inequality might emerge, which may or may not conform with the maxims of a good society and which may or may not carry a moral sanction.[4]

Another possibility would be to adopt the axiom that people in the original state should act 'as if' their earnings capacities were unknown to them. As distinct from a requirement to act as if risk-aversion was infinite (case (3)), this requirement has a meaningful axiomatic foundation. To overlook one's earnings capacity is to act without self-interest. Provided that risk-aversion is in fact infinite (case (4)), maximin is arrived at and in a more meaningful fashion than in case (1), since the element of tension is introduced by acceptance of the veil of ignorance. Note, however, that the maximin solution works only if risk-aversion is in fact infinite. Since this is a forced assumption, we are pushed to case (5), where maximin does not follow or to case (6), which is open to the objections raised previously against case (3).

We are thus left with the conclusion that the veil of ignorance hypothesis—though appealing if accepted while abilities are known—is not enough to carry the day. Maximin follows only if combined with an 'as if' acceptance of infinite risk-aversion. Since this is an artificial formulation, we again conclude that maximin (and its acceptance in the original state) should be deduced directly from the more general axioms (such as equal worth, self-esteem, stability and harmony) already contained in Rawls' system, rather than be derived from a model of optimising under uncertainty. The uncertainty model, if such an exercise is to be retained, then changes its nature. Maximin becomes the predetermined variable in the system, and the role of the model is merely to find the pattern of risk-preference under which maximin (or some other justice norm) would follow from optimisation under uncertainty. In short, the veil of ignorance hypothesis is attractive as a device for securing a disinterested view of the good society, but the formulation of justice as a problem of optimising behaviour under uncertainty, while fun and games for the economist, does not solve the essential issue.

## THE LEISURE TRADE-OFF

Economists in dealing with the issue of redistribution have been aware of the interaction between (1) how the pie is to be sliced and (2) its size. Writers such as Edgeworth, Sidgwick and Pigou concluded in the utilitarian tradition that maximum welfare would call for an equal distribution of a given pie, provided that equal income utility schedules could be applied to all individuals. But they hastened to temper this conclusion by noting that excessive redistribution might reduce the level of income available for this purpose. Thus, maximum welfare would call for some degree of inequality. This problem of trade-off being the very kind of issue that the tools of economic analysis were designed to explore, the economist's contribution to the justice problem is evident, as is their affinity for Rawls' difference principle, which deals with precisely this issue. Whereas the utilitarian principle of maximum total or average welfare can be applied even in the absence of such a trade-off, the maximin rule is squarely based on this contingency.

While a person's welfare depends on his consumption of both goods and leisure, the nature of things is such that redistribution can be expedited through the transfer of goods or income only.[5] But though there can be no redistribution of leisure, the party subject to an income tax may substitute leisure for goods (or income). As a result, redistribution of income via an income tax under maximin must cease at the point (or inequality be permitted to exist up to the point) beyond which there would be no further gain to the individuals at the bottom of the scale. Income tax rates imposed on high-income recipients must not be carried beyond this threshold.[6] The maximin rule, by focusing on this contingency, renders the formulation of redistribution more realistic, but again I wonder whether it should be assigned so strategic a role in a theory of justice.

My question to the philosopher is whether maximin as the requirement of fairness should be defined narrowly so as to (1) permit individuals with higher earnings ability to undertake defensive leisure–good substitutions, or more broadly so as (2) to require them to surrender part of their potential welfare?[7] In case (1) individuals at the lower end of the scale will be left with a lower level of welfare than in case (2). As a pragmatic matter it is of course much easier to implement (1) than (2), but Rawls' just society, as set in the original condition, is not a prescription for how benevolent dictators should deal with their malevolent subjects.[8] Rather it is to lay down a moral principle, based on voluntary consent. This being the case, should not the rule of fairness be extended to the more demanding second interpretation?

Since a person's welfare is a function of both his goods and leisure, the equalisation rule should include both components. But if this view is taken in the original position, the trade-off problem loses its sting. Goods–leisure preferences remain accounted for, but the trade-off ceases to pose a barrier to equalisation. Although the tax subsidy adjustment is still in terms of income as the vehicle of transfer, the adjustment is made not by income tax but in lump-sum fashion, so that there is no substitution effect. The very feature from which maximin derives, i.e. the practice of defensive leisure substitution and the resulting concept of excess burden, is thus removed. While I have always thought that the concept of lump-sum taxes and transfers is of little use in considering the practical problem of distributional adjustment, a solution that may be described in such terms seems appropriate to the philosopher's construct of original position.[9]

Moreover, implementation of the maximin rule under defensive leisure substitution is troublesome not only with regard to vertical equity but also in horizontal terms. While this aspect has been generally neglected in economic models of maximin by postulating identical utility functions (risk–leisure preferences) for all individuals, differences exist, and problems of horizontal equity arise. Implementation of maximin thus leads to a redistributive system that, among individuals with equal earnings ability, favours those with a high preference for leisure. It is to the advantage of recluses, saints and (non-consulting) scholars who earn but little and hence will not have to contribute greatly to redistribution. Assuming that they have a substantial unused earnings capacity, it would seem reasonable, from the point of view of fairness, to require them to allocate more of their time to income-earning activities in order to contribute more to redistribution.

The question remains, however, whether this would not interfere unduly with liberty. Rawls seems to suggest that such is the case. Society, so he argues, is not entitled to compel those with greater talents to work for the less favoured. This would involve too great an infringement of liberty. Society can only say 'that the better endowed may enjoy their position only in terms that help others' [Rawls, 11, p. 145]. But much depends on how the term 'enjoy their position' is interpreted. If it is taken to include consumption of goods only, Rawls' caution is needed, lest the talented be asked to work 24 hours, while transferring most of their income to the less talented who enjoy leisure. But if enjoyment is interpreted to include both goods and leisure, this contingency does not arise. The taxpayer's loss of leisure due to more work reduces his welfare just as the transfer recipient's gain of leisure raises it, thus narrowing the remaining need for income transfer. While the high-ability person gives up both goods and leisure, this is merely the outcome of his free choice between them, made in response to the lump-sum tax. It is difficult to see why there should be a more severe infringement of his liberty if participation in equalisation is based on both goods and leisure potentials than if it is based on goods only. The prior concern for leisure, it appears, is not needed in the context of a just solution, although it is appropriate if relative positions are viewed in terms of goods only. This may be the best one can do in practice, but not for a theory of justice. Here it leaves the maximin rule and the income tax mechanism of implementation a second-best solution only.

## NOTES

1. I am aware that Rawls means the application of the maximin principle to be more general than to the distribution of goods only. The present note, however, is limited to this aspect, without claiming that its reasoning would apply to other objects of choice, e.g. choice of religion. For economic applications of the model see Phelps, [9]; and Cooter and Helpman [3].
2. For what appears to be the first formulation of this proposition, see Harsanyi [6]; also Harsanyi [7]. A similar formulation was used by Vickrey [12].
3. The implicit assumption throughout is that differential abilities will be translated into corresponding income differentials by application of some factor pricing rule, e.g. compensation in line with marginal productivity.
4. Edgeworth [5, p. 102] surmises that such bargaining would lead to a modification of the utilitarian (greatest happiness) solution such as to 'conduct the greatest sum-total welfare of both parties, subject to the condition that neither should lose by the contract'.
5. Our use of the term 'leisure' simply refers to useful uses of time for purposes other than income-earning activity or the consumption of goods. It does not in any way carry the connotation of uselessness. See 'Time in economic life,' especially the comment by Baumol [2].
6. Throughout this discussion (including Rawls' own work as well as discussion in economic journals) it is assumed, rather strangely, that the income tax reduces work effort. This may or may not be the case, depending on the magnitude of income and substitution effects for both taxpayers and transfer recipients.
7. Mirrlees points out [8, p. 208] such an ideal solution is not feasible, but some improvement over the income tax should be possible.
8. Implementation of (1) suggests that taxes should be based on potential rather than on actual income. This would require evaluation of leisure-time as well as of income lost due to acceptance of lower-paying jobs. The latter aspect in particular becomes increasingly important the higher is the level of affluence and hence the greater the tendency to substitute job-pleasantness for income. It would not suffice, therefore, to relate the tax to hours worked as well as to income. (See Mirrlees [8, p. 208] where only the hours aspect is noted.) However this may be, there remains the question of what is to be equalised; and as shown in the following note, equalisation of potential income is not the correct solution.
9. To illustrate the solution, consider two people $H$ and $L$ with high and low earnings capacities and similar goods–leisure preferences as well as 'utility levels'. Let $AB$ in Figure 15.1 be the opportunity line for $H$, while $AC$ is that for $L$. To simplify, assume that these returns to work are constant and independent

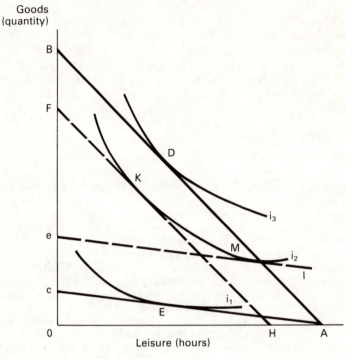

Goods
(quantity)

Leisure (hours)

*Figure 15.1*

of each other. In the absence of any adjustment, *H* chooses point *D*, while *L* chooses point *E*. Having larger amounts of both goods and leisure, *H* enjoys a higher level of welfare. To secure equalisation of welfare, *H* is called upon to pay a lump-sum tax that, measured in goods, equals *BF*, while *L* receives a lump-sum subsidy equal to *GC* = *BF*. Thus, the opportunity line for *H* drops to *FH*, that for *L* rises to *GI*, with *H* choosing point *K*, and *L* choosing point *M*. Both are located on the same indifferent curve and enjoy the same level of welfare, although *H* consumes more goods than *L* and *L* consumes more leisure than *H*. This solution may be thought of as a tax on income and leisure, imposed at the proper rate by an omniscient referee. Or, more suitably in Rawls' context, we may think of *H* and *L* in the original state as *agreeing* upon *K* and *M* as the just solution where, as Rawls puts it, the higher earnings capacity of *H* is translated into a social asset.

This reasoning, of course, involves interpersonal utility comparison, but so does maximin, since as Arrow and others have noted a comparison is needed to determine who is in the worst position. [Arrow, 1, p. 254]. In the absence of interpersonal utility comparison, one may derive a utility frontier corresponding to various patterns of lump-sum taxes and transfer between *H* and *L* and then choose the optimal point on a basis of a social welfare function. This, however, will not do in the philosopher's context, where the derivation of this function is precisely the point at issue.

It may be noted, finally, that the above solution is superior to (a) using a lump-sum-type tax-transfer scheme to equalise actual income; (b) using such a scheme to equalise potential income; or (c) using a system of income taxes and subsidies so as to equalise actual income or, which amounts to the same, to equalise the net wage rate or potential income. Solutions (a) and (b) are efficient but do not equalise welfare, while (c) equalises welfare but is inefficient. The above solution (which taxes potential income and leisure at rates so as to equal welfare) meets both these requirements.

# REFERENCES

[1] Arrow, K. (1973), 'Some ordinalist utiliarian notes on Rawls' *Theory of Justice'*, *Journal of Philosophy*, LXX.
[2] Baumol, W. (1973), 'Time in economic life', *Quarterly Journal of Economics*, LXXXVII.
[3] Cooter, R. (1974), 'Optimal income taxation for transfer payments under differential welfare criteria', *Quarterly Journal of Economics*, LXXXXVIII.
[4] Dworkin, R. (1973), 'The original position', *University of Chicago Law Review*, XL, p. 537.
[5] Edgeworth, Y. (1925), *Papers Relating to Political Economy*, vol. II (London, Macmillan), p. 102.
[6] Harsanyi, J. (1953), 'Cardinal utility in welfare economics and theory of risk-taking', *Journal of Political Economy*, LXI.
[7] Harsanyi, J. (1959), 'Cardinal welfare, individual ethics and interpersonal comparisons of utility', *Journal of Political Economy*, VXIII.
[8] Mirrlees, J. (1971), 'An exploration in the theory of optimal income taxation', *Review of Economic Studies*, XXXVII, p. 208.
[9] Phelps, E. (1973), 'Taxation of wage income for economic justice', *Quarterly Journal of Economics*, LXXXVII.
[10] Rawls, J. (1971), *A Theory of Justice* (Cambridge, Mass., Harvard University Press).

# 16 Adam Smith on Public Finance and Distribution*
## 1976

Adam Smith, in the *Wealth of Nations*, paints a sweeping panorama of economic activity, public as well as private. While focus is on the private sector and markets are guided by the invisible hand, Smith was no economic anarchist. Governmental activity forms an inherent part of his system of natural liberty. As laid out in the introduction to Book V, the sovereign must provide for a system of laws which assures the sanctity of property and sets the rules by which exchange and the division of labour can flourish. Moreover, provision must be made for defence, public works have to be undertaken, and public education must be provided for the common people. Were I to report on how Smith viewed the provision of public services, the conduct of my 'allocation branch' of the budget, I might have viewed Chapter 1 of Book V as a forerunner to the modern theory of social goods. Even though his view of the matter was not as incisive as that of Hume, externalities might well be built into the Smithian system, setting a limit to what the invisible hand can handle.[1] But my assignment is to deal with the distribution and not the public service function of the fiscal system and on this aspect very little is to be found in the *Wealth of Nations*. My task, therefore, must be to inquire why the distribution issue was so largely omitted from Book V. Thereafter, I shall sketch how, Adam Smith notwithstanding, this issue became a major concern of fiscal theory, how distribution-oriented policies came to assume strategic, if not dominant, importance, and how our past master might have felt about these developments.

## DISTRIBUTION IN SMITH'S FISCAL SYSTEM

Before examining Smith's view of the fiscal system, it is well to take a look at the fiscal environment in which he worked. A sketch thereof is given in Table 16.1. At the beginning of the decade in which the *Wealth of Nations* appeared, the British national income was approximately £130 million.[2]

---

* In Wilson, T. and Skinner, A. (eds) (1976), *The Market and the State, Essays in Honour of Adam Smith* (Oxford, Clarendon Press), © Oxford University Press 1976.

*Table 16.1 The structure of public finances in 1770 (in £000)*

| | | | |
|---|---|---|---|
| A. *Expenses* | | | |
| Net expenditures, United Kingdom (1770) | | | |
| 1. Debt charges | | 4836 | |
| 2. Defence | | 3863 | |
| 3. Civil List | | 898 | |
| 4. Other civil government | | 927 | |
| 5. | Total | ——— | |
| | | | 10 524 |
| 6. Expenditures on poor relief (1776) | | 1531 | |
| 7. assumed for 1770 | | | 1300 |
| County expenditures (1792) | | | |
| 8. Jails; vagrants, constables | | 113 | |
| 9. Bridges | | 33 | |
| 10. Other | | 77 | |
| 11. | Total | 223 | |
| 12. assumed for 1770 | | | 150 |
| | | | ——— |
| | | | 11974 |
| | | | |
| B. *Receipts* | | | |
| Receipts, United Kingdom (1770) | | | |
| 14. Customs | | 2841 | |
| 15. Excises | | 5139 | |
| 16. Stamps | | 336 | |
| 17. Post Office | | 162 | |
| 18. Land and assessed taxes | | 1796 | |
| 19. | Total | ——— | 10274 |
| 20. Poor Rates receipts (1776) | | 1720 | |
| 21. assumed for 1770 | | | 1500 |
| 22. County and police rates (1792) | | 218 | |
| 23. assumed for 1770 | | | 150 |
| | | | ——— |
| 24. Estimated total, 1770 | | | 11924 |

*Source*:
Lines 1–5: Mitchell [14, p. 390]
Line 6: Ibid, p. 410.
Line 7: Ibid.
Lines 8–11: Ibid, p. 411.
Line 12: Ibid.
Lines 14–18: Ibid, p. 388.
Line 20: Ibid, p. 410.
Line 21: Ibid.
Line 22: Ibid, p. 411.
Line 23: Ibid.

With public expenditures of £12 million, the expenditure to national income ratio stood somewhat below 10 per cent, a ratio not very different from that prevailing up to World War I. Of the expenditure total of £12 million, 40 per cent went for debt service and 33 per cent for military purposes (1770). Of the remaining 27 per cent, £1.3 million went for poor relief, leaving £1.9 million for other purposes, half of which was accounted for by the civil list. Poverty-related programmes were thus a major expenditure item, accounting for nearly half of what is left after deducting the 'uncontrollable' outlays of interest and defence. Yet there is no consideration of the finance of poor relief in Book V, and Smith's earlier critique [24, vol. 1, p. 137] of the settlement laws is directed against the resulting immobility of labour without consideration of the adequacy of support levels. With poor relief provided in kind, transfer payments as a category do not appear in Smith's fiscal system. Only in his treatment of education does he consider public responsibilities toward the poor. He notes the need for public education as a means of relieving the condition of the common people, suffering from the dulling effects of industrial labour, and argues in favour of extending the Scottish system of publicly-supported parish schools to England [24, II, p. 270]. However, this goes to prove the exception rather than the rule, there being little or no concern with distributive expenditure policy in the rest of Smith's fiscal system. Nor did he view taxation as a redistributive device, since tax equity, as we shall note presently, was interpreted in benefit rather than ability terms.

How can this omission be explained, given the image of Adam Smith as so worldly-wise and generous a thinker? The answer may be found in the twofold constraint imposed by (i) the system of moral sentiments in which Smith and his time viewed the conduct of society, and (ii) the system of economic relationships by which he held the state of distribution to be determined. Neither was amenable to the inclusion of distribution issues in the system of public finances and both must contribute to explain their omission.

## Distribution in the *Theory of Moral Sentiments*

Adam Smith's view of what today would be called distributive justice cannot be garnered from the *Wealth of Nations*, or certainly not from this source alone. Though this work is rightly considered his supreme achievement, he was also the author of a *Theory of Moral Sentiments*. While the *Theory* was published 17 years earlier, it would be a mistake to consider it a youthful aberration, lest the more hard-headed author of the *Wealth of Nations* be embarrassed thereby. Certainly, Smith himself did not take this view, since the *Theory* underwent six revisions, the last being published in 1790, the year of his death. In order to understand what is not said in the *Wealth of Nations*, I must begin, therefore, by considering what was said in the *Theory of Moral Sentiments*, inviting, as it were, the older brother to the birthday party.[3]

Adam Smith, the moral philosopher, weaves in this work an intricate web of motivations, values, and rules of conduct. While man is more concerned with his own happiness than that of others, his tendency to selfish action is constrained by his desire for approbation by the 'impartial spectator' [25, p. 162]. Reflecting the opinion of others and 'his representative, the man within the breast', the spectator will monitor one's conduct and induce one to respect certain virtues including those of justice, prudence, and beneficence.

*Justice*, in Adam Smith, is seen in commutative rather than distributive terms. It is a 'negative virtue', which consists of the duty not to injure someone else [25, p. 169]. Offence against justice is resented by the observer and calls for punishment. The claim to justice can be enforced by the injured party. *Prudence*, 'the capacity to take care of oneself' is not 'one either of the most endearing or of the most ennobling of the virtues', yet it is considered respectable and approved by the observer [25, p. 353]. Indeed, 'the sober and deliberate action which it demands, the willingness of that prudent man to sacrifice present satisfaction in expectation of the future', is the fuel which drives economic progress and which generates the wealth of nations. Prudence, as socialised self-interest, has a strategic place in the natural order of things and as such differs from mere selfishness. *Beneficence*, finally, is the highest of all virtues.[4] The extension of generosity, affection and kindness is a voluntary act which, as distinct from justice, cannot be enforced. Given freely, it secures the applause of the impartial spectator. But man is capable of limited beneficence only. It is extended most readily to family and friends, followed by neighbours and perhaps the nation, but hardly to humanity at large. Love of humanity, though the greatest of virtues, is hardly in man's grasp. Perfection is not within reach, and prudence distrusts 'the man of system' who pursues utopian goals and cannot suffer deviation from his 'ideal plan'. He is more likely to create disorder than to do good [25, p. 380].

Smith's structure of moral sentiments, like that of his friend Burke, thus rests on a conservative position. But though man is entitled, by the Lockean system of natural liberty, to the fruits of his labour, beneficence retains a major role.[5] While expressed mainly in terms of friendship, sympathy and esteem, there is no suggestion that beneficence might not also take the form of material support. Why, then, does not this expression of virtue find a place in Smith's view of the fiscal system? Its absence is explained by the voluntary nature of beneficence, a virtue which will be rewarded with sympathy but cannot be enforced. Transfers to the less fortunate, though laudable in Smith's moral system, must be of the voluntary or Pareto-optimal type, calling for implementation by charity rather than by a mandatory process of budgetary redistribution.[6] People may choose to share their riches with their neighbours, but they cannot demand that others do so. The virtue of giving is with the giver and the view of equality as a social good is disallowed. The voluntary exercise of beneficence in turn is limited by human frailty, so that the scope of charity is restricted.

The pressure on beneficence is relieved, however, by two further considerations. One is psychological in nature, and holds that the state of distribution has little to do with the level of welfare because little is gained from the consumption of luxuries. The other derives from the economic order which leaves only a limited degree of freedom in affecting the state of distribution. On both counts, the significance of distributive concern (*qua* economic beneficence) is thus reduced.

## Distribution and Welfare

Consider first the unimportance of excessive possessions. The individual's unceasing desire for wealth, so Smith tells us, is based on a deception. The landlord who surveys the riches of his fields and in imagination himself consumes the whole harvest, does not realise that the 'capacity of his stomach bears no proportion to the immensity of his desires, and will receive no more than that of the meanest peasant' [25, p. 304]. In later terms, the marginal utility of income is taken to fall to zero after a certain minimum level is reached. Smith thus rejected the view of his friend Hume [10, II, p. 229], who recognised that the gains to the poor, from redistributing a given total income, would exceed the losses of the rich. What then is the motivation behind industry and the striving for wealth? 'Do they imagine,' so Smith asks, 'that their stomach is better or their sleep sounder, in a palace than in a cottage?' 'The contrary,' so he answers, 'has so often been observed, and indeed, is so very obvious ... that there is nobody ignorant of it' [25, p. 113]. The true motivation, rather, is provided by the desire to win the admiration and notice of others. Only kings are fit for happiness or tragedy; the poor man is ashamed of his lot and goes unnoticed. This Veblenesque drive explains why men undergo the toil and anxiety which they must suffer to improve their lot, and in the process, give up 'all that ease, all that careless security, which they otherwise could enjoy'. But the deception thus worked by human avarice has its positive function: it lends stability to the social structure and provides the driving force 'which rouses and keeps in continual motion the industry of mankind' [25, p. 303]. The gain, it appears, is not in wealth itself but in the dynamic process of enhancing it. In short, inequality serves an important function and happily does so at little opportunity cost.

## The Economic Laws of Distribution

I now turn to the second constraint on distribution policy, which is posed by the functioning of the economic system. Here we have two models to deal with, one dominant in the *Theory of Moral Sentiments* and the other in the *Wealth of Nations*. Both shade into each other, but there are important differences as well.

Beginning with the *Theory of Moral Sentiments*, Smith's view is that by the nature of things, a more or less egalitarian end result ensues, no matter how unequal may be the start. Viewing equity in terms of consumption rather than income, he argues that the rich can consume but little more than the poor. The rest of the riches they must distribute among those who provide

the different baubles and trinkets which are employed in the economy of greatness; all of whom thus derive from his luxury and caprice the share of the necessities of life which they would in vain have expected from his humanity or his justice. The soil maintains at all times nearly that number of inhabitants which it is capable of maintaining. The rich ... consume little more than the poor ... Though they mean only their own conveniency ... They are led by an invisible hand to make nearly the same distribution of the necessaries of life which would have been made had the earth been divided into equal portions among all its inhabitants; and thus, without intending it ... advance the interest of the society, and afford means to the multiplication of the species. When providence divided the earth among a few lordly masters, it neither forgot nor abandoned those who seemed to have been left out in the partition ... In ease of body and peace of mind all the different ranks of life are nearly upon a level, and the beggar, who suns himself by the side of the highway, possesses that security which kings are fighting for [25, p. 304].[7]

The economic reasoning of this remarkable passage lends itself to various interpretations. The argument is not simply that because the rich can consume only little, little is taken away from the poor. (One wonders, in this context, how large a share of national output went, at Smith's time, into the consumption of baubles and trinkets.) It is held also that population size will adjust itself to what the land can produce so that improved means of production, in the long run, will not raise wages rates but merely expand population. This is the Malthusian-like mechanism, which in amended form reappears in the *Wealth of Nations*. Moreover, it is *because* the rich pay for the production of baubles and trinkets that the poor can earn the necessities of life. Presumably, they could not do so (or population would have to be smaller) without there being a demand for luxuries by the rich. But why could not the resources used to produce trinkets be used to produce amenities for the poor? Is it that the trinkets (or the emulation called forth by their possession) are needed as a reward for entrepreneurial industry, or is there a pre-Keynesian hint of potential under-consumption, due to incapacity of the poor to generate sufficient demand? Here, as in other passages, there are many facets to Smith's reasoning and it is not easy to disentangle them.

Viewed as an expression of moral sentiments, one wonders whether the quoted passage would have satisfied the impartial observer. He might well have viewed it as an apologetic for not confronting the issue of distributive justice more squarely; or he might have taken it to reflect Smith's Calvinist dislike of trinkets, leading him severely to underestimate the elasticity of demand for opulence, not unlike in this respect to the low esteem in which a more recent colleague holds the modern pleasures of affluence. However this may be, it is significant to note that Smith did not rest the case simply by reference to the natural law of entitlement and just acquisition. Rather, the invisible hand is invoked—this being one of the two instances where, to my knowledge, he does so—to show that inequality is, after all, less unequal and avoidable than it seems to be.[8]

Turning to the richer and more complex analysis of the *Wealth of Nations*, we now find the issue of distribution viewed as a theory of factor shares, rather than one of inter-individual assignment. As such it is an integral part of the theory of value, with product and factor prices linked in a general equilibrium system. At the same time, factor shares in the late eighteenth century reflected economic classes, more nearly so than they do today, so that the economic theory of factor pricing also doubled as a social theory of distribution among economic groups.

Moreover, the theory of factor shares is now seen in a dynamic setting. In the long run, population size, via changes in the rate of infant mortality [24, vol. I, p. 81], still responds to any deviation of actual from subsistence wage, until the latter is restored. But two further considerations apply, both of which are favourable to labour: (i) while the capital stock increases, the demand for labour rises and with the resulting increase in labour supply lagging behind, wage rates are temporarily increased. It is not the level of the capital stock that matters, so Smith argues in his chapter on wages, but its rate of increase [24, vol. I, p. 71]. (ii) In the process, there may result an upward shift in what is considered an acceptable subsistence. This will retard population increase and permit the new equilibrium to be reached at a higher wage rate.

In combination, these two provisos may be read as compatible with a marginal productivity theory of wage determination, but taken separately they differ in their implication. Whereas the gains under (i) are contingent on continued growth, those from (ii) would remain even if expansion ceases. However this may be, Smith points with satisfaction to the fact that British wages have risen well above the subsistence level [24, vol. 1, p. 75] and that increased productivity has permitted the frugal peasant to live as well as an African king [24, vol. 1, p. 14]. The poor, as well as the rich, stand to gain from economic expansion, although it is not evident how the share of the poor will fare in the process.

We are left with two models of distribution theory which yield rather different results. In the *Theory*, the poor remain poor but distribution does not matter greatly because excess consumption is useless. In the *Wealth* they can gain from economic development and such gain is applauded. This makes it somewhat difficult to identify the 'true Mr Smith', but both versions are similar in that neither leaves much scope for adjusting the state of inter-individual distribution.

## Smith's Welfare Function

Before proceeding to the application of this analysis to tax policy, let me speculate briefly on how Smith would have written an individual's utility function and how he would have approached the design of a social welfare function.

A person's happiness, so Smith might have argued, would be a function of (i) the necessities of life which he consumes, including some conveniences and superfluities which are enjoyed by even 'the meanest labourer' [25, p. 112]. To this would be added (ii) the satisfaction gained from the exercise of beneficence, as well as (iii) that derived from the envy of others for one's riches, offset more or less by the additional toil and burdens assumed in securing it. Finally, there might be a term reflecting (iv) the pride or satisfaction derived from being a part of the harmonious order which the system of natural liberty provides.

Asked further to write the social welfare function reflective of his natural order, Smith, after protesting so unproductive an activity, might well have adopted the utilitarian pattern of assigning a weight of 1 to each individual, and he might not have objected to comparing levels of utility or happiness. But he would have found no occasion to assign differing social weights to successive units of income since he thought such differentials to be spurious. The marginal utility of income schedule as we have seen drops to zero after a certain level of income is reached.

Turning to the social welfare function, would welfare be viewed in terms of average or total welfare? Smith does not offer an explicit discussion of the 'utilitarian' formula of maximum happiness for the largest number (the *Wealth of Nations* somewhat preceded Bentham's formulation) but he did call his major work the *Wealth of Nations* and not the *Wealth of Man*. Moreover, the economic process of accumulation (more about which later) is said to 'serve the interest of Society, and afford the means to the multiplication of the species' [25, p. 304]. But even if population growth were added as a term to the social welfare function, Smith's linkage between welfare and distributional change would operate via its effects on accumulation and population size, rather than via the effects of redistribution among a given population. Yet, it is precisely the latter that is the essence of the modern distribution problem.

## Implications for Tax Policy

How, then, does his theory of factor pricing and income shares relate to the role of tax policy, and especially its bearing on the state of distribution? The first of his four maxims of taxation (equality, certainty, convenience of payment, and economy in collection) demands that the tax system be equitable, but equity is defined as distributional neutrality:

The subjects of every State ought to contribute toward the support of the government, as nearly as possible, in proportion to their respective abilities, that is in proportion to the revenue which they respectively enjoy under the protection of the State. The expense of government to the individuals of a great nation, is like the expense of management to the joint tenants of a great estate, who are all obliged to contribute in proportion to their respective interests in the estate [24, vol. 2, p. 310].

This passage may be read as either an ability to pay or a benefit-based view of tax equity. The 'that is' clause nicely begs the issue since if ability-to-pay depends on income, and income is earned under the protection of the state, the two versions may be said to yield the same result. But other passages suggest that he ranked the benefit principle in the primary role. Moreover, Smith calls for a distribution of the tax burden in *proportion* to income, with a slight nod in the direction of progression [24, vol. 2, p. 327]. Finally, we note that equity is seen in terms of income (i.e. 'revenue from *all* sources'), rather than in terms of consumption. Indeed, consumption taxes are criticised because 'they do not always fall equally or

proportionably upon the revenue of every individual' [24, vol. 2, p. 378].
Contrary to his view of utility *qua* consumption in the *Theory*, Smith now
sides with the Haig–Simons rather than the Fisher–Kaldor school of tax
base theorists.

Given the premise of proportional rates, Smith would have no need to
call for a global-type income tax. A schedular-type tax, with wages
excluded but all other schedules subject to the same rate, would do. He did
not, however, support an income tax as he opposed the taxation of profit
income, and his anti-income tax position lent authority to the case against
Pitt's income tax of 1799 [Kennedy, 12, p. 149]. This followed from his
notions of tax incidence as based on his theory of factor shares. A tax on
wages, so he argues, would be 'absurd and destructive' because it would
either come to be absorbed by the landlord in reduced rent as in the case of
agricultural labour or by the consumer as in the case of industrial labour
[24, vol. 2, p. 349]. With wages at the subsistence level, a decline in the net
wage below this level calls forth a decrease in labour supply, with the gross
wage rising until the net wage is returned to the old level. As a result, the
return to other factors is reduced and this being the case, they might as well
be taxed in the first place.[9] The underlying assumption is that the wage rate
cannot fall below subsistence, even though this may be at a customary
rather than a minimum level. Evidently, the acceptable minimum can rise
in the process of development, but thereafter cannot be depressed.
However this may be, the population response is still the key factor in the
argument.

The rent of land, on the other hand, is a fit object of taxation. The land
tax ranks high, as 'it does not appear likely to occasion any other
inconvenience to the landlord, except always the considerable one of being
obliged to pay the tax' [24, vol. 2, p. 318]. Essentially the same holds for
taxes upon the produce of land which finally are also paid by the landlord.
Taxes on the rent of houses are divided between the ground and building
rent component of the base. The tax on ground rent is borne by the owner
of the land, but the tax on building rent causes capital to move to other
uses, with the burden passing to the landlord and the consumer of housing.
In all, taxes on house rent are good taxes even though they may bear more
than proportionally upon the rich.

Taxes upon profits, finally, are of questionable merit. That part of profits
which is needed to pay interest is in the nature of a rent income, so that the
tax thereon cannot be passed on. The tax is economically feasible but its
administration would call for an intolerable inquisition. The remaining part
of profits 'in most cases ... is no more than a very moderate compensation'
and is needed to reward the employer for his risk and efforts [24, vol. 2,
p. 331]. Such taxation would interfere with the reward for prudence and
retard economic growth. Profits, therefore, are not a proper subject of
taxation.

Turning to taxes on consumable commodities, a distinction is drawn
between taxes on luxuries and taxes on necessaries, defined to include 'not
only those things which nature, but those things which the established rules

of decency have rendered necessary to the lowest rank of people' [24, vol. 2, p. 355]. Taxes on necessaries operate in the same manner as a direct tax upon the wages of labour and are self-defeating. 'The middling and superior ranks of people, if they understood their own interest, ought always to oppose all taxes upon the necessaries of life, as well as all direct taxes upon the wages of labour' [24, vol. 2, p. 357]. They themselves must pay such taxes. Taxes upon salt, leather, soap and candles are rejected accordingly. Taxes upon luxuries, however, are paid by the consumer. Though not paid in proportion to all revenue received, they permit the individual flexibility in his tax payments. They are 'perhaps, as agreeable to the three first ... maxims ... as any other' [24, vol. 2, p. 379], and though they offend the fourth, this is unavoidable and must be taken into the bargain.

This summary, to be sure, does not pretend to offer a full evaluation of Smith's incidence analysis. While the chapters on incidence reflect inconsistencies inherent in various parts of Smith's distribution theory, they are nevertheless impressive in their heroic endeavour to view the problem of incidence (as the Physiocrats had done) in general equilibrium terms. A splendid but defective model of factor pricing, to paraphrase Schumpeter in his 'Review of the Troops', produced positive if mistaken answers to incidence theory.[10] For our purposes the upshot of the matter is that there are only two viable tax bases, i.e. rent and luxury consumption.

The burden of approved taxes thus seems to fall on the progressive side of Smith's proportionality rule. Landlords with the highest income are hit from both the income sources and the spending uses side. Profit recipients, the next highest group, pay on the spending side only but are taxed relatively heavily on luxury consumption. The common people in turn pay no tax, except through their limited consumption of amenities. With incidence thus determined by the nature of economic forces, the first maxim has only limited application. Taxes, it would seem, have to be placed where the economy can absorb them.

But theorising aside, what was the actual tax structure which existed in Smith's time? One-third of revenue (see Table 16.1) was derived from taxes falling on the rent of land and housing, while the other two-thirds came from customs duties and excises. With levies on malt, beer and sugar the main revenue producers, the tax structure relied to a significant degree on items below the luxury level [Dowell, 5, p. 207]. However, Smith thought of these as amenities rather than necessities, with taxes thereon borne by the consumer. While the impact of the tax structure in its reliance on customs duties and excises was not as equitable as he might have liked it to be, he thought it preferable to the continental system. Moreover, in matters of applied tax policy Smith was rather pragmatic. After the good taxes have been fully utilised, so he tells us, the less desirable ones must be resorted to.[11]

While Smith does not discuss expenditure incidence, his logic would have led to similar conclusions on the expenditure side. Leaving aside the difficult question of how to allocate the benefits from defence and debt service, remaining outlays, as noted before, were in substantial part directed at the very poor (workhouses), with the remainder going largely to the very rich (Civil List). But in the context of his economic system, Smith would have been led to conclude that poor relief in the end could not raise the standard of living of the poor but merely siphon income from the landlords and sustain a larger population. In short, there was little economic scope for the exercise of beneficence through the budget, even if redistribution through the mandatory use of taxation had been defensible. Moreover, by retarding the rate of growth, the lot of the poor might well have been worsened.

## THE POST-SMITH RECORD

Having sketched the role of redistribution in Smith's view of the public sector, I can find little which anticipates subsequent developments, be it at the level of fiscal theory or of practice. The mechanism of population response, so central to his incidence theory, ceased to function or became reversed, and consumer stomachs learned to expand in line with the vast increase in per capita income that occurred in the western world. While the relationship between the size of the pie and its slicing remained an acute issue, the range of distributional policy options proved much greater than the Smithian view had suggested. Along with this development, the strictures of natural law, which would guarantee innate property rights in differential ability and inherited wealth, gave way to a more flexible view of what the optimal state of distribution should be. All this combined with the rise of popular democracy, a shifting balance of political power, and rising fiscal centralisation to render distributional concerns of growing importance to fiscal policy.

### The Distribution Issue in Fiscal Theory

Just as the theory of social goods is an extension of the benefit view of tax equity, so is the theory of fiscal redistribution an extension of the ability-to-pay doctrine. Though the benefit theory need not be incompatible with progressive taxation, the rising case for progressive taxation, as a measure of redistribution, belonged to the ability to pay tradition. While earlier writers had interpreted ability to pay to call for regressive, proportional or progressive taxation,[12] a more systematic interpretation of the doctrine began only with John Stuart Mill. Construing taxation according to ability to pay as taxation which imposes equal sacrifice, Mill [13, p. 804] called for equal proportional sacrifice, mistakenly thinking that this would also result in least total sacrifice. Matters were straightened out by Edgeworth [6, vol. 2, p. 100], who distinguished between equal absolute, equal proportional, and equal marginal sacrifice, and who noted the equivalence of the latter as an equity rule with least total sacrifice, thus coinciding with the criterion of fiscal efficiency. These concepts were developed further by Pigou [19] who thought equal absolute sacrifice the proper equity rule. However, there was no simple and obvious relationship between the various equity rules and the case for progressive taxation. Assuming comparable and equal marginal utility of income schedules, equal marginal sacrifice would call for maximum progression (levelling incomes down from the top until the necessary revenue is reached) provided only that marginal utility falls as income rises. Equal absolute sacrifice in turn would call for progressive, proportional or regressive rates depending on whether the elasticity of the schedule exceeds, equals or falls short of unity. Equal proportional sacrifice, finally, poses a more complex case so that no simple relationship follows. But though it seems reasonable to assume that marginal income utility declines, there is no intuition regarding the rate of decline, thus leaving the issue of progressivity (and with it appropriate changes in the distribution of income) an open question.

This theory of tax equity thus leads to a wholly inconclusive position. Beyond this, it came to be attacked on more basic grounds. The *old* welfare economics, of which ability to pay theory was an inherent part, came to be rejected in its entirety because the very premise of interpersonal utility comparison came to be considered non-operational and meaningless (a critique by which I was never wholly persuaded). The *new* welfare economics proposed to deal with problems of welfare in terms of efficiency only, while shunning issues of distribution. Distribution, to post-Robbins economic theory, became a non-issue. Society would benefit if A gains without a loss to B, and this was about all that could be said. A social welfare function was designed which would record a gain in welfare as a move to the efficiency frontier, thus separating welfare economics as an efficiency issue from any justice content.

But economics as a social science cannot entirely detach itself from major social problems. It is not surprising, therefore, that economists are now in the process of replacing the new with a still *newer* welfare economics. A social welfare function is postulated which (i) values the utility derived by various individuals of equal income equally, and (ii) assigns social weights to the marginal utility of income, letting these weights decline as income rises. Consequently, the crude measurements of inequality by such devices as the Gini coefficient may be supplemented by a more meaningful measure which reflects the social gain that can be obtained from equalisation [Atkinson, 21, p. 244].

In the newer welfare economics, the framework of the old sacrifice theory is essentially re-established, with the difference (perhaps more formal than real but satisfying the scientific conscience of the profession) that it avoids the hurdle of interpersonal comparison and empirical determination of income utility functions. The new approach, however, makes some important additions. Discussion of the fiscal distribution issue is no longer restricted to the allocation of tax burdens, with revenue limited to the size of the public service budget, but is seen in more general terms. The target becomes optimal income distribution, the design of an optimal tax-transfer system, not merely the optimal collection of a fixed amount of revenue. Moreover, the new analysis systematically allows for the efficiency costs of redistribution, those responses which Pigou had referred to as announcement effects and which linger in the shadows of Smith's fourth maxim. Concurrent with this development in economic analysis, philosophers have re-examined the distributional implications of the contractarian tradition and have focused on a maximin rule of distribution [Rawls, 20].

Given this framework and based on certain assumptions, devotees of the newer welfare economics have been busy computing what would constitute an optimal state of distribution and the required scope of redistribution [Atkinson, 1; Sheshinski, 23]. These results have given a more concrete flavour to the debate, but they depend on the nature of the underlying assumptions, mainly (i) the shape of the social welfare function by which outcomes are evaluated, (ii) the distribution of earnings capacity, the results of which are to be adjusted, and (iii) the shape of a uniform utility function, maximisation of which determines the individual's response (in choosing between goods and leisure) to tax and transfer policies. Finally (iv), a linear tax function is assumed. The results suggest that the optimal degree of redistribution even under the extreme Rawlsian criterion of maximin (where a zero value is assigned to gains obtained by anyone but the lowest on the scale) is less than might have been expected, but these results depend on the underlying assumptions. In particular, I remain uneasy about the arbitrariness which is introduced in choosing a particular (Cobb–Douglas or constant elasticity) utility function, in assuming it to be uniformly applicable to all individuals, and in operating with a linear tax schedule only. I appreciate that these assumptions are needed to formulate a workable model and I admire the mathematical ingenuity which went into this construction, but I remain as yet hesitant to draw policy conclusions. Nevertheless major progress is being made, and one wonders how Adam Smith would have viewed it. Two responses may be ventured.

First of all, Smith would have held that the utility function by which short-run labour supply is determined permits a goods–leisure trade-off only above subsistence, and that the long-run schedule must allow for population response. Second, Smith would have felt very uneasy about the simplified leisure–goods trade-off on which the current models are based. He would surely have argued that the response will differ between various types of labour and that effects upon the dynamic role of entrepreneurship and capital accumulation must be distinguished from effects on the supply of common labour. Finally, and most important, he would have rejected the very notion of an optimal distribution of income which is to be attained by a process of non-voluntary redistribution. For him the state of distribution, as noted before, was set by the system of natural liberty (property rights in the fruits of one's ability and industry) and the objective forces of the economic system (factor pricing and population response), an order which was to be amended only by voluntary redistribution based on the virtue of beneficence, but not by budgetary meddling. Given redistribution of that type, efficiency costs do not arise, so that the problem of dead-weight loss would be limited to the response to taxes imposed to finance public services. For such finance, the benefit principle would apply, with a compromise to be reached between equity and the other three maxims. The newer welfare economists would be applauded in implementing the fourth maxim, but this would only be part of the story.

## The Distribution Issue in Fiscal Practice

If Adam Smith would have been displeased with the introduction of mandatory redistribution schemes into fiscal theory he would have been dismayed by the revolutionary changes in fiscal practice which occurred over recent decades. These developments are shown in Tables 16.2a and 16.2b using the US and UK as illustrations, with more or less similar pictures to be found in other western countries. We note that budget patterns changed relatively little over the century and a half following the *Wealth of Nations*. The share of the public sector in GNP was not much higher in the 1920s than at the time of Adam Smith, but drastic changes began in the 1930s and gained pace in the post-war years. The construction of the modern welfare state, heralded in the mid-1940s by Beveridge's *Full Employment in a Free Society*, placed social service expenditures in the centre of budgetary policy. What had seemed hardly worth mentioning in the *Wealth of Nations* became the core of the fiscal issue. The public sector share (see Tables 16.2a and 16.2b) rose from below 15 per cent of GNP in the mid-1920s to a 1974 level of 33 per cent for the US and 44 per cent for the UK. The share of the social expenditure items in total public expenditures rose from around 30 per cent to 50 per cent or more, with a substantially higher ratio if defence and interest are excluded from the base. Indeed, this increase in social service expenditures accounted for the entire gain in the rising ratio of public expenditures to GNP which has occurred (especially in the US) over the last two decades. To be sure, a substantial part of the growth has been in transfers, so that the real share of government in GNP has not expanded accordingly. But this is only a natural by-product of the rising importance of distributional considerations, and does not detract from their increasing weight in budget patterns.

A similar, though less pronounced, development has occurred on the tax side of the budget picture, where the rise of the direct tax share in total tax revenue signalled increased reliance on progressive taxation. Using again the US and UK as points of reference, this development is shown in Table 16.3. In the UK the income tax share rose from 36 per cent in 1913 to over 40 per cent in later years, an increase which occurred at the cost of the share contributed by local rates. In the US the income tax share rose from 11 per cent at the beginning of the century to 30 per cent in 1927 and 50 per cent today. The sharp increase which occurred during World War II was largely at the cost of the property tax share, reinforced by a decline in the contribution of indirect taxes. These developments, combined with the increasingly progressive rate structure of the income tax, suggest a

*Table 16.2a Rise of social expenditures: (a) United Kingdom*

|  | 1770 | 1890 | 1910 | 1938 | 1955 | 1974 |
|---|---|---|---|---|---|---|
| *As percentage of GNP* | | | | | | |
| Public expenditures, total[a] | 12 | 9 | 13 | 30 | 37 | 44 |
| Total, excl. defence and interest | 3 | 5 | 8 | 17 | 23 | 35 |
| Social services | 1 | 2 | 4 | 11 | 16 | 25 |
| Transfers | n.a. | 1 | 1 | 7 | 7 | 15 |
| Purchases[b] | n.a. | 8 | 12 | 23 | 30 | 25 |
| | | | | | | |
| *As percentage of public expenditures* | | | | | | |
| Social insurance and assistance | n.a. | n.a. | n.a. | 17 | 16 | 21 |
| Education | n.a. | n.a. | n.a. | 9 | 11 | 13 |
| Other social services[c] | n.a. | n.a. | n.a. | 11 | 16 | 23 |
| Total, social services | 13 | 22 | 31 | 37 | 43 | 55 |
| Transfers | n.a. | 7 | 13 | 21 | 26 | 35 |
| Purchases | n.a. | 93 | 87 | 79 | 74 | 57 |
| | | | | | | |
| *As percentage of public expenditures* *excl. defence and interest* | | | | | | |
| Social insurance and assistance | n.a. | n.a. | n.a. | 30 | 26 | 27 |
| Education | n.a. | n.a. | n.a. | 15 | 17 | 17 |
| Other social services | n.a. | n.a. | n.a. | 20 | 27 | 30 |
| Total, social services | 43 | 40 | 50 | 65 | 70 | 74 |
| Transfers | n.a. | 13 | 21 | 37 | 42 | 44 |

*Sources*: For 1775 see Table 16.1. For 1890–1955 see Alan T. Peacock and Jack Wiseman, *Growth of Public Expenditures in the United Kingdom* (Princeton University Press, 1961), pp. 83, 86, 92. For 1974 see CSO (1975) *National Income Bluebook*, Table 52. A GNP base at market price of £82,000 million is used. Using a market price base of £70,000 million, the over-all expenditure ratio is 40 per cent.
  [a] Excludes (1) lending and borrowing, and (2) public corporations which, in a more detailed analysis, should be partly included.
  [b] Includes interest on public debt
  [c] Includes outlays on health, housing and food subsidies.

widening departure from Adam Smith's rule of proportionate taxation, at least on the surface. However, in recent years there has developed a significant counter-tendency, i.e. the rising importance of the payroll tax, especially in the revenue structure of the United States.

In order to measure the overall distributive effects of taxation, a comparison must be drawn between the pre- and post-tax distributions of income; or, preferably, the existing post-tax distribution may be compared with that under a proportional tax structure. This is a speculative undertaking involving theoretical judgement regarding incidence, supported in part by only limited empirical evidence. In some instances, especially with regard to the corporation and property taxes, there remains substantial room for controversy, and long-run results may differ from those applic-

*Table 16.2b Rise of social expenditures: (b) United States*

| | 1902 | 1927 | 1940 | 1950 | 1960 | 1973 |
|---|---|---|---|---|---|---|
| *As percentage of GNP* | | | | | | |
| Public expenditures, total | 7 | 10 | 18 | 23 | 27 | 32 |
| Public expenditures, excl. defence and interest | 5 | 8 | 14 | 13 | 15 | 23 |
| Social services | 2 | 3 | 5 | 6 | 9 | 15 |
| Transfers | n.a. | n.a. | 3 | 5 | 15 | 10 |
| Purchases[a] | n.a. | n.a. | 15 | 18 | 22 | 22 |
| | | | | | | |
| *As percentage of public expenditures* | | | | | | |
| social insurance, assistance, and other | 7 | 7 | 14 | 10 | 18 | 30 |
| Education | 18 | 22 | 16 | 15 | 14 | 18 |
| Total, social services | 25 | 29 | 30 | 25 | 32 | 48 |
| Transfers | n.a. | n.a. | 15 | 25 | 19 | 30 |
| Purchases[b] | n.a. | n.a. | 85 | 75 | 81 | 70 |
| | | | | | | |
| *As percentage of public expenditures, excl. defence and interest* | | | | | | |
| Social insurance, assistance, and other | 10 | 19 | 18 | 18 | 33 | 39 |
| Education | 25 | 17 | 21 | 27 | 25 | 23 |
| Total, social services | 35 | 36 | 39 | 45 | 58 | 62 |

*Sources*: See R. A. Musgrave and P. B. Musgrave (1970) *Public Finance in Theory and Practice* (McGraw-Hill, New York), 2nd edn, p. 137.

[a] Interest is included in purchases.

[b] The overall expenditure ratio for 1974 is 33 per cent, and the ratio excluding defence and interest is 24 per cent. 1973 rather than 1974 figures are used because the necessary breakdown for the latter is as yet unavailable.

*Table 16.3 Composition of tax structure (all levels of government)*

| | United Kingdom[a] | | | United States[b] | | | |
|---|---|---|---|---|---|---|---|
| | 1913/14 | 1938/39 | 1974/75 | 1902 | 1927 | 1950 | 1974 |
| Direct | 36% | 42% | 43% | 11% | 31% | 53% | 49% |
| Indirect | 31 | 28 | 29 | 37 | 18 | 24 | 17 |
| Local rates | 33 | 17 | 10 | 52 | 49 | 13 | 12 |
| Payroll | – | 12 | 18 | – | 2 | 10 | 22 |
| Total | 100 | 100 | 100 | 100 | 100 | 100 | 100 |

*Sources*:

[a] See A. R. Prest, *Public Finance in Theory and Practice*, 5th edn, pp. 168, 199, and for 1974, *C.S.O. Annual Abstract* (1975), Tables 330 and 331.

[b] See R. A. Musgrave and P. B. Musgrave, *Public Finance in Theory and Practice*, 2nd edn. p. 208; and US Department of Commerce, *Survey of Current Business* (July 1975).

able to the short run. Nevertheless, the typical conclusion is that the tax structure as a whole (and Adam Smith would have been pleased with this) tends to be proportional over the larger part of the income range. Such is the case for estimates based on British [3, 16], US [17, 15] and Swedish [7] data. The British estimates, which exclude corporation tax and allocate rates in line with rental expenditures, show some degree of progression for household incomes up to £800 (1973 levels) but become more or less proportional above this level. The US data, which include all taxes and are available for a variety of incidence assumptions, follow a more or less similar pattern. Progression depends in particular upon the treatment of the corporation and the property taxes, but remains modest even if the most favourable assumptions for progressive results are made. Given a more or less proportional effective rate curve, it is not surprising that the Gini coefficient applicable to post-tax income is but slightly more equal than that applicable to pre-tax income.

Turning to the expenditure side of fiscal redistribution, the rise of transfer payments and of social services has made for an increasingly redistributive pattern. Estimates for a variety of countries, including UK, US and Sweden, show the benefit to income ratio to decline sharply as income rises. While a host of new difficulties arise in an attempt to allocate expenditure benefits, it is evident that they cannot be neglected. Indeed, the major redistributive effects of budget policy operate via the expenditure side. Expenditure equity, it appears, is more important than the traditional focus on tax equity.

But it is not enough to consider the tax and expenditure sides in isolation. To obtain the net result, both sides must be combined. Relating the net of benefit and taxes to earnings (before tax and transfers), 1973 data for the UK show a net benefit rate falling from 700 per cent at the lower end of the scale to zero at an income level of about £1200 and a rising net burden rate thereafter, reaching 26 per cent above a £3750 level US estimates for 1968 present a similar pattern with the breakeven point at around $8000, approximately the mid-point in the family earnings scale. Throughout, the post-budget distribution of income (earnings plus expenditure benefits minus taxes) is more equal than the distribution of earnings only (excluding benefits and before deducting taxes), and throughout the net gain in equality is substantially larger than if the comparison is limited to taxation effects only.

Nevertheless, the overall impact as measured by the change in Gini coefficient is still modest. This had led observers to note that the redistributive process involves a great deal of churning with a relatively small net effect. This, however, overlooks the fact that the resulting increase in the percentage of income received by, say, the lowest decile or quartile in the income scale is very substantial. As weighted by a social welfare function, the resulting degree of equalisation thus proves much larger than suggested by the resulting unweighted change in Gini coefficient.

Smith might have been pleased with this result, finding support of the poor closer to his virtue of beneficence than a more broadly-based egalitarian goal. But, in line with the winds of current thought, he would have stressed the linkage between distribution policy and accumulation, arguing that all factors stand to gain from more rapid growth, which growth may well be retarded by redistribution. Even so, he would have to revise his view of the mechanism by which the distribution issue is related to growth, as well as his set of moral sentiments by which the case for reduced inequality can be argued or rejected. The wealth of nations, as Smith well knew, is not independent of its distribution; but the same wealth, in the last resort, belongs to the individuals that comprise the nation and thus cannot be assessed without assignment among them.

## NOTES

1. Hume [11, III, ii, 7] offered an uncannily modern conception of the social goods problem including the absence of preference revelation and the freerider issue. Peacock [18].
2. We use 1770 (rather than 1776) as our reference point so as to view the fiscal structure as it was prior to the subsequent expansion in defence outlays. The British national income for 1801 was estimated at £232 million. See Mitchell [14]. With prices about doubling between 1770 and 1800 (ibid., p. 468) this was equivalent to about £160 million in terms of 1770 prices. Allowing for the growth in real income from 1770 to 1800, this seems in line with Hollander's [9] 1770 estimate of £127 million.
3. Indeed, an analysis of his view of public finances and certainly of his view of the role of the state should allow for the *Theory of Moral Sentiments* as well as for the *Wealth of Nations*. The otherwise fine contributions by Peacock [18] and Stigler [27] suffer from drawing on the latter work only. For a fuller interpretation of Smith, drawing on both works, see Recktenwald [21].
4. In Smith's system [25, II, 1] it is the virtue of beneficence, rather than that of justice, which bears close relationship to distributive justice.
5. Smith [26, p. 149] sets forth various ways of acquiring property, viewing entitlement to the fruits of one's labour in a Lockean spirit. However, Smith the practical man is impatient with the abstract construct which derives natural law from the condition which prevails 'in the state of nature—as there is no such state existing'. See also [24, vol. 17, p. 123].
6. This aspect of inter-individual utility interdependence has received intensive consideration in recent years. See Hochman and Rogers [8].
7. The 'all is for the best' flavour of this passage foreshadows Mrs Alexander's nineteenth-century hymn, 'All things bright and beautiful, all creatures great and small, all things wise and wonderful, the Lord God made them all. The rich man in his castle, the poor man at his gate, God made them, high or lowly, and ordered their estate.'
8. The other occurs in the discussion of product markets [24, vol. 1, p. 421].
9. More specifically, Smith argues that it is better to tax these other sources because the maintenance of net wages at subsistence will call for a percentage

increase in the wage rate which exceeds the rate of tax. While the latter point is correct, it hardly justifies the conclusion that *therefore* it is better to use other taxes in the first place.
10. Schumpeter [20, p. 161], when evaluating the Ricardian model, noted that 'it is an excellent theory that can never be refuted and lacks nothing but sense.' [5, iii. 207].
11. See Smith [24, ii. 390]. Given this premise Smith (contrary to Stigler's stricture) did allow for revenue adequacy as part of his system of tax maxims.
12. For a survey of this literature see Seligman [22].

# REFERENCES

[1] Atkinson, A. (1973), 'How progressive should income tax be?', in *Economic Justice*, ed. Phelps, E. (New York, Penguin Books).
[2] Atkinson, A. (1970), 'On the measurement of inequality', *Journal of Economic Theory*, 2.
[3] Central Statistical Office, *Economic Record*, December 1974.
[4] Cooter, R. and Helpman, E. (1974), 'Optimal income taxation for transfer payments, under different welfare criteria', *Quarterly Journal of Economics*, LXXXXVIII.
[5] Dowell, S. (1965), *History of Taxation and Taxes in England* (New York, Kelley).
[6] Edgeworth, F. (1929), *Papers Relating to Political Economy* (London, Macmillan).
[7] Franzen, P., Lovgren, K. and Rosenberg, I. (1975), 'Distribution effects of taxes and public expenditures in Sweden', *The Swedish Journal of Economics*, 77.
[8] Hochman, H. and Rogers, J. (1969), 'Pareto-optimal distribution', *American Economic Review*.
[9] Hollander, S. (1973), *The Economics of Adam Smith* (Toronto, University of Toronto Press), p. 127.
[10] Hume, D. (1752), *Essays and Treatises on Several Subjects* (London, Jones).
[11] Hume, D. (1740), *A Treatise on Human Nature* (Oxford, Clarendon Press).
[12] Kennedy, W. (1913), *English Taxation, 1640–1799* (London, Bell).
[13] Mill, J.S. (1848), *Principles of Political Economy* (London, Longman Green).
[14] Mitchell, B. (1962), *Abstract of British Historical Statistics* (Cambridge, Cambridge University Press), p. 366.
[15] Musgrave, R., Case, K. and Leonard, H. (1974), 'The division of fiscal burdens and benefits', *Public Finance Quarterly*.
[16] Nicholson, J. (1974), 'The distribution and redistribution of income in the United Kingdom', in *Poverty, Inequality and Class Structure* ed. Wedderburn, D. (Cambridge, Cambridge University Press).
[17] Pechman, J. and Okner, B. (1974), *Who Bears the Tax Burden?* (Washington D.C., The Brookings Institution).
[18] Peacock, A. (1975), 'The treatment of the principles of public finance in the *Wealth of Nations*, in *Essays on Adam Smith*, ed. Skinner, A. and Wilson, T. (Oxford, Oxford University Press).
[19] Pigou, A.C. (1928), *A Study in Public Finance* (London, Macmillan).
[20] Schumpeter, J. (1951), 'The review of the troops', *Quarterly Journal of Economics*.

[21] Recktenwald, H. (1975), 'Adam Smith, Heute und Morgen', *Kyklos* XXVIII.
[22] Seligman, E. (1894), *Progressive Taxation in Theory and Practice* (New York, American Economic Association).
[23] Sheshinski, E. (1973), 'The optimal linear income tax', in *Economic Justice*, ed. Phelps, E. (New York Penguin Books).
[24] Smith, A. (1784), *The Wealth of Nations*, ed. Cannan, E. (London, Macmillan).
[25] Smith, A. (1759), *The Theory of Moral Sentiments*, ed. West, E. (New Rochelle, Arlington House).
[26] Smith, A., *Lectures on Jurisprudence*, ed. Cannan, E. (Oxford).
[27] Stigler, G. (1976), 'Smith's travels on the ship of state', in *Essays on Adam Smith*, ed. T. Wilson (Oxford, Oxford University Press).

# 17   Alvin Hansen[*]
## 1976

Alvin Hansen was born in 1887 in Viborg, South Dakota, the youngest child in a family of Danish immigrants. Growing up in the tightly-knit set of a small farm community, he disliked farm chores but compensated with an early interest in learning. In this he was encouraged by his widely-read grandfather, a former Baptist minister, who kindled Alvin's lasting interest in history and introduced him to the wider world. The early school years were spent in a one-room schoolhouse, where the eager child was able to cross rows and listen in on the more advanced lessons. Responding to his mother's stricture that something new must be learned each day, he saw academic pursuits as a welcome escape from farm work and as an alternative way of meeting the high expectations that his community had placed upon him. Travels as choirboy with a local evangelist marked the religious setting of his early childhood. Smilingly, in his later years, he would refer to himself as 'just a simple farm boy', suggesting wonder at where his good fortune had taken him, no less than pride in his early community's values, the importance of work, and the directness of tasks that had to be met, if the farm or, for that matter, the US economy was to thrive.

Because Viborg lacked local facilities, Alvin proceeded to Sioux Falls Academy for his high school education, the first of two students from his area to attend high school and the first to continue on to college. The choice of college was made when G. H. Durand, a Harvard graduate and Kittredge student, visited Viborg to recruit for Yankton College. A small Congregational school, Yankton proved a rich experience, highlighted by the study of Shakespeare under Durand and of history under George Warren. Aware of Alvin's interest in social problems and his great promise (Alvin had received a freshman award as the most outstanding student), Warren encouraged him to undertake graduate work in sociology. Studies, however, had to be interrupted for two years to lay the financial basis for continued education. As a school principal and superintendent in Lake Preston (1912–13), Alvin is said by his former students to have been an inspiring teacher, in the classroom no less than as coach of his newly

---

[*] *Quarterly Journal of Economics*, Vol. XC, (1976).

created basketball and debating teams. There was no such thing as lack of time for either himself or others. It is only those who are hard-pressed for time, so he would tell his students, who can succeed in life.

Although Warren had encouraged him to do graduate work at the University of Chicago, his Yankton credentials proved more readily acceptable at the University of Wisconsin. He thus proceeded to Wisconsin in 1914, where John R. Commons and Richard T. Ely directed his interests into economics. In Commons' workshop, then engaged in providing the raw materials for the *History of Labor in the United States*, Hansen was impressed with the importance of careful attention to data and institutional settings. 'Caring for the real problems', as he later referred to it, was what mattered. In 1916 Hansen married his wife Mabel, a cheerful and sturdy companion for many years to come. In the same year he accepted an instructorship at Brown University, where he stayed for three years. His dissertation was completed during the Brown years. An empirical study of business cycles in the United States, Great Britain and Germany, this work foreshadowed a lasting interest in macroeconomics. The PhD was granted in 1918, and the thesis was published in 1921, after what the department considered to be much-needed stylistic revisions.[1]

While at Brown, Hansen offered a course under the auspices of the Newport YMCA, enthusiastic reports on which led Ely to recommend him (so Hansen thought) for a newly-opened position at the University of Minnesota. The Hansens moved to Minnesota in 1919 and remained there for nearly 20 years. Somewhat surprisingly, Hansen's teaching assignments during his Minnesota years were largely in Labour Economics and in Principles. The latter gave rise to joint authorship with Frederic B. Garver, of *The Principles of Economics* [2], a micro-oriented and demanding introductory text in the neoclassical tradition. At the same time Hansen's own research interests and studies (his daughters report their father as working late into the night) continued in macroeconomics, leading to publication of his *Business Cycle Theory* [4]. A survey and analysis of the state of the art, this volume established Hansen as a major figure in the profession, but as yet gave little indication of what was to come. While Hansen discussed the underconsumption theories of Foster and Catchings extensively, his analysis was unsympathetic to their view. What they thought to be the crucial dilemma of oversaving, so Hansen argued, could be solved by appropriate monetary policy. The basic difficulty, rather, was to be found in society's tendency to accumulate capital without saving, thus giving rise to inflation followed by subsequent collapse.

In 1928–29 Hansen was awarded a Guggenheim Fellowship and spent a year travelling in Europe, interviewing numerous economists, especially in Germany and England. This trip provided him with a wide range of professional acquaintances abroad, an experience that he continued to cherish and expand upon in later years. The material gathered during the trip laid the basis for *Economic Stabilization in an Unbalanced World* [5]. While this study did not as yet recognise how deep the Depression would finally be, it was characteristic of the flavour of Hansen's later work. The book ranges widely over current policy issues, including reparation payments, international capital flows, unemployment insurance and population problems; and each issue is met in a head-on fashion, searching for the causes of the disturbance and proceeding to seek a solution.

The early 1930s also brought the beginning of policy activities outside the campus, activities that for the subsequent decades would come to occupy an increasing share of Hansen's time. Hansen meant to be an educator to the world outside the campus (presidents, senators, businessmen, union leaders, voters) no less than to his students. In this he succeeded. His first Washington assignment was as Director of Research for the Commission of Inquiry on National Policy in International Economic Relations (1933–34), followed by service as economic advisor to Secretary Hull, assisting in the development of trade agreement programmes then undertaken in the State Department (1934–35). On loan from the State Department, Hansen came also to be drawn into the discussion of the Social Security Programme in the fledgling New Deal. In this he was joined by Edwin Witte, with whom he had been a graduate student at Wisconsin and who had become Executive Director of Franklin D. Roosevelt's Commission on Economic Security. Hansen's earlier work on unemployment insurance in Minnesota provided a useful basis for this new task.

The mid-1930s brought two major changes in Hansen's life. Harvard University had been given a grant in 1936 to establish a Graduate School of Public Administration and two Chairs were to be filled, designed 'to direct the work in the social sciences at Harvard more specifically and effectively toward the larger problems of policy and administration with which modern governments are confronted' [1]. Hansen's record as a policy economist eminently qualified him for the new position, and he, together with Heinrich Bruening, last democratic Chancellor of the Weimar Republic were selected as the first appointees. Hansen had no difficulty in accepting the new position, as he considered Harvard one of the two major centres of economic teaching. After moving to Harvard in 1937 as the first Littauer Professor of Political Economy with a joint appointment in the new School of Public Administration and the Department of Economics, Hansen expanded his activities at a rapid pace. Moreover, it was during this period that his views on macroeconomics underwent a profound change. The Depression had reached unexpected depth and the appearance of Keynes' *General Theory* in 1936 had opened new vistas. Hansen's early review of the work [7] had been less critical than most, although far from enthusiastic, as yet failing to recognise the fundamental importance that the new framework was to achieve. But his breakthrough to the new perspective came soon thereafter and matured in the context of the fiscal policy seminar. Offered jointly with John H. Williams, the first Dean of the newly established Graduate School, the seminar became the core of Hansen's teaching activities. Much as Commons had done earlier, Hansen made the seminar the workshop in which the new concepts of Keynesian economics were hammered out and tested, the forum in which the Harvard School of macro policy was formed. Driven by Hansen's keen enthusiasm for the new ideas, his eagerness to learn no less than to teach, and tempered by John Williams' friendly scepticism, the seminar left a deep impact on the future development of macroeconomics and public policy in the United States. The new insights of economic science and the plight of the depressed economy combined to give a sense of unique importance to this venture. The new tools were at hand, and if properly used they would provide a solution to the key problem of unemployment. The early years of the fiscal policy seminar thus became the high point of Hansen's teaching, and the ideas and friendships formed during this time retained a central position in his future work.

Stated in his *Full Recovery or Stagnation?* [8] and propagated in his testimony at the TNEC hearings (1939), Hansen's case for expansionary fiscal policy became a central issue in the public policy debate of the late 1930s. As a member of the Advisory Commission on Social Security (1937–38), he broke with the Wisconsin group in opposing the reserve approach as detrimental to the employment situation. In 1937 he was elected President of the American Economic Association, and a systematic reformulation of his earlier position on business cycle theory was presented in *Fiscal Policy and Business Cycles* [11].

During the war years, Hansen became Chairman of the US–Canadian Joint Economic Commission (1941–43), designed to coordinate the economic war effort of the two countries. From 1940 to 1945 he served as Special Economic Advisor to the Federal Reserve Board, where Marriner Eccles proved a kindred spirit in supporting policies leading to the enormous wartime expansion in employment and output. Moreover, his position at the Board provided him with a helpful base for pursuing his many other interests, including support for his research at Harvard. The battle for full employment had to be continued, and the counter-offensive, built around the alleged dangers of a rising public debt, had to be met. Strategic contributions were made to the important economic developments of the early post-war years, such as the monetary reconstruction of Bretton Woods, which was to align international with domestic stability, and the Employment Act 1946, which was to lay the basis for prosperity at home.

In his presidential address of 1938 Hansen set out the theme that the unemployment of the 1930s was not to be seen as a passing problem, but rather as a structural change inherent in the nature of advanced economic development [9]. Declining population growth and disappearing economic frontiers, combined with a rising rate of saving, he believed, would create a lasting problem of deficient demand that in turn would have to be met by expansionary fiscal measures. The same perspective was retained in his thinking about the post-war setting when, after a brief interval of inflationary pressure, the same tendencies would again dominate the picture. Harking back perhaps to his earlier interest in Sombart's view of 'structural change' (his travel notes suggest that discussions with Sombart had been a high point in his European trip of 1929) and to his long-standing interest in the historical setting of social affairs, the Keynesian concept of underemployment equilibrium was thus extended into a theory of economic stages and development. The central role of inflation and stagflation in the post-war decades was not foreseen, but such is the fortune of most historical prediction.

The goal of full employment was central, but there were other matters of importance. Paralleling Galbraith's position, Hansen argued for more adequate provision of public services, especially at the local level, and for federal responsibility in equalising fiscal capacities and in providing the necessary financing [10]. Nor was there any doubt about the value premises for these goals. Improving the economic lot was a first prerequisite to improving the human condition; and though he considered high employment the key to social progress, this was not his only concern. He also sought to realise 'the democratic ideal of providing for all individuals a reasonable approach to equality of opportunity' [10], and though he thought it neither possible nor desirable to demand complete equality, he felt it 'highly important to eliminate such gross disparity as now exists'. Emphasis was to be on opportunity in jobs, rather than on welfare. Social justice was important, but too self-evident to men of good will (and who would care about the rest?) to need much exposition. Given this basis, Hansen was pragmatic and non-ideological in his approach. The invisible hand should be grasped where useful, but alone it was not enough, and public policy was needed. Choosing wise solutions would be difficult; but solutions could be found, and reasonable men would join in implementing them. The economic and social problem, as he saw it, was not a zero-sum game, but rather one that could be resolved by understanding and cooperation. It was this basic approach to economics as a calling, no less than his specific contributions to analysis and policy, that made so great an impression on his students and associates.

After his retirement from Harvard in 1956, Hansen was invited to continue his research and teaching activities at a variety of institutions. He travelled widely, developed an interest in painting, which he pursued systematically as he had done with other tasks, and continued his readings in history. As throughout his life, he continued to enjoy exploring the variety of ideas and means by which people live and society functions. The Hansens continued their residence on Juniper Street, Belmont until 1973. They then moved to the home of their daughter Marian Merrifield in Alexandria, Virginia, where with his wife Mabel he spent his last few years and where he died on 7 June 1975.


## NOTES

1. Even though Hansen was to become the major proponent of the Keynesian system in the United States [14], there appears to have been no close personal association between the two men. Hansen's less than enthusiastic reception of the *General Theory* had been preceded by an earlier critique [6] of Keynes' *Treatise on Money*, in which Hansen uncovered an error in the first fundamental equation, a discovery, which as a non-mathematician, he viewed with some amusement.

# REFERENCES

[1] *First Annual Report of the Graduate School of Public Administration*, (1937) (Harvard University Press), p. 3.

[2] Garver, F. B. and Hansen, H. A. (1928), *Principles of Economics* (Boston, Ginn).

[3] Hansen, A. H. (1921), *Cycles of Prosperity and Depression in the United States, Great Britain and Germany: A Study of Monthly Data 1902–1908* (Madison, University of Wisconsin Press).

[4] Hansen, A. H. (1927), *Business Cycle Theory: Its Development and Present Status* (Boston, Ginn).

[5] Hansen, A. H. (1932), *Economic Stabilization in an Unbalanced World* (New York, Harcourt Brace).

[6] Hansen, A. H. (1932), 'A fundamental error in Keynes' *Treatise on Money*', *American Economic Review*, XXII.

[7] Hansen, A. H. (1936), 'Mr Keynes on underemployment equilibrium', *Journal of Political Economy*, XLIV, no. 5, October.

[8] Hansen, A. H. (1938), *Full Recovery or Stagnation?* (New York, Norton).

[9] Hansen, A. H. (1939), 'Progress and declining population', *American Economic Review*, XXIX, March.

[10] Hansen, A. H. and Perloff, H. S. (1944), *State and Local Finance in the National Economy* (New York, Norton).

[11] Hansen, A. H. (1941), *Fiscal Policy and Business Cycles* (New York, Norton); for a later statement see also *Monetary Theory and Fiscal Policy* (1949) (New York, McGraw Hill).

[12] Hansen, A. H. (1938), *Full Recovery or Stagnation?* (New York, Norton).

[13] Hansen, A. H. (1941), *Fiscal Policy and Business Cycles* (New York, Norton); for a later statement see also *Monetary Theory and Fiscal Policy* (New York, McGraw Hill).

[14] Hansen, A. H. (1953), *A Guide to Keynes* (New York, McGraw Hill).

# 18   Economics and the World around It*
## 1980

Economic theory, in Joan Robinson's phrase, is a box of tools. This makes a good beginning, but leaves open the question of what the tools are to be used for and who is to use them. During my years in Ann Arbor, I was too busy making tools to raise such epistemological questions, as were my colleagues. Ken Boulding completed the third edition of his *magnum opus* and was getting ready to disown it; Gardner Ackley and Warren Smith were revising the Keynesian model to allow for the eventuality of a sloping LM curve; Wolf Stolper had discovered that factors as well as products can move across borders; Bill Haber and Hal Levinson demonstrated that unions after all do raise wages; Dan Suits and Larry Klein were building the world's first man-sized econometric model; George Katona and Jim Morgan were dressing *homo economicus* in human clothing; Shorey Peterson was dispensing no-nonsense elementary economics; Bill Palmer was expounding Chamberlinian market structures; Harvey Brazer was exploring why governments act the way they do; and I was inventing my theory of public finance, interrupted only by occasional trips to Lansing to discuss the state of the state with Governor Soapy Williams. All this was to refurnish the box with a final set of tools, Michigan-made, ready to take care of any pipe that might burst or any wiring that might short-circuit. Thirty years later I am a bit more doubtful, as I suppose are my friends and comrades of those golden years. As one grows older it becomes more tempting to theorise about theories than to invent them, and I do not apologise for that. Both activities are needed and have their role.


## DETERMINANTS OF ECONOMIC THEORY

Economic theory, so we tell our students, is to instruct us about the relationship between dependent and independent variables in the economic system. But what about reversing the process and taking economic theory as the dependent variable? What then should we expect to find on the right side of the equation? The answer has to be catholic since

---

* In *Economics and the World around It (1980)*, ed. S. Hymans, (Ann Arbor, University of Michigan Press).

280

single-cause explanations are sure to be wrong. To express this spirit while maintaining a workable framework for my paper, I shall distinguish between three lines of causation, including (1) the internal logic of theoretical development, (2) the changing technical, institutional and social setting in which the economy operates, and (3) the role of value or ideology.

In the first place, economic theory, in the spirit of Schumpeter's *History of Economic Analysis*, may be seen as driven by an internal dynamics of scientific advance. Simple hypotheses turn into more concise formulations and provide deeper insights. Answers to old problems lead to new ones and an expanding theoretical structure emerges. To illustrate, follow the trail from early perceptions of diminishing returns, over the law of variable proportions to today's sophisticated production functions. Or consider the mutation of Quesnay's tableau into multiple-sector input–output models, the maturing of the Walrasian system into Arrow–Debreu theorems on the existence of competitive equilibrium, and the path from early wage funds to modern demand theories. While a continuing process, this refinement of analytical tools has proceeded at an uneven pace, with periods of slow progress along established lines (ordinary science in Kuhn's sense) interrupted by major breakthroughs (changes in paradigm if you wish). Identifying the paradigm changers is an attractive parlour game for economists (Smith, Ricardo, Marx, Menger, Wicksell, Schumpeter, Keynes, and who else?) which I shall not play here, but I should note that my concept of internal progress is not limited to puzzle-solving activity, but also includes the vision of new puzzles.

Secondly, refinement of analytical tools offers an important key to the history of economic thought but unfortunately (or, happily, depending on where you stand) it is by no means the entire story. Surely, allowance must be made for the fact that economic activity (unlike the solar system) operates in a rapidly changing environment, this being one of the ways in which economics and astronomy differ. Such changes may be technical or demographic in nature, or they may involve the institutions, in which the economic process is conducted. The changing environment, by posing new problems, calls for new tools with which to resolve them. Adam Smith's concern with the division of labour was enlivened by the concurrent development of manufacture, Ricardo's interest in comparative advantage was linked to the debate over the Corn Laws, Keynes' macroeconomics responded to the experience of the Great Depression, theories of imperfect competition reflected the development of new market structures, the rising cost of energy now poses new problems in factor substitution, and so on. Many of the great contributors to economic theory were involved in the affairs of their time and even contributed to the course of events. The development of economic theory may thus be viewed as the manufacture of tools designed to meet demands derived from the course of changing events. When toolmakers lag behind changing demand (witness their default in the current debate over inflation) economics and economists suffer in reputation, and rightly so.

My third line of causation deals with the role of changing value systems. This might have been included as a further aspect of environmental change, but I prefer to consider it a distinct factor. The role of values, in my view, is not simply one of apologetic ideology or superstructure. That role exists, but beyond it values enter as a distinct variable with an exogenous quality of their own. Their effectiveness in shaping events depends on their holder's ability to promote them, be it by writing books, access to the media, or through political power. The market place of ideas is as imperfect (if not more so) as that for goods, but this does not reduce the importance of ideas. As time goes by, I have been increasingly impressed by the connection between the theories which particular economists produce and their values. Why otherwise could it be that the work of one set of theorists is directed at showing that velocity is more stable than the multiplier, that the Coase theorem takes care of externalities or that expectations are rational, while the work of another set aims to show that the multiplier is more stable, that Pigouvian taxes are required and that expectations are a matter of outguessing or of animal spirit?

By pointing to the importance of values, I do not mean to argue that economists cheat, although sometimes they do. Rather, I follow Max Weber's contention that it is quite proper for the investigator to let his or her choice of hypothesis be influenced by values, provided that the testing proceeds along objective lines. What matters, as Schumpeter put it, is whether the answers are right, not why the question was posed. Nevertheless, value considerations, by influencing the choice of problems under investigation, have much to do with how economic theory advances. Since ideological cycles are of the Kondratieff rather than the Kitchin type, this is an important factor, perhaps not over infinity but over quite substantial periods.

Having defined these three lines of causation, let me briefly respond to some objections which may arise. Some may wish me to stay with my first point; deal with the internal logic of theoretical development and leave it at that. External events should not be permitted to divert the pure theorist's concern with the true essence of economics, i.e. the efficient use of scarce resources, conceived as a formal proposition. Nor should economists feel called upon to address such amorphous concepts as value (excepting, of course, value in exchange) or distribution, a matter to be left to social philosophers or, even worse, to sociologists. I understand that message, but I disagree. Economics should be more than engineering and consulting training. If it is to be a social science, it cannot be sealed off from the world around it.

Others may well take the opposite view, pleased that I have added a second and third perspective, but disagreeing with my distinguishing so sharply between them. I am sympathetic, but plead inability to do better, at least in the context of this paper. The ultimate goal, to be sure, is to develop a general social theory in which various dimensions of the social process are linked in interaction. Economics has an important niche in such a system, but so do other aspects of the social sciences (psychology, social philosophy, politics) and no single perspective (not even economics) can claim to be the centrepiece. The Michigan tradition has not been unaware of this; and notwithstanding the current trend of the profession to the contrary, I hope that it will continue to be the case. At the same time it must be admitted that a general social theory is almost impossible to devise. Not because there would be too many equations but because there is no common unit of account, nor is there a common mechanism of interaction through which the various dimensions of the system can be linked. Some heroic attempts to do so have been made, including Adam Smith's in his *Theory of Moral Sentiments*, and Karl Marx in his theory of social change, but both present a vastly oversimplified and, in their own ways, biased view of how society really functions. Max Weber, wiser and aware of the multidimensional nature of the social process, avoided such oversimplification, but consequently failed to arrive at a workable system. However this may be, I shall for now have to focus on economic theory as if it were the centrepiece, and consider how its development has responded to my three forces.

More specifically, I shall apply this framework to examining the development of public sector economics. This has been closest to my own work and also one of the most lively and expanding areas of retooling. Since the 1920s, when Lord Robbins declared economics the science of the marketplace, there has been a growing involvement of economic theory with non-market transactions. Public sector economics has become a major and integral part of economic theory. This development responded to a rapid growth of the public sector in western market economies, as well as to an ideological climate which (from the 1930s to the early 1970s) was supportive of governmental participation in economic life. Most leading economists during this period were in the liberal camp. In viewing this development, I will make use of my distinction between the allocation, distribution, and stabilisation aspects of the public sector. Though much criticised, this tripartite approach has been widely accepted and remains, I believe, essentially correct.

## ALLOCATION ASPECTS

Beginning with the allocation aspects, the most important development of modern economics has been the theory of social goods. While dating back to Wicksell's writings of the 1890s and Lindahl's extension of 1919, the modern era begins with my retelling their story in the late 1930s and with Samuelson's restatement of the mid-1950s. In this restatement social goods, i.e. goods involving non-rival consumption, were incorporated into the model of Pareto-efficient resource use, thereby establishing them as honourable members of the community of economic phenomena, and worthy of the theorist's attention. The principles of welfare economics were generalised to encompass the phenomenon of externalities, a fine illustration of how economic theory develops out of its internal logic.

But the linkage between stating efficiency conditions and reaching efficient outcomes (produced in the case of private goods through a market mechanism) remained undefined. Since social goods must be made available free of direct charge (marginal cost for additional users being zero) provision for such goods cannot be accomplished through the market mechanism. An alternative process is needed to secure preference revelation. To overcome the freerider problem, this has to be a political process, involving mandatory compliance. By disavowing this part of the problem as a hopeless morass, Samuelson's initial formulation placed social goods theory into a somewhat barren context, a context from which (notwithstanding my efforts and those of a few others) it has had difficulty emerging. Stating efficiency conditions for social goods was a fundamental first step, but tools are as good as their use and the pay-off is in learning how to apply them. Budgetary provision based on mandatory implementation of a voting rule leaves some participants dissatisfied, so that the outcome will not be optimal. But this is no occasion for setting aside the issue. The real problem, in economics as in other aspects of life, is how to avoid tenth-best solutions if fifth-best outcomes can be obtained. The development of a theory of public choice has been helpful and recent models of cheat-proof voting systems may prove an important step. Nevertheless, much remains to be done along these lines.

As distinct from the endogenous nature of social goods theory, the development of cost-benefit analysis offers a prime illustration of demand-induced supply of economic tools. Though calling for the resolution of theoretical issues (e.g. how to derive the proper rate of discount) this enterprise has been an eminently practical one. While somewhat discredited by over-enthusiastic attempts at detailed application, it nevertheless offers a most useful step toward translating the theory of public economics into efficient practice. Such is the case even though the recipe-book approach to cost-benefit analysis can be applied only after the menu has been written. And to write the menu for social goods, the problem of benefit measurement must first be resolved. This qualification, however, is rendered less serious by the fact that public expenditures frequently, if not typically, involve provision for mixed rather than for pure social goods. Moreover, even in the latter case, cost-benefit analysis offers a useful framework in which to analyse the problem.

Since the 1960s, there has been a shift in attention from the provision of social goods to the avoidance of social bads, such as those caused by environmental pollution, for example. External costs, like external benefits, are not accounted for by the market and hence in need of correction. Once more this is not an entirely new development, at least not to those of us who remember Pigou's *Economics of Welfare* with its proverbial smoke nuisance case. The principles are the same as for social goods theory; only the application differs. The sudden growth of environmental concern and, with it, the growth of environmental economics may be seen as a response to the increasing incidence of pollution—another illustration of demand-induced tool supply. Some such increase has occurred, especially with regard to automobile pollution, but there is more to the dramatic rise of environmental economics than that. It also reflects the ideological anti-system mood of the 1960s, dwelling as it were on an inherent weakness of the market with its neglect of external cost and the belief that there is a common entitlement to, or sanctity in, the benefits of nature.

The trends in public sector economics which I have noted so far support the proposition that action by the public sector is needed to correct for market failure. While this has been the dominant trend from the 1930s to 1960s, the 1970s have brought a sharp reversal. Instead of viewing the government as acting efficiently in correcting market failure, the dominant vision seems to be of government acting inefficiently and disturbing the functioning of the market. The new theme is government, not market, failure. In part, this again reflects the internal logic of theoretical development. As one compartment of the tool-box is filled, the emptiness of another becomes apparent and it cannot stay so for too long. Thus, in the wave of theorising about what efficient government should do, theorising about what makes government behave as it does is not neglected. While the Marxist tradition in its concern with fiscal sociology and the role of the state had always been aware of this aspect, mainstream analysts had given it only minor attention. Government, so we had assumed, would attempt to implement the wishes of the voters as well as it could, especially if following our advice on what to do.

A positive theory of public sector behaviour, though not necessarily a theory of public misbehaviour, was thus in order. Yet it is not surprising that the new development took the latter form, precisely because it coincided with a sharp value shift in the ideological spectrum. The emergence of a new generation of conservative intellectuals which we have witnessed over the last decade has been an important event and has had a massive impact on public sector economics. Indeed, public sector economists have been in the vanguard of that development. As I see it, their modelling of government behaviour in terms of monopolistic bureaux and agenda-setters takes a rather one-sided view. Policy-makers, like businessmen, may be expected to act as maximisers, if that term simply denotes purposeful behaviour. But it is wrong to assume that the same purpose (i.e. profits) is the object of maximisation in all cases. There is more than 'one game in town' and to model government behaviour in terms of profit-maximisation is to build government failure into the model. Moreover, such modelling leads to faulty policy prescription. Nevertheless, the new theory of government failure has been an important development which in time, and under a more balanced perspective, should contribute to a better understanding of the public sector.

## DISTRIBUTION ASPECTS

Turning now to the public sector's role in distribution, economic theory was quick to develop and to refine a theory of factor shares. At the outset, this theory was not without social content, as the relevant parties (land, labour and capital) did reflect the then significant pattern of social stratification. But before long the theory of distribution became a theory of efficient factor pricing, interesting as a part of welfare economics and to some degree as a description of market behaviour but only loosely related to the quite different question of how the fruits of economic activity are or should be distributed among the members of the community. Yet the latter issue plays a central role in what economic activity is about. Viewed from the perspective of the social scientist it may well be *the* central issue. However hard it may try, economic theory cannot for long neglect this half of the problem.

Under the old welfare economics (from, say, John Stuart Mill over Edgeworth to Pigou) the rationale of distribution policy, and its application to progressive taxation, was seen in terms of equal and comparable marginal utility of income schedules. Dan Suits used to tell me that this was a nonsense proposition since I would be unable to show him the laboratory where utility is measured. I never quite believed him, and still do not, but his came to be the view of the profession. The great retreat to Pareto-efficiency was underway, with distribution issues, somewhat like naughty children, banned from the professional table. But not for too long, since distribution soon reappeared in the guise of the social welfare function. (Let me note that my story here uses the novelist's licence in somewhat distorting historical timing, but remains essentially correct.) This, however, was to restate the problem rather than to resolve it. Without telling us how the social welfare function is derived, and bedevilled further by Arrow's proposition that there is no consistent way of derivation anyhow, all this remained at a rather formal level. None the less, distribution issues were readmitted and theorists were spared further embarrassment by the comparability assumption.

The social welfare function, after its triumphant entry in the late 1930s, kept a rather low profile during the first three decades of its life, but has moved back into the forefront of discussion of late. Interestingly enough, this has come in response to the writings of social philosophers, mainly John Rawls' *Theory of Justice*. Justice as fairness, Rawls argued, requires a state of distribution in line with maximin, permitting inequality only to the extent that its retention improves the position of the least favoured. Economists found much to criticise in this formulation (including the assumption of total risk-aversion and the zero valuation of welfare losses from taxation incurred above the minimum) but it gave rise to an interesting debate over how the shape of the social welfare function could be derived from underlying value premises about social justice. I for one have found this a fascinating interaction between economic theory and theories of non-market value. Its timing was in line with the rapidly rising level of transfer payments by the public sector and the debate over such issues as the negative income tax and welfare reform.

A subsequent and recent development in the tool-kit of distribution economics has been the application of optimal taxation theory to the income tax. This has also reflected a resumption of earlier themes. Edgeworth had qualified his conclusion in favour of equalisation (the minimum total sacrifice rule) by reference to incentive effects; and Pigou, in his discussion of tax burden distribution, had pointed to the existence of what he called announcement effects. Moreover, it was Pigou whose queries induced the first formal statement by Ramsay. But only recently have efficiency costs of redistribution moved to the centre of the discussion. Since continuing redistribution from A to B cannot be sustained by lump-sum transfers (that least useful if most popular tool of welfare theory) the efficiency cost involved in such transfer must be allowed for. This development offers another illustration of theoretical advance driven by the internal logic of the system. My generation of tax theorists has paid much attention to the distribution of the tax burden, in terms of both horizontal and vertical equity, but we have tended to view the burden in terms of revenue collected, thus disregarding the efficiency cost of excess burden. Correction for this benign (or, as others might see it, malign) neglect was due. But the change in emphasis is also a good illustration of the ideological base from which questions are asked. For one thing, concern with the efficiency cost of redistribution appeals to a conservative position as it limits the scope for such policies. For another, the new generation of efficiency-oriented tax theorists shows little distress over the disappearance of horizontal equity from the analysis, a disappearance which follows from the assumption (shared by most optimal tax theory) of identical utility functions. My mathematical friends tell me that to allow for such differences would render the problem unmanageable. Yet this issue was central to the more equity-oriented analysis of my generation. I do hope that a mathematical genius who can reintroduce it will come along.

## STABILISATION ASPECTS

Turning to fiscal concerns with macro policy, we find perhaps the most dramatic and interesting story of continuing retooling. The macro vision of Adam Smith was one of economic growth, driven by accumulation and thrift. The state had a role in certain areas of public investment (bridges, harbours, canals) but that was all. Ricardian revisionism was less optimistic, with growth declining toward the stationary state and Malthusian subsistence. The state was assigned no role except as a spendthrift whose scope should be minimised. Both views involved a smooth journey along a predetermined path, with Say's law assuring the clearing of markets, and controlling traffic along the way. There was no occasion for stabilisation policy in the modern sense. With Marx concern shifted to conflicts and contradictions, of both a short- and long-run nature, within the system. Stabilisation would be called for but, by the nature of the capitalist state, could not be forthcoming in an efficient form. Wicksell's vision of the natural rate of interest focused on the equilibrating mechanism of the modern economic system and the role of financial markets therein, thus laying the groundwork for modern macro and stabilisation theory. Robertson, and Keynes in his *Treatise*, continued in that vein, whereas business cycle theorists such as Hayek extended the structural tradition of Ricardo and Marx. Next came the Keynsian revolution, a piece of economic history for those who study now, but the dominant event of my generation's academic childhood. The *General Theory* obviously was a response to the policy needs of the Great Depression. But beyond this, so it seemed, it also offered a fundamental breakthrough in economic understanding. It had disproven the classical system and elevated deficit finance as *the* solution to the problem of macro policy. Later on, the neoclassical synthesis of the 1950s provided a *rapprochement* between the Keynesian and the classical view, leaving the continuing battle between the two schools somewhat of a tempest in the theoretical teapot. Moreover, the neoclassical synthesis dislodged the expenditure side of the budget from its unique position as a stabilisation tool, making it clear that aggregate demand control can be accomplished from either the tax or the expenditure side, or for that matter by monetary tools.

Since then we have witnessed a near replacement of short-run macro theorising by econometric model-building. This reflected the strategic role of lags in short-run economic change, a role first noted in Duesenberry's consumption lags (also a product of Michigan economics) and in Metzler's contribution to the Hansen *Festschrift*. But when all is said and done, lag structures cannot be derived theoretically but are an empirical matter, making it difficult to construct useful models without an empirical base. Moreover, the econometric approach has been made possible by the development of computer technology, illustrating how the content of economic theory responds to changes in the technology of theorising. The transformation of stabilisation policy into econometrics has helped, but has also had its problems—not so much because it is the wrong way in which to go, but because as yet the tools are unequal to the task.

Another important development has been a renewed concern with the long-run issues of economic growth. This is not surprising. The short-run nature of the Keynesian model with fixed capital stock was inadequate and had to be amended to allow for capital accumulation and for growth, a factor which had been so central to the classical system. In the early phases of this development, as reflected in the Harrod–Domar model, there was a hope that reintroduction of growth could be combined with the insights of Keynesian economics, but this was not to be. Instead, growth theory returned the analysis to the context of a wholly flexible classical model, as if disturbances did not exist. With the Malthusian doom removed by the pill, society is free to choose its growth path into the future. Disturbances are considered irrelevant in the long run, which is not only wrong but also, as Keynes noted, of limited concern. All this has important bearing on the role of public policy. With the emphasis on growth, the impact of fiscal policy shifts from aggregate demand to the composition of output and in particular to the level of private investment. As I shall note presently, this has involved important implications for the politics of fiscal policy. Moreover, the nature of the growth model has direct bearing on what can be accomplished by fiscal policy. Given a growth model of the Solow type, fiscal policy can affect the level of output but not the long-run rate of growth, thus limiting its usefulness.

A painful parallel to the ultra-classical nature of modern growth theory is found in the current theory of inflation. Disregarding earlier models of inflation, which emphasised the dynamic aspects of adjustment lags, current models centre on tracing a hypothetical adjustment to a non-existent equilibrium rate of inflation, thereby missing the essentially dynamic nature of the problem. Economic theory progresses, but like other human endeavours, not necessarily along a straight line.

The most recent development in macro theory has been an emphasis on rational expectations, reflecting as it were a delayed reaction to the Keynesian emphasis on uncertainty and irrational behaviour. Once more we see how in filling one section of the box the next one is discovered. Ordinary science then requires that it also be filled. The new tools need to be explored even if in the end they do not turn out to be very useful. I believe such to be the case when it comes to the application of the new approach to the role of fiscal policy. The proposition is that consumers' responses to tax and deficit finance will be the same because taxes needed for future debt services are capitalised. This seems to me a quite unrealistic assumption, so that the conclusion is not a particularly useful addition to our kit of tools. I should add in all fairness that there is a central assumption in traditional fiscal theory which is subject to a similar objection. This is the assumption, which most of us have been accustomed to use, that government adjusts tax and expenditure levels in a rational fashion. Thus, built-in revenue responses are taken to be stabilising in an inflationary setting, as is an increase in tax rates, but such is not the case under an alternative and at times more realistic model, where government expenditures tend to move with tax revenues. One of the difficulties in recent years has been precisely this perverse type of behaviour.

Enough has been said to show how the development of macro theory and of fiscal policy tools has responded to both the logic of internal development and to changes in the setting of the economy. Once more a word may be added regarding the role of values. As a preliminary, what *is* macro theory, anyhow? After distinguishing between partial and general equilibrium aspects of micro theory, what remains there to be explored? Taking the model of a perfectly functioning market system, full employment prevails automatically and the market sets real wages so as to equate the demand supply for labour. Similarly, the system automatically achieves an optimal rate of growth as the time-preference of consumers is equated with the marginal product of capital. A policy issue arises only with regard to money supply. Economists in rare agreement reject the commercial loan theory and hold that a central bank is needed to control the money supply. But given a well-behaved classical system, this task is trivial. The central bank should simply let the money supply expand with real output. Macro theorists may investigate how the rate of growth would change if the time preference of consumers did differ, but that would be a limited pursuit.

For macro theory to be fun, there must be disturbances in the system. That is to say, *macro theory is essentially a theory of market failure.* As such, its link to ideological factors becomes evident. The exhilaration which early Keynesians experienced in proving Say's law to be wrong is a good illustration. So is the almost touching satisfaction which marketeers derive from restoring the honour of their system by reference to the Pigou effect. If only wages and prices were perfectly flexible, there could be nothing wrong with 'the system as such'—the working of the Pigou effect would, sooner or later, restore the economy to full employment. Essentially the same 'as if' argument reappears in postulating a long-run vertical Phillips curve with a constant equilibrium rate of inflation at full employment.

Value aspects also enter into how various instruments of stabilisation policy are viewed. In the early stages of Keynesian economics, stabilisation policy was directed at expanding demand. Moreover the instrument of expansion was seen in raising government spending. Celebration of the balanced budget multiplier came later, as did recognition that expansion can also be accomplished via tax reduction. The fiscal approach came thus to be associated with large budgets, with the liquidity trap a welcome excuse for expanding the public sector. Hence it is not surprising that fiscal policy advocates were to be found in the liberal camp. Now that the problem has become one of restriction, stabilisation policy via expenditure adjustment (downwards) emerges as a conservative cause. Checking inflation becomes a massive argument for cutting back the budget, notwithstanding the fact that demand restraint may contribute little to stabilisation and that the primary source of demand expansion may be in the private sector—in consumer credit, for example.

Similar considerations apply to the rise of 'supply-side economics', both in the context of long-run growth and in dealing with inflation. Having more in the future is, of course, to everybody's advantage, but the question is who gets less in the present. Growth-promoting policies in a market economy must strengthen incentives for saving and investment. Deterring effects of taxation upon incentives depend upon marginal rather than average rates, and the same applies with regard to the marginal tax rates which are implicit in transfers that decline with income. Incentive policies, therefore, tend to be anti-redistributive and differ in this respect from stabilisation policy which may be held distributionally neutral. The concern with growth and supply-side economics thus has strong political implications. These are evident for issues of distribution policy but go well beyond them. Emphasis on growth is in line with the ethos of capitalism, the heroic role of the entrepreneur and the entitlement to individual effort. What on the surface appears a purely economic issue—that raising the growth rate by $x$ per cent requires the rate of capital formation to be increased by $y$ per cent, for example—is but the tip of a much larger iceberg of political, social and cultural change.

## CONCLUSION

Looking back at the preceding discussion, it is not surprising to find that public sector economics lends itself especially well to exploring how economic analysis responds to the changing world around it. We have seen that the development of analytical tools in important respects follows its internal logic, but we have also seen that other factors such as changes in social or economic setting and in value systems must be allowed for as well. Failure to do so reduces what is inherently a social science to the much less interesting (if perhaps simpler) world of physics. Taking this view, it is unnecessary to add that I have misgivings about how our science has been moving. The growth of mathematical tools in recent decades has contributed greatly to the rigour of economic analysis, but it has also moved this analysis along lines to which mathematical rigour can best be applied. Technique and substance are not unrelated, nor are they without bearing on the role of values.

As noted before, I have been increasingly impressed with this role, not in the sense that its presence leads to false analysis, but in the sense that values pose the questions which are asked. In particular, I think that there are two value sets which are of key importance. One is how one relates to the phenomenon of the invisible hand. The other is how one views the issue of social justice. I begin with the former, the role of the invisible hand in securing an efficient outcome through the mechanism of a competitive market. Though commonplace in our thinking, this is a truly extraordinary concept. As an intellectual proposition, I still find it astounding—indeed, mind-boggling—that the self-interested action of millions of individuals should automatically lead to a result which is efficient for the community as a whole. I have been told that this surprise is naive because efficiency is defined so as to reject the non-market outcome, but such is surely not the case. The phenomenon is extraordinary, especially since it does not hold in other spheres of social interaction. But it does not follow that a system, guided by the invisible hand, must be the best of all worlds. To some, it would appear a magnificent working of deistic design (as in Adam Smith's *Theory of Moral Sentiments*) while to others it poses a strange paradox. If the nature of things is such that man will be most social by being selfish, then how can a moral social order be established? The former will seek to demonstrate that most real-world phenomena lend themselves to market solutions, thereby reducing the need for state intervention. The latter will be inclined to show that phenomena such as externalities do not permit solution by market process so that a political type of social interaction is required.

Similar considerations arise with regard to views of social justice. Some will hold that a person is entitled to the fruits of his or her labour, while others will hold that talents should be considered common property in the good society. The former will be inclined to verify the hypothesis that redistribution policies carry a heavy excess burden, while the latter hope to show the burden to be slight. And even after the cost has been agreed upon, as it should be in the course of objective analysis, observers will differ on the price which should be paid. No wonder, then, that value-based formulation of problems, combined with objective research in their resolution, has had a major effect on the development of economics, and in particular on the economics of the public sector.

# 19 Liability Rules, Efficiency and Equity*
## 1980

## INTRODUCTION

During the century, the legal doctrine on product liability has moved towards shifting the locus of liability from consumer to producer and towards extending its scope to inclusion of damages not due to specific product failure or to negligence on the producer's part. Moreover, there has been a tendency towards coverage of third parties not in contractual relation to the producer. While the former extensions remain within the world of private goods and markets, the latter deals with an externality or social good type of situation.

## THE CONTRACTUAL SETTING

In choosing between consumer liability (*CL*) and producer liability (*PL*) both efficiency and equity considerations must be allowed for. Whereas the legal move towards producer liability has been based largely on equity grounds, economists have emphasised the efficiency aspects and have presented three sets of conclusions, i.e. (1) that the choice between *PL* and *CL* does not matter because the response of the market leads to similar outcomes in either case; (2) that *CL* is preferable because it leaves the consumer with a wider choice, and (3) that liability should be placed where the cost of risk-bearing is cheapest, pointing mostly to *PL*. Our purpose is to specify the settings under which the various conclusions apply.[1]

### Perfect Markets
Consider a consumer good which, with a known probability distribution and independently of frequency or manner of use, generates a risk of damage to the user. Assume further that perfect competition prevails in both product and risk markets. Under such conditions, *CL* and *PL* lead to identical results.

* With Elisha A. Pazner (1980). Originally published in *Public Finance, Finances Publiques*, Vol. XXXV, 1. pp. 1–12. Reprinted with the permission of the Foundation Journal Public Finance.

Under *CL*, the *consumer* will obtain his product at a lower price than under *PL* but incur a risk in the process of using it. If the degree of risk-taking involved exceeds his total demand for risk (at the going rate of return for risk-taking) he will compensate by insurance; if the risk involved is insufficient, he will supplement it by other risks, say through purchase of lottery tickets. Under *PL* the consumer will have to pay more but can consume his product without risk. He will therefore meet his demand for risk-investment entirely by the purchase of lottery tickets. His net risk position will be the same in both cases as will be the terms under which risk-taking is undertaken. The opposite situation applies to the *producer*. Under *CL* the producer incurs no product risk and satisfies his entire demand for risk-taking by the purchase of lottery tickets. Under *PL* he incurs a product risk. If the risk thus incurred exceeds his demand for risk taking, he may compensate by taking out insurance. If the product risk is insufficient, he may supplement it by the purchase of tickets. Either party will incur the desired level of risk, whatever the liability rule. Assuming perfect markets the return to risk and the cost of insurance will be equated by arbitrage and the same terms will be available to all. Limitations imposed upon risk involved in the consumption or production of particular products do not matter as they can be compensated for by adjustments in other risks or insurance.

In terms of a demand–supply diagram, a switch from *PL* to *CL* will result in a drop of the product supply schedule by the cost of 100 per cent insurance. This will be the case whether or not the producer chooses to purchase such insurance under *PL* since his retention of product risk involves an equivalent opportunity cost. The switch will also result in an equal drop of the demand schedule, independent of whether the consumer will now purchase insurance or not. As a result, the amount purchased remains unchanged. The case is analogous to that of a unit tax which leads to identical results whether imposed on the demand or the supply side of the market. Both consumers and producers were satisfied with their risk position under *PL* and remain so after the switch to *CL*. Only the mix of risks (product risk, insurance, lottery tickets) changes.

Not only does it follow that both *PL* and *CL* lead to efficient solutions but the solutions are identical, leaving the choice between *PL* and *CL* a matter of indifference on equity as well as efficiency grounds.

## Blocked Access to Risk and Insurance Markets

As against this conclusion, James Buchanan [8] has made a case in support of *CL*, based on the proposition that under *CL* consumers, by purchasing insurance, have the option of selecting levels of insurance or residual degrees of risk which are in line with their particular degrees of risk-aversion. Under a system of *PL*, they are effectively coerced into buying a fully-insured product. Such is the case because, under *PL*, the producer must compensate the consumer for the full damage and hence charges the consumer with the full insurance cost. As a result, the consumer must link purchase of the product with the purchase of full insurance. His options are curtailed and this imposes a welfare loss.

In terms of our demand and supply diagram, substitution of *CL* for *PL* will lead to a drop in the supply schedule by the full amount of the 100 per cent insurance cost. On the consumer's side, the demand schedule will also drop, but this drop will fall short of the full insurance cost. Purchase of the product now gives consumers the opportunity to take risk, which they can do by taking less than 100 per cent insurance. This renders the product more attractive to consumers, especially if their risk-aversion is low. As a result, the amount of product purchased will increase, the increase being the larger, the lower is the consumer's risk-aversion. *CL* is superior on efficiency grounds because it removes the limitation on consumer choice (i.e. restraint on risk-taking) which was imposed by *PL*. This conclusion, we may add, does not depend on the fact that *PL* typically involves 100 per cent liability, but would also hold (with reduced force) for a partial but fixed liability share under *PL*.

While *CL* is more efficient under these conditions, is it also preferable on equity grounds? It is evident that the outcomes now differ and that consumers as a group gain from substitution of *CL*. This follows since their options are increased. Producers, on the other hand, are deprived of their market for rendering insurance services to consumers, tending to worsen their position.[2] If on the average consumers have a lower income than producers this may be taken to involve an equity gain, but such need not be the case. Much depends on the product in question (who consumes it) and on the groups of producers that are involved in supplying it. Moreover, the gain to particular households will depend on their degree of risk-aversion. Substitution of *CL* will be especially advantageous to households which spend a relatively large share of their income on risky products and which have low risk-aversion. It is not evident that these must be low-income households.[3] Risky products are consumed throughout the income scale. While damages from oil stoves accrue typically to low-income households, plane accidents are a high-income hazard. Nevertheless, for many products (e.g. stoves) the cheaper quality tends to be riskier and low-income households will buy the cheaper quality. This supports the presumption of unequalising effects, but in the end the issue is an empirical one and cannot be answered without closer investigation.

Buchanan's case for *CL* is appealing but the conclusion rests entirely on the implicit premise that consumers do *not* have any access to the risk (lottery) market whereas producers do. The opposite result follows if the blocked access to risk-taking (the lottery market) applies to the producer's side. The shift from *PL* to *CL* then causes the demand schedule to fall by the full (100 per cent) insurance cost, while the supply schedule declines by a lesser amount. As a result, the amount sold declines, the reduction being larger, the lower is the suppliers' risk-aversion. In this case, *PL* is more efficient because *CL* limits the producer's option to take risk, and the equity aspect involves a gain in the position of producers relative to that of consumers. Which rule is preferable, therefore, depends on the empirical question of access to risk markets and the respective degrees of risk-aversion.

## Differential Risk and Insurance Markets

In the preceding section we have dealt with an all-or-nothing situation, where one side has access to risk markets which permits it to compensate for risk positions involved in the product while the other side has not. Turning to a more realistic setting, we must allow for a situation where both sides have access to risk markets, but where the costs of risk-bearing differ.[4]

Such differences may arise because lower resource costs are involved. Producers may enjoy economies of scale in time and negotiation costs, while entering into insurance agreements. Or, differences may come about because producers and consumers deal with separate risk-insurance markets, and are confronted by different returns to risk-taking and insurance costs. This may reflect differences in supply–demand conditions in the two markets, or differences in their respective market structures. In particular, assume that the return to risk-taking on the producer's side is higher (the pay-off on lottery tickets is better and insurance costs are lower) than on the consumer's side. Substitution of *PL* for *CL* will then be an efficient move because the increase in supply price reflecting producers' insurance cost (at 100 per cent insurance) falls short of consumers' savings in full insurance costs.[5] Thus Calabresi is correct in concluding that *PL* is preferable on efficiency grounds, provided that the cost of insurance is lower (or the pay-off on lottery tickets higher) on the producers' than on the consumers' side. Since this is likely to be the case, Buchanan's conclusion in favour of *CL* (based on the extreme case of zero risk return to the consumer) is reversed, the revised presumption on efficiency grounds being in favour of *PL*. Moreover, contrary to the Buchanan case, both sides stand to gain from using *PL*.

## QUALIFICATIONS FOR CONTRACTUAL CASE

The preceding analysis of the contractual case must now be qualified by the introduction of some additional considerations.

### Structure of Product Market

So far our reasoning was based on the assumption of competitive product markets. Will the results change if market imperfections are allowed for? Returning to our analogy with the unit tax, we noted that it is a matter of indifference in competitive markets, whether a unit tax is imposed (or liability is placed) on the seller's or the buyer's side of the market. The same holds for the case of pure monopoly. They may change, however, for alternative behaviour assumptions, e.g. oligopoly practices or for firms which aim to implement a target rate of return or follow objectives of sales maximisation. In such cases, substitution of *PL* for *CL* may not leave the outcome unchanged, even if a single market for risk-taking is postulated. Substituting *PL* for *CL* may cause the supply price to rise by more or less than the producer's full insurance. Prediction of outcomes becomes more complex and welfare comparisons become more difficult to apply.

## Unequal Information

Up to now we have assumed that all parties are fully informed with regard to damages. If consumers are less well informed, as is likely to be the case, *PL* may well be superior on efficiency grounds. Such may be the case even though no misrepresentation or fraud is involved. Assuming other and more easily understood sources of risk-taking to be available to consumers, the more efficient solution is secured by combining safe products with such other risk outlets. The alternative of combining *CL* with transmission of full information to the consumer involves implementation costs which are avoided by *PL*.

## Variable Product Mix

We now allow for the fact that similar products may be produced with different probabilities of damage. Will the range of available risk levels be affected by the choice between *CL* and *PL*? Assuming competitive markets, outcomes will again be the same. Under *CL*, consumer preferences will be registered in the product quality market. Confronted with the choice of buying cheaper and riskier products combined with higher insurance, and more costly and safer products combined with lower insurance, consumers will choose what they consider the most desirable combination. The safer product replaces the riskier one where the increase in cost falls short of the insurance saving. Under *PL*, producers will minimise costs of producing products at any level of safety and make them available after adding the corresponding insurance costs. The incentive to develop risk-reducing technologies is the same under *CL* or *PL*, so that allowance for product variability does not change our earlier conclusions.

Nor does allowance for product variability affect the conclusion for the Buchanan case, where consumers have no access to risk markets. *PL* still restricts the consumer to purchasing what to him is a no-risk product, with the actual risk content of the product determined by the cost of safety devices relative to the cost of insurance available to the producer. The conclusion that *CL* is superior to *PL* still stands. As we allow both consumers and producers access to risk markets but differential insurance costs, the introduction of product variability reduces the importance of such cost differentials, but it remains more efficient to place liability at the side at which the cost is lower.

## Damage Dependent on Product Use

The preceding discussion was based on the assumption that the contingency of damage is independent of the product use by the consumer. In most instances such will not be the case. The likelihood of damage will depend upon the frequency of use and/or the care with which the product is used. This adds a new and important dimension to the problem. The deterrence effects of liability rules must now be allowed for.

Deterrence effects are not absent under *PL*. If the average level of damage is higher, the supply price of the product will be higher as well and this will deter its purchase. But under *CL*, the *individual* consumer is given a further incentive to minimise damages, i.e. either to reduce his frequency of use or to use greater caution. Under *PL* consumers lack this incentive since producers are fully liable. They act as freeriders since the average damage which determines the supply price will not be affected (assuming fairly large numbers) by their particular behaviour. Under *CL*, individual behaviour is affected, so that *CL* is superior in cutting back damages to the efficient level.

It remains to be noted that this advantage of *CL* (the individualised deterrence effect) will depend on the type of insurance that is available to the consumer. No such effect is left if insurance is compulsory and a person's individual performance has no effect on his insurance cost. Such remains the case even if there is differentiation of premiums in relation to broad categories of users such as age groups since such differentiation does not relate to the performance of particular members of the group. The deterrence effect remains operative, however, where insurance is voluntary and where performance rating is considered in setting the insurance premium. Depending on the insurance setting, deterrence considerations may establish an efficiency presumption in favour of *CL* although this must be tempered by the cost (and in some cases even the feasibility) of fault-finding. The case for no-fault car insurance is based on the hypothesis that additional accident costs fall short of the cost of fault-finding or that the establishment of fault is frequently impossible. Moreover, car accidents frequently involve third parties, a matter to be considered presently.

From the point of view of deterrence effectiveness, the distinction between causation through frequency of use and causation through negligence in use may not be of major importance, but it is relevant in the equity context. Traditionally, producer liability was applied in the absence of user negligence only. Entitlement to compensation was considered to exist only if the damage was not the user's fault. Equity and efficiency thus led to the same liability policy, at least with regard to the negligence element in causation. Movement of the law away from emphasis on negligence and fault, and extension of *PL* to claims by the consumer independent of his conduct, sacrifices the efficiency aspect of deterrence and substitutes what would seem to be a less persuasive concept of entitlement. The no-fault approach thus rests on the proposition that the cost of fault-finding exceeds not only additional damage cost but also the loss attributed to a less satisfactory view of entitlement [Keeton, 5]. Justice like other good things in life is costly, and its procurement becomes part of the allocation decision.

## CONCLUSIONS

The preceding review of the role of liability rules in a contractual setting has yielded the following conclusions:

1. The choice of liability rules is a matter of indifference if both consumers and producers have equal access to a single and competitive risk and insurance market. The solutions are identical on both efficiency and equity grounds.
2. Buchanan's finding in favour of *CL* is based on the assumption that consumers cannot compensate for *PL* by increased risk-taking elsewhere while producers (under *CL*) can compensate by lottery tickets. Given this assumption, *CL* is preferable on efficiency grounds. Moreover, *PL* favours consumers relative to producers but there is no clear presumption that it favours low- over high-income groups.
3. Allowing for differential access to risk markets for both consumers and producers, the efficient solution is to place the insurance liability at the side at which the cost of risk-bearing is less. Both consumers and producers stand to gain thereby.
4. These conclusions are not altered for pure monopoly, but may come to differ if alternative modes of market behaviour are allowed for.
5. Allowing for imperfect and differential information regarding product risks strengthens the case for *PL*.
6. Assuming perfect markets, these conclusions are not affected by allowance for product variability.
7. Linkage of damage to frequency and care of use introduces deterrence as an additional consideration. The role of insurance differs depending on whether it is mandatory and whether premium costs are related to the performance of the insured. While deterrence considerations speak in favour of *CL*, the costs of fault-finding must also be allowed for.

## THE THIRD PARTY PROBLEM

We have seen how in the privity case (where the parties are related by contract) the contingency of damage and the nature of legal liability rules will be reflected in the terms of the contract. Depending on the circumstances the outcomes (with regard to efficiency and equity) may or may not be invariant to the liability rules, but the market will respond to the risk of damage. In the third party case, damages result to others who are not parties to the contract. Because of this, they are not reflected automatically in the pricing system of the market. They become externalities which fail to be internalised by the pricing system, so that inefficient results ensue. As against this, Ronald Coase has noted that such need not be the case. The parties, so the argument goes, will find it in their interest to engage in voluntary bargaining and this process will lead to an efficient result [Coase 4]. Moreover, the resulting resource allocation will be efficient whatever the liability rule. A system of mutual bribes will lead to an outcome similar to that established through market adjustments in the contractual case. This line of reasoning has had a massive impact upon the application of economic reasoning to legal thinking, especially in connection with the role of regulation.[6] But it is subject to various limitations.

Provided that only a small number of people are involved in the third party case, bargaining may take place, but it does not follow that liability rules do not matter. Several qualifications are in order: (1) The bargaining process need not yield efficient results. The outcome depends on the relative bargaining strength of the two parties and upon the strategies, including threats, that are used. (2) The choice of strategies and hence the outcome may differ under $CL$ and third party liability. (3) Even if the bargaining outcome is efficient under either $CL$ or third party liability ($TL$), the solution differs from an equity point of view. Under $TL$ the third party must bribe the consumer to desist, while under $CL$ the consumer must bribe the third party to permit him to continue the damaging activity.[7] Thus, even if the bargaining process should lead to efficient results in either case, the distributional implications differ. Consumers will opt for $TL$ while the third party is better-off under $CL$. This is in contrast to the contractual setting where the choice of liability rules was a matter of indifference with regard to distributional aspects as well. The difference arises because in the contractual case risk enters into the determination of the contract terms, whereas the third party does not enter into a contractual relationship.

This much for the small number case. Frequently, the third party problem is not limited to small numbers and this changes the situation drastically. As numbers increase, be it on one or both sides of the activity, the bargaining mechanism falters and eventually becomes inoperative. 'Transaction costs become infinite', to use a widely applied, if misleading, phrase, and damages to the third party remain unaccounted for.[8] A new instrument must be used to internalise the damages in order to secure efficiency; and a technique other than setting liability rules (e.g. a budgetary transfer mechanism) must be applied to deal with the equity aspects.

We now consider a situation where the purchase of a product by $A$ results in damages to $B$, $C$, ... $N$. Consumption of the product thus generates an external cost which should be internalised. For this purpose, a tax may be imposed either on the producer or on the consumer.[9] With the rate of tax properly chosen, the production and consumption of the product will be cut back to its efficient level, i.e. where at the margin the cost of producing it plus the damage cost to the third party will be equal to the benefit derived by $A$ as measured by its price.

This principle is clear enough but application is difficult. In order to set the proper rate of tax, the damage must be valued. In the large number case such valuation is hard to obtain. The trouble is analogous to that posed by the freerider problem in the case of social goods. Just as individuals will tend to understate their evaluation of such goods, so they will tend to overstate the damage. In the context of a legal (as distinct from economic) perspective there is the further issue of inalienability. The entitlement to certain contingencies may be absolute, i.e. the required compensation infinite. In this case, the solution calls not only for curtailment but for abandonment of the damaging activity.

Now consider the equity aspect. As the activity is cut back, damages to the third party are reduced, but a residual degree of damage remains. On efficiency grounds, retention of this level of damage to the third party is called for, but this gives little comfort to the third party. Whether the third party should be compensated for such remaining damage is an equity question, a matter of entitlement, which is to be dealt with as a separate issue.[10] If quiet is considered a matter of entitlement, the victims of jet noise should be compensated for remaining damage. But the efficiency case for cutting back third party damage (reducing jet noise by imposing a tax on jet flights) stands, even if the entitlement to compensation is denied. The tax should be imposed because (due to the large numbers involved) the efficiency objective of reduced noise cannot be achieved through negotiation.

Once more the difference between the small and large number case need be noted. As long as numbers are small, the efficiency objective might be met (more or less perfectly) by negotiation between the third party victim and the consumer, while the equity issue remains to be resolved by formulating the liability rule. Such rules, as noted before, need not be of the all or nothing (100 per cent) variety. They may be a partial (< 100 per cent) rule reflecting, as it were, partial entitlement. In the large number case, the effluent charge takes the place of negotiation in achieving efficiency and the equity issue, in line with the state of entitlement, must be handled separately by budgetary compensation. The tax burden placed on the consumers is determined by the cutback which is required on efficiency grounds rather than by the amount required to compensate the third parties for the remaining damage. If the revenue from the tax or effluent charge is insufficient to compensate for remaining damages, full implementation of consumer liability requires a further tax to be imposed on the intra-marginal use of the activity by consumers.

In dealing with the third party case, we have argued that the consumption of product $X$ by consumer $A$ causes damage to, $B$, $C$, ... $N$, and thus results in an external cost. But the very existence of a third party situation means that the two sides are involved in letting this cost come about. The driver would not hit the pedestrian if the latter had not been in his way. He would not have bent the driver's fender and would not have been injured. In some sense, the cause of the accident must have a reciprocal base. The murderer and his victim are, in a sense, involved in a joint happening. This poses an equity rather than an efficiency problem. As far as efficiency is concerned, the scale of both activities (driving and walking) should be lowered. A cutback in the former results in response to the tax while a cutback in the latter results by permitting some activity (and hence probability of pedestrian damage) to continue.

One way of looking at the basis for compensation is to argue that the third party should be compensated if it was not at fault and then to define absence of fault in terms of entitlement to pursue the activity without disturbance. Another way of interpreting fault is in terms of departure from prudent exercise of the activity in question. The driver then is at fault if he does not live up to some defined standard of careful driving, while the pedestrian is at fault if he does not exercise prudence in walking. Entitlement is then limited to conducting the activity (walking or driving) in a prudent fashion (given some statutory definition of prudence) and compensation will be paid only if injury occurs, even though prudence has been exercised.[11]

## NOTES

1. For general discussions of the problem see [8]; McKean [6]; Calabresi [2].
2. Since the rearrangement is efficient, compensation could be paid by consumers to producers so as to leave both parties better off, but such compensation will in fact not be paid so that the adjustment involves a redistribution towards consumers.
3. This appears to be Buchanan's reasoning [8, pp. 66, 67], who argues that low-income consumers buy risky products because they 'can ill afford to purchase a high degree of risk avoidance'. This may be correct but appears to overlook that the poor consumers' inability to purchase is general and does not only relate to risk-avoidance.
4. This is the aspect of the problem which is given central position by Calabresi [2], who argues that the liability should be placed upon the party which is the cheaper risk spreader. However, his concept of cheapest risk-spreader lacks precision and is much broader than the differential insurance costs noted above, as it includes distributional effects and the desire to minimise economic disruption. As distinct from differentials in insurance cost, it might also be suggested that the problem is not only one of access to risk markets but that there may be a qualitative difference between the risk which is intrinsic in the product and other risks, such that the one cannot be compensated for by the other. However, such incommensurability would apply to the insurance aspect as well as to the supplementary taking of other risks. The fact that insurance is taken therefore, permits us to reject this view.
5. Again it does not matter what the actual level of insurance will be. While consumers under CL may have chosen to insure at less than 100 per cent, they may compensate for the mandatory increase in the degree of insurance by purchasing more lottery tickets. Similarly, producers will charge for the cost of 100 per cent insurance, even though they may only partially insure.
6. The general impact of the argument has been to feed the currently fashionable case against regulation. While the actual performance of regulatory authorities may provide ample reason for scepticism regarding regulatory accomplishments, application of the Coase-type argument has led to an over-optimistic appraisal of what will happen in the absence of regulation.
7. For a discussion of liability rules in the third party context, see Calabresi and Melamed [3].
8. Interpretation of the difficulty as involving 'infinite transaction costs' is suggestive of an excessive cost of time spent in negotiation or mail charges needed. It does not bring out the more crucial aspect of strategic behaviour. With large numbers, any one individual cannot secure a significant reduction in

the damage risk and therefore has no incentive to negotiate. Accounting for third party damage now poses a freerider problem, similar to that encountered in the provision of social goods.

9. Whether the tax is placed on the producer or consumer is a matter of indifference as long as the external cost (damage to third parties) is independent of the mode of use. If the damage is a function of frequency and care of use, the tax should be imposed on the consumer, provided that the rate of tax is related to the mode of use. The argument is similar to that made in support of *CL* on deterrence grounds.

10. The question arises whether payment of compensation will not interfere with securing the cutback in activity which is needed as a matter of efficiency. Such interference is avoided provided that damage is not compensated for at the margin. See Baumol [1].

11. Using a time dimension, entitlement to compensation can be made contingent upon having exercised prudent care in anticipating future contingencies. In this connection, see Michelman [7, p. 1165].

# REFERENCES

[1] Baumol, W. J. (1972), 'On taxation and the control of externalities', *American Economic Review*, Vol. 62, No. 3, pp. 307–22.

[2] Calabresi, Guido (1970), *The Cost of Accidents* (New Haven, Conn., Yale University Press).

[3] Calabresi, G. and Melamed (1972), 'Property rules, liability rules and inalienability: one view of the cathedral', *Harvard Law Review*, Vol. 85, No. 6.

[4] Coase, R. (1960), 'The problem of social cost', *Journal of Law and Economics*, Vol. 3, pp. 1–44.

[5] Keeton, R.E. (1965), 'Conditional fault in the law of torts', *Harvard Law Review*, Vol. 78.

[6] McKean, Roland N. (1970), 'Products liability: implications of some changing property rights', *Quarterly Journal of Economics*, Vol. 84 November, pp. 611–26.

[7] Michelman, Frank A. (1967), 'Property, utility and fairness: comments on the ethical foundations of just compensation law', *Harvard Law Review*, Vol. 80, No. 6, pp. 1165–258.

[8] 'Symposium on products liability: economic analysis and the law', (1970), *University of Chicago Law Review*, Autumn, pp. 1–141.

# 20    Private Labour and Common Land*
1983

Theories of distributive justice follow three major traditions. Natural law
theorists view a person as entitled to the fruits of his labour. Justice
prevails if each receives the value of his product. Utilitarians hold that
reason calls for distribution based on the maximising rules of welfare
calculus. A third tradition rejects personal talents as a basis for desert. Just
distribution is to be deduced from principles of fairness, agreed upon in the
original position. My purpose here is *not* to compare these approaches or
to choose among the ethical premises on which they rest. Rather I shall
deal with the entitlement approach only and take its premises as given.[1]
More specifically, I shall focus on the tension which arises within a dual
view of entitlement, where private entitlement to the fruits of one's labour
is combined with common entitlement to the fruits of land.

The entitlement doctrine is of particular interest to the historian of
economic thought who is not embarrassed by the interaction of analysis
and value. It has provided an ethical framework for economic theory from
medieval doctrine on usury over Adam Smith's natural order and Karl
Marx's surplus value to J. B. Clark's view [4] of marginal product as a just
return. If justice calls for reward in line with value created, determination
of factor shares matters not only for the theory of production but also for
the implementation of distributive justice. Economists, to be sure, have
been annoyed by this nexus. Marx wanted his doctrine of surplus value to
be understood as an objective fact of capitalist production, not as a moral
basis for social critique. George Stigler in turn criticises Clark for having
linked marginal productivity theory to just distribution. Its significance as
an economic theory should be seen in relation to efficient resource use and
to the theory of production, not as legitimisation of market ethics.[2] Later
welfare economics, be it of the Pigou or Samuelson–Bergson variety, heeds
this separation and bypasses the relationship between factor pricing and
entitlement to distributive shares.[3] Yet the notion that justice calls for
compensation in line with productive contribution remains very much a
part of our social mores.[4] Indeed, it may well be considered the dominant

---

* In *State and Local Finance: The Pressure of the Eighties* (1983), ed. G. Break, (Madison,
The University of Wisconsin Press).

304

norm. *Re*distribution by definition follows distribution and is the exception to the rule.

The same goes for the perception that 'land' or natural resources in general differ from other factors. On the one hand, economic analysis has extended the concept of rent to all factors, viewing it as a generally applicable phenomenon of inelastic supply. On the other hand, land has retained its special place in the common man's view of property rights. This difference arises not because of differences in supply elasticity or spatial mobility, but because land is outside man and, as a matter of 'natural right', is seen as held in common. The modern concern with environment and the right to oil resources and ocean wealth are cases in point, as is the ongoing debate over property taxation. Traces of the dual entitlement rule thus remain embedded in popular mores, and a review of its doctrinal development is more than a historical exercise. We begin with the seminal presentation by Locke [9],[5] turn to its recent restatement by Nozick [16], and then step back to its essential role in the earlier system of Henry George [6].

## LOCKEAN ENTITLEMENT AND THE PROVISOS

Locke's theory of property begins with the proposition that man has the right to self-preservation and hence to the things which 'nature' yields for his subsistence.[6] For this purpose nature was given to mankind to be used in common: 'Whether we consider reason or revelation—'tis very clear that God, as King David says, has given the earth to the children of men, given it to mankind in common' [Locke, 9, p. 327, s. 25].[7] But man, so Locke continues, also has property in his person: 'Every man has a property in his own Body and the Work of his Hands, we may say, are properly his' [9, p. 328, s.27]. The two entitlements interact because labour yields fruit only when mixed with land. Man, to obtain fruits from his labour, must obtain property in the crop which he raises: 'Whatever then he removes out of the State that Nature has provided—he has mixed his labour with, and joined to it something that is his own, and thereby makes it his Property' [9, p. 329, s. 27]. But there are limits to the produce which a man may extract from land. They are given by two provisos which to me seem among Locke's most intriguing passages.[8]

The first proviso holds that no one can accumulate more goods than he can use without wastage: 'As much as any one can make use of to any advantage of life before it spoils; so much he may by his labour fix a property in' [9, p. 332, s. 31]. Since produce spoils, this limits accumulation and thereby the utilisation of land. The second proviso adds that a person has a right to the produce which he extracts from land 'at least where there is enough and as good left in common for others' [9, p. 333, s. 33]. Both provisos are inoperative while land is abundant. Without scarcity of land, the spoilage proviso has no distributive bite but merely prohibits waste as an offence against nature. The 'as good' proviso as well is satisfied as long as the supply of land is abundant. Man can freely mix his labour with 'new' land without pre-empting its use by others, thereby satisfying the 'as good' condition. Locke thus shows how property could exist in the state of nature prior to civil society, and do so without offending against the common entitlement and its provisos.

But how does Locke deal with the tension which arises when land becomes scarce? Now that the crop becomes the joint product of private labour and scarce (but common) land, can the cultivator still lay sole claim to it? Viewed in the context of a barter economy, Locke's answer would have had to be no. With land scarce, the 'as good' proviso would come into play and restrict the private property in land. But he did not foresee that this condition would occur. The 'wild woods and uncultivated wastes of America', he tells us, still beckon with a safe margin of uncultivated land [9, p. 336, s. 37].

Land becomes scarce only with the use of money and the resulting drive for accumulation. But the use of money as a means of exchange and store of wealth now permits a person to hold more land than he needs for his own use, and to do so without spoilage.[9] The surplus crop may be sold and wealth may be accumulated in the form of money. The spoilage limitation to private ownership of land is thus removed. True enough, but Locke further holds that tacit consent to the use of money also suspends the common claim to land and permits its unlimited private possession. This conclusion only follows if the 'common claim' is viewed as a derivative of the non-spoilage proviso. As we read Locke's earlier invocation of the common claim, be it by 'reason or by revelation', this is not a permissible interpretation.[10] A better explanation is needed to show why Locke suspends his principle of common claim.

One possible explanation lies in Locke's observation that private ownership of land increases accumulation and adds to the nation's wealth, which in the end will be to everyone's benefit [9, p. 343, s. 50]. Perhaps so, but it seems strange for Locke to sacrifice the common claim to land— introduced first as a God-given natural right—to so utilitarian a considera- tion. This is strange, especially since private accumulation could proceed in terms of money and of capital goods, even though the common claim to land was preserved.

To make Locke's reasoning stick, one would have to reinterpret his initial postulate of common claim to land. Rather than as a natural right in itself, the common claim would have to be seen as derived from the right to self-preservation.[11] One could then argue that with the use of money and trade, self-preservation no longer requires access to land; and thus reinterpret the 'as good' proviso as referring to produce rather than to land itself. The objection that a utilitarian argument is used to override a right would then be overcome. But once more, this interpretation seems incompatible with Locke's invocation of scriptures and natural law, when presenting his initial doctrine of common claim to *land in particular*. As we read Locke, he meant to say that the fruits of land only were to be shared, while leaving private entitlement to the fruits of one's labour. Such a dual entitlement rule does not interfere with the right of self-preservation, but merely influences how total output is to be divided and to what assets private title can be attached.

However this may be, it is not our purpose here to speculate on Locke's precise reason for abandoning the common claim and his 'as good' proviso.[12] Rather, let us consider the consequences of strict adherence to Locke's initial model as we read it, that is, consider a situation of scarce land with the 'as good' proviso in full force. That part of output which is contributed by labour—a part which Locke considers to constitute most of the total [9, p. 339, s. 42]—belongs to the worker. The remainder, which is contributed by land, belongs to the common. The question is how to distribute the common share among the workers. Since God gave land 'to the use of the industrious', not to the idle, the Lockean model might distribute rent in proportion to labour input [9, p. 333, s. 34]. Workers, as it were, participate in two roles: (1) as claimants to the fruits of labour, and (2) as co-workers of land and co-claimants to rent. With (2) assigned in proportion to (1), workers receive the entire product in line with wages. Under this rule, the common claim to land would not change the distribution pattern set by wages. Workers cultivating a given plot would divide the output in line with labour inputs, so that in fact there would be no need for splitting the two shares at all. But this conclusion only follows if assignment to the 'industrious' is considered appropriate. If instead the common claim were interpreted as, say, an equal per capita division, the distribution of rent would have an equalising effect. But even then, differential labour income would permit inequality to arise. Acceptance of common entitlement to the fruits of land does not make Locke an egalitarian.

It remains to fit capital into the Lockean scheme. Locke notes the use of financial capital as essential to production with interest a necessary return due to its unequal holding [19, p. 52]. But he does not present a full view of the role of real capital as a factor of production. Rather, the labour that was needed to make the plough must be charged to labour [9, p. 346, s. 43]. There has thus developed an interesting controversy over whether or not Locke held to a labour theory of value, but we shall bypass this here. Rather, let us consider claims to factor shares in an updated Lockean model, which allows for returns to both capital and labour.

How may entitlement to the return of capital be assigned? Presumably Locke would have argued that the saver is entitled to this return in response to his contribution, just as the worker is entitled to his wages. Labour would no longer receive the entire product other than rent. The consideration remains: How would the claim to rent now be distributed? Should the suppliers of capital share in the bounty of nature, and if so, should rent be distributed in line with capital and labour shares? If labour benefits from 'mixing' with land, so does capital. If reward to the

'industrious' is now applied to both saving and work, the solution would
again be one of sharing rent on a matching basis, leaving rent once again a
distributionally neutral factor.

However this may be, a rule is needed to define factor shares. A theory
of entitlement in line with productive contribution requires this contribution to be determined. Not only must the common share of rent be
separated out, but the remainder must be divided between capital and
labour. Assignment in line with factor pricing in a competitive market is
one such rule. Moreover, it has the further qualities of (1) being in line
with efficient resource use, and (2) being open to implementation through
a competitive market.[13] J. B. Clark, when presenting his marginal productivity theory at the close of the last century, believed in this triple union of
justice, efficiency, and competitive markets. The requirement of competitive markets, to be sure, is not spelled out in Locke. His discussion of
natural price well preceded the modern view of price determination as the
function of both cost and demand conditions. Yet he thought of a fair
market price as determined by the interaction of many sellers, a formula
quite compatible with the spirit of competitive markets [19, p. 60].

## NOZICK'S JUSTICE IN HOLDING

Similar problems persist in Nozick's reformulation of the Lockean model.
Nozick [16, p. 10] launches his argument from Locke's proposition that
man has a right to act freely as he wishes but within the bounds of nature,
that is, man is subject to Locke's condition that 'no one ought to harm
another in his life, health, liberty, and possessions.' Justice in holding
exists, so Nozick argues, if possessions are justly acquired in line with (1)
the principle of just acquisition and (2) the principle of just transfer
[p. 191]. The theory of justice is thus formulated as a process theory. A
just state of distribution is one that has come about through a just process,
and his theory of justice is conceived as a historical theory. He then
contrasts this with what he calls end-state theories, according to which a
just distribution is one that meets a predetermined pattern.

But justice in acquisition precedes justice in transfer. The rules of just
acquisition are thus of fundamental importance to Nozick's entire argument and not a mere 'additional bit of complexity' as he suggests [16,
p. 174]. Nozick does not invoke Locke's proposition that God has given
land to man for use in common, but begins with the broader maxim that
the law of nature forbids actions which harm others. Property rights in 'a
previously unused thing' cannot be acquired if 'the position of others no
longer at liberty to use the thing is thereby worsened' [16, p. 178]. The
'previously unused things' include Locke's land and natural resources, but
other items such as inventions are added in. Locke's 'as good' proviso, so
Nozick notes, was designed to prevent such unjust acquisition; and he
draws the conclusion—avoided by Locke—that after land becomes scarce,

literal interpretation of the proviso causes the existing entitlement structure to collapse by a principle of regression [16, p. 180].

Nozick tries to meet this difficulty in various ways. One of them is to follow Locke in noting that private property in scarce land contributes to economic progress which benefits *all*, even those who no longer can obtain use of land. Thus private property in scarce land is said to be compatible with the *intent* of the Lockean proviso. This consideration, so Nozick notes, is not introduced as a utilitarian suspension of a basic right. Rather it is allowed because (similar to a previously noted reading of Locke) the common claim to land was never meant to be absolute but derived from the right to 'things'. As a second line of defence, Nozick suggests that the share in property holdings which is traceable to unjust appropriation of land is minor, so that the difficulty applies to only a small part of the prevailing property structure. Perhaps so, but this hardly resolves the principle at issue.

Finally, and most interesting, Nozick suggests that the proviso be restated in less demanding form. A distinction should be drawn between two ways in which a person's position can be worsened. *A* taking a piece of land as property may (1) reduce *B*'s ability to use land freely which he previously so used, or (2) reduce *B*'s ability to acquire new land. A stringent interpretation prohibits both outcomes, whereas a weaker version would prohibit the first one only [16, p. 176]. Nozick accepts the weaker version as sufficient for his theory of just acquisition. The regression problem may then be avoided by one further adjustment: the addition of a 'base line' date and a general amnesty for unjust acquisitions that preceded it [16, p. 177]. We are left with an interesting but still unsatisfactory solution. Drawing the base line is an arbitrary matter and amnesty begs the issue of justice in original acquisition. Without a just basis from which to start, the concept of just process remains a somewhat hollow construct. However this may be, let us accept the base line plus amnesty version and consider the requirements of just process thereafter.

Clearly, just transactions should be voluntary in nature, requiring the consent of both parties.[14] But this is not sufficient. As Nozick [16, p. 181] puts it in his colourful way, 'each owner's title to his holding includes the historical shadow of the Lockean proviso on appropriation.' Transactions must not leave anyone worse-off than the base line position. *A* may not, as formulated in situation (1) above, purchase the only waterhole in existence and then charge what he wishes. If he were to do so, his property in the well would not be justly acquired. But Nozick suggests that the free operation of the market system will not actually run foul of the proviso, that is, type (1) situations will not be prevalent. At the same time, *A* may, as formulated in situation (2), manufacture pins and sell them more cheaply than *B*, thereby driving *B* out of business and leaving him less well off. The difference between situations (1) and (2) is that the former involves the holding of scarce resources and thus violates the proviso, whereas the latter does not.

But what if a third type of situation arises, where $A$, after buying out $B$, establishes a monopoly in pins and thus hurts $C$ who must pay more? This would be no offence against Nozick's concept of just transaction, as I understand it. I have two difficulties with this conclusion. For one thing, the meaning of entitlement, as a matter of natural right, can hardly be made contingent on what market structures happen to develop in the post-base line period. Yet this will be the case if exchange is defined simply in terms of noncoercion.[15] A person's return is determined by his real wage, and this depends not only on what is offered but also on the structure of the labour and product markets in which he deals. For another thing, specification of permissible terms of trade is crucial for the relationship between efficiency and justice. Both criteria are met if the permissible terms of exchange are restricted to competitive markets; but they conflict if justice is taken to require noncoercion only. Exchanges may then proceed in non-competitive markets and the benign scheme of the market as an invisible hand process—both just and efficient—breaks down. This basic issue cannot be avoided by *assuming* that all markets are competitive or that only negligible departures occur. Anti-trust policy, for instance, will be just or unjust (as well as efficient) depending on how the concept of just transaction is defined.

Similar problems arise with regard to externalities, be they of the cost or benefit variety. If $A$ is damaged by $B$'s activities (such as the construction of a nextdoor factory which creates a smoke nuisance), does the rule of justice call for compensation?[16] In the modern world, which abounds with externality and third-part problems, it is clearly unsatisfactory to define entitlement and just property rights in terms of a model which consists of contractual relations only. By assuming away market imperfections and externalities, a much too simplified picture is drawn. We can hardly criticise Locke, who wrote 300 years ago, for overlooking these complications. But Locke recreated should allow for them.


## HENRY GEORGE AND THE UNEARNED INCREMENT

Nowhere has the antinomy between the common claim to land and the private claim to the fruits of one's labour been carried so far as in the writings of Henry George. His approach differs from that of Locke and Nozick in various ways. For one thing, the common claim to land is given as a fundamental right, as seen in the Biblical–natural law tradition, not as a mere derivative of the right for subsistence. Next, he accepts the full consequences of the proviso by calling for public appropriation of the returns to land. Finally, and most important, he does not see private ownership of land as necessary for economic progress. On the contrary, he is concerned with 'the evils which, as modern progress goes on, arise from the greater and greater inequality in the distribution of wealth', and he considers private ownership of land to be the major cause of this evil.

Public appropriation of rent offers a simple and sufficient remedy. It 'will substitute equality for inequality, plenty for want, justice for injustice, social strength for social weakness, and will open the way to grander and nobler advances of civilisation.' Expediency joins justice, so he concludes, in the case for abolishing the private ownership of land [6, pp. 329, 367]. Note that his immediate case is directed only against inequality which results from the private ownership of *land*. Apart from land, George was a staunch defender of private property and its role in economic progress. However, with private ownership of land the major cause of inequality, its removal would go far to abolish inequality at large.

The rightful basis of property, so George argues, is the right of man to himself: 'Thus there is to everything produced by man's exertion a clear and indisputable title to the exclusive possession and enjoyment which is perfectly compatible with justice as it descends from the original producer in whom it is vested by natural law' [6, p. 334].[17] These laws 'are the decree of the Creator'. Without directly claiming the authority of Locke, George's basic premise of entitlement is the same as that of the eighteenth-century writers, combining natural law with divine sanction.[18] Man is rightfully entitled to the fruits of his exertion by labour only. Property may be transferred legitimately after it has been acquired, but just acquisition of a good has to be based initially on the input of one's labour.[19] The worker cannot claim private property in land, since land does not embody labour. Private ownership of land permits the owner to appropriate the produce of another person's labour as the price that person must pay for permission to labour [p. 341]. It is thus incompatible with the very principle of entitlement to the fruits of one's labour. Public appropriation of the return to land is thus just. He proposes that this be done by a confiscatory tax on the rent of land rather than outright public ownership [p. 406].[20] Improvements, however, are not to be taxed, since capital earnings are a just return.

To show how the evil of private ownership of land increases with economic progress, George must show how the rising share of rent creates poverty. The first step is to examine how factor shares are determined. Rent is defined along Ricardian lines as the excess of product over that which the same labour input can secure from the least productive land in use [6, p. 168]. 'Wages and interest,' so he argues, 'do not depend upon the produce of labour and capital, but upon what is left after rent is taken out; or upon the product which they could obtain without paying rent—that is from the poorest land in use' [p. 171]. This may be taken to suggest a general equilibrium system in which all factor shares are mutually determined, but the fuller exposition also carries overtones of the physiocratic notion that land is the basic source of output, with the return to land determined first and the other factors receiving what is left.

Turning to interest as a return to capital, George rejects the view that interest is a return to waiting, and that wages are 'advanced' by capital. Rather, it is the current output of labour that sustains capital formation. The consequence of an increase in the number of workers is not that a given wage fund must be spread more thinly. On the contrary, increased labour gives rise to increased capital. Interest, according to George, is paid because the use of the tools of production increases the efficiency of labour. 'The advantage which is given by the lapse of time springs from the regenerative forces of nature' [6, p. 367]. He thus does not admit that capital formation requires a diversion of labour from the production of current output to that of tools and that this involves waiting, which enters as a cost of production. Yet, he considers the return to capital as a legitimate return. It is only the income from land that is to be in common. The reasoning is puzzling. If the 'regenerative forces of nature', which stem from capital, are created by the input of labour, why then should not the return of capital also accrue to the worker?

Having developed his theory of factor shares in a static setting, George proceeds to his major theme, which is the rising share of rent in the course of economic growth. In line with the classical tradition, he begins with the impact of population growth. He does not, however, follow the Malthusian doctrine that increasing population, via diminishing returns on land, leads to poverty. This doctrine is unacceptable to George, because its prognosis of inevitable property would contradict the benevolence of nature and provide an apologetic for injustice [6, p. 185]. In order to disprove Malthus, George argues that rising population (with technique constant) will result in increasing efficiency due to greater division of labour [p. 223]. Rising population, therefore, need not lead to Malthusian subsistence. Per capita income may remain constant or may rise.

At the same time, George also wishes to show that the share of rent will increase in the process, so as to stress the necessity of public ownership of land. How can the two outcomes be combined? His reasoning is somewhat obscure, as no clear distinction is drawn between rates of return and factor shares. However, his result might be rationalised as follows: The efficiency gain (due to greater division of labour made possible by rising population) might be viewed as raising the efficiency units embodied in an hour of work, thus resulting in an upward shift of the marginal product of labour schedule. At the same time, the rising ratio of labour to capital lowers the marginal product by moving down along the schedule. Combining both changes, the marginal product of labour and the wage rate might remain constant or rise, even though the share of rent increases. His result is thus conceivable, but it implies a rather extreme view regarding the continuing gains from the further division of labour made possible by population growth.[21]

But the picture changes as improvements in the arts are allowed for. Improvements will increase wealth, which will raise the demand for land and bring inferior land into cultivation. As a result, rent will rise. Moreover, it will rise so as to increase its share in national income, with most all income eventually being absorbed by rent and wages tending toward the poverty level. To reach this conclusion, George seems to argue that innovations will be land-using but labour-saving [6, pp. 749ff.]. Resulting changes in the capital share are not allowed for, nor is the possibility that improvement in the arts will raise the productivity of labour and/or of capital at the margin of cultivation. Although deeply concerned with the problem of inequality, George is thus led to neglect inequalities which may arise from the ownership of capital.

The Georgian economic model, as will be apparent from this overview, is driven by single-minded determination to demonstrate that the rental share must rise, and to do so while rejecting the Malthusian argument. If the outcome is unconvincing and the reasoning at times obscure, it should be kept in mind that *Progress and Poverty* was written at a time when the new doctrine of marginal productivity was just beginning to emerge. Moreover, George, as a visionary and a populist, was not given to reading contemporary 'professors' and wished to reinvent economic theory in his own image [8, pp. 193, 210].

Having shown that private ownership is both illegitimate and harmful, George unhesitatingly proceeds to the conclusion that the rent of land should be taxed away. He does not worry about how past injustice can be undone. While the return to improvements is carefully excluded, all rent of land should be appropriated forthwith. This should be done even where land was acquired in good faith and paid for by present owners out of justly acquired earnings. George thus rejects Mill's insistence that present owners be compensated if future increments of rents are socialised [6, p. 366; Mill, 13, Book II, ch. 2, s. 5).[22] George argues that such a proposal would be better than nothing as rents rise, but it would be insufficient. By the same token, George would have rejected Nozick's base line approach. The drawing of rent, so George notes, 'is not merely a robbery in the past; it is a robbery in the present' [6, p. 365]. If compensation were paid, both workers and capitalists would continue to lose their just reward. Given the premise of common entitlement, this is correct, but it does not meet the difficulty that the original robbers and the present owners are not one and the same. The question of how to rectify unjust gains which are capitalised remains unresolved, as does that of removing past inequities of taxation.

After rent has been appropriated by common entitlement through land taxation, there remains the question of who is entitled to receive it. George argues that all should share the bounty equally and that by using the land tax to finance the budget, rent would become 'equally distributed in public services' [6, p. 440]. Of course, the Georgian position need not hold that the entire receipts from the land tax must be used for public services. If some revenue is left over, it might be distributed to the public, presumably on a per capita basis—much as is now done in some oil-rich jurisdictions. But what if revenue from the land tax does not suffice to finance the required level of public services? It is here that the claim of *single* taxers becomes untenable. While it might be conceivable that the prevailing level of property tax revenue could be obtained by including only land in the base, it would be totally impossible to finance all tax revenue from this source.[23] Perhaps this situation was not visualised by George, who saw the rental share increasing rapidly without anticipating a correspondingly large increase in the size of the public sector. But though the term 'single tax' has done the Georgian case a disservice, the fact that other taxes are needed as well is no reason not to begin with land as the preferred base.

Economists have been generally favourable towards the taxation of rent, but for different reasons. With land inelastic in supply, the taxation of rent permits public funds to be obtained without the deadweight loss which accompanies other forms of taxation. In fact, economic theory suggests that the same be done with regard to all rents, that is, returns in excess of those needed to solicit the factor supply. Labour on this basis would receive its marginal return for the last hour, while the intra-marginal surplus or rent would be subject to tax. By including the rent to all factors, the available tax base would vastly exceed that offered by land rent only, and even a large budget could be financed without deadweight loss. This is an appropriate prescription in the context of economic efficiency, but it has nothing to do with the entitlement doctrine which stipulates a common claim to the rent of land but *not* to the economist's rental component of labour.

In all, George must be given credit for carrying the premise of dual entitlement to its logical conclusion. This is more than can be said for the two other authors here examined. The weakness of his doctrine lies in its exaggerated claim that land ownership constitutes *the* dominant cause of inequality, and that land taxation should be viewed as *the* single tax. It is because of these claims that the doctrine lost credibility, except in the inner circle of close followers.


## CONCLUSION

The purpose of this chapter has been to examine the internal logic and economic implications of a dual theory of entitlement, not to defend it as an ethical doctrine or to advocate its policy implications. The sense that a person is entitled to the fruits of his or her labour has long antecedents and is still widely reflected in or, indeed, dominates how people feel about property. The further sense that the contribution of land is received in common is also of ancient vintage and, though less fully shared, continues to enter into contemporary mores about property rights.

For economic analysis, the dual entitlement theory enters in two ways. First, if the worker is entitled to the fruits of his or her labour, a theory of factor shares is needed to lend operational meaning to this dictum. The question then is whether the economist's resolution in terms of efficient factor pricing also provides the ethically appropriate principle of imputation. The answer to this determines whether or not justice and efficiency coexist. Secondly, the economist's generalised concept of rent as intra-marginal gain, applicable to all factors, differs from the distinct role of land in the entitlement context. In that context the peculiar characteristic of land does not rest on its inelastic supply, but results because the claim to its factor share is held in common. The economist's case for generalising the tax on rent as an efficiency device does not follow from the entitlement framework.

There are important differences in the approach to dual entitlement among the authors I have dealt with. A first difference relates to their interpretation of how absolutely the common entitlement is to be viewed. Locke first establishes the common claim to land as a divine and natural right, but then abandons it to the needs of a monetary economy. Nozick takes the basic right to land (and resulting obligation not to leave others worse off) more seriously. But in the end he also bypasses the issue of just acquisition through his base line–amnesty construct. George alone considers the common entitlement to be absolute and draws the inevitable conclusion that society should appropriate the rent of land. A further difference pertains to the consequences of private ownership of land. Locke and Nozick both view such ownership as essential to economic growth and welfare. For Locke this suspends the proviso, while for Nozick the common claim is redefined as derived only. For George, on the contrary, private ownership of land is evil in its economic consequences. Thus justice and expediency coincide in calling for its termination.

The dual entitlement doctrine shows the intricate way in which the economic theory of factor shares has been interwoven with the ethical theory of property rights. Economic analysis, to be sure, may view the theory of factor shares as unrelated to the ethics of distribution, and the spirit of modern economics will do just that. Where concerns with distribution enter, they do not come in via factor pricing. Yet, the theory of factor pricing, as it developed through the marginal productivity doctrine, evolved in a culture in which entitlement to earnings played a central role in just distribution. Like it or not, this relation has remained alive in the public mind, and there is much to be said for thinking it through in rigorous terms, including allowance for imperfect markets, for externalities, and for the special role of land in the entitlement doctrine.

## NOTES

1. For a critique of the underlying premises, see Nagel [14].
2. See George Stigler's critique [18] of J. B. Clark, whose 'naive production ethics' is blamed for 'the popular and superficial allegation that neoclassical economics was essentially an apologetic for the existing economic order' (p. 297).
3. This point is stressed in Clark and Gintis [3].
4. See *President's Economic Report* [17, p. 137].
5. Page references are to the revised edition, with section numbers of Book II also given.
6. The Lockean doctrine, as presented here, is based on his exposition in ch. V of the *Second Treatise*. For more comprehensive appraisals of the Lockean system which are of special interest in our context, see McPherson [10], Vaughn [19] and Clark [1; 2].

7. Locke's reference is to Psalm CXV:xvi, which reads, 'The ... heavens are the Lord's, but the earth hath he given to the children of men.' Note that the stipulation of 'given it to mankind in common' is Locke's own addition and hence hardly unimportant in interpreting his text.

8. For a less favourable view, see Viner [20].

9. For an argument that accumulation without spoilage is possible even in a barter economy, see Weymark [21, pp. 282–90].

10. For a contrary view, see Vaughn [19].

11. This explanation is suggested by McPherson [11, p. 213].

12. McPherson [11] suggests that Locke's relaxation of his initial limitation of property rights (limiting property to the fruit of one's *own* labour only) was needed to accommodate his desire to provide an apologetic for the capitalist system. Vaughn [19, p. 106] suggests that his support of private accumulation only reflected his recognition that everyone would gain thereby. Clark [1; 2] views the Lockean system as disapproving of great inequality and claims that Locke is among the originators of the liberal theory of justice.

13. An alternative union of justice and efficiency might be obtained by a system in which all rents, including those of land and labour, are taxed away and considered to be held in common. This would still be efficient, because the return at the margin would not be affected. At the same time it would be considered just if the entitlement doctrine were changed to grant entitlement to compensation for work disutility only. But though a possible reformulation, this is not what the Lockean entitlement doctrine had in mind.

14. Nozick [16] recognises one exception, however, where individuals do not wish to join the voluntary protective association (the minimal state) and are forced to do so. However, compensation must be paid.

15. There is the further question of how the concept of coercion is defined. Nozick's essay [15] on coercion leaves the answer problematical. Nozick states that exchanges between buyers and sellers cannot 'normally' be considered coercion [p. 447], but beyond this no reference to the problem of coercion in market transactions is made. However, in distinguishing between threats and offers in other settings, certain analogies arise. Thus Nozick considers a situation where $P$ announces that he will do such and such if $Q$ does $A$. Whether this is to be considered an offer or a threat (coercion) to $Q$ depends on whether $P$'s intervention will make the outcome of $Q$ doing $A$ better or worse than it otherwise would be in the 'expected' course of events. The term 'expected' is used as a straddle between 'predicted' and 'morally required'.

    Given the criterion that expected outcomes render a transaction non-coercive, the question remains whether the transactor is or is not entitled to expect competitive markets. The issue remains unresolved by the expectation criterion.

16. An expectation criterion similar to Nozick's is suggested by Michelman [12], who proposes that entitlement for compensation be made contingent on the damage being unexpected.

17. See also note 7 above.

18. For a more extensive discussion of values as derived from natural law, see George's controversy with Henry Spencer [7].

19. See also Collier [5].

20. George does not consider the question of how the market can function as an allocator of land if there is a 100 per cent tax on rent, reducing the value of land to zero. However, in one passage [p. 347], he refers to levying a tax so as to 'very nearly' absorb rent, which may allow for a management fee.

22. John Stuart Mill, in his discussion of property, distinguishes between property in land and property in other things: 'The essential principle of property being to assure to all persons what they have produced by their labour and accumulated by their abstinence, this principle cannot apply to what is not the produce of labour, the raw material of the earth.' Property in land is justified only to the extent that the owner improves it. 'When private property in land is not expedient, it is unjust.' But compensation must be paid if the state decides to take over land. See Mill [13, ch. 2, 86].

23. Taking land values as 40 per cent of total real estate value, the high estimate of the share as given by Manvel [11], it would be necessary to raise the effective rate of property tax by a multiple of 2.5. With a mill rate of close to 4 per cent and a yield of, say, 5 per cent, 100 per cent taxation of land rent would be approximated. Allowing for the fact that property tax revenue provides little over 10 per cent of total (federal, state, local) tax revenue, the impossibility of the single tax proposition is evident.

# REFERENCES

[1] Clark, Barry S. (1980), 'John Locke and the origins of the liberal theory of justice', Working Paper No. 30 (University of Wisconsin–La Crosse; Bureau of Business and Economic Research).

[2] —— (1981), Review of Karen Iverson Vaughn, *John Locke: Economist and Social Scientist*, in *Eighteenth Century Studies: A Bibliography*.

[3] —— and Herbert Gintis (1978), 'Rawlsian justice and economic systems', *Philosophy and Public Affairs*, 7, 4 Summer: 307.

[4] Clark, J. B. (1899). *The Distribution of Wealth* (New York, Macmillan).

[5] Collier, Charles (1979), 'Henry George's system of political economy', *Hope*, 2, 1.

[7] —— (1955), *A Perplexed Philosopher* (New York, Robert Schalkenbach Foundation).

[8] George, Henry Jr. (1960), *The Life of Henry George* (New York, Robert Schalkenbach Foundation).

[9] Locke, John (1963), *Two Treatises of Government*, ed. P. Laslett. rev. edn. (New York, Mentor Book, New American Library).

[10] McPherson, C. B. (1962), *Possessive Individualism* (New York, Oxford University Press).

[11] Manvel, Allen D. (1968), *Three Land Research Studies*, Research Report No. 12 (Washington, DC The National Commission on Urban Problems).

[12] Michelman, F. I. (1966), 'Property, utility and fairness: comments on the ethical foundations of "just compensation" law', *Harvard Law Review*, 80: 1165–258.

[13] Mill, John Stuart (1921), *Principles of Political Economy, Book II*, ed. W. J. Ashley (London, Longmans, Green).

[14] Nagel, T. (1975), 'Libertarianism without foundations', *The Yale Law Journal*, 85.

[15] Nozick, Robert (1969), 'Coercion', in *Philosophy, Science and Method*, ed. S. Morgenbesser, P. Suppes and M. White (New York, St Martin's Press).

[16] —— 1974), *Anarchy, State, and Utopia* (New York, Basic Books).

[17] *President's Economic Report* (1974), (Washington, D.C., US Government Printing Office), January.

[18] Stigler, George (1941), *Production and Distribution Theory* (New York, Macmillan).
[19] Vaughn, Karen Iverson (1980), *John Locke, Economist and Social Scientist* (Chicago, University of Chicago Press).
[20] Viner, Jacob (1963), 'Possessive individualism as original sin', *Canadian Journal of Economics and Political Science*, 29 (November): 548–66.
[21] Weymark, John A. (1980), 'Money and Locke's Theory of Property', *History of Political Economy*, 12, 2:282–90.

# 21 Samuelson on Public Goods*
## 1983

The modern theory of public goods may be dated from June 1954, when Samuelson's *Pure Theory of Public Expenditures* appeared [31].[1] Never have three pages had so great an impact on the theory of public finance. They spawned a large body of literature with many variations on the theme, but the basic model had been set. The conditions of Pareto-optimality had been expanded to include public goods and the optimum optimorum based on a social welfare function had been restated accordingly. At the same time—and Samuelson made this clear from the outset—his model was not designed to show how the optimum might be arrived at in practice. At the formal level of welfare theory all was resolved, but much remained and remains to be done to put the theoretical jewel to practical use. To place Samuelson's contribution in perspective, I begin with a sketch of fiscal theory up to 1954. I shall then summarise and examine his basic model, to be followed by a review of its major offshoots.

## ANTECEDENTS

The history of doctrine, here as in other contexts, defies pedantic chronology. New ideas arise, overlap the old, and progress in discontinuous fashion. We may thus date the pre-history of public goods theory from 1776 (Adam Smith) to 1928 (A. C. Pigou), with history overlapping from the 1880s (Sax and Mazzola) to 1954 (Samuelson), and post-history thereafter.

### Pre-history
Unlike most of his classical successors, Adam Smith did not view the economics of public finance as merely a matter of minimising the evils of taxation. Book V of his *Wealth of Nations* gives more space to the expenditure than to the tax side of the budget. Public expenditures had a positive and important role to play. Maintenance of the courts, defence, justice and free education for the poor were needed. Beyond this, the sovereign's duty

---

* In Paul Samuelson and Modern Economic Theory (1983), ed. E. C. Brown and R. Solow (New York, McGraw-Hill). Thanks are due to James Buchanan for helpful comments.

is that of erecting and maintaining those public institutions and those public works, which, though they may be in the highest degree advantageous to a great society, are, however, of such a nature, that the profit could never repay the expense to any individual or small number of individuals, and which it therefore cannot be expected that any individual or small number of individuals should erect or maintain [38, p. 168].

Smith thus recognised the occurrence of market failure due to the peculiar nature of public goods, as well as the resulting need for public provision. But he did not go on to explore what it is in the nature of public goods that causes this difficulty to arise, evidently unaware of Hume's uncannily modern characterisation of the freerider problem [11, p. 159]. Nevertheless, these early insights should have sent the theory of public goods off to a running start, but such was not to be. Classical economists who followed showed little appetite for examining the economic nature of public goods. With few exceptions, they addressed the tax side of the budget only. Ricardo in particular considered public expenditures inherently wasteful, endorsing Say's dictum that 'the very best of all plans of finance is to spend little'. John Stuart Mill gave much space to the design of an equitable tax structure but paid little or no attention to expenditure analysis.

Such was the case even though the benefit strand of equity theory could not quite escape its implicit linkage to the expenditure side. Taxation according to benefits received was a natural outgrowth of Lockean contract theory, in which civil society is formed for the protection of justly acquired property. 'The subject of every state', so Adam Smith noted, 'ought to contribute towards the support of government as nearly as possible in line with their respective abilities; that is, in proportion to the revenue which they respectively enjoy under the protection of the state'. Taxation according to benefit received thus involves the central notion of a *quid pro quo*, of taxation as a just price paid for services rendered. But the proper scope for such services, as indeed the role of the state, was considered as minimal. Emphasis was on how to distribute the cost of a given budget in line with the recipients' gains, rather than on how its composition and size should be determined. Benefit theorists differed, however, in what they considered the relationship between benefits and income [20, chs 4, 5]. Some, including Mill, held that the benefit rule would call for regressive taxation as the poor are in greater need of protection, while others argued that the rich have more wealth to protect, thus calling for progressive rates. In either case, reference was to the *amount* of protection needed, rather than to different valuations that poor and rich would place on a given amount. Both groups also adhered to the Lockean notion that returns to effort establish a just distribution, so that redistributive taxation is ruled out. The benefit doctrine thus had an essentially conservative appeal.

Ability to pay theorists in turn disregarded expenditures altogether. They thought to determine a fair distribution of the tax burden quite independent of how the money is spent. The tax burden, as a matter of equity, should be distributed in line with 'ability to pay'. Beginning with

John Stuart Mill, this was restated as requiring an imposition of equal sacrifice, [18, p. 805] and subsequent refinements were added by Edgeworth and Pigou [10, ch. 5; 27, ch. 5]. They distinguished between equal-absolute, proportional and marginal sacrifice, with the latter doubling as an equity and welfare-maximising rule. Pigou's formulation moreover, introduced dead-weight loss into the burden concept, thereby foreshadowing recent developments in the theory of optimal taxation. But the ability to pay doctrine lost professional credibility with the advent of the new welfare economics from Robbins on and its banning of cardinal utility comparisons from theoretical analysis. The practice of such comparisons, however, survived in the public mind, as did the notion that taxes should be distributed fairly.

Contrasted with the conservative appeal of the benefit doctrine, the ability to pay approach was favoured by liberal writers who were not averse to income redistribution. Distribution of the tax burden by ability to pay was generally interpreted to call for progressive taxation, although, as Samuelson showed in an early footnote, this is by no means a foregone conclusion. All depends on how equal sacrifice is defined and on the shape of the income utility function [30, p. 227].

**History**

Pigou's primary concern in fiscal theory was with the design of the tax structure, in line with the ability to pay approach [27, Part IV]. We have therefore grouped him under the pre-history caption. This grouping, however, needs qualification because his treatise also contains a brief but important chapter on expenditure theory. In this chapter, he calls for both sides of the budget to be linked by the efficiency requirement that provision for public goods should be carried to the point where marginal social benefits come to equal marginal social costs [27, ch. 5][2]. This was an advance over the ability to pay tradition as it overcame the taxation-only bias that had characterised that approach. In its abstract and normative tone, it indeed resembles the spirit of Samuelson's later contribution. But unfortunately Pigou did not go beyond stating his unexceptionable rule. He did not address the question of why certain goods need be provided through the budget, and he made no serious attempt to define the nature of public goods. As Samuelson noted, it is surprising that the author of *The Economics of Welfare* did not carry his theory of externalities to his later study of fiscal problems. [33, II p. 1233]. Nor was he aware of the new doctrine that had developed in the continental writings of the 1880s and 1890s when the newly-emerged doctrine of marginal utility came to be applied to public finance. Public, like private, goods, so the new argument went, should be evaluated in line with their utility to the consumer. Thereby the basis for modern public goods theory was laid and economic analysis, interpreted as the theory of efficient resource use, was expanded to nonmarket phenomena. Though beginning with Sax, the modern definition of public goods may be traced to Mazzola. Writing in 1890, he recognised the indivisibility of public services as their distinguishing characteristic, the fact that 'consumption can not be divided up' [16, p. 42]. Since consumers differ in incomes and tastes, this indivisibility 'constitutes a technical reason' why uniform pricing would leave some with more and others with less than the marginal utility that they derive. [ibid]. Uniform pricing, therefore, would contradict society's natural tendency to use resources for maximum satisfaction. To secure it, he continues, governments charge multiple prices, 'so that each pays for these goods according to his own evaluation'.

While Mazzola thought of the efficient tax price as resulting from the maximising behaviour of consumers, he recognised that evaluation does not come about automatically through a market process. Rather, it is entrusted to governmental agencies. When their policies are dominated by the interests of particular classes or groups, the natural equilibrium of welfare maximisation is disturbed and dissatisfaction results. The equilibrating process of the competitive market is replaced by that of the political system. Though open to criticism in details, Mazzola's formulation was nevertheless an important advance. His model served as a stepping-stone for Wicksell's analysis and already contained the essential elements of Lindahl's subsequent pricing solution. Since it was dissatisfaction with this solution that 30 years later induced Samuelson's reformulation, we may observe an intriguing if discontinuous intellectual lineage from 1890 to 1954.

Wicksell, writing in 1896, accepted Mazzola's central thesis of 'equality between the marginal utility of public goods and their price' as an efficiency rule. But he rejected the further contention that this result comes about when each taxpayer succeeds in maximising his utility. Mazzola's rule as a requirement of tax policy 'is really meaningless' [ibid, p. 81]. The reason lies in the 'freerider' behaviour, a term that came later but a concept that was clearly grasped by Wicksell: 'Since the taxpayer's own outlays on public services will have no significant effect on total supply, he will pay nothing.' The necessary equality between marginal utility and tax price 'cannot be achieved by the action of individual taxpayers'. Rather, it must be brought about by consultation between all taxpayers, a process which Mazzola did not describe. In Wicksell's view, 'this is precisely the question which ought to be decided' [ibid, p. 82].

In addressing this issue, Wicksell considers the possibility that an enlightened ruler (not unlike Samuelson's ethical observer) succeeds in implementing the general welfare, but he drops this as an unlikely solution. Majority rule under representative democracy is even more likely to fail, since the representatives will be as selfish as their constituents. The solution must be sought in a voting system in which each expenditure project is paired with alternative taxing patterns. If the expenditure project creates utility that exceeds its cost, so Wicksell argues, one of the combinations is likely to find unanimous acceptance [ibid p. 90], Budget decisions should therefore be made on a unanimous basis. This will not assure that Mazzola's criterion is met, but it will provide a fair approximation. Having proposed his stern requirement of full unanimity, Wicksell then dilutes it and calls for a rule of only 'approximate unanimity of decision—absolute unanimity may have to be ruled out for practical reasons' [ibid, p. 92]. This weakens Wicksell's case, especially since no definition of 'approximate' is given and the nature of the 'practical reason' is not described.

Wicksell also adds a 'necessary, although ultimately only an apparent, exception to the principle of unanimity and voluntary consent as the basis for just taxation'. This exception arises because 'it is clear that justice in taxation tacitly *presupposes* [italics added] justice in the existing distribution of property [ibid, p. 108] and income. There can be no true *quid pro quo* in paying for public services if what the taxpayer surrenders is not properly his. If the prevailing property order is 'in open contradiction with modern concepts of law and equity, then society has both the right and duty to revise the existing property structure'. But here the unanimity requirement has to be suspended 'since it would obviously be asking too much to expect such revision even to be carried out if it were made dependent upon the agreement of the persons primarily involved' [ibid, p. 109]. Wicksell, at the same time, cautions against excessive interference of this sort but the essential methodological point is made: Just distribution precedes the just financing of public services and the two are viewed as distinct steps. As we shall see presently, this poses one of the fundamental points of disagreement between his and Samuelson's formulation.

We now come to Lindahl's contributions as the last step towards the completion of history. Lindahl, writing in 1919, presented what later became known as the voluntary exchange solution. Two parties, A and B, advance their offer curves for public goods, defining the maximum fraction of the total cost that they would be willing to assume at various budget sizes. An equilibrium is established at the intersection of the two curves, where their marginal evaluations add up to total cost [ibid, p. 169]. As shown later on by Bowen, the same solution may be arrived at as the intersection between the supply schedule (recording marginal cost to the community as a whole) and a hypothetical market demand schedule, in this case by vertical rather than horizontal addition of individual schedules [2, p. 177]. Tax prices thus determined leave each taxpayer in a position where price ratio equals marginal rates of substitution. Social good pricing is similar to private good pricing in this respect, but the social good case combines different prices with equal quantities, while the private good case combines equal prices with different quantities.

Lindahl's pricing solution thus resembles that visualised by Mazzola and accepted as a norm by Wicksell. He differs from Wicksell in that he takes this pricing rule to come about as the result of voluntary bargaining, be it among two parties or among a number of individuals who strike successive bargains. His 'standard solution' is achieved if 'power is distributed evenly in relation to the existing property order' [45, p. 172]. If political power differs, a solution more advantageous to one or the other party will result. But in all, the political process may be expected to approximate the standard case. Following Wicksell, Lindahl notes that the solution will reflect the consequences of a given property order. For the pricing solution to be just, the property order must also be considered such, since, so he quotes Wicksell, 'it would obviously be nonsense to speak of a just portion of an unjust whole' [ibid, p. 227].

## THE SAMUELSON MODEL

Such was the state of the debate in 1954 when, after a hiatus of 35 years, Samuelson's model appeared. There had been no mention of public expenditures in his *Foundations* and only a cursory footnote reference to taxation. The excursion into expenditure theory was undertaken, so we are told, to illustrate the usefulness of mathematical economics, rather than as the outcome of our author's long-standing and substantive concern with the problem. It was induced also by his 'dim remembrance' of the Lindahl diagram in my maiden paper which, a few years earlier, had brought the voluntary exchange model and its unrealistic setting to the attention of the English (only) reading public [36, III p. 492; 19]. Yet, his brief initial contribution proved to be among his most important pages.

The model is too familiar to require more than a brief summary. The problem that is posed and solved is how to allocate resources efficiently in a setting that includes public as well as private goods. Public—or, as referred to initially by Samuelson, collective consumption goods—are defined as goods for which each person's consumption is related to the total by a condition of equality, not summation, as for private goods. Given the production possibility frontier and taking individual preferences for public and private goods to be known, the set of Pareto-efficient solutions is arrived at. The efficiency conditions are shown to differ from those of private goods. For the latter, the marginal rate of transformation in production equals that of substitution in consumption, which is the same for all consumers. For public goods the marginal rate of transformation equals the sum of the marginal rates of substitution and these may differ among consumers. Given the set of efficient solutions (with each defining the mix of output between public and private goods, and the allocation of private goods among consumers), the best among them (the 'bliss point', as Samuelson put it) is chosen by application of a social welfare function.[3]

This formulation differs from its precursors in important respects. The theory of public goods is now viewed as an extension of the conditions of Pareto optimality and no longer as modelling or reforming the process by which budget policy is determined. Most important, the derivation of efficiency conditions is separated from the process by which an efficient budget may in fact be arrived at. By introducing an ethical observer to whom preferences are known, the revelation issue is bypassed and the problem is solved without reference to such institutional baggage as a prevailing distribution of income, taxes, or expenditures. This is quite in line with Samuelson's earlier statement of welfare maximisation in a private good setting [3, ch. 8]. While the competitive market may be used as an implementation device for this setting, the efficiency conditions do not derive from the existence of market institutions. Similarly, those for public goods are defined independent of budgetary or voting institutions.

In this setting, Lindahl pricing ceases to be *the* solution and becomes but a special case of the general model. As Samuelson shows in a later paper, the observer may play the Lindahl game by using a 'pseudo-demand analysis' to compute the equilibrium. [36, III, p. 496]. He will begin with some particular distribution of money income, derive each individual's corresponding pseudo demand curve, and then provide for public goods in line with what people wish to buy at Lindahl prices. This solution will be efficient and reflect a point on the utility frontier. But the outcome may not be optimal. The observer then applies a set of lump-sum taxes and transfers to achieve another income distribution and repeats the experiment.[4] Doing so for all possible distributions will trace the entire utility frontier. Finally, the best point is chosen on the basis of the social welfare function. Postulating a distribution of income and playing the pricing game is a possible way of solving the problem, but a cumbersome one. The proper distribution of income has to be arrived at simultaneously with the allocation pattern and the chosen set of Lindahl prices, so that nothing is gained by introducing a distribution of money income at the beginning. The observer will save time by proceeding directly with his optimisation problem. Moreover, if a distribution of income *is* introduced, the observer need not charge Lindahl prices. The prices that are charged need not equal the consumer's marginal rate of substitution. The solution will be efficient, provided only that marginal rates of substitution aggregate to that of transformation [17].

Having separated the analytical problem of maximisation sharply from that of implementation, Samuelson faults Wicksell for not drawing his distinction with sufficient clarity. In particular, he takes issue with Wicksell's proposition that just taxation must be preceded by a just distribution of income [36, III, p. 495].[5] Clearly, Wicksell's proposition is mistaken if viewed within the context of Samuelson's own model. But this is not what Wicksell was after. His concern was with the mechanism of preference revelation and with improving the fiscal institutions through which this mechanism operates. It was not with the derivation of efficiency conditions in a setting that assumes preferences to be known. Once preferences are not given, a voting mechanism must be used to induce preference revelation; to do so a given distribution of income must prevail. Moreover, if the voting solution is to be optimal as well as efficient, the correct, or as Wicksell called it, the 'just' distribution of income must prevail to begin with. But how can this be if, as Samuelson holds, the distribution issue must be resolved simultaneously with that of public goods alloction? In my view (although I have not persuaded Professor Samuelson of this), the circularity is broken by introducing an additional equation [Musgrave 21, p. 106]. In the private good setting, and with preferences unknown, the competitive market may be used as a computation device. This being the case, *the* proper distribution of income is that which yields the optimal result given the use of marginal cost pricing through the market system. For the case of public goods, that distribution of money income is proper or 'just' which yields the optimal solution (an efficient outcome and a distribution of welfare in line with the social welfare function) given *that* pricing rule which is approximated by the voting process. While there is more than one efficient pricing rule, I find it reasonable to postulate that the voting process should be designed to approximate Lindahl pricing. This permits parallel treatment of public and private goods prices in setting the proper distribution of (real) income, and allows the voter-consumer to think symmetrically about his or her 'purchases' of public and private goods.

All this, to be sure, does not matter in Samuelson's pure model where the issues of allocation and distribution intrinsically overlap and must be resolved simultaneously. Given the omniscient referee and the global task that Samuelson assigns to him or her, there is no prior state of distribution and hence no issue of 'redistribution'. Allocation decisions need not be compromised by distributional concerns. As noted before, the referee may while away time by using a 'pseudo-demand algorithm to compute equilibrium', but all the Pareto-optimal solutions may be traced out readily by manipulating the pattern of lump-sum taxes and transfers [36, III, p. 497]. At a more realistic level, however, this ideal tax-transfer system is not available. Lump-sum redistribution in an ongoing economy is but a fiction of the theorist's imagination. Redistribution policies in the real world cause distortions, leaving the 'feasible utility frontier' along which policy may move from a given initial position well inside the true frontier of the pure model. Redistribution in kind, such as expenditures on health, may then involve less distortion and hence be better than a tax-transfer scheme. In his response to Margolis, Samuelson thus dissociates himself from 'the type of liberal who would insist that all redistributions take place through tax policies and transfer expenditures' [32, II p. 1232]. A second-best solution is all that there is to be had, but the reference point remains that of the pure model. Real transfers and subsidies become the counter-part to selective commodity taxation, from Pigou's query to Ramsey's theory on to today's optimal taxation theory.

This, however, is hardly the reason why transfers in kind are used so widely. In a brief departure from neoclassical tradition, Samuelson notes that 'paternalistic policies may be voted upon themselves by a democratic people because they do not regard the results of spontaneous market operations as optimal [ibid.]. I take this to recognise the existence of what I have called merit goods, a concept that has recently reappeared in relation to distribution, especially in Tobin's concept of 'specific egalitarianism' and views of equity in categorical rather than simply vertical terms [20, 22, p. 83; 40]. But these are exceptions, out of bounds for Samuelson's theory of public goods, which squarely rests on an individualistic social welfare function. The same goes for modern fiscal theory in general, including most of my own work. Whether or not marginal rates of substitution are additive is no reason why private preferences should or should not be respected. Yet, there are exceptional situations in every society where the public interest is taken to override private preferences, be it with regard to the provision of otherwise private or of public goods. Such types of interference, if this be the right term, make take budgetary form and should have their place in the body of fiscal theory rather than be excluded by definition.[6]

Turning now to the mechanism of preference revelation, Samuelson applauds Wicksell for rejecting the hypothesis that revelation can be secured through a decentralised market mechanism [36, III, p. 501]. But he denies as naive Wicksell's proposition that an optimum will be promoted by voting upon issues that combine the tax and expenditure sides of the budget [ibid.]. Bundle-voting, to be sure, will not eliminate strategy, but in my view Wicksell's prescription retains much merit. By coupling both sides of the budget, the voter is confronted with the fact that public services involve an opportunity cost. Specification of his tax price at given service levels imposes a constraint that facilitates rational choice, and, I suspect, limits the scope for profitable misrepresentation. Indeed, better linkage of tax and expenditure decisions may well be the key to reform of legislative fiscal procedure. Samuelson's call for 'corrosive nihilism' may be helpful 'to puncture the bubble of hopeful thinking', but things are not all that bad [ibid]. The democratic process, after all, functions not too badly and it may be improved by constructive reform. Samuelson himself concedes as much:

My doubts do not assert that passably good organisation of the public household is impossible or unlikely, but merely that theorists have not as yet provided us with much analysis of these matters that has validity or plausibility. If I stimulate someone to resolve my doubts, that will make two people happy [ibid].

Have these doubts been resolved by recent work on a voting system under which self-interested individuals will choose not to cheat? [7; 7a]. Beginning with a prevailing distribution of income, suppose that cost shares in the budget are assigned among individuals in some arbitrary fashion and independent of their preferences, true or as revealed. Suppose that the budget is to be financed by a head tax. Individuals are then asked to record their maximum-offer schedules for various budget sizes, aggregate 'demand' is determined in Bowen fashion by vertical addition, and output is set at the intersection of the aggregate demand with the supply schedule. The solution will be efficient provided that individuals will report their true demand schedules. They will be induced to do so by a tax (payable in addition to the cost share) that renders misrepresentation unprofitable. Each individual will pay a Clarke tax (named after its inventor) equal in amount to the loss of consumer surplus suffered by others because he chooses to vote rather than to abstain. This will induce him to reveal his true preferences because cheating will increase his Clarke tax by more than he can hope to gain from pushing the budget size towards his preferred level. This outcome is not surprising. If true preferences are revealed, the allocation decision will fall on the utility frontier. Cheating moves the solution inside. What A may gain from misrepresentation must fall short of what B and C lose. Misrepresentation therefore does not pay if A must pay compensation through the Clarke tax. While the proceeds are retained in the budget rather than paid out to B and C, this does not reduce the deterrent to A.

As much as I would like to, I cannot share the claim that the Clarke mechanism disposes of the revelation issue, thereby resolving the freerider problem that for centuries has haunted fiscal theory [42, p. 1145]. To begin with, the tax does not do away with distortions that arise from strategic behaviour through the formation of coalitions. It deals with isolated cheating by individual voters only. Samuelson's call for nihilism may still hold. But there are difficulties even short of this. If cost shares are to be assigned in arbitrary fashion, net gains or losses from public services must be compensated for elsewhere in determining distributional adjustments, and voters will be aware of this. While it has been suggested that the Clarke tax approach may be used to determine Lindahl prices, [ibid., p. 1156] I see no basis for this. Moreover, the feasibility of the approach depends on the numbers involved. In the small-number case, the administrative costs are limited and the pressure imposed by the Clarke tax may be substantial. At the same time, coalition strategies are readily feasible. In the large-number case, the Clarke tax will prove very small and one wonders whether its pressure can suffice to induce voters to comply with the rather demanding task of filing their offer curves. Moreover, for the large-number case one wonders how the schedule can be collected and processed and individual Clarke taxes be assigned. It has been suggested that these difficulties might be avoided by reliance on sampling, but this seems more feasible for determining the budget size than for assigning Clarke taxes.

In all, the Clarke mechanism leaves serious problems of implementation, quite apart from the theoretically intriguing (and hence much discussed) fact that the government must somehow dispose of its Clarke tax receipts. While progress is made, it can hardly be said that the issue has been resolved. Samuelson's scepticism remains relevant, and it is a matter of regret that he himself did not undertake to lift it. Had he done so, we would undoubtedly be further in translating his theoretical vision into an operational pattern.

## DESCENDANTS

Samuelson's pure theory of public expenditures has become the basis for numerous variations and extensions, some of which we note in this final section.

## Polar Cases and Blended Models

Samuelson initially offered his theory of public expenditures as a 'polar case model of government', to be contrasted with the traditional individualistic model of general equilibrium [32, II, p. 1226]. In subsequent writings, however, he distanced himself from the polar case concept. To be sure, the polar case did not require that the public good, while being equally available to all, should be equally useful to each consumer. On the contrary, what may be highly beneficial to A may be useless or even a social bad to B [ibid.]. But the polar concept becomes dubious when questioning how widely the condition of equal availability to all is in fact applicable to the range of public goods and services. In response, Samuelson conceded that in many instances there exists some 'element of variability in the benefit that can go to one citizen *at the expense* of some other citizen' [ibid., p. 1232].[7] In most instances, the nature of public services reflects a 'blending of the extreme antipodal models' [32, II, p. 1232]. Subsequently, he went further and jettisoned the 'polar' public good concept altogether. Instead, he proposes a knife-edged definition of a pure private good as entering into the utility function of one particular consumer only. All the rest (that is, goods that enter two or more utility functions) falls into the public good domain by virtue of involving some consumption good externality [36, III, p. 501]. This permits Samuelson to stress the essential analytical similarity of all externality cases, from national defence to decreasing cost industries. Yet subsequent authors have found it useful to distinguish between particular externality situations and the policy problems that they pose.

To begin with, A's consumption of x may enter B's utility function in various ways. It may do so because B enjoys A's well-being without B's own consumption intake being affected. B feels better if A consumes more milk or, generally, has a higher income. *Or*, B may benefit because A's consumption gives rise to a spillover that grants a similar benefit to B. A's inoculation reduces B's risk of infection, albeit less so than would B's own inoculation [26]. External benefits result but in diluted form. Both interactions are more or less similar formally and may be allowed for readily by the observer, but the innate difference ('psychological' utility interdependence in the one case and 'physical' benefit spillover in the other) may be significant in their policy implications.[8] Moreover, the presence of dilution bears on the degree of market failure. As the degree of dilution becomes larger, it will become worthwhile for both A and B to treat x as if it were a private good and bid for it at the market. The degree of market failure is reduced and public policy now calls for a subsidy rather than total provision through the budget. Since partial externality may be viewed as the typical case, it may well be argued that a general theory of budgetary provision should be a theory of subsidy rather than one of full financing. Determining the appropriate degree of subsidy, to be sure, once more involves the problem of preference revelation and the troublesome issues of voting strategy that this implies.

Another instance, also addressed by Samuelson, arises in the case of public goods that are subject to crowding or congestion [36, III, p. 510; 27]. Were it not for the lumpiness factor, such goods could be provided efficiently through the market, and where divisibility can be approximated by successive units of the facility (for example, additional cinemas), provision might in fact be left to this mechanism. But where lumpiness is substantial, the charge appropriate to reducing congestion to its optimal level will hardly be that which also recovers the capital cost of the project.

A further case that has received much attention relates to public goods whose benefits are spatially limited. Such benefits are available equally to all residents of a particular area, but not (or at a lower level only) to outsiders. Thus a distinction arises between national, regional, and local public goods. This feature has been the basis for an extensive theory of local finance, at both a normative and a positive level [39]. In the normative context, local public goods theory has dealt with the problem of optimal club size, as well as with the equilibrating process, by which a system of clubs or fiscal jurisdictions is established [4]. The resulting theory of fiscal location has been among the most productive offsprings of public goods theory, even though weakened by inadequate integration with other aspects of location theory. At the positive level, local fiscal theory has focused on location choice in response to fiscal variables as a mechanism ('voting by feet') through which preference revelation may occur. But, as Samuelson notes, the optimality of the outcome will depend on the preference configuration. Not everyone may get what he or she wants so that the optimal solution cannot be achieved without application of a 'given determinate' social welfare function. Moreover, 'there is a political and ethical question whether groups of like-minded individuals shall be free to run out on their social responsibilities and go off by themselves' [33, II, p. 1238]. Once more there may be dimensions to fiscal theory that reach outside the neoclassical framework.

It remains to note the somewhat curious fact that contributions to the theory of public goods have focused almost entirely on consumption goods. Samuelson's original reference, as noted before, was to collective consumer goods. In subsequent papers, reference changed to public consumer goods and then simply to public goods, but the initial emphasis on consumer goods remained and had a lasting impact. Yet, public provision for capital goods is of no less importance and, especially in the context of developing countries, may well be more important. While the implications for efficiency conditions are analogous to those for consumer goods,[9] policy considerations differ. To the extent that public provision takes the form of intermediate goods that enter private production, benefit determination is simplified because the resulting cost reduction and consequent consumer responses may be measured in the market. Costs may be internalised by appropriate taxes and the freerider problem does not arise.

## Public Sector Failure

Samuelson's theory of public goods, by mirror-image, was a theory of market failure. Central to his argument is the proposition that there exists no decentralised market mechanism by which the optimal solution can be obtained. His pure model shows how optimal action by the public sector can remedy the failure of the market. This focus on market failure has now given way to a counter-offensive, as attention is directed at problems of public sector failure.[10] The Hegelian pendulum has swung and history is on the march again, but with a reversed course.

As one line of attack, it is argued (a) that the voting process does not yield optimal results and (b) that it involves a systematic bias towards overexpansion. Regarding (a), Samuelson may indeed be viewed as a harbinger of the new wave. While stressing the presence of market failure, he also takes a pessimistic view regarding the approximation of an optimal solution through voting. He differs, however, with the new school's conclusion regarding (b), that the voting process carries a systematic bias towards over-expansion [41; 6]. Given the vagaries of strategic behaviour, he finds (and I think correctly so) that the deviation from optimality may be in either direction [36, III, p. 501]. The only basis on which there is a presumption towards overexpansion is the assumption that 'transaction costs' for proponents of projects fall short of those for opponents.

However this may be, recent theorems on government failure have gone beyond voting bias and have focused on the role of bureaucracy as a third and independent factor in the fiscal process. The bureaucrat (once thought of as a civil servant) is viewed as a force whose action will distort the outcome even if preference revelation could be secured effectively through a system of (otherwise) Downesian democracy.

In sharp contrast to the classical role of bureaucracy as viewed by Max Weber [44, p. 21], the modern bureaucrat is seen as maximising her own utility function, featuring above all the size of her bureau. Moreover, she is said to possess powerful instruments by which to accomplish her goals. Confronting the legislature with all or nothing budget requests, she pushes enactment of programmes which exceed the optimal level of activity [25]. Similarly, by controlling the agenda of issues on which voters are allowed to vote, she may restrict the agenda to programme levels that exceed the optimum [15]. Allowance for the role of public officials in decision making is all to the good, but I doubt the realism of the new model, including its behavioural assumptions, as well as the institutional framework in which it proceeds. Insufficient attention is paid to the existence of a budgetary process through which programme choices are weighted and to the power of the electorate in imposing its will if governmental behaviour moves too far out of line.

Going beyond the diagnosis of public sector failure, the new approach seeks for remedies to offset what it considers to be the built-in bias of prevailing institutions. Thereby it follows the Wicksellian tradition of focus on procedural reform. However, what I take to be questionable diagnosis also leads to questionable remedies. These involve restraining actions of various forms, including tax and/or expenditure limitations at the constitutional level, increased majority requirements, limitations as to choice of revenue sources, and so forth. As I see it, more neutral improvements in budget procedure, such as Wicksell's quest for tax and expenditure linkage and superior project evaluation, are much to be preferred [5, ch. 10; 3]. Nevertheless, the new approach offers an important addition to the economics, or better, the politics, of public goods. Proceeding in the tradition of microeconomics, it may be viewed as a complement, rather than an alternative, to Samuelson's model.

Both approaches are neoclassical in spirit and may be contrasted with the quite different perspective provided by the Goldscheid–Schumpeter tradition of fiscal sociology [23]. According to the latter, the formation and functioning of fiscal institutions is viewed as the outcome of group interaction and as a reflection of the broader social and economic structure of society. Maximising behaviour of individuals enters but is far from the entire story. As Samuelson well recognised in retitling his second paper from 'The' to 'A' theory of public expenditures, fiscal theorising may not yield a unique solution. But whatever its future course, 1954 will surely remain a landmark date in the theory of public finance.

## NOTES

1. Page citations from Samuelson are to reprints in his *Collected Scientific Papers*, with volume in roman numerals. To permit focus, this paper is limited to Samuelson's contribution to the theory of public goods, thus omitting some other writings in public finance, especially his paper on the theory of capital income taxation [34, III, p. 179].
2. The same may be said for earlier continental attempts to prescribe a proper balance between private and public outlays. Thus Schäffle's law of proportional expenditures implied a principle similar to that advanced by Pigou [Schäffle, 37] but the needs to be covered by the state were taken to be given as group needs. Adolf Wagner similarly balanced the advantages and costs of public services [Wagner, 43] but he left it to political science to determine the proper range of state activities.
3. For the basic model, see [31, II, ch. 92] and [32, II, ch. 93]. For its further development, see [33, II, ch. 94] and [36, III, ch. 172].
4. See Johansen [12] for application of the Lindahl solution to alternative income distributions.
5. Samuelson [36, III, p. 495] suggests that Wicksell confuses two concepts of justice: (1) justice in distribution so as to secure maximum bliss—the utilitarian approach, and (2) justice in permitting a person to secure optimal use of a given income—the approach implicit in considering a Lindahl price as just. I wonder whether Wicksell was indeed confused on this point. Given the need for securing preference revelation via a given distribution of income, both concepts of justice are needed and have to enter in an interdependent fashion.
6. For the outlines of an alternative approach see Colm [8; 9].
7. It is precisely this feature that has led me to describe the key characteristic of public consumption goods as involving non-rival consumption [21, p. 126], a term that Samuelson considers somewhat doubtful. Samuelson does not, however, use the term 'jointness in consumption' as characterising the nature of public goods, a condition that is neatly distinguished from that of jointness in production [35, III, ch. 168].

8. The efficiency conditions for the two cases are not identical. See Roskamp [25].
9. For a discussion of public capital goods, see Kaizuka [13].
10. Among a large and rapidly growing literature, see Buchanan [5] and Borcherding [1].

# REFERENCES

[1] Borcherding, T. E. (ed.) (1977); *Budgets and Bureaucrats: The Sources of Public Sector Growth* (Durham, N.C., Duke University Press).
[2] Bowen, Howard R. (1948); *Toward Social Economy* (New York, Rinehart).
[3] Brennan, G. and J. M. Buchanan (1980); 'The logic of the Ricardian equivalent theorem', *Finanzarchiv*, 38 (1).
[4] Buchanan, James M. (1969); 'An economic theory of clubs', *Economica*, 32, February.
[5] —— (1974), *The Limits of Liberty* (Chicago, University of Chicago Press).
[6] —— and Gordon Tullock (1962); *The Calculus of Consent* (Ann Arbor, University of Michigan Press).
[7] Clarke, E. H. (1971), 'Multiple pricing of public goods', *Public Choice*, 11, Autumn.
[7a] —— (1972),'Multiple pricing of public goods: An example', in S. Mushkin (ed.); *Public Prices for Public Products* (Washington, Urban Institute).
[8] Colm, Gerhard (1927); *Volkswirtschaftliche Theorie der Staatsausgaben* (Tübingen, J. C. Mohr).
[9] —— (1955); *Essays in Public Finance and Fiscal Policy* (New York, Oxford University Press).
[10] Edgeworth, F. Y. (1925); 'The pure theory of taxation', *Papers Relating to Political Economy*, Vol. II (London, Royal Economic Society).
[11] Hume, David (1740); *A Treatise of Human Nature*, III, L. A. Selby-Bigge (ed.), (Oxford, Clarendon Press, 1958).
[12] Johansen, Leif (1965); *Public Economics* (Amsterdam, North-Holland).
[13] Kaizuka, Keimei (1965); Public goods and decentralization of production', *Review of Economics and Statistics* 47, February.
[14] Lindahl, Eric (1919, 1928): excerpts translated in R. A. Musgrave and A. Peacock (eds) (1958), *Classics in the Theory of Public Finance* (London, Macmillan).
[15] Mackay, R. J. and C. L. Weaver (1979); 'On the mutuality of interests between bureaus and high demand review committees: a perverse result'. *Public Choice*, 34 (3–4).
[16] Mazzola, Ugo (1890); excerpts translated in Musgrave and Peacock *op cit*.
[17] McGuire, Martin C. and Henry J. Aaron (1969); 'Efficiency and equity and optimal supply of a public good'. *Review of Economics and Statistics*, 51, February.
[18] Mill, John Stuart (1847); *Principles of Political Economy*, Ashley edn (London, Longmans, 1909).
[19] Musgrave, Richard A. (1938); 'The voluntary exchange theory of public economy', *Quarterly Journal of Economics*, 53, February.
[20] —— (1959); *The Theory of Public Finance* (New York, McGraw-Hill).
[21] —— (1969); 'Provision for social goods', in J. Margolis and H. Guitton (eds); *Public Economics: An Analysis of Public Production and Consumption and*

*their Relations to the Private Sectors: Proceedings of a Conference Held by the International Economics Associations* (London, Macmillan).

[22] —— and Peggy B. Musgrave (1973); *Public Finance in Theory and Practice*, 3rd edn (New York, McGraw-Hill).

[23] —— (1980); 'Theories of fiscal crisis: an essay in fiscal sociology', in H. J. Aaron and M. J. Boskin (eds), *The Economics of Taxation* (Washington, Brookings Institution).

[24] —— (1981); 'Leviathan Cometh, or Does He?', in H. Ladd and N. Tideman (eds); *Control of Public Expenditures* (Washington, Brookings Institution).

[25] Niskanen, W. (1971); *Bureaucracy and Representative Government* (Chicago, Aldine).

[26] Oakland, William (1969); 'Joint goods', *Economica*, 36. August.

[27] —— (1972); 'Congestion, public goods and welfare', *Journal of Public Economics*, 1, November.

[28] Pigou, A. C. (1928); *Studies in Public Finance* (London, Macmillan).

[29] Ricardo, David (1817); *The Principles of Political Economy and Taxation* (London, Dent, 1911).

[30] Roskamp, Karl (1975); 'Public goods, merit goods, private goods, Pareto optimum, and social optimum', *Public Finance*, 30, No. 1.

[31] Samuelson, Paul A. (1947); *Foundations of Economic Analysis* (Cambridge, Mass., Harvard University Press).

[32] —— (1954); 'The pure theory of public expenditure', *Review of Economics and Statistics* 36, November; *Collected Scientific Papers*, II, ch. 92.

[33] —— (1955); 'Diagrammatic exposition of a theory of public expenditure', *Review of Economics and Statistics* 37, November; *Collected Scientific Papers*, II, ch. 93.

[34] —— (1958); 'Aspects of public expenditure theories', *Review of Economics and Statistics* 40, November; Collected Scientific Papers, II, ch. 94.

[35] —— (1964); 'Tax deductibility of economic depreciation to insure invariant valuations', *Journal of Political Economy*, 72, December; *Collected Scientific Papers*, III, ch. 179.

[36] —— (1969a); 'Contrast between welfare conditions for joint supply and for public goods', *Review of Economics and Statistics*, 51, February; *Collected Scientific Papers*, III, ch. 168.

—— (1969b); 'Pure theory of public expenditure and taxation', in Margolis and Guitton *op cit.*; *Collected Scientific Papers*, III, ch. 172.

[38] Schäffle, Albert (1873); *Das gesellschaftliche System der menschlichen Wirtschaft* (Tübingen, Germany).

[39] Smith, Adam (1776); *The Wealth of Nations* (New York, Modern Library, 1937).

[40] Tiebout, Charles (1956); 'A pure theory of local expenditures', *Journal of Political Economy*, 64, October.

[41] Tobin, James (1970); 'On limiting the domain of inequality', *Journal of Law and Economics*, 13, October.

[42] Tullock, Gordon (1959); 'Problems of majority voting', *Journal of Political Economy*, 67, December.

[43] —— and Nicholas Tideman (1976); 'A new and superior principle of public choice', *Journal of Political Economy*, 84, December.

[44] Wagner, A. (1883); *Finanzwissenschaft*, Part 1, 3rd edn (Leipzig). See also excerpts in Musgrave and Peacock, op. cit.

[45] Weber, M. (1920); in H. Gerth and C. Mills, *From Max Weber: Essays on Sociology* (New York, Oxford University Press, 1946).

[46] Wicksell, Knut (1896); excerpts translated in Musgrave and Peacock, op. cit.

# 22   Pathway to Tax Reform*
## 1984

Stanley Surrey was a leader in our generation of tax reformers, a generation that believed with Justice Holmes that good government is vital to a democratic society and that fairness in taxation is an essential part thereof. Though not given to philosophical discourse on social mores, Stanley laboured relentlessly in pursuit of fairness. For all of us who worked with him over the decades, his tireless dedication to the public interest was an inspiration. His Treasury years in particular stand in shining contradiction to the caricature of the self-serving bureaucrat that now dominates the media and academic models of government.

What, then, was the good tax system toward which Stanley Surrey wanted to lead us? Not surprisingly, an abstract summation is difficult to find: tax reform deals in specifics, and in the end it is these that matter. Nonetheless, a unifying theme runs through his work, and it can best be seen by focussing on the federal income tax. World War II vastly increased the demand for federal revenues, and this demand was met by expansion of the income tax. What had been only an upper class levy became a mass tax and the mainstay of the revenue system. Focus on federal taxation, therefore, meant focus on the income tax.

By this time, tax theorists had come to view income as the best measure of ability to pay. A correct and workable definition of taxable income thus became the key to a fair distribution of the tax burden and hence the centre of Stanley's concern. His view of taxable income was rooted in the Schanz-Haig-Simons concept of accretion. Income was to be defined as total accretion to wealth or, stated differently, as the sum of consumption and increase in net worth. This broad-based concept of income came to be accepted by most tax economists in the postwar decades as the basis for tax equity, both horizontal and vertical. But Surrey, ever the pragmatist, stopped short of going the whole way. While ultimately relying on the accretion concept, he allowed for feasibility in administration and for considerations such as the 'generally accepted structure of the income tax' and 'widely accepted definitions of income.' [Surrey, 1984]. Thus, he tolerated the omission of certain components of income even if inclusion would be required by the Schanz-Haig-Simons scheme. Items like imputed

---

* *Harvard Law Review* (1984), 98, No. 2. Copyright © 1984 by The Harvard Law Review Association.

rent on owner-occupied residences, the value of the domestic services of stay-at-home spouses, unrealised capital gains, and the receipt of gifts and inheritances accordingly remained outside Surrey's list of offenders. But other omissions from the tax base could not be condoned in good conscience. These included the deduction of mortgage interest and charitable contributions, the exclusion of interest on state and local government securities, and the partial exemption of realised capital gains. Even medical deductions were to be disallowed. Such tax preferences, which Stanley was the first to label 'tax expenditures', were to be excised from the Code, and their removal was to be the central focus of tax reform. Where justified, the policy objectives underlying such deductions might then be implemented more openly, efficiently, and effectively through direct-expenditure programmes. To push this idea, Stanley championed a tax-expenditure budget, and legislation requiring the listing of such expenditures in the budget was passed in 1971.

But history also has its sense of humour, and it must be reported that although Stanley championed the removal of tax expenditures in 1970, ten years earlier he had been the godfather of the investment tax credit. At that time, he served as chairman of Senator John F. Kennedy's task force on tax reform, and the Senator wished to propose an investment incentive in the course of his campaign against Vice President Nixon. Rather than bow to pressures for accelerated depreciation, the task force proposed an investment credit. The credit would be more explicit and less distorting in its effects on investment; moreover, it would leave the way open for subsequent reform towards economic depreciation. There was even the utopian thought of applying the credit only to marginal investment, but this idea was soon ruled out by more practical minds. When the task force met with the President-elect to report its findings, Kennedy asked what the investment gain per dollar of revenue loss would be. So blunt and direct a question had hardly been expected, but I ventured that a ratio of 2 to 1 might not be far off. This resolved the immediate situation and subsequently did not prove too bad a guess.

Another of Stanley's characteristic departures from the purist's approach was his view of the corporation tax. According to the Simons model, which is accepted by most tax economists, the corporation is viewed as merely a funnel through which income passes to the shareholders, and not as a taxable entity in its own right. Retained earnings are thus to be imputed to the shareholder, and the corporate taxation of distributed income is to be considered the withholding of personal tax. Stanley never accepted this view, and maintained his support for an absolute corporation tax. He found it unacceptable, I presume, to view the corporation as a powerful decision-making unit on the one hand, yet as a mere conduit (for tax purposes) on the other.

The essence of Surrey's work, however, is not conveyed by featuring a few key issues. His great strength lay in his ceaseless ability to apply consummate craftsmanship to a never-ending stream of specifics and to give the smallest issues as much attention as the largest. Economists working with him learned to understand that tax measures must be formulated not only as general propositions, but also as provisions that allow for the vagaries of institutional structures and the technical problems that arise in the process of implementation. Thus, a legislative proposal emerging from the Treasury's Office of Tax Analysis (the domain of economists) might be vetoed as impractical by the Office of the Legislative Council (the lawyers' unit), or it might be returned for more realistic modification. There were endless sessions in the Treasury's large conference room, where, pressed by Stanley's interrogation, economists and lawyers interacted in thrashing out policy proposals. But the interdependence was mutual. Just as economists had much to learn from Stanley, so he came to rely heavily on their advice. Exactly what would be the effect of this or that measure? Was it justified by sound economics? What would be its cost to the Treasury? Who would bear the burden? Having posed the questions, he would not be satisfied with equivocal answers. When the Secretary needed a decision, Stanley expected the economist to know.

The same drive for solutions pervaded his teaching career. In our joint offering of the Seminar on Federal Taxation at Harvard Law School, I had the pleasure of witnessing his skill at the Socratic method. Questions would be posed and answers solicited, one after another, until finally the structure of the argument was laid bare and the correct solution was found. A brilliant exercise in teaching and learning it was indeed, and yet it was more than that: Stanley attacked the problems raised in Langdell Hall with the same sense of urgency that he brought to his work in his D.C. office at 15th and Pennsylvania.

I have told friends that, after working with Stanley for decades, I cannot recall our ever having talked at length about anything but taxation. Yet he was a good friend—warm and charming even when pursuing the most technical of issues. For a generation of tax theorists, he provided a bridge between the principles of analysis and the realities of tax reform. And though not all our hopes have yet materialised, the final payoff, as he would now assure us, will someday come.

# REFERENCES

Surrey, S. (1973), *Pathways to Tax Reform* (Cambridge, Mass., Harvard University Press).

# 23　A Brief History of Fiscal Doctrine*
## 1985

## INTRODUCTION

There are many ways in which a history of ideas may be written. One is a strict chronological accounting, moving from year to year and encompassing the entire subject. Another is to proceed on an author-by-author basis, focusing on what the main contributors had to say. Then there is the option to select major themes and to see how they evolved, thus taking a number of runs down (or up) the time-path of doctrinal development. I have chosen the latter option as most appropriate to accommodate the wide range of issues to be covered in a history of the fiscal theory. They are here arranged in five essays, dealing with the theory of public expenditures or of social goods, equity principles in taxation, efficiency conditions in taxation, tax shifting and incidence and finally the macro aspects of fiscal policy. Hopefully, this arrangement will set forth both the internal structure of fiscal doctrine and its historical development. But beyond this, there is no single or correct view of intellectual history. Such a history, in both selection and arrangement, is bound to reflect the perspective of the time in which it was written, as well as that of the author in whose prism past events are collected.

The history of fiscal doctrine, perhaps more than that of any other aspect of economics, carries a particular fascination. On the one hand, it reflects the advance of analytical economics, an enrichment of the tool-box, to use Joan Robinson's terms, which may then be applied to the solution of fiscal problems. As we shall see, the key fiscal tools were in fact forged by a line of great general theorists, not fiscal specialists. This line ranges from Smith over Ricardo, Mill, Depuit, Edgeworth, Wicksell, Pigou and Keynes to Samuelson. The close linkages between general and fiscal theory is most evident for the analysis of tax incidence, which at each stage reflects the prevailing theory of price and distribution. The analysis of tax equity was affected profoundly by the growth of utility theory. The rise of Paretian welfare economics permitted the modern analysis of social goods. The

* In *Handbook of Public Economics* (1985) Vol. I, ed. A.J. Auerbach and M. Feldstein (Elsevier Science Publishers B.V., North-Holland).

advent of Keynesian economics placed the role of budget policy in a new perspective, and so forth.

But there is more to a history of fiscal doctrine than the tools of economic analysis. The history also responds to changing economic and social institutions. With the decline of feudalism, the property income of the Crown had to be replaced by taxation; and as the rise of modern legal and financial institutions came to be reflected in the tax structure, the complexity of tax structure analysis increased vastly. The growth of popular democracy, in turn, altered what is viewed as the appropriate range of governmental functions, with budget policy replacing the barricades as the area of struggle among group and class interests.

Changing social philosophies and values, finally, also have their bearing on the development of fiscal doctrine. The displacement of Lockean rules of entitlement by the utilitarian model of Bentham greatly altered the premises of tax justice; and the rise of egalitarian philosophy proved a major factor in the growth and significance of transfer payments. Single-minded economists may find these cross-currents disturbing, but to this observer they add sparkle to what even without them would be an intriguing story.

For reasons of space, but also substance, our analysis begins with Adam Smith and *The Wealth of Nations*. This, to be sure, is not the beginning of fiscal doctrine. The Physiocrats had their theory of taxation and the Cameralists had written explicitly on the administration of public finances. However, Smith offers a convenient point of departure to trace the emergence of modern thought. The major issues are already present and neatly arranged, from the duties of the prince to provide public services to appropriate ways of raising the necessary revenue. What follows over the next two centuries are variations, if dramatic ones, on his essential theme. At the other end of the scale, we shall carry the story up to the 1960s. Given our space constraint, our treatment has to be selective, both as to issues and authors. It is hoped, however, that the reader will be encouraged to pursue matters further on his own account.[1]

## PUBLIC GOODS

The core of fiscal theory addresses the question of what public services should be provided by the public sector, and how much. Our first task, therefore, is to examine how this question has been addressed as fiscal theory developed. Not surprisingly, it is here and in matters of tax equity that approaches have differed most widely, in contrast to the theory of incidence which does, and the newer role of fiscal policy which should, offer a more uniform body of thought.

### The Duties of the Sovereign

The operation of the public sector, as developed by the classical economists, is seen in the context of a natural order which calls for reliance on and non-interference with the market. Public provision and taxation for its finance is called for only where exceptional circumstances demand it. A definition of these circumstances is attempted, but the tools for precise analysis were still lacking. An essential feature of the classical approach, still widely followed, is that the economics of expenditures and taxation are pursued as separate issues: while benefit taxation was viewed as the ideal, the bulk of tax revenue and hence tax analysis had to be examined in a context of ability to pay, with the required total set from the expenditure side.

## Adam Smith

Adam Smith, in concluding his critique of mercantilist policy, sets out the 'obvious and simple system of natural liberty that will establish itself of its own accord' once governmental restraints are withdrawn (Smith, 1776, vol. II, p. 184). The prince, therefore, is 'discharged from any duty of superintending the industry of private people'. But the system of natural liberty still needs the prince. It requires him to perform three duties, 'duties of great importance indeed, but plain and intelligible to common understandings'. These duties are, first, to protect society against invasion from abroad; second, to protect every member of society from the injustice of every other member; and third, to provide certain institutions and public works. Having staked out these three functions, Smith examines each in detail. Interesting and cogent observations are offered on how these functions have grown and how they should be conducted, but the core issue of why they must be undertaken by the prince (read public sector) remains unsolved.

The discussion begins with defence. As the art of defence becomes more complex, self-protection becomes impossible and even reliance on a militia inadequate. Efficient defence, based on the division of labour, calls for a professional and standing army. But Smith does not go beyond this to question why this army must be maintained by the prince rather than by private providers. Next, Smith shows how the administration of justice is needed to safeguard life, limb and property against internal offence. The more property there is, he argues, the more inequality there will be, and the more costly will the protection of property become. Yet, its provision is essential to the functioning of the market system.

Smith then examines how justice should be administered to assure impartiality, and how its finance may be secured without burdening general revenue. Once more he does not address why the administration of justice must be public rather than private. Perhaps no special explanation seemed needed to justify the public conduct of defence and justice. Though a proponent of the market, Smith was not an unbounded libertarian.[2] He did not believe that civil society could be based on market forces only. Natural liberty requires a framework of security and legal rules, and government is needed to provide it. Smith's view of the world may be read between the lines of the *Wealth of Nations*, but is developed in detail in his earlier work, *The Theory of Moral Sentiments* (1759). It is in this earlier work that Smith the moral philosopher presents an extremely complex and subtle structure of human interaction. Comprising a multiplicity of forces and motivations, individuals guided by the invisible hand are led to interact so as to produce a socially desirable outcome. In this interaction, benevolence as well as self-interest has an important role to play.

Turning to the expense for education, both university and elementary education are considered. The finance of university education is examined in its bearing on the quality of teaching, with scathing comments on how public financing and endowment lead to laziness and abuse once faculty is paid without relation to services rendered to their students (Smith, 1776, vol. II, p. 249). Major concern, however, is with elementary education. Here public support is needed because division of labour, as it progresses, leads to monotonous and simple tasks, a specialised dexterity which is 'acquired at the expense of the intellectual, social and martial virtues' of the labouring population (ibid., p. 267). For moral as well as economic and military reasons, government must take some pain to prevent this process, and this calls for public provision of elementary education. Implicit in the argument is that education involves externalities, but once more the criteria of publicness is not addressed in explicit form.

The need to do so arises only when Smith turns to the provision of public works. Here a criterion had to be established to determine just which public works government should undertake. Such a criterion is offered in a preamble to the section on public works:

The third and last duty of the commonwealth is that of erecting and maintaining those public institutions and those public works which, though they may be in the highest degree advantageous to a great society, are, however, of such a nature that the profit could never repay the expense to any individual or small number of individuals, and which it therefore cannot be expected that any individual or small number of individuals should erect or maintain (ibid., p. 539).

As is evident from this passage, Smith recognised that market failure occurs in the provision of certain goods, goods which it does not pay the individual to provide. But we are not told just why this is the case. Nor do we receive an explanation in the more detailed discussion that follows, much of which focuses on how finance can be arranged by fees, so as not to burden general revenue. We thus have to rely largely on the preamble. Much can be read into it, including the key concepts of joint consumption, externalities, and freerider behaviour which enter the modern view of social goods. But none of these is made explicit, so that it would be unduly generous to attribute them to Adam Smith. Nevertheless, his passage is not hostile and indeed amenable to these later developments. It contains the important premises that there exist certain functions which for *objective* (not ideological) reasons need be provided for by the public sector.

Unfortunately, however, Smith appears to have overlooked a strikingly insightful passage in Hume's *Treatise of Human Nature* (1739), a treatise which had appeared over 30 years prior to the *Wealth of Nations*. Hume describes how two neighbours might agree to drain a meadow but how a thousand persons cannot reach such agreement, as each will try to lay the whole burden on others. Political society overcomes this difficulty by reliance on magistrates whose interest it is to reflect the interests of [Hume (1739, p. 539)]:

any considerable part of their subjects. ... Thus bridges are built ... by the care of the government which tho' compos'd of men subject to all human infirmities, becomes, by one of the finest and most subtle inventions possible, a composition, which is, in some measure, exempted from all these infirmities (p. 539).

Here, as in other instances, an idea running ahead of its time finds no response until the situation is ripe, and then springs up at once in many places.

### David Ricardo

Leaving Adam Smith, it is disappointing to find that nothing is to be said in this context about Ricardo. Although his concern with the affairs of the government was paramount, he dealt with the effects of taxation on the private sector only. There is nothing to be found on public expenditures in his treatise, except his approving quotation of the 'golden maxim' of J.B. Say, 'that the very best of all plans of finance is to spend little, and the best of all taxes is that which is least in amount' (Ricardo, p. 159). The same view appears in his scathing rejection of Owen's proposal for workhouse reform (*Collected Works*, vol. VIII, p. 46).

### John Stuart Mill

John Stuart Mill, our next author, viewed society through a quite different window. Concerned as he was with the works of the early socialists such as Fourier, Owen and Sismondi, he addressed the proper scope of government in detail. Like Smith, he held that '*laissez-faire* should be the general practice: every departure from it, unless required by some great good, is a certain evil' (Mill, 1848, p. 952). But also like Smith, he found important instances where a departure is called for. These instances are divided into 'ordinary' and 'optional' functions. The ordinary functions include above all position for a legal system which secures life, limb and property, a security which is prerequisite for the system of *laissez-faire*. But beyond this, 'there is a multitude of cases in which governments, with general approbation, assume powers and execute functions for which no reason can be assigned except the simple one, that they conduce to general convenience.' As examples he cites not only coinage and the setting of standard weights, but also paving and lighting of streets, erection of harbours, lighthouses and dykes. The range of functions seems to be left wide open, limited only by the rule that 'interference of government should never be admitted but when the case of expediency is strong' (ibid., p. 800).

Though sceptical whether a specific principle of demarcation can be developed, he nevertheless tries to set forth the conditions under which the principle of *laissez-faire* and reliance on individual choice may be interfered with. Three such situations are noted: (1) Individuals may be unable to evaluate the utility of certain products. Thus children may be required to undergo elementary education. (2) Individuals lacking foresight may undertake irrevocable contracts and need to be restrained. (3) Regulations may be needed where individuals delegate decisions to managers, whose interests differ. Regulation of stock companies is thus called for, especially of monopolies in whose profits governments should share.

Coming closer to the economic content of publicness, he addresses 'matters in which the interference of law is required, not to overrule the judgment of individuals—but to give effect to that judgment: they being unable to give effect to it except by concert, which concert again cannot be effectual unless it receives validity and sanction from the law' (ibid., p. 963). Suppose, so he argues, that it is advantageous to reduce the working day from 10 to 9 hours. The individual worker cannot do so, nor can it be accomplished by agreement among them, as particular individuals will find it convenient to break the agreement. Hence legislation may be required. As a further illustration, he points to colonisation. Individual colonies will wish to appropriate as much land as possible, while it would be to the advantage of the colonists to require newcomers initially to work as hired hands (the Wakefield system) so as to permit more intensive cultivation of specific parcels. Mill thus recognises, implicitly at least, the existence of a prisoner's dilemma and freerider problem, conditions which require public intervention.

He also notes cases in which 'acts done by individuals, though intended solely for their own benefit, involve consequences extending indefinitely beyond them, to interests of the nation or posterity' (ibid., p. 970). A case in point is again colonisation, which requires regulation in line with the permanent welfare of the nation. The same principle, so he continues, 'extends to a variety of cases wherein which important public services are to be performed, while yet there is no individual especially interested in performing them, nor would any adequate remuneration naturally or spontaneously attend their performance.' A voyage of exploration might produce benefits of great public value, yet 'there is no mode of intercepting the benefit on its way to those who profit by it, in order to levy a toll for the remuneration of its authors.' Thus, 'no one would build lighthouses from motives of personal interest, unless indemnified and rewarded from a compulsory levy by the state' (ibid., p. 975). Mill's explanation why certain goods require public provision thus moves beyond Adam Smith's generalisation, but still falls short of precise formulation. Emphasis is on the difficulty of collecting tolls, an argument also advanced subsequently by H. Sidgwick. Indeed, it was not until a hundred years later that the lighthouse problem (Coase, 1974) was placed in its proper perspective, i.e. that fee finance of social goods would be inefficient even if fees could be collected. Nevertheless, both Smith and Mill were aware that the nature of certain goods requires public provision, even though they assigned primacy to the market and flayed the inefficiency of governmental action.

## The public economy as *Staatswirtschaft*

The traditions of British authors, from Adam Smith on, viewed the market as the rule and the public sector as the exception, needed to step in if and where a specific market failure occurs. The tradition of continental and in particular of German authors was to view the economic system in dual terms, with the public sector (*Staatswirtschaft*) equal in birthright to the private sector (*Privatwirtschaft*). This difference in emphasis had various roots. British fiscal theory emerged from the background of the Lockean model, a society based on individual entitlements and free exchange, guided by the beneficent rule of an invisible hand. The continental approach emerged from the Cameralist teaching which had developed rules for the conduct of public affairs in the enlightened state. Kant's view of the state as limited to its productive function had been superseded by the Hegelian vision of the state as 'immaterial capital'; and the Historical School's approach to economics, dominant in the closing decades of the nineteenth century, invited a view of growing state activity as a natural outcome of the historical process. Moreover, a sympathetic view of the public sector was supported in Germany by the rising concern of academic economists (the so-called pulpit socialists) with matters of social welfare.

Among major contributors to this view of public finances we may note Dietzel, Schäffle and Wagner. Dietzel (1855) addressed the role of the state as a producer of public goods, the critical feature of indivisibility (already vaguely noted by Mill) requires the same quantity to be available to all consumers. Since the marginal utility of the same quantity differs among them, the equating process calls for differential prices to be charged. Thus benefit taxation—greatly broadened from its Hobbesian origin as payment for protection—becomes the 'supreme law of the fiscal economy' [Musgrave and Peacock, 1958, p. 81].

With public expenditures linked to consumer evaluation, the basis for the modern theory of public goods was laid. But, not surprisingly, this early formulation had its shortcomings. By framing the efficiency rule in terms of benefit taxation, attention was diverted from specifying just how indivisibility affects efficiency conditions, conditions which may be met with or without benefit finance. It would be over half a century for these conditions to be worked out. Moreover, by focusing on the benefit rule as an analogue to market pricing, attention was diverted from the political, not market, process needed to reach an efficient solution. Not that the Italians were unaware of this problem. Mazzola noted that budgetary decisions are made by agencies, but held that agencies must act so as to satisfy voters, lest political equilibrium be disturbed (ibid., p. 44). De Marco, viewing the income tax as a subscription price, thought it to secure a fair solution. While the analogy to a market solution was central, the concept of a competitive political process was also present.

### Knut Wicksell

This was the aspect of the problem which drew Wicksell's attention and solicited his seminal contribution to the theory of public finance (Wicksell,

1896; see also Musgrave and Peacock, pp. 72–118). Wicksell accepted the new doctrine that provision of public goods should be designed to maximise individual satisfaction, and that the benefit rule would accomplish this. But then two concerns arise.

A first reservation relates to the equity implications of benefit taxation. Justice may be said to be served if consumers pay in line with their marginal evaluation but, so he adds, 'it is clear that justice in taxation presupposes justices in the existing distribution of property and income' (p. 143; Musgrave and Peacock, p. 108). Wicksell thus views distributive justice as primary, but then separates it from justice in taxation as payment for the cost of public services, a separation to which we will return later on.

Notwithstanding this qualified endorsement of the benefit rule, Wicksell did not consider it a realistic option. Indeed, he rejected as 'really meaningless' (ibid., p. 81) Mazzola's new model. Analogy to the market, so he argued, was inapplicable since individuals would not reveal their preferences without injection of a political process. With large numbers the offer of capital, both fixed and 'immaterial', with public credit an important instrument of economic growth, Schäffle (1867) advanced his rule of 'proportionate satisfaction' of public and private wants, anticipating Pigou's formulation of the mid-1920s. Wagner (1883), the leading figure of his time, formulated his law of expanding state activity, based on technical factors such as increased density and urbanisation, as well as a growing acceptance of social policy objectives in fiscal affairs. This line of thinking, moreover, exerted considerable influence on American scholars, who at that time tended to do graduate work in continental and particularly German universities. This influence is apparent as one compares the basic American texts of Adams (1899) with its British counterpart of Bastable (1892).

## Subjective Value and Public Provision

But though the Cameralist tradition of German authors had provided a more open-minded view of the public sector, it did not furnish an economic theory of public goods. Such a theory emerged only after the basis had been laid in the 1880s, when the analysis of subjective utility had grounded value theory on the demand side. This new approach, as developed by Menger and Jevons, was soon to find its application to the budget. Thereby the analysis of public provision was placed in an entirely new perspective. Focus was no longer on the duty of the sovereign, but on the demands of the individual consumer. The public sector appeared no longer as an awkward, albeit necessary, exception to the laws of economics. The same principles of efficient resource use were now to be applied to both the public and the private sphere. Integrated into the general theory of value, public sector economics was legitimised.

### Marginal utility
The breakthrough emerged in the 1880s from the contributions of Austrian and Italian writers, among whom Sax (1883), Panteleoni (1883), Mazzola

(1890) and de Viti de Marco (1888) may be noted.[3] While nuances differed, the essence of the new doctrine was this: Given the preferences of individuals, welfare is maximised by having each equate marginal utility with price. This basic efficiency rule applies to both public and private goods. To be sure, there is a difference: In the private good case, goods are sold at a uniform price, with individual consumers equating price and marginal utility by quantity adjustment. In the case made by any one individual has no significant effect on total supply so that consumers 'will pay nothing whatsoever' [Musgrave and Peacock, 1958, p. 81]. Wicksell, as did Hume 150 years earlier, thus clearly recognised what later came to be known as the freerider principle. Impatient with the assumptions of altruistic and omnipotent behaviour [Wicksell, 1896, p. 90], the real problem as he saw it was to design a practicable process which will approximate an optimal outcome. Ideally, consumers would be asked to vote on bundles of options combining a complete set of budgets and tax shares, with provision based on that bundle which carries unanimous support [Musgrave and Peacock, 1958, p. 92]. Since this ideal situation is impracticable, Wicksell settles for a rule of approximate unanimity, but stresses the need to protect minority rights. He thus laid the basis for a normative approach to voting models, a problem which has again become a subject of lively discussion in recent years.

## The Lindahl Price

The story continues with the appearance of Eric Lindahl's doctoral dissertation (1918) written under the auspices of Wicksell.[4] Lindahl visualises two consumers who must share in the cost of a public good. The more A pays, the less B will have to pay. Given the cost schedule for the product, A's offer curve may thus from B's point of view be translated into a supply curve, and vice versa. The two curves are plotted and their intersection determines the quantity to be supplied. At this solution each pays a tax price (the famous Lindahl price) equal to the value of the marginal utility which he derives, with the sum of the two tax prices adding up to the cost of the product (Musgrave and Peacock, 1958, p. 89).

One wonders how pleased Wicksell was with this formulation of his student. Certainly, the Lindahl price (i.e. benefit taxation) was efficient, but the market analogy inherent in the Lindahl diagram was precisely what Wicksell had objected to most in Mazzola's presentation. While a bargaining solution might be reached in the small number case, it hardly need be the efficient one. More important, the analogy does not extend to the large number case, where preferences are not revealed, reducing the Lindahl schedules to 'pseudo demand curves', as referred to later on by Samuelson (1954). Lindahl, of course, was aware of these limitations. He notes that the intersection solution is reached only on the assumption of 'equal bargaining power' and, in his later writings expanded upon the political setting in which the budget determination occurs (Lindahl, 1928; Musgrave and Peacock, 1958, pp. 214–32). Nevertheless, the concept of the Lindahl price and its initial demand–supply presentation, has remained his key contribution.

## Pigouvian Externalities

The Austrian and Italian models of fiscal analysis and the Wicksellian interpretation in voting behaviour did not enter the purview of English-language authors for over half a century. Continuing the classical tradition, an *ad hoc* approach to the delineation of expenditure functions prevailed from Mill to the 1920s. Marshall had little to say on the subject, nor did Jevons apply his marginal analysis to the public sector. Bastable's *Public Finance* (1892), the major English-language treatise, offered little advance over Mill, even in its later edition of 1903. Various categories of public expenditures are discussed but little attention is paid to the nature of publicness and how they are able to be determined.

Thus it was not until Pigou's *Economics of Welfare* (1920) that a new perspective was introduced. This perspective emerged from the concept of externalities, central to the Pigouvian distinction between social and private net product (Pigou, 1920, ch. 9). The private net product measures the internalised costs and benefits which are recorded in market price. The social net product will be larger when further benefits accrue to persons other than those engaged in the sales transaction; and it will be smaller if costs are imposed on third parties, costs which need not be compensated for and hence are not reflected in price. Where social benefits are in excess of private, a bounty need be paid to allow for the addition (external) benefits which are not reflected in market demand. Where social costs exceed private cost, a tax is in order. Thus fiscal instruments become a mechanism of adjusting for externalities, be they of the benefit or cost type.

Where a bounty is appropriate, its magnitude will depend on the spread between private and social product. Thus Pigou notes that a moderate bounty to farming may be suitable if farming yields the 'indirect service of developing citizens suitable for military training … . A more extreme form of bounty, in which a governmental authority provides *all* the funds required, is given upon such services as the planning of towns, police administration, and sometimes, the clearing of slum areas.' Having advanced this close to providing a criterion for public provision, it is frustrating to find that Pigou does not proceed to do so. Yet the logic of this argument suggests that public provision (i.e. a full bounty based on tax finance) is needed where the private net product is zero and the social net product absorbs the entire value.

Nor did Pigou offer an explicit linkage between externalities and social goods in his subsequent *Study in Public Finances* (1928). This volume, as we shall see presently, made major contributions on the theory of taxation, but gave only brief attention to the expenditure side of the budget. A distinction is drawn between transfers and exhaustive expenditures leading to a principle of expenditure allocation, similar to Schäffle's (1880) much earlier rule of proportional satisfaction. Within a given budget size, the programme mix is to be adjusted so as to balance the marginal benefits derived from various projects; and in determining the size of the budget, the marginal benefits from public outlays are to be equated with those from private outlays. Such would be the simple formula if the community was a unitary being (ibid., p. 52). Since it is not, and since the desire of any one taxpayer to contribute depends on the contribution of others, government, as the agent of its citizens collectively, must exercise coercion upon them individually. This coercion creates indirect costs which must be allowed for. But though the need for coercion is noted, there is no consideration of the mechanism by which it will inform government how individuals value social goods. Pigou, evidently, was still unaware of what had been contributed by the Austrians and Swedes three decades earlier. His contribution, however, was to place the extreme case of 'full bounty' into the broader spectrum of externalities, which may differ in degrees and kind, i.e. may range from 'mixed' social goods to the polar case of full external benefit.

## Pareto-effficiency with public goods

It was not until 1938 that the continental discussion of the 1880s and 1890s was brought to the attention of the English- (and only English) reading part of the profession (Musgrave, 1938). Howard Bowen's (1948) vertical addition of demand curves for social goods reinvented Lindahl's earlier formulation, and the breakthrough came with Samuelson's (1954, 1955) two three-page papers on the subject. Carrying a benefit–page ratio without rival, at least in the literature of fiscal theory, these papers met the long-delayed need for a rigorous integration of social goods into the conditions of Pareto efficiency. Thirty years later, his solution may seem evident to the well-trained senior, but at the time it offered a giant step forward.

### The Samuelson model

Addressing the implications of indivisibility and joint consumption for Pareto efficiency, Samuelson assumed that there exists an omniscient referee to whom individual preferences are known. Based on this information, given resources and technology, the referee then determines a set of optimal solutions, each involving a mix of output between private and social goods and a division of the former among consumers. Each solution reflects different positions of welfare for particular consumers with the optimal solution or 'bliss point', chosen by application of a social welfare function. The set of efficient solutions meets the condition of equality between the sum of differing marginal rates of substitution in consumption and the rate of transformation in production. It differs from the case of private goods where the marginal rate of substitution is the same for all consumers and equal to the rate of transformation. Social goods are thus amenable to the same (if somewhat altered) principles of efficiency as private goods, to be dealt with as a sub-case of the Paretian rule.

How did this formulation relate to the Wicksellian system and its use of benefit taxation as an efficiency rule? The two approaches are similar in that both yield efficient solutions. The Lindahl price, approximated by the Wicksellian voting system, is also among the solutions which meet Samuelson's efficiency conditions. But the approaches differ in dealing with distribution.

For Wicksell, a distribution of money income and charging of tax prices is essential. Preferences must be determined by voting, in line with a pattern of effective demand based on a given distribution of money income. In Samuelson's (1969) model, money income and taxes may be inserted, but they are not needed and only clutter up the problem. Given an omniscient referee whose preferences are known, the referee may proceed directly to the solution. Having determined the set of efficient solutions, he then resolves the distribution problem by applying a social welfare function. Optimal distribution is determined in terms of welfare positions. The Wicksellian model begins as just noted with a distribution of money income; and this distribution must be just to begin with if the voting process is to arrive at tax prices which are 'just' as well as efficient. But how can a just distribution of money income be taken as predetermined when the distribution of welfare (which is what matters) depends on relative prices (including those of public goods) as well as on money incomes? The appearance of circular reasoning is resolved, however, once the voting rule is allowed for in determining the distribution of money income, and determination of the voting rule is added as a further equation in the system (Musgrave, 1969; 1984, p. 67). Multiple policy objectives may then be resolved in an interdependent fashion, including a benefit tax-based allocation branch which provides for social goods, and a tax-transfer-based distribution branch which secures the desired distribution of money income (Musgrave, 1959, ch. 1).

*Extensions and additions*

The modern discussion of budget determination thus involves two traditions, both valid and compatible with each other but addressing different aspects of the problem. The analytical neatness and abstract formulation of Samuelson's model meets the pure spirit of Paretian welfare economics and as such has invited the attention of economic theorists. The greater realism of the Wicksellian approach has offered a more workable stepping-stone to the problems of budget policy. Subsequent work has drawn on both traditions. Among the most important extensions, the following are noted briefly, leaving further discussion to subsequent chapters of this volume where the current state of the art is examined:

(1) Extension of the Samuelson model has focussed on examination of non-polar cases, such as benefit spillover and congestion (Oakland, 1971, 1972), as well as on the conditions under which private supply of public goods is feasible (Demsetz, 1970).

(2) The Pigouvian analysis of external effects, and in particular external costs, has become a central aspect of growing concern with pollution and environmental economics (Baumol and Oates, 1975).

(3) Much attention has been given to the analysis of local public goods and the implications of spatial benefit limitation (Tiebout, 1956). Based on Tiebout's hypothesis of voting by feet, the feasibility of Tiebout equilibria has been examined and tested in empirical work (Oates, 1972). A theory of fiscal federalism based on a theory of clubs (Buchanan, 1965) was developed.

(4) Empirical research has been directed at estimating expenditure functions for government, based on the hypothesis that the political process approximates the preferences of consumers as expressed by their voting behaviour. Utilising median voter models (Downs, 1966) and cross-section data for state and local government, such research has become a rich area of fiscal analysis (Inman, 1978).

(5) Wicksell's primary concern with the political mechanisms by which fiscal decisions are reached was extended in the context of voting theory (Black, 1948), and a model of democracy viewed in analogy to a political market (Downs, 1955). Early optimism was soon dampened by Arrow's demonstration that an unambiguous social welfare function cannot readily be determined (Arrow, 1951), and fiscal issues played a central role in the rapid development of public choice theory (Mueller, 1979).

(6) As distinct from normative considerations, a new direction of fiscal analysis emerged as a positive theory of government behaviour (Buchanan and Tullock, 1962). Critical of public sector growth, the new model centred on the propositions (a) that the voting process is biased towards over-expansion, and (b) that this bias is accentuated by the desire of bureaucrats and politicians to maximise their budgets (Buchanan, 1975; Niskanen, 1971; Borcherding, 1977). The role of government is seen not as a servant of majority preferences but as a self-interested actor in its own right. Attention shifted to a theory of 'government failure' and resulting need for governmental restraint, countering in Hegelian fashion the earlier concern (underlying Pigouvian externalities and public goods theory) with market failure and the need for remedy by governmental action. This analysis, though very different in content, might be viewed as a resumption of interest in fiscal sociology which, 50 years earlier, had been pursued in the context of Marxist thought (Goldscheid, 1917; see also Musgrave and Peacock, 1958).

## Cost-benefit analysis

It remains to note a further and more operational approach to the economics of public expenditures. Moving to the forefront of fiscal work in the 1960s cost-benefit analysis was designed to provide a practical basis for evaluating 'public works and development projects of a sort for which measures of value can be established empirically' (Eckstein, 1961, p. 440). This episode thus matched the partial approach of tax theorists who, as we shall see presently, dealt with the tax side of the budget only, while disregarding the expenditure side (Musgrave, 1969, p. 103).

While cost-benefit analysis became the vogue in the 1960s, its begin-nings, in important part, date back over a century to the work of Jules

Dupuit. Drawn to the problem as an engineer in the Corps des Ponts et Chaussées, he was the first to pursue cost-benefit analysis on a rigorous basis and indeed anticipated the essence of much that was to come later (Dupuit, 1844; Vickrey, 1968). In particular, he developed the concept that benefits are measured by the area under the demand curve, not by what is actually paid. The next major contribution appeared nearly 100 years later when Hotelling (1938, p. 158) formulated the case for marginal cost pricing: 'The efficient way to operate a bridge,' so he argued, 'is to make it free to the public, so long at least as the use of it does not increase to a state of overcrowding'. (1938, p. 158). The common assumption 'that every tub must stand on its own bottom' is rejected, and the rationale for subsidies to increasing cost industries is given. Beginning in the late 1930s, the US government adopted standards for cost-benefit analysis of water projects, and studies of cost effectiveness blossomed in the Department of Defence during World War II.

Beginning with the late 1950s, an extensive literature on cost-benefit analysis emerged and became the vogue of the 1960s (Layard, 1972). Theoretical interest centred on problems such as the choice of an appropriate discount rate, measuring the opportunity cost of capital withdrawal from the private sector and the introduction of shadow prices (Marglin, 1963; Harberger, 1969; Feldstein, 1973). By the end of the 1960s or early 1970s, the major analytical issues had been resolved and cost-benefit analysis had become an important tool of applied fiscal analysis.

## EQUITY IN TAXATION

In the preceding section, our focus has been on the development of expenditure theory, a development which in large part proceeded independent of the taxation side of the fiscal process. The classics first examined the obligations of the prince and then turned to tax analysis. With benefit taxation applicable to only a small part of the revenue total, criteria of 'good taxation' for most of the revenue had to be developed independent of expenditures. Pigou once more dealt with the expenditure side in terms of externalities, then took up taxation theory as a separate issue. Samuelson's model, to be sure, covered both the uses and sources side of the fiscal picture, but at a level of abstraction which did not involve tax institutions. Thus only the Austrian approach and its Wicksellian extension opted for a simultaneous solution to both sides of the budget equation. Taxation theory similarly developed largely in isolation from the expenditure side. Such was the case with the classics, with the Schanz–Simon approach to income taxation and now replays in the context of optimal taxation theory.

Criteria for 'good taxation' found an early statement in Smith's (1776, vol. II, p. 310) famous 'maxims'. Among them Smith includes equality, certainty, convenience of payment and economy in collection as most important. Equality or equity in turn was interpreted along two lines, i.e.

that contributions should match benefits received, and should also reflect ability to pay. In both camps, there emerged a long debate over whether burden distribution should be proportional or progressive, with the ability doctrine more open to egalitarian interpretation. Moreover, it was necessary to specify an index by which benefit and ability to pay is to be measured.

## The benefit doctrine

The benefit approach to tax equity was congenial to the political philosophers of the Enlightenment, such as Hobbes, Grotius and Locke. With legitimacy vested in the hand of the governed, the contractarian model would call upon them to pay the state for protection received. Under the Lockean concept of entitlement, each person had property in the fruits of his labour (Locke, 1690, p. 327), an entitlement compatible with taxation as payment for services rendered but not with state-taking on other than a *quid pro quo* basis. Smith's (1759) grand design for the human condition, as painted in his earlier work, fitted squarely in this pattern.

The first of his famous maxims of taxation states the rule of tax equity as follows:

The subject of every state ought to contribute towards the support of the government, as nearly as possible, in proportion to their respective abilities; that is, in proportion to the revenue which they respectively enjoy under the protection of the state. The expense of government to the individuals of a great nation, is like the expense of management to the joint tenants of a great estate, who are all obliged to contribute in proportion to their respective interests in the estate. In the observation or neglect of this maxim consists, what is called the equality of inequality of taxation (Smith, 1776, vol. II, p. 310).

While the maxim begins with ability to pay, its thrust is in the direction of a benefit rule. As stated in the last lines, equality in taxation calls for payment in proportion to one's interest in the public estate. Placing Smith in the benefit camp, while somewhat controversial, also matches his repeated call for fee finance in the expenditure chapters, including a timely admonition that professors be paid in line with student attendance (ibid., p. 249).

While contribution is to be in proportion to revenue received, Smith then qualifies this in various ways. Most important, he excludes wage income needed for subsistence. A tax on subsistence wages (as we shall see below) would have to be absorbed by higher-income consumers or by landlords. Its imposition would be 'absurd and destructive' (p. 350). He thus shares the view, frequently held by early advocates of proportional taxation, that a subsistence minimum (then necessarily in the form of wages) should be exempt. A further exemption arises in connection with a tax on house rents. Smith supports such a tax, even though it would in general fall upon the rich, adding 'that in this sort of inequality there would perhaps not be anything very unreasonable. It is not very unreasonable

that the rich should contribute in proportion to their revenue but something more than in that proportion' (p. 337). Smith once more is too wise a
man to permit neat classification as an all-out advocate of proportional
taxation.

Benefit theorists, however, were far from unanimous in support of any
particular pattern of rates. Most of the early contractarians, such as
Hobbes and Grotius, supported the proportional view, as did Bentham,
subject to the exemption of subsistence wages. Sismondi, Rousseau and
Condorcet, among others, favoured progression. Robespierre rejected
progression as insulting to the poor, while John Stuart Mill (though
rejecting the benefit rule) thought it called for regression; the poor, so he
noted, are most in need of protection and thus would have to pay most
(Mill, 1848, p. 805). The question, who benefits most, it appears, was not
easily resolved. (See Seligman (1908, part II, ch. 2)).

In past no less than current controversy, disagreement frequently reflects
a difference in the question that is asked; but unhappily, the question is not
readily defined until the problem is resolved. The issue, in the interpretation of the benefit rule, is whether focus is on the cost of the service
rendered to a particular person, or whether it is on what a person (given his
or her income and preferences) would be willing to pay. In the latter case,
the benefit tax as we have seen becomes a Lindahl price; and the issue of
progressive taxation then hinges on the income and price elasticities of
demand—factors which depend on the particular services in question and
cannot be generalised upon for the budget as a whole (Buchanan, 1964).
Others have questioned whether Lindahl pricing meets the spirit of the
benefit rule. Thus Myrdal has suggested that benefit taxation should be in
line with total (not just marginal) benefit received. Interpreted in this
fashion, benefit taxation would still be 'efficient' but would yield surplus
revenue which would then have to be disposed of in other ways (Myrdal,
1953).

## The Ability to Pay Doctrine

The ability to pay doctrine also claims a long history. As with the benefit
doctrine, views on the resulting burden distribution varied. Montesqieu
and Say found in favour of progression, while early observers such as
Bodin deduced a proportional rate (Seligman, 1908, part I, ch. 3).

The modern doctrine may be said to begin with John Stuart Mill's
formulation. Writing in the 1840s, Mill responded to a wholly different
philosophical and political setting than had Adam Smith. Representative
government had progressed and the accepted functions of the state had
broadened. Bentham's utilitarian framework had replaced natural law and
the Lockean view of entitlement had given way to a new concept of
distributive justice.[5] The case had been made as early as 1802, that welfare
from a given income total would be maximised by equal distribution
(Bentham, 1830); and the concept of justice, to quote Mill (1848, p. 805),
came to 'consist not in limiting but in redressing the inequalities and

wrongs of nature'. Moreover, 'government must be regarded as so pre-eminently the concern for all, that to determine who is most interested in it is of no real importance.' The just pattern of taxation, therefore, is not to be derived from the expenditure side of the budget, but is to be based on a general rule of social justice.

Mill defines equal treatment as follows:

For what reason ought equality to be the rule in matters of taxation? For the reason that it ought to be so in all affairs of government. As a government ought to make no distinction of persons or classes in the strength of their claim on it, whatever sacrifices or claims it requires from them should be made to bear as nearly as possible with the same pressure upon all, which it must be observed, is the mode by which least sacrifice is occasioned on the whole ... means equality of sacrifice (ibid., p. 804).

Mill, then, interpreted equal sacrifice to call for a proportional tax on income above subsistence, in line with Pitt's income tax and its 3 per cent rate. Following Bentham, he feared the disincentives of progressive income tax rates but (unlike Bentham) he favoured sharp progression in inheritance taxation. While mistaken in equating 'equal' with 'least total' sacrifice, his concern with the latter anticipated the subsequent shift from equity to efficiency aspects of sacrifice doctrine. His main contribution was to have posed the problem of equity in terms of equal sacrifice, thus setting the framework for half a century of subsequent discussion.

Nearly 50 years later, the argument was resumed by F. Y. Edgeworth. Edgeworth (1897, p. 101) begins with 'the purest, as being the most deductive form of utilitarianism, from which Bentham reasoned down to equality'. He then deduces equal marginal or least total sacrifice as the optimal solution, not as a principle of distributive justice but on a game theoretical basis. Edgeworth considers two self-interested parties, contracting in the absence of competition:

In this setting, neither party in the long run can expect to obtain the larger share of the total welfare ... . Of all principles of distribution which would afford him now a greater now a smaller proportion of the sum-total utility obtainable on each occasion, the principle that the collective utility should be on each occasion a maximum is most likely to afford the greatest utility in the long run to him individually ... . The solution to this problem in the abstract is that the richer should be taxed for the benefit of the poorer up to the point at which a complete equality of fortunes is attained (p. 103).

He does not explain why the individual player should agree to this solution, but intuition might have suggested an argument in line with Hasyani's (1953) maximisation of expected utility under the veil of ignorance.

Edgeworth thus not only applied the equal marginal sacrifice rule to distributing the cost of public services but he extended it into a system of transfers resulting in an equal distribution of income. But having thus sighted the 'acme of socialism', he finds it 'immediately clouded over by doubts and reservations' (p. 104). The detrimental effects of the extreme solution are noted, including reduction in output and, here quoting Mill, threats to personal liberty. Thus 'minimum sacrifice, the direct emanation of pure utilitarianism, is the sovereign principle of taxation; [but] it requires no doubt to be limited in practice' (p. 106).

In addition to minimum sacrifice, two other species of the 'hedonistic theory of taxation' enter. These are the rules of equal absolute and equal proportional sacrifice, as first explored by the Dutch economist Cohen Stuart (1889) (Musgrave and Peacock, 1958). Given Bernoulli's assumption of a unit-elastic marginal utility of income curve, the two rules call for proportional and progressive taxation, respectively. More or less elastic schedules respectively call for progressive and regressive rates for equal absolute sacrifice, with proportional sacrifice not amenable to a simple solution of this sort. Suspecting the decline of utility to be more rapid than Bernoulli suggests, Edgeworth concluded that both rules require progression, but once more we are warned that 'other utilities' must be allowed for as well, and that this prohibits rigid application of either sacrifice rule.

Writing as a contemporary of Edgeworth, a generally similar position was taken by Henry Sidgwick. Benefit charges should be applied where possible, but the principle of payment in line with services received is of limited applicability. Where it cannot be applied, the 'obviously equitable principle—assuming that the existing distribution of wealth is accepted as just or not unjust—is that equal sacrifice should be imposed on all' (Sidgwick, 1883, p. 562). He takes this to call for exemption of a minimum income, but hesitates to favour progressive rates as these may become excessive and unduly depress capital formulation. But given that concern with capital formation is the reason for limiting progression, a case is made for the exemption of saving and the taxation of luxury goods.

Along with this debate among British economists, the case for progressive taxation was argued by Adolf Wagner, the German fiscal economist noted earlier for his 'law of expanding state activity'. Also writing toward the close of the nineteenth century, Wagner distinguished between (1) a purely financial, and (2) a social welfare principle (*sozialpolitisches Prinzip*) of taxation. The former calls for proportional taxation in the finance of public services, while leaving the distribution of income unchanged. It is then supplemented by the latter, which calls for progression to reduce income inequality. With the development of modern society, Wagner expected this development to expand and viewed it with less concern than did his English contemporaries (Wagner, 1883).

The discussion of ability to pay then lapsed, but was resumed in Pigou's *Studies in Public Finance* (1928). Pigou accepted least sacrifice as an absolute principle of taxation, viewing it as counterpart to the general rule that public policy should be directed at maximising welfare. He explored tax formulae applicable to various equity rules and arrived at conclusions similar to those of Edgeworth. Like Edgeworth, he found no convincing basis on which to choose between equal absolute and equal proportional sacrifice, with preference again given to the equal marginal sacrifice rule.

Conclusions regarding progressivity, from Edgeworth to Pigou, had been based on the assumptions (1) that utility is comparable across individuals and measurable in cardinal terms; (2) that there exists a known marginal income utility schedule; (3) that this schedule shows marginal utility to decline with income; and (4) is identical for all people. Doubts regarding (3) and (4) had been raised by Edgeworth and Pigou, but the fundamental break with (1) did not come until the 1930s. At that time, the feasibility of interpersonal utility comparison was rejected (Robbins, 1932; 1938), and modern welfare economics was restated in terms of Pareto-optimality. A welfare gain could be recorded only if there was an improvement in A's position without worsening that of B or, less demanding, if A's gain was sufficient to permit potential compensation of B. Having thus advanced (or retreated) to the impeccable shores of Pareto-efficiency, the rug was pulled out from under the older sacrifice doctrine. The distribution of the tax burden, henceforth, would be a matter of social ethics or politics, but no longer of economics.

But the issue of distribution proved too basic to be excluded from economics for ever, and the distribution of the tax burden proved too central a part of public finance to be permanently expunged from its books. Distributional considerations soon re-entered via a social welfare function (Bergson, 1983). Assuming its shape to be given, the social welfare function was applied in the context of social goods theory, so as to determine the 'bliss point' on the utility frontier (Samuelson, 1954). It soon reappeared in the use of distributional weights in cost-benefit analysis (Weisbrod, 1968) and more recently in optimal income tax rates. By postulating a welfare function which reflects social value judgement (arrived at by a political process as based on the social preference of individual voters), the disputed premise of cardinal measurement and comparability is avoided. But the heart of the matter, we venture to suggest, was not changed as much as is commonly thought.

In concluding this review of equity doctrines, we note that while the ability to pay view of tax equity does not allow for benefit considerations, ability to pay considerations may enter into the benefit doctrine. They will not do so as long as benefit differentials are viewed in terms of differences in service levels provided to the rich and the poor. Thus, as Adam Smith saw it, the rich should pay more because they have more carriages to protect than the poor. But ability to pay enters once it is seen that the rich will value the benefit per carriage more highly than do the poor, as reflected in differential Lindahl prices. The later interpretation, and with it a linkage between benefit and ability to pay doctrines, also enters in the Wicksellian context where tax prices are needed for purposes of preference revelation.

## The Index of Equality

So far we have traced the debate over how taxpayers with differing levels of capacity should be taxed. This leaves open the question of how this capacity should be measured. The answer has to be viewed in historical terms, as it depends on the prevailing economic institutions and objects of taxation which may be taken as representative of ability to pay. The answer also depends on the availability of 'tax handles', i.e. objects of taxation which can be reached by fiscal administration. From the Middle Ages to the Elizabethan Poor Laws, 'faculty' had been interpreted as property and this was still the case in early colonial taxation. Specific forms of property, such as cattle, windows or carriages, in turn served as indices for property at large. There then occurred a gradual shift to a broader view of property; and beyond it, faculty came to be interpreted as income, viewing the tax base in terms of flows rather than stocks. The development of tax bases may thus be seen to reflect the institutional changes which accompanied the rise of modern industrial and financial society. Schumpeter (1918), in particular, viewed the rise of the income tax as a corollary to the growth of capitalism and a pecuniary economy. The increasing complexity of economic institutions in turn was reflected in the emerging technical discussion over how the specifics of income taxation should be defined.

### The income base

Income, as measure of taxable capacity, dates back to Adam Smith and before. But the concept of the comprehensive income base emerged only slowly. Certain sources of income, it appeared, could not be taxed, even if an attempt were made to do so. Thus the Physiocrats viewed the rent of land as the only feasible tax base, simply because land was considered the only genuine source of income (Quesnay, 1760). The classics, from Smith to Mill, took a broader view of the income base, but still thought it useless to tax subsistence wages or necessities, as such taxes would have to be passed on to rent or profits. Thus only rent, profits and income flowing into luxury consumption remained as eligible sources of taxation. With taxation of profits involving undue meddling, causing capital flight (Smith, 1776, vol. II, p. 333), and detrimental to growth (Ricardo, 1817, p. 94), the viable tax sources were reduced to rent and income used for luxury consumption.

The modern idea of a comprehensive and global income tax as the best index of equality and taxable capacity only emerged towards the close of the nineteenth century. Intensive discussion of the income concept, especially by German authors, then led to the concept of accretion, first proposed by Georg Schanz (1896) and subsequently introduced into the American literature by Haig (1921). With a person's income defined as the money value of net accretion to his/her economic power, the measurement of taxable income was made tax-specific and distinguished from the concept of income shares in the context of national income accounting. Pioneered by Neumark (1947) in Germany and Simons (1938; 1950) in the United States, the development of a broad-based income tax came to occupy much of the tax literature over the following decades. With accretion as the guiding concept, specific issues of tax base measurement could be dealt with in coherent form, covering such items as the treatment of capital gains independent of realisation, the integration of corporate source income into the income tax base, the economic measurement of depreciation, and so forth (Seligman, 1914; Vickrey, 1947, Pechman, 1959; Musgrave, 1967; Shoup, 1969; Goode, 1977). The comprehensive income tax base thus became the banner of tax reform in the United States, designed to secure equal treatment of taxpayers with equal income (horizontal equity) as well as to provide a global base on which progressive rates could be assessed in a meaningful fashion (vertical equity). How much impact this movement has had on the actual income tax is a different matter, but it clearly provided the focus of analysis and delight for a generation of tax economists in the United States.

In contrast, British public finance literature was reluctant to embrace the accretion concept. The schedular approach to the income tax was deep-rooted. Ursula Hicks (1947), following J. R. Hicks' analysis in *Value and Capital*, still defined income so as to exclude windfall gains. Similarly, a Royal Commission of the mid-1950s rejected the usefulness of establishing criteria for an income concept, with a minority view in favour of the accretion approach joined by Kaldor (1955). More recently, however, the accretion concept and comprehensive base approach has gained acceptance (Prest, 1975; Kay and King, 1978), but with it there emerged an alternative approach to broad-based taxation in the form of consumption.

### The consumption base

Though emphasis among tax economists had traditionally been on the income base, the case for consumption as index of equality also claims a long ancestry. Thus, over three centuries ago, Hobbes stated the equity case for the consumption base as follows:

Equality of imposition, consisteth rather in the equality of that which is consumed, than of the riches of the person who consumes the same. For what reason is there, that he which laboureth much, and sparing the fruits of his labour, consumeth little should be more charged, than he that living idly, getteth little and spendeth all he gets; seeing the one has no more protection from the Common-wealth, than the other. (Hobbes, 1651, p. 386)

Adam Smith, while featuring income in his first maxim, subsequently retreated to rent and luxury consumption as the appropriate bases. Ricardo, bypassing the issue of equity, prevailed against the taxation of income which would be returned to capital. It was thus left to John Stuart Mill to lay the modern basis for the consumption-base doctrine. Beginning with an income-based view of sacrifice, Mill rejected preferential treatment of temporary as against permanent income, but not all income was to be treated alike. Suppose there are two people with the same income, so he argued. One is a wage earner, has no capital and must save for old age. The other has interest income and need not save as his capital will provide for retirement. The wage-earner, so Mill argued, has less left for consumption, and to treat him equally, his savings should be omitted from his tax base:

If, indeed, reliance could be placed on the conscience of the contributors, or sufficient security taken for the correctness of their statements by collateral precautions, the proper mode of assessing an income tax would be to tax only that part of income devoted to expenditure, exempting that which is saved. For when saved and invested (and all savings, speaking generally, are invested) it thenceforth pays income tax on the interest and profits which it brings, notwithstanding that it has already been taxed on the principal. Unless therefore savings are exempted from income tax, the contributors are twice taxed on what they save, and only once on what they spend .... The difference thus created to the disadvantage of prudence and economy is not only impolitic but unjust (Mill, 1848, p. 813).

Mill concluded that savings should be exempt if this can be administered without abuse, but was sceptical that this can be done. As a more practical solution, he suggested that 'life incomes' be taxed at only three-quarters of the rate applicable to 'incomes of inheritance'.

While Edgeworth conducted his analysis of sacrifice doctrines in income terms, the case for the consumption base—in theory, if not in practice—was made by distinguished theorists such as Marshall (1927), Fisher (1909), Einaudi (1912) and Pigou (1928). With the exception of Fisher, these authors argued the case in principle, but, like Mill, did not think a personalised tax on consumption to be practicable. The first detailed proposal for practical implementation was made by Fisher (1942), and a second by Kaldor (1955). As the readers of this chapter are well aware, the expenditure tax recently moved to the centre of the academic tax discussion (Pechman, 1980). While its fate in the arena of actual tax policy remains to be seen, the idea of personalised and progressive expenditure tax freed consumption taxation from its previous association with regressive burden distribution, an association which had prevailed as long as consumption taxes were viewed as *in rem* taxes on retail sides.

## Unjust Enrichment

Before leaving the topic of tax equity, we briefly return to the income base. This is to note views that certain types of earnings should be singled out for taxation, not because they reflect a higher ability to pay, but because the recipient is not entitled to them. Thus, Aristotle and Thomas Aquinas, while defenders of property, questioned the legitimacy of interest income (Schumpeter, 1954, p. 82); and though this scruple disappeared later on, there remained a presumption that 'earned' income might be given preference over 'unearned' income, as indeed has been the case until recently with the earned income exemption under the US income tax.

The main instance of differentiation, however, was with regard to land. This thought goes back to John Locke who, in quoting Scripture, distinguished between the fruits of labour to which a worker is entitled and the fruits of land which God gave to man to be held in common (Locke, 1698, Book 11, ch. 5). The same theme was taken up with John Stuart Mill who noted that there were certain exceptions to uniform taxation, 'consistent with that equal justice which is the groundwork of the rule' (Mill, 1948,

p. 817). Such is the case with regard to rent from land. The ordinary progress of society increases the income of landlords who have no claim, based on the principle of desert to this accession of riches. Introduction of a penalty tax on prevailing land values, so argued Mill, would do injustice to the present owners; but an extra tax on increments is appropriate, provided they reflect the progress of society rather than the industry of the owner. This discussion was continued by Edgeworth and Marshall who, while agreeing, stressed the difficulty of isolating external effects (Edgeworth, 1887, p. 216).

The same theme was continued by Henry George, whose single tax doctrine swept the United States in the 1880s and 1890s (George, 1880). While a staunch defender of private property, George viewed the entitlement to land as held in common. Impressed with rapid gains in land values at his time, he viewed such gains as *the* source of inequality and social injustice. Following Herbert Spencer, his case for a 100 per cent tax on the rent of land was more drastic than Mill's, as it was to apply to entire land values and not only increments therein. George thus became the founder of the single tax movement, a movement which was subsequently supported by Brown (1918), and still continues. As will be noted, land as the prime base of taxation was to receive further endorsement on efficiency (as distinct from equity) grounds. As shown in the later literature, the taxation of natural resources has remained a problem of great interest.

Nor is this the only instance in which selective taxation of certain sources of income has been argued in the name of tax justice. The taxation of wartime profits under an excess profits tax, for instance, has been common practice. While the concepts of accretion and global base have been central to the equity rule, the underlying premise of general entitlement has been subject to certain qualifications. Changing views on tax equity must indeed be understood in the context of philosophical views regarding the nature of property, individual entitlement thereto, and the relationship of the individual to the state. Thus, there is a vast gap between the neo-Lockean view of taxation as 'forced labour' (Nozick, 1974, p. 169) and, say, Justice Holmes' view of taxation as the cost of civilisation.


## EFFICIENCY IN TAXATION

But equity is not all there is to the construction of a good tax system: efficiency also matters, and here economic analysis takes over. Adam Smith, in his fourth maxim, counsels that 'every tax ought to be so contrived as to take out and to keep out of the pockets of the people as little as possible, over and above what it brings into the public treasury of the state' (Smith, 1776, vol. II, p. 311). Reference is to the cost of tax administration, obstruction to industry, the burden of penalties, and odious examinations. Taxes should be 'as little burdensome to the people' as possible. John Stuart Mill quotes Smith with approval but finds that no elaboration is needed. At one point, Mill (1948, p. 803) almost recognises that payment of similar amounts under different taxes may impose differential burdens, but then backs away from this conclusion. Edgeworth, as noted before, accepted least total sacrifice as the utilitarian solution, but also warned that the 'productional' consequences of taxation may outweigh 'distributional' requirements. At some point 'the utilitarian must sadly acquiesce in inequality of taxation' (Edgeworth, 1897). Similar views were expressed by most early contributors to the equal sacrifice debate, although concern with potential loss of output and reduced growth was more serious in some cases (Bastable, 1892, p. 311) than in others (Adams, 1899, p. 351). However, reference was to loss of output rather than to dead-weight loss.

The modern formulation of efficiency in taxation was anticipated once more by Dupuit (1844). As noted earlier, Dupuit anticipated modern utility theory by exploring the conditions under which a public works project should be undertaken. In the process he developed (or came close to developing) the concept of a demand curve, and measured the net loss from a tax diagrammatically by the triangle which after Marshall became the standard picture of excess burden. Indeed, Dupuit already recognised that the net loss is proportional to the square of the tax base. But Dupuit's insight was far ahead of its time, as was that of Gossen's (1854) early vision of marginal utility analysis.

The concept of consumer surplus reemerged 40 years later in the works of the marginal utility theorists such as Wieser, Menger and Jevons, Jenkin (1871), as noted below, was the first to use demand and supply curves in incidence analysis, and to show how the burden of a tax exceeds the amount of revenue collected. Marshall (1890, Book III, ch. 6), during the same period, developed the concept of consumer surplus on his own terms and warned of the underlying assumption of constant marginal utility of income. He then applied the concept to tax analysis. Inquiring whether competitive equilibrium produces maximum welfare, he suggested that welfare may be raised by giving a bounty to decreasing cost industries while taxing those with increasing cost. In a footnote, he added that the 'net loss' (now referred to as excess burden, dead-weight loss, or efficiency cost) of a product tax would be larger for the case of a luxury than for a necessity since demand tends to be more elastic (Marshall, 1890, p. 467). Ever since, the concept of consumer surplus has played a key role in tax economies— first in the evaluation of particular taxes, and recently generalised in the theory of optimal taxation.

Marshall's application of consumer surplus to taxation was by way of illustrating general principles of price theory, as was the case for most of his analysis. The efficiency implications of taxation were given central focus only 30 years later. Pigou (1928, Part II, ch. 5), after discussing sacrifice rules as had Edgeworth, proceeded to an explicit analysis of 'announcement effects'. As a tax is introduced, a taxpayer finds his options changed and adjusts his behaviour accordingly. This results in 'announcement burdens' or loss of consumer and producer surplus (Pigou, ch. 6). The announcement burden of an income tax will be larger if a given revenue is drawn from a particular taxpayer under a progressive rate schedule than under a proportional one. But for a given total revenue to be obtained, the use of a less progressive rate schedule requires taxpayers with lower incomes to be taxed more, leaving the net effects on announcement burdens questionable. With labour supply seen to be generally inelastic, Pigou concludes that distributional considerations should be given the major weight.

But the principle of least sacrifice calls for the exclusion of saving from the income tax base. Inclusion, so he argued correctly, taxes future consumption at a higher rate than present consumption. This offends the principle of least sacrifice. It does so, so his argument continues somewhat strangely, because saving is the more elastic use of income and should, if anything, be taxed at a lower rate (Pigou, 1928, p. 138). Efficiency considerations thus call for an expenditure tax. But Pigou holds a progressive expenditure tax unworkable and thus opts for exclusion of investment income as an equivalent solution. To avoid unjust windfalls, this exclusion is limited to earnings from future investment income only, a proviso which anticipates the transition problems in the expenditure tax debate to follow 50 years later (Pechman, 1980). Other situations may also arise where announcement considerations call for discrimination against certain sources of income. Thus the unimproved value of land is a prime source of taxation, as there are no announcement effects. And so are unanticipated windfalls. However, once more, care need be taken lest sudden introduction of a high land tax discriminates against old holders.

Addressing the bearing of demand and supply elasticities on the announcement effects of product taxes, Pigou was aware of the complexity of the problem and concluded that a 'more powerful engine of analysis is needed' to construct an optimal system. This analysis was provided by F. P. Ramsey who, in response to Pigou's inquiry, laid the basis for what has now come to be known as the theory of optimal taxation. Ramsey (1927) demonstrated that

the optimal system of proportionate tax yielding a given revenue will cut down the production of all commodities in equal proportions. Assuming labour supply to be fixed, this will be achieved by uniform proportional taxes; but with labour supply variable, differential *ad valorem* rates will be called for, depending on the elasticities of demand and supply.

But differentiation between products causes distributional inequities among taxpayers with equal income but different tastes. Given this further conflict between equity (now within the income group) and efficiency, Pigou (1928, p. 132) suggests that progression be applied via the income tax, supported perhaps by some luxury taxation. He thus stresses the importance of taste differentials, a factor destined to be largely neglected by the optimal taxation to follow 50 years later.

While the contributions of Pigou and Ramsey laid the basis for the modern theory of optimal taxation, its current formulation was slow in coming. The first major contribution, following Pigou (but evidently unaware of Pigou's and Ramsey's writing) was that of Hotelling (1938). Departing from Dupuit's work, Hotelling derived the superiority of a lump-sum over an excise tax in general equilibrium terms, based on ordinal analysis and without using the concept of consumer surplus. More questionably, he then extended this conclusion to claiming superiority of an income over an excise tax. In subsequent writings, this superiority became accepted doctrine. It remained so until Little (1951) showed that the earlier conclusion had depended crucially on the assumption of fixed labour supply and that, with labour supply variable, no such *a priori* judgement could be drawn. As recognised later (although not noted by Little), allowance for a variable goods–leisure choice invalidates the *a priori* case for ranking a general consumption ahead of a general income tax. Focus on the importance of the goods–leisure choice pointed to product complementarity with leisure as key factor in the selection of an efficient tax base (Corlett and Hague, 1953).

With these foundations laid, Harberger (1964) carried the argument beyond theorising into the empirical measurement of dead-weight losses for particular taxes. Thus the analysis of excess burden was moved to an applied base and has been actively pursued since then. At the theoretical level, it was not until 1971 that the model of optimal taxation, visualised 50 years earlier by Ramsey, was resumed and expanded (Diamond and Mirrlees, 1971). Optimal taxation then became the centre of tax theoretical work in the 1970s.

## SHIFTING AND INCIDENCE

Economists have for long been aware that there exists a difference between the point at which taxes are imposed (their 'statutory' incidence) and the 'final' point at which burdens come to rest. The transition or shifting process has been at the centre of tax economics from the Physiocrats on. Indeed, the development of incidence theory closely reflects the development of economic theory at large. Developments in the theory of tax incidence have mirrored the advances of price and distribution theory, including both their general and partial equilibrium settings.

### The Precursors
The first general equilibrium model was that of the Physiocrats and it also spawned the first well-defined incidence theory. But the discussion of incidence dates further back. Hobbes' proposal for a tax on expenses, made in 1651, was based on the premise that such a tax falls on consumers. The growth of excises that was to follow focused the early debate on such taxes. Leading up to the furore created by Walpole's excise reform of 1733, a wide variety of views emerged. Thomas Mun (1664) argued that taxation of necessities would not only raise their price, but also cause wages to rise

accordingly. The final burden would thus fall on the rich. Sir William Petty (1667), in what was the first English treatise on tax theory, held that all excises, even those on necessities, will be borne by consumers. This was the case even for consumers of necessities. For some this was reason to reject such taxes as inequitable; but others (including Petty) thought it to be a virtue. A tax on necessities, so they argued, would reduce laziness, add to output, and in line with the contemporary doctrine favouring low wages, would thus be to the advantage of the British economy. Anticipating Physiocratic doctrine, John Locke (1692) held that all taxes, including excises on necessities, would be borne by the landlord. The landowner cannot shift a tax on land since such a tax does not change the 'tenant's bargain and profit'. A tax on necessities raises wages and thereby the cost to the farmer who, in turn, is able to pay less rent to the landlord.

There is thus a wide range of early opinion based on diverging views regarding the shape of labour supply, including vertical and backward bending. Moreover, many points featured in later discussion already appear in one or another part of this early debate. These include allowance for how tax revenue is spent, the concept of capitalisation, the idea that old taxes are good taxes, and a warning that excessive rates will reduce revenue. However, the views are advanced mostly in *ad hoc* terms and will not be pursued here. The interested reader is referred to Seligman's (1899, Book I) scholarly account.

As noted before, rigorous incidence theory begins with the Physiocratic model of income generation, and its first vision of an equilibrating economic system (Schumpeter, 1954, part II, ch. 4). According to this model, only land was able to produce a net product (Quesnay, 1758). Labour could merely produce an output needed to maintain itself; and the capitalist's return, net of compensation for risk, was similarly limited. With land the only factor capable of producing a surplus, it followed that land could be the only lasting source of taxation. Taxation of wages or of products could only lead to economic decline without any lasting revenue gain to the Crown. The sensible way to tax, therefore, was to proceed directly to a tax on land. The Physiocratic model thus led to a warped view of incidence, less realistic indeed than the *ad hoc* theorising which had gone before. It is not surprising, therefore, that Turgot, while an ardent proponent of the doctrine, made no attempt to introduce the single tax on land during his tenure in office.

With one extreme leading to its opposite, we may note here the theory of Canard (1801), celebrated at its time, that the search for rents of surplus leads to a diffusion of tax burdens which continues until the burden is shared equally by all participants in the exchange. The burden of taxation, so he held, results from the disturbance caused by this adjustment process and vanishes as the tax comes to rest. Hence, the conclusion that 'every old tax is good; every new tax is bad' (Seligman, 1899, p. 162).

## The Classics

The system of the classical economists, like that of the Physiocrats, centred on the division of output among factor shares. But the essentially two-factor model of the Physiocrats was now extended to include capital, reflecting the change in perspective from an agricultural to a manufacturing economy. Focus on the return to the three factors not only served as a central analytical tool to explore the laws of value and production, but also dealt with the division of output among the major classes—landlords, capitalists and workers—which defined the social and economic structure of the times. A view of incidence theory as distribution of the tax burden among these factor shares, therefore, not only fitted the analytical scheme but also provided a political economy of taxation.

In addition to adding the third factor of capital and manufacture, the classical model also broadened the framework of tax analysis by tracing taxation effects through the price adjustment of the market and by drawing a distinction between short- and long-run responses. In this broadened setting, the classics remained true to the Physiocratic tradition of viewing incidence in the context of a truly general equilibrium system. Moreover, the assumption of infinitely elastic labour supply was largely retained, at least in the longer-run context, so that the expanded model still yielded a set of relatively simply solutions.

### Adam Smith

The heart of classical incidence analysis is to be found in the work of David Ricardo, but his analysis responded to the pattern developed by Adam Smith. It is thus well to begin with that version as developed in *The Wealth of Nations* (Smith, 1776). After presenting his maxims, Smith in a series of chapters offers a detailed discussion of the major taxes, including their incidence.

Not surprisingly, the story begins with a tax on the rent of land. If imposed directly on the landlord, so Smith asserts without further explanation, the tax will be absorbed in rent. The same result obtains if the tax is levied on the tenant. The tenant is charged a rent equal to the amount by which the value of his output exceeds what he needs to maintain himself (Smith, 1776, vol. I, p. 145). Thus he cannot absorb the tax and deducts it from his rental payment. 'The landlord is in all cases the real contributor' (Vol. II, p. 313). While arriving at a valid conclusion, the reasoning still rests on a Physiocratic notion of net product, rather than on a view of rent as an intra-marginal return. This is evident when Smith arrives at a faulty result for the tax on agricultural produce. Such taxes, Smith (p. 321) asserted, 'are in reality taxes upon rent', and like taxes on rent they are eventually paid by the landlord. The essential distinction between a tax on rent and a tax on agricultural produce was not as yet recognised.

A direct tax on the wages on labour, so Smith continues, cannot be borne by the worker. The wage is set by the cost of subsistence and therefore cannot be reduced. If the tax is on the wages of agricultural labour, the farmer (as employer of such labour) must pass it back to the landlord through reduced rent. The outcome is similar to that of a tax on agricultural produce. If the tax is on the wages of manufacturing labour, the manufacturer will add it to price. What happens next depends on whether the taxed labour is engaged in the production of luxury goods or necessities. In the former case, the tax is borne by the consumer. In the latter case, the consumer, already living on a subsistence wage, cannot absorb the tax. Wages must rise and the tax once more is passed back to the landlord in the form of reduced rent. Smith thus concludes as follows:

> Taxes upon necessities, so far as they affect the laboring poor, are finally paid, partly by landlords in the diminished rent of their lands, and partly by rich consumers, whether landlords or others, in the advanced price of manufactured goods. [Therefore] the middling and superior ranks of people, if they understand their own interest, ought always to oppose all taxes upon the necessities of life, as well as direct taxes upon the wages of labour (p. 357).

Smith notes that the 'middling and superior ranks of people' should not only be indifferent between taxes on luxuries and rent, which they pay directly, and taxes upon wages and necessities which they must absorb indirectly; they should indeed prefer the former. The reason, it appears, is that the latter are taken to raise prices by more than tax, thereby imposing an additional burden.

The conclusion that wages and necessities cannot be taxed conflicts with Smith's (1776, vol. I, p. 71; vol. II, p. 384) recognition that subsistence may be more or less liberal, depending on whether the demand for labour is increasing, stationary or declining. Given this range, he might have noted that circumstances may allow for a reduction in the market wage net of tax, on at least a temporary basis. His focus, however, is on the longer run, where the wage returns to its subsistence level. If reduced below that level, population would fall, economic advance would be retarded, and the revenue base would be lost.

Next consider Smith's view of a general tax on profits. Profits or the 'return from stock' are divided into compensation for trouble or risk of employing the stock and into interest which belongs to the owner. The former cannot be taxed, as entrepreneurs also seem to have their subsistence wage. The part which reflects interest, however, is likened to rent (p. 331). 'With the quantity of stock or money in the country, like the quantity of land, being supposed to remain constant, the same after tax as before', Smith (p. 352) concludes that interest, like rent, can absorb taxation. The assumption that stock remains constant, however, is qualified by subsequent counsel against its excessive taxation as causing undue inquisition and capital flight.

Taxes which are imposed on profits of particular industries, finally, are passed to the consumer, as capital will be withdrawn until the tax is recovered in higher prices (p. 310). Smith thus recognised that returns will be equalised across industries, but he mistakenly interpreted this as burdening the consumer rather than as spreading the tax among all uses of capital.

### David Ricardo

We now turn to David Ricardo, the main architect of the classical system of incidence theory.[7] Ricardo's central concern with taxation is evidenced by the very title of his major work, the *Principles of Political Economy and Taxation* (1819). The market, so Ricardo held, does best without interference; but, unhappily, public expenditures are made and taxes are needed to finance them. Thus interference is inevitable: 'It is here then that the most perfect knowledge of the science is required.' Indeed, 'political economy, when the simple principles of it are once understood, is only useful as it directs governments to right measures of taxation (*Collected Works*, vol. VIII, p. 132).

All taxes, so Ricardo notes at the outset, are either paid from income or from stock. But government expenditures are 'unproductive consumption'. They add neither to capital nor provide for advances to labour. Therefore if such expenditures are financed by taxes which fall on revenue, i.e. reduced private consumption, the national capital remains unimpaired; but if such consumption is not reduced, taxes must fall on capital, and eventually distress and ruin follows (ibid., vol. I, p. 151). No neater formulation of the supply-side view of the budget could be desired.

Following the pattern laid out by Adam Smith, Ricardo then turns his attention to particular taxes, taking a critical view of earlier doctrine. A *tax on rent*, or a land tax levied in proportion to rent, does not apply to marginal land which yields no rent. Since this is the land on which the price of produce is determined, a tax on rent cannot be reflected in that price and must be borne by the landlord. The conclusion is similar to that of Adam Smith, but the reasoning differs. The Physiocratic view of land as the basic source of income is now replaced by rent as an intra-marginal return which does not affect price.

With this clarification, Ricardo proceeds to correct Adam Smith's conclusion that a *tax on raw produce* is borne by the landlord. By raising the cost of produce at the margin of cultivation, such a tax also raises the price of produce. Hence the tax is not paid by the landlord but by the consumer. Such at least is the case until further adjustments, similar to those of a tax on manufactured products, are allowed for. As noted previously, such a tax, if on necessities, cannot be borne by the consumer.

Ricardo's most intriguing argument applies to a *tax on wages*. As a wages tax is imposed on the worker, nominal wages must rise. This must be the case since labour supply is fixed in the short run and the wage rate is at subsistence. As wages are raised, profits are reduced. Suppose now that as nominal wages rise, the employer comes to recoup his profits by raising prices. This would call for a further rise in wages so as to maintain the real wage at subsistence, generating a further increase in prices, and so forth. Ricardo (*Collected Works*, vol. I, p. 225) rejects this reasoning as 'indefensible', as it suggests that the tax is paid by no one. To determine where the tax falls, he views the problem in terms of resource use. If total output is fixed and part thereof is transferred to government, some other use of resources must be cut. But these cuts cannot be in the wages fund. Since government engages in unproductive consumption (consumption which does not add to necessary advances to labour), since labour supply is fixed and since wages are at subsistence, the wages fund (circulating capital) must remain intact.[8] Therefore, the only resource uses that can be cut are consumption by capitalists and the stock of fixed capital. Since both are paid for out of profits, this is where the tax must fall.[9] Any attempt to recoup the increase in wages by raising price only requires further wages increases and will not help.

Much the same reasoning applies to a *tax on profits*. Such a tax cannot be recouped in higher prices because this would require an increase in wages, nor can wages be reduced since the wages fund must be kept intact to compensate the fixed labour supply at its subsistence wage. Since 'a tax on wages is in fact a tax on profits', so Ricardo (*Collected Works*, vol. I, p. 226) concludes, 'I should think it of little importance whether the profits of stock or the wages of labour were taxed'. Turning finally to a tax on manufactured products, much depends on whether the product is in the form of necessities or luxuries. A tax on the former must again fall on profits, whereas a tax on the latter can be absorbed in reduced consumption of the well-to-do.

Given the *short-run* context in which labour supply and hence the wage bill in real terms is held fixed, Ricardo thus arrives at these two conclusions: (1) taxes on rent, profits and luxury products are absorbed by the payee, whereas taxes on wages and necessities are passed on to and borne by profits; and (2) the resource release from the private sector must be either in reduced consumption of landlords and capitalists, or in their reduced contribution to the maintenance or expansion of the fixed capital stock. But the story does not end here. In the *longer run*, reduced accumulation will result in a decline 'in society's demand for labour' (*Collected Works*, vol. I, p. 222). As a result, population declines— Ricardo (p. 218) quotes Malthus with approval—until the wages fund is distributed among fewer workers and the market wage has been returned to its natural level of subsistence. Thus, a new equilibrium is established at a lower level of population. The net real wage rate is restored, rent is reduced, and there is a lower capital stock. Taking the *very long* view, profit taxes hasten the arrival of the stationary state, as the net (after-tax) return to capital reaches zero at an earlier point and (returning to the Physiocratic outcome) only rent remains as a taxable income.

This, to be sure, is a simplified version of a highly complex system in which many additional factors are involved. Thus, Ricardo considers how adjustments to a partial tax will differ depending on whether the industry is intensive in fixed or circulating capital, how adjustments to profit and commodity taxes will differ depending on whether the output of precious metals (the monetary standard) is included in the tax base or not, on how the role of trade is affected, and on how government spent the funds. Due to these complications and abundant quarrels with other authors, it is difficult to draw out the core of his argument. Our summary therefore cannot but involve interpolation and interpretation. (See also Shoup, 1960).

From the perspective of later analysis, the system is biased by conducting most of the arguments under the assumption of fixed labour supply and subsistence wage, supplemented in the longer run by a Malthusian labour-supply response. Nevertheless, Ricardo offers an impressive structure of micro and macro analysis. Schumpeter (1954, p. 473) may have been uncharitable, therefore, in disposing of the Ricardian model as 'an excellent theory that can never be refuted and lacks nothing save sense'. Indeed, as we shall see below, it has only been in recent years that incidence analysis on a Ricardian scale has been resumed in the context of neoclassical growth models.

## The Marginalists

Adam Smith and Ricardo, of course, were not the only classical economists who wrote on the incidence of taxation. Others to be noted in a more detailed accounting include McCulloch (1845), who stressed the 'reproductive effect of taxation', and Mill (1849), who restated the Ricardian position in a more flexible fashion and extended its application to international trade. However, the essential theme has been given with Adam Smith and Ricardo, so that we may proceed directly to the next stage, i.e. the rise of marginalism and the modern view of factor pricing.[10]

The revolution in economic analysis which occurred in the closing decades of the nineteenth century began with the recognition of utility as a determinant of value. Value was no longer derived from input of labour but from utility in use; and demand, based on relative utilities, was assigned a strategic role in setting relative product prices. This advance was followed by application of marginal analysis to factor pricing and the theory of distribution. The return to labour was no longer determined by a subsistence wage and the Malthusian mechanism of adjustment was dropped. The rule of capital as a factor of production, dealt with ambiguously by the classics, was given specific content. The return to capital and saving was now seen as compensation for contribution to increased productivity via roundaboutness in production. The pricing of all factors in line with their marginal product thus became subject to one and the same principle of compensation. 'The theories of the values of labor and of the things made by it', as Marshall (1890) put it in the introduction to his *Principles of Economics*, 'cannot be separated: they are parts of one great whole; and what differences there are between them even in matters of details, turn out on inquiry to be, for the most part, differences of degree rather than of kind.' The new model was bound to revolutionise incidence doctrine, just as the classical formulation had superseded that of the Physiocrats.

### Fleming Jenkin

A first and striking contribution was made by Jenkin (1871) (see also Musgrave and Shoup, 1959). Drawing on Jevons' presentation of marginal utility curves to show gains from trade, Jenkin interpreted these as offer curves in relation to price. He was thus the first to have viewed incidence analysis in terms of supply and demand curves, with taxes resulting in shifts therein. He then uses this newly-found apparatus to show how the burden of a unit tax is divided between buyers and sellers, and how the injury to each exceeds the tax paid. The total loss for each then depends on the slopes of the demand and supply curves. The terminology, to be sure, was not as yet in terms of consumer and producer 'surplus'; and the concept of elasticity remained to be introduced. Nevertheless, the substance of Jenkin's analysis was essentially the same as may be found in textbooks of today.

*Leon Walras*
While Jenkin was the first to apply marginal analysis to incidence theory in a partial equilibrium setting, it is not surprising that Walras (1874), in his *Elements of Pure Economics*, was the first to apply it in the context of general equilibrium.

Walras concluded his treatise with a chapter on taxation. Incidence is viewed in the context of an interdependent set of factor and product prices. Taxes on the three factors (land, labour and capital) are examined, as are taxes on products. A distinction is drawn between partial and general taxes. While taxes are not formally entered into the set of Walrasian equations, the general argument and its conclusions are in line with modern doctrine.

The incidence of a tax on capital income (i.e. on interest, as there are no profits in competitive equilibrium) will depend on how saving responds. Since this cannot be predicted, 'we may as well assume that the incidence of the tax falls on the capitalist' (Walras, 1874, p. 454). A tax on wages, similarly, will depend on the response in labour supply, which once more cannot be foreseen. Special attention is given to taxes on capital which apply unequally to various uses. Two effects are distinguished. Suppose that the tax is imposed on rental income from housing. Capital in the housing industry will decline, rentals will rise and tenants will bear the burden. But this is not all and Walras continues as follows:[11]

Hence a tax on house rent would work out like a tax on consumption—or at least in part, for, if we look at the matter closely, we observe that a portion of the burden is borne by the capitalist. Since some of the capital goods previously employed in the construction of houses will be transferred to all sorts of other employments, a general decline in the rate of income (from capital goods) will result, and this decline will be to the detriment of all capitalists including home owners and to the advantage of all consumers, including tenants. One could, therefore, inquire into the extent to which the consumers thus recover, through the decline in the prices of other services and products, what they lose by the rise in house rents (p. 455).

Given a somewhat modern interpretation, Walras thus distinguished neatly between (1) how the depressing effects of the tax on net capital income are generalised among capital in all uses, and (2) how consumers are affected by more or less offsetting 'excise effects'. The modern theory of property tax incidence (Mieszkowski, 1972) has its antecedent.

The incidence of product (or indirect) taxes, finally, will be borne partly by the consumers of the taxed product and partly by the owners of the productive services which are employed in their manufacture. The outcome, therefore, is extremely complex, depending on the conditions of demand and supply in the particular markets. Walras's discussion, while held in fairly general terms, is unobjectionable, to be improved upon only in its specifics in later analysis.

### Knut Wicksell

Wicksell's primary contribution to fiscal theory, as noted earlier, is related to the voting process as a mechanism of preference determination. However, his fiscal treatise begins with an extensive analysis of incidence. Wicksell (1896, p. 5) opens with two methodological observations of importance. First, he rejects the term 'shifting' as misleading, because it suggests that A, the initial payee, passes part of the tax to B and so forth until the entire tax (equal to revenue) is distributed among a chain of payees. This is misleading, because the burden at any one stage may exceed the amount of tax paid, so that the total burden may exceed the total tax. Dead-weight loss, in modern language, should be allowed for. Secondly, he notes the confusion encountered in earlier analysis, which combines the expenditure and tax sides of the budget. While the pattern of government demand matters, this should be separated from the analysis of tax incidence. To do so, government expenditures should be held constant and the incidence of alternative taxes (collecting the same revenue) should be compared. That is to say, incidence should be conducted in differential terms (see also Musgrave, 1959, p. 212).

Wicksell then turns to a tax on monopoly profits. Based on Cournot's (1838) much earlier work (see also Musgrave and Shoup, 1959), he shows that a tax on profits cannot be shifted. For the case of product taxes, he further shows that the increase in price needed to obtain a given revenue will be smaller under an *ad valorem* than under a unit tax. The *ad valorem* approach, therefore, imposes a lesser burden and is to be preferred.

Wicksell's major concern, however, was not with changes in product prices but with the classical problem of incidence among social classes and factor shares. A new formulation was needed, as the Ricardian model of a fixed wages fund, divided among a fixed labour supply, had been discarded by the advances of marginal analysis. Wicksell (1896, p. 35) attempted to fill the void by application of Böhm Bawerk's capital theory. Beginning with the simplest case, he assumes a two-factor model, including labour and capital only, engaged in the production of a single product. Moreover, labour supply and the capital stock are fixed. The only question is how the capital stock is to be used, i.e. how long the 'average period of production', $t$, should be. As $t$ is lengthened, the productivity of labour is increased, and for any given wage the producer will choose that period for which the rate of interest is maximised. But the wage rate, equal to $k/t$, where $k$ is the capital stock, must fall as $t$ is increased. In combination, these two relationships establish an equilibrium position, determining $t$ as well as the wage and interest rate.

Wicksell then uses this model—with its peculiar mixture of marginal productivity and wage fund-setting—to examine incidence. A tax on income, be it on wages or on interest, will have no effect on the optimal period. The wage and interest rate are unchanged and the tax is absorbed by the payee. But a product tax will affect the outcome, as it is equivalent to an increase in the cost of labour and hence leads to a lengthening of $t$. Both interest and wages are reduced as a result, with the outcome depending on the shape of the production function or relation between $t$ and labour productivity. By assuming a one-product model, Wicksell thus bypasses the issue of how incidence is affected by partial taxes and differing production functions. He does, however, amend his model by introducing land and allowing for variable capital and labour supply.

## Alfred Marshall

Marshall frequently used the analysis of tax changes to 'throw side-lights on the problem of value' (Marshall, 1890, p. 412).[12] In particular, tax illustrations are used to show how the nature of return to capital depends on the length of time under consideration. Returns obtainable from a given stock or machine are in the nature of quasi-rents, and taxes thereon (like taxes on the rent of land) cannot be shifted. The situation differs, however, in the longer run, when supply is variable. The return to capital is no longer a rent and the tax enters as a cost. Emphasis on the distinction between short- and longer-run adjustments may thus be considered one of his major contributions to incidence analysis. Marshall again shows how a tax on monopoly profits cannot be shifted, while a tax on the monopolist's product leads to adjustments. Once more, general and selective taxes are distinguished.

Special attention is given to the incidence of local rates (Marshall, 1901). A distinction is drawn between 'onerous' rates, which leave the property without benefits and 'beneficial' rates which are reflected in public improvements. He notes that capital movement in response to local differentials relates to the *net* of the two, but such movement is not considered substantial. Incidence is shown to differ for taxes on sight or building values and once more the adjustment process and the resulting incidence depend on the length of period allowed for.

## F. Y. Edgeworth

Next in our parade of early neoclassical incidence theorists, Edgeworth's (1897) contribution is to be noted. This contribution is distinguished by its systematic approach. Combining assumptions regarding fixed and variable supply, fixed and mobile uses of factors, and increasing and decreasing cost, the incidence of product taxes under various combinations is explored. Special attention is given to 'peculiar cases' which arise under conditions of complementarity among products in consumption and production. He thus presents the famous 'Edgeworth's paradox' where it is shown that imposition of a tax on first-class fares may lead to a reduction in both first- and third-class fares (Edgeworth, 1897, p. 93; Hotelling, 1932).

Enriched by lovely illustrations of changing slopes drawn from hiking trips in the French Alps, Edgeworth exhibits virtuosity in addressing fine points of incidence.

*Enrico Barone*

Finally, we note Barone's (1899) ingenious application of marginal utility analysis to determine the effects of a tax on work effort (see also Musgrave and Shoup, 1959). Primus, producing for his own use, will work so as to equate the marginal utility of output or $x$ with the marginal disutility of work or $c$. Maximum utility is established at the maximum difference between $U(x) - C(x)$, i.e. where $u(x) = c(x)$. After a lump-sum tax is introduced, this becomes $u(x - a) = c(x)$. The marginal utility of $x$ curve shifts to the right and intersects the marginal utility of work curve at a higher level of output. If, however, the tax is proportional to output, the difference to be maximised equals $U(x - tx) - (Cx)$. The optimal value of $x$ is given by $(1 - t) u(x - tx) = c(x)$ and $x$ may rise or fall. Barone thus anticipates later results arrived at by the distinction between income and substitution effects. Moreover, he shows that output will increase or decrease, depending on whether the elasticity of the marginal utility schedule at the pre-tax equilibrium exceeds or falls short of $1 - t$.

## Later developments

These and other contributions to incidence theory during the closing decades of the last century had provided the major breakthrough. Subsequent developments offered improvements built on that base. We shall note very briefly some of the steps in this development, by no means complete but leading up to the current state of the art.

*Imperfect competition*

We have noted repeatedly how innovations in price and value theory came to be reflected in incidence analysis. A prize exhibit is provided by the work on product tax incidence which flourished in the late 1930s, following the birth of imperfect and monopolistic competition (Robinson, 1933; Chamberlin, 1938). Robinson, in developing the principles of imperfect competition, made extensive use of tax analysis, restating and expanding on Cournot's earlier work on monopoly taxation and even designing a tax device by which to correct monopolistic practice. This was followed by a spate of papers, exploring the relation between unit and *ad valorem* taxes under competition and monopoly, and given varying cost and demand conditions (Fagan and Jastram, 1939; von Mering, 1942).

*Income and substitution effects*

In the earlier discussion, it had become evident that the incidence of factor taxes will differ, depending on how factor supplies respond to a reduction in the net rate of return. The tools for addressing this problem were refined with the distinction between income and substitution effects (Hicks, 1938,

p. 31) and its application to tax analysis. Since the two effects work in opposite directions, it followed that no *a priori* conclusion can be drawn whether factor supplies will fall or rise, a conclusion which had already been reached by Barone. Going further, subsequent analysis pointed to a significant difference between proportional and progressive rates. Since the substitution effect depends on marginal and the income effect depends on average rates of tax, factor supply will tend to be lower under a progressive tax (Hicks, 1939), but not necessarily so since subsitution of a progressive for a flat schedule not only raises marginal rates of tax for some but also lowers them for others (Musgrave, 1959, ch. 11).

*Risk*
The taxation of capital income, by reducing the net rate of return, may reduce saving and the supply of capital, following reasoning similar to that for a tax on wages. But the return to investment is not certain. Rather, it is the expected value of probable gains and losses. The effect of a tax thus depends on how probable gains and losses are dealt with. If the tax law is such as to assure loss offset (be it by carrybacks, carryovers or refunds), government becomes a participant in both possible gains and losses and the outcome is not readily predicted (Simons, 1938; Lerner, 1943; Domar and Musgrave, 1944; also Musgrave and Shoup, 1959). Examination of taxation effects thus leads into portfolio analysis and investment choice (Tobin, 1958; Feldstein, 1969).

*Depreciation*
Also relating to the definition of taxable income from capital, much attention has been directed at the treatment of depreciation. The effective rate of tax is shown to depend on the nominal rate and the time pattern at which depreciation is allowed (Brown, 1948). Depreciation rules, unless carefully designed, may lead to differential effective rates of tax for industries with different assets lives. Thus the analysis of depreciation was directed at both the use of accelerated depreciation as tax incentive and at devising a depreciation rule which would be neutral among investment. Economic depreciation as the neutral method emerged (Samuelson, 1964) and the topic resurfaced fifteen years later when it was given new currency in the context of neutrality of tax incentives (Harberger, 1980) and of inflation (Auerbach and Jorgenson, 1980).

*General equilibrium*
Recent developments of incidence theory have moved towards a rigorously formulated general equilibrium approach. As we have seen, the classics had such an approach, but the underlying model was incomplete (a lack of capital theory) and unrealistic (the population response). The development of marginal productivity analysis at the close of the last century required a new model. It was recognised that taxes on any one factor may affect returns to other factors, as well as relative product prices; and that taxes on any more product may affect the prices of other products as well

as factor returns. Returned to the general equilibrium perspective (Brown, 1924), incidence analysis came to be viewed in differential terms, with any particular tax substitution affecting both the uses and sources sides of their accounts (Musgrave, 1959).

Mathematical models of general equilibrium incidence made their appearance (Shepherd, 1944; Meade, 1955) and took hold with Harberger's (1962) model of corporate tax incidence. This was the first model to offer a general yet workable approach. The burden of a profits tax on one industry is shown to be distributed among labour, capital and consumers, depending on certain characteristics of the taxed industry relative to those of tax-free industries. Assuming the elasticity of substitution of capital for labour to be unity in both industries, factor shares are unaffected and the tax is absorbed by profits, including profits in both taxed and tax-free industries. The analysis is directed at an intermediate period with capital allowed to move, but the total capital stock is held fixed. Moreover, perfect capital mobility and competitive markets are stipulated. Based on this model, a wave of theoretical and empirical work developed and is still in process (Mieszkowski, 1969).

*Growth models*

Appearance of the neoclassical growth model (Solow, 1956) was followed by introduction of tax variables, thus opening a new dimension of incidence analysis (Krzyzanisk, 1967; Feldstein, 1974). Thus incidence theory closed the circle by returning to the long-term perspective of the classics. With focus directed at effects on factor shares under conditions of steady growth, earlier conclusions from comparative statics were changed. Incidence under steady growth is shown to depend on savings propensities as well as on elasticities of factor supply. Thus, substitution of a tax on capital income for an equal yield tax on labour income will (1) leave part of the burden on labour, even if both factor supplies are inelastic, provided that the propensity to save out of capital income is higher; and (2) will leave capital with the entire burden, even if labour supply is elastic, provided that propensities to save are the same.

*Empirical studies*

Empirical studies of tax incidence began slowly but recently exploded under the impact of newly available computer technology. Among the early work, mostly directed at income tax, we may note the Colwyn Report with its contributions by Coates (1927), as well as studies of income tax effects on labour supply (Break, 1957) and on saving (Harberger and Bailey, 1969; Break, 1974).

At the same time, empirical studies tracing the actual incidence of particular taxes from observed data remained relatively scarce. An early attempt at econometric estimation of corporation tax incidence concluded that there may be substantial shifting (Krzyaniak and Musgrave, 1963), but the outcome of this and subsequent studies remained controversial (Harberger *et al.*, 1967).

While the concern of classical analysis had been with the distribution of the tax burden by factor shares, this was no longer the relevant consideration for purposes of policy analysis. With the change in social structure, attention had shifted to the distribution of the burden among individuals or households arranged by income brackets. A systematic attempt at assessing the distributional effects of the entire tax system along these lines begins with a study by Colm and Tarasov (1940), continued by Musgrave *et al.* (1951), and leading up to the comprehensive work by Pechman and Okner (1974). The methodology underlying this family of studies was to test the implications of various shifting hypotheses by estimating the distributional effects which would result. Product taxes are imputed to consumers, income taxes to the suppliers of factors, and alternative assumptions are applied regarding the incidence of the corporation and property tax. Proceeding along similar lines, attempts were made to allocate the distribution of expenditure benefits, thus aiming to arrive at a pattern of 'net distribution' through the budget (Musgrave *et al.*, 1974).

Among various shortcomings of this methodology, it has been noted that the approach is based on shifting hypotheses rather than on empirical evidence as to actual shifting. Also, the approach has been criticised for being limited to a partial equilibrium setting (Prest, 1955). Taxes are assigned to either the uses or sources side of the taxpayer's account, while neglecting second-round effects. Moreover, dead-weight losses are disregarded. In defence of this methodology, it has been argued that the distributional impact of first-round effects will dominate and that the implications of alternative shifting assumptions may be tested readily.

In recent years, a new approach to general equilibrium estimation has emerged, based on the tradition of the Harberger model and made possible by the advances of computer technology. Taxation effects are estimated in the context of a general equilibrium system, based on production functions and elasticities as deduced from prevailing output and price relationships (Shoven and Whalley, 1984). Thus, the complete chain of secondary effects is included and dead-weight losses are allowed for. However, the outcome still depends on the quality of the parameters which are built into the model. Moreover, it cannot be claimed that the model estimates the observed outcome of actual tax changes. Rather, it simulates the results which emerge on the assumption that adjustments proceed in a perfectly competitive and flexible economy.

## STABILISATION AND DEBT

Up to the 1930s, fiscal economics, with few exceptions, dealt with the effects of budget policy on alternative uses of resources and the distribution of income. This analysis, as we have seen, was conducted in the context of a full-employment economy. Much attention was given to fiscal effects on the division of output between capital formation and consumption, and thereby on growth; but by the nature of the underlying macro model, effects on the level of employment were outside the confines of analysis. With the 'Keynesian revolution' of the 1930s (Klein, 1947), aggregate demand became a major factor in determining the level of employment; and with it budget policy gained a new and strategic role. The stabilisation function was added to the more traditional aspects of budget policy, and fiscal policy moved into the centre of macroeconomics. Most of the fiscal literature of the 1930s and 1940s was directed at exploring this new dimension.

## Fiscal policy and stabilisation

While this phase of fiscal analysis gained dominance with the rise of Keynesian economics, it also had its antecedents.

### Early Keynesians

Aggregate demand was of concern in mercantilist thought, and Sir James Steuart (1767, vol. II, pp. 642, 644), writing a decade before the *Wealth of Nations*, argued that stagnant money 'lent to government, is thrown into a new channel of circulation—thereby to augment the prominent income of the country'. Then there was that 'brave army of heretics, Mandeville, Malthus, Gesell and Hobbson who, following their intuition, have preferred to see the truth obscurely and imperfectly rather than to maintain error, reached indeed with clearness and consistency and by easy logic, but on hypotheses appropriate to the fact' (Keynes, 1936, p. 371).

That central hypothesis, of course, was Say's law (1821), i.e. the proposition that there could be no general glut since, commodities being exchanged against commodities, supply would create its own demand. Malthus (1820, p. 316), the chief heretic among the classics, was critical of 'Mr. Say, Mr. Mill, and Mr. Ricardo, the principle authors of these new views'. An adequate level of 'effectual demand' is needed, so Malthus argued, to sustain output:

But if the conversion of revenue into capital pushed beyond a certain point must, by diminishing the effectual demand for produce, throw the labouring classes out of employment, it is obvious that the adoption of parsimonious habits beyond a certain point, may be accompanied by the most distressing effects at first, and by a market depression of wealth and population afterwards. (Malthus, 1820, p. 326)

His primary problem with saving, it appears, was not that funds will be withheld from the expenditure stream, as in the Keynesian model. Rather it was that too much is spent on capital formation, leaving consumer demand insufficient to absorb the increase in potential output that results. In consequence, profits will fall and accumulation will decline. Balance may be restored but only after distress has occurred. Malthus thus explains the depression which followed the Napoleonic wars by underconsumption. Of particular interest in our context are certain implications which Malthus draws for budget policy. If the problem is one of deficient consumer demand, budget policy can be helpful. Consumer demand might be raised by redistributing income towards 'those classes of unproductive consumers who are supported by taxes' (Malthus, 1820, p. 410). Moreover, budget policy can be harmful if consumer demand is reduced by excessively rapid repayment of public debt. Having noted this much, Malthus (p. 411) hastens to add that property rights must not be violated by redistribution, and assures the reader that he is not 'insensible to the great evils of public debt'.

Malthus, along with Sismondi, was among the first to advance an under-consumption theory of crisis. Marx offered a related doctrine and under-consumption theories reached high fashion in the writings of the 1920s. (For a discussion, see Hansen (1927), McCord Wright (1942), Keynes (1936), ch. 23.) However, these contributions paid little attention to the role of the public budget, nor did monetary theories of business cycles of that period.

### The Keynesian model

Analysis of budgetary effects on employment enter the public finance literature only in the mid-1930s, when the stage had been set by Keynes' *General Theory of Income and Employment* (1936). The impact of Keynesian economics on fiscal theory profoundly changed its focus. Whereas the problem had been to observe resulting shifts in resource use, concern now was with effects on its overall level. With employment seen to depend on aggregate demand and with budget policy a direct contributor thereto, budget policy became a critical determinant of the level of employment. This new function of budget policy was the more important because departure from full employment was seen no longer as a temporary aberration, but a central tendency of the economy. A continuing tendency towards oversaving (Keynes, 1936, p. 31) and stagnation (Hansen, 1938; 1941) was expected to prevail, with expansionary fiscal policy called for on a sustained basis in order to maintain high employment in a mature economy. Moreover, fiscal policy was not only one but *the* policy instrument with which to remedy the problem of underemployment. Monetary policy at least in the earlier depression phase of Keynesian economics was rendered ineffective by the existence of a liquidity trap. Aggregate demand, like a string, could not be pushed up by monetary expansion, but it could be pulled up by government outlays.

The Keynesian case for deficit finance, from the beginning, was doubly controversial. Not only were the underlying analytics questioned, but the model carried political and ideological implications which contributed to the heat of the debate. If fiscal expansion had to be secured via increased government expenditures, it would also add to the size of the public budget. Moreover, the central proposition that private saving may be a public vice offended deeply-held values based on puritan tradition. The notion that different principles of prudence applied to the public and the private sector ran counter to the concept of a society based on the beneficial interplay of individuals in the market.

In the course of time, the extreme view of the early Keynesian model was moderated, and the supreme powers of fiscal policy were tuned down. However, its role in stabilisation remained a key factor. The field of 'public finance', traditionally a subject in micro economics, became part of macro teaching and macro issues claimed dominant attention. No attempt can be made here to trace the development of macro theory from the 1930s to 1960s, not to speak of entering into the current debate. Rather, we limit ourselves to a brief look at certain macro issues which arose in the context of fiscal policy. Among the major contributors to the development of the fiscal policy concept we may note Alvin Hansen, whose fiscal policy seminar, conducted at Harvard during the late 1930s, was the mainspring of the new approach in the United States (Hansen, 1941) and, in Great Britain, Beveridge's (1945) programme for full employment in a free society was to be the blueprint for macro policy in the post-World War II years. In the United States, the Employment Act 1946 made it the President's responsibility to 'promote maximum employment, production, and purchasing power' and, as added in 1953, 'a dollar of stable value'. It also established the Council of Economic Advisors to pursue these goals.

*Multiplier analysis.* Central to the role of fiscal variables in the Keynesian model was their treatment in the multiplier formula. Initially this was thought of as the multiplier effect of an increase in 'government investment', observed while holding tax revenue constant. By adding government purchases, the level of autonomous expenditures would be raised, thus offsetting a higher level of private sector saving and permitting a higher level of income. The measurement of the fiscal multiplicand was explored (Clark, 1935; Currie and Krost, 1939; Villard, 1940), based on the assumption of a fixed level of investment. Samuelson's (1939) multiplier–accelerator model then expanded multiplier analysis to include investment effects and to examine the pattern of resulting income fluctuations. While initial emphases had been on increases in government purchases, subsequent analysis admitted tax reduction as a second device, leading to the analysis of alternative packages of tax and expenditure changes which would secure the same overall leverage effect (Beveridge, 1945; Hansen, 1945; Musgrave, 1945; Samuelson, 1948).

In line with the early focus on excess savings as the villain, the creation of a public deficit (public dissaving) was first seen as an essential feature of fiscal leverage. It therefore came as somewhat of a shock when it was demonstrated in the early 1940s that even a balanced budget increase could exert a leverage, albeit with a multiplier of unity only (Gelting, 1941; Salant, 1942; Havelmo, 1945). Within a short time span the 'balanced budget theorem' had been advanced independently in a number of places, a nice illustration of how what was once unthinkable becomes commonplace when the time is ripe (Salant, 1975). Examination of the multiplier time period (Metzler, 1948) and further exploration of various policy lags followed (Friedman, 1948), and the estimation of multiplier effects became a central part of the newly-developed breed of econometric models (Klein and Goldberger, 1955).

*Fiscal structure*. The newly-formed role of fiscal policy also placed the quality of various taxes in a new perspective. Taxes which fell heavily on consumption would carry a larger (negative) multiplicand than those falling on saving and thus do less damage to the leverage of the budget. Thus full-employment policy was linked to progressive taxation. A tax on undistributed profits was enacted briefly in 1937 (Colm, 1940) and the feasibility of a tax on hoarding, linking back to Gesell's idea of stamped money, was considered (McWright, 1942).

Given these new uses of tax and expenditure instruments in the context of macro policy, the question arose how they could be reconciled with the traditional fiscal objectives, i.e. the provision for needed public services and the design of an efficient and equitable tax structure. Keynes (1936, p. 220) was pleased to shock his bourgeois readers by noting that even the construction of pyramids or the digging of holes would increase the national income, without adding that constructing a useful highway may be even better. Lerner (1943), in his 'functional finance' doctrine, viewed taxation merely as a means to reduce the purchasing power of the public in contrast to its traditional role of transferring resources to the public sector. This author, concerned with avoiding distortions due to conflicting objectives of various policy functions, proposed a 'three-branch model' in which various functions of the budget could be reconciled and be performed in a compatible fashion (Musgrave, 1959, ch. 1). Changes in fiscal leverage, in that context, would be expedited primarily via changes in tax rates with government purchases set so as to meet the need for public services at a full-employment level of income. These considerations, we may add, are no less relevant in the current setting where macro considerations point in the direction of budgetary restriction.

*Built-in flexibility*. By the late 1940s, a distinction emerged between the stabilising effects of the fiscal system which arise as the result of discretionary changes in fiscal parameters and those which arise automatically in response to changes in the level of economic activity. Measures of built-in flexibility were devised and the comparative flexibility of various taxes was explored. Critics of discretionary policy held that changes in fiscal leverage should be limited to those which result automatically, while setting the level of tax rates so as to balance the budget at full employment (Friedman, 1948; Committee for Economic Development, 1947). Others held that discretionary changes cannot be dispensed with.

Over time it appeared that built-in flexibility might not be an unmixed blessing. Whereas the automatic decline in revenue in the course of a recession would be helpful, the automatic increase in the upswing, or a secular increase in response to growth might generate a fiscal drag (*Economic Report of the President*, 1962; Heller, 1967).

*The neoclassical model*
The economic experience of World War II, with its massive growth in the budget and rise in GNP, had demonstrated the powers of expansionary

policy under wartime conditions, and during the 1940s thinking about post-war policy projected a continued need for expansionary fiscal measures. As it turned out, the post-war decades produced a much stronger economy, and with it reinstated monetary policy as an effective policy tool. The approximate mix of fiscal and monetary policy was examined in the context of a 'neoclassical' policy model, designed to accommodate both monetary and fiscal policy variables and to allow for the effects of unbalanced budgets (deficit or surplus) on the structure of claims (Samuelson, 1951). Various degrees of monetary and fiscal tightness (or ease) could be combined to achieve the same level of aggregate demand but they would differ in the resulting mix of consumption and investment with a tight fiscal and easy money mix more favourable to growth. There would also be a difference in balance of payment effects, with the tight money and easy fiscal mix yielding the more favourable results. Adding selective instruments when needed, policy tools would be adequate, if wisely used, to achieve various macro policy goals.

The high point of optimism regarding the New Economics (Heller, 1967) and the powers of stabilisation policy was reached in the first *Economic Report* of the Kennedy Administration (1962) and the recovery following the tax cuts of 1964. Thereafter, the changing economic scene, with its shift in concern from unemployment to stagflation, produced a setting less favourable to the powers of fiscal policy. With it, changing perspectives on macro theory and the ensuing monetarist–fiscalist debate called for reconsideration of earlier tenets. Thus a new chapter was opened, but one which extends beyond the timespan of this essay.

## Public debt

The economics of public debt, the final topic to be considered here, has been among the most controversial parts of fiscal doctrine. In some measure, this reflects its strategic role in fiscal politics. Resort to debt finance is said to facilitate spending, remove public outlays from taxpayer control, and burden the future. The very proposition that the rules of prudence in private debt accumulation may not apply to the public sector offends, as noted before, the image of a natural order based on the rules of the market. But beyond this, subtle problems of economic analysis arise, problems which are still (or better, again) at a debatable stage.

### Debt burden and future generations

Central to the debate is the issue whether the burden of the debt is paid for by future generations. The mercantilists thought not. Credit was viewed as a creation of wealth and outstanding debt was no burden. As stated by Melon (1734), an associate of John Law, public debts, if domestically owed, are debts which the 'right hand owes to the left'. Pintus, Voltaire and Condorcet took similar positions. The growth of French and British debts in the eighteenth century, however, produced a more critical view. Thus Montesquieu and Hume rejected Melon's proposition as specious

(Hume, 1742). Smith (1776, vol. I, pp. 410–412) similarly rejected the transfer argument as 'sophistry of the mercantile system' as well as the mercantilist view that the national debt is an addition to the nation's capital. Debt finance may be needed in wartime, or on other special occasions, but tax finance is to be the general rule. Tax finance will be drawn largely from funds otherwise used in the employment of unproductive labour, whereas loan finance will divert funds from the maintenance of productive labour, thus impairing the country's capital stock (Smith, 1776, vol. II, p. 410). Moreover, the burden of tax finance is felt at once, thus creating taxpayer resistance and providing protection against public waste.

Ricardo's contribution to debt theory has regained recent attention as the 'Ricardian equivalence theorem'. Hidden in a chapter on commodity taxes in the *Principles* (1817, p. 244) and restated in his essay on the *Funding System* (1820, p. 187), he offered this intriguing contribution to debt theory: Suppose, so he argues, that £20 million has to be raised to pay for the expenses of a year's war. In the case of tax finance, let a particular individual be called upon to pay £2000, or 1/10,000 thereof. In the case of loan finance, and with interest of 5 per cent, £1 million per annum must be paid in interest to the lenders. Of this, our taxpayer is asked to pay £100. Under tax finance, he could have borrowed from the same lenders to finance his tax of £2000, being left once more with an annual charge of £100. From the taxpayer's point of view, the two methods are therefore equivalent.

Put in modern terms, Ricardo concludes that the taxpayer in the loan finance case discounts his future tax liability and finds his net worth reduced as it would be under tax finance. 'In point of economy', there is no real difference 'between the two modes' (1820, p. 186). The burden of the war is paid for by the taxpayer during the year in which it is financed, be it in his role of paying £2000 at once or as assuming a tax obligation of £100 per annum. Future interest payments, therefore, are only transfers among the future generation and impose no burden.

But having posed this argument as holding 'in economy'—meaning, we take it, on the assumption of perfect foresight and rational behaviour— Ricardo hastens to reject it as unrealistic. Asked to pay the full £2000 in the case of tax finance, the taxpayer will endeavour at once to 'save speedily' that amount from his income. Under loan finance, he has to pay only £100, and will thus 'consider that he does enough' by saving this lesser sum 'and then deludes himself with the belief that he is as rich as before'. In short, 'loan finance is a system which tends to make us less thrifty—to blind us to our real situation' (1817, p. 247).

Tax and loan finance both involve the diversion of resources to wasteful use, but they differ in their effect on capital formation and hence on the position of future generations. Saving and capital formation are reduced as tax finance is replaced by loan finance, and the future generation *is* burdened by having a lower income. Ricardo's rejection of the equivalence theorem could not be more explicit, and it is strange that the equivalence theorem could now be presented under his banner (Shoup, 1960; Driscoll, 1977).

The economics of public debt also received lively attention among continental authors. German writers, tending towards a more favourable view of the public sector, saw the growth of public debt with less alarm. Dietzel (1855), impressed with the economic advance of Great Britain, attributed it to the rapid growth of public debt. Equating growth of public debt with public capital formation, he viewed the former as a sign of growing national wealth. Public capital formation, moreover, would include not only the real but also the 'immaterial' capital of the state, such as the existence of legal institutions. Notwithstanding his over enthusiastic view of state outlays, he anticipated future thought by calling for loan finance in the case of capital and tax finance in the case of current outlays. A similar, though more cautious support, of public debt was advanced by Wagner (1883, p. 184), whose views on the growth of public expenditures we previously encountered. The Italian literature of the 1890s—that decade of flourishing fiscal theory—accepted and elaborated upon the Ricardian equivalence theme (de Viti de Marco, 1893); and, for a review of the Italian literature, Buchanan (1960). The leading French, British and American texts (Leroy-Beaulieu, 1906; Bastable, 1892; Adams, 1892), however, adhered to the view that debt finance reduces private capital formation and thus places a burden on future generations by reducing the capital stock which is bequeathed to them.

This view was shaken by the impact of Keynesian economics. Not only would creation of debt be a necessary by-product of fiscal expansion needed to secure high employment, but outstanding debt would pose no serious subsequent problem. The old doctrine that interest payments constitute a transfer from the right to the left hand now reappeared as 'we owe it to ourselves'. Public debt, so Lerner (1948) argued, differs from private debt because the latter is owed 'to others' whereas the former is owed to citizens of the 'same nation'. Creation of national debt, therefore, is no subtraction from national wealth, nor do interest payments by members of a future generation reduce the national income of that generation.

To be sure, tax finance of interest payments might induce burdensome disincentives and dead-weight losses. But, so Lerner argued, tax finance of interest charges is not needed, since interest payments may in turn be loan financed. Tax finance becomes necessary only after interest payments become so large, relative to earnings, that further loan finance would become inflationary. At this point, a large national debt might become a serious problem, but he did not think this situation likely to arise. The wealth effect of growing debt reduces the propensity to save and thus terminates the need for further debt expansion, leading to an equilibrium level of public debt at full employment.

Essential to this view of debt and interest burdens is the assumption of an underemployment economy which calls for aggregate demand to be raised by fiscal expansion. Government borrowing activates funds (recall our earlier reference to Sir John Steuart), but does not reduce private investment. Hence there are no depressing effects on future generations by leaving it with a reduced capital stock. Given an extreme Keynesian model with fixed investment and excess saving, this conclusion follows, just as the opposite conclusion (that loan finance burdens future generations) is appropriate for a full-employment model.

While the case for deficit finance (increase in debt) came to be accepted as an appropriate employment policy, concern with the burden of interest service and its effects on future generations continued. This fear was allayed, however, by the proposition that interest burden was a function of the ratio of interest bill to GNP, rather than its absolute level. Given a constant ratio of deficit to GNP and constant yields, the ratio of interest bill to GNP also approaches a constant level (Domar, 1944).

Subsequent discussion returned the argument to a full-employment setting. Attack on the 'new orthodoxy' (i.e. the 'we owe it to ourselves' proposition) was led by Buchanan's (1958) subjective approach. There can be no initial burden, so he argued, since lenders are not called upon to contribute anything. Thus no burden is imposed in the initial period. Future taxpayers, however, are burdened by having to finance interest payments. Thus burden transfer occurs. Others continued to stress reduced capital formation and the burden which it imposes as the future generation as a whole is left with a reduced capital stock (Shoup, 1962). With future tax payments needed to finance interest service equal to the loss of capital income, the two formulations yield essentially similar results.

The difference between loan and tax finance was thus left to depend on resulting differences in resource withdrawal from consumption and capital formation. (For major contributions to this debate, see Ferguson, 1964). The fact that loan finance may involve burden transfer, however, is not necessarily an argument against it. In the context of public capital formation, transfer of burden via loan finance may serve as an instrument of intergeneration equity and a rationale for a capital budget approach (Musgrave, 1959, p. 562). A further equity-oriented case for loan finance may arise in the context of war finance, where the use of 'refundable taxes' permits a post-war correction of inevitably heavy wartime burdens on low income groups (Keynes, 1939).

*Public debt and liquidity structure*

Apart from the differential implications of tax and loan finance, much attention was given during the 1940s and 1950s to how an outstanding debt should be managed. The two major issues were the choice between marketable and non-marketable bonds, and the maturity structure of the debt. With the former essentially a question of distributional outcome, the latter led into the linkage between fiscal and monetary theory. With issuance of debt viewed as a purchase of liquidity, the Treasury should choose between short- and long-term issues so as to minimise the cost of securing a given reduction in liquidity (Rolph, 1957). Short-term debt, being closer in nature to money, would buy less illiquidity than long-term debt and hence be worth more to the Treasury.

The proposition that debt issue reduces liquidity was questioned, however, as debt policy came to be viewed in the context of general portfolio choice (Tobin, 1963). Moreover, attention was given to the fact that the choice of maturities so as to minimise interest cost involves not only the prevailing term structure of rates, but also anticipation of future changes therein (Smith, 1970). Finally, there was the question of how maturity structures of different lengths would affect the stability of the market. Long-term debt would avoid the hassles of refinancing but would result in larger fluctuations in the market value of outstanding bonds, thereby increasing the risk of 'disorderly conditions', especially in the case of monetary restrictions. With the drastic shortening of the debt in the post-war decade, these issues which once were lively topics have largely disappeared from the discussion.

## CONCLUSION

This closes our account of the evolution of fiscal theory. Over the two centuries here surveyed, the economics of public finance has grown enormously both in breadth and sophistication, moving with and benefiting from the growth of economic analysis at large, but also contributing thereto. This growth, however, has been far from linear, with insights cropping up, dropping out, and reappearing when their time had come. But great progress has been made. Yet, the basic problems have remained the same. The questions of what public services should be provided, how they should be financed, and what role government should play in the macro conduct of economic affairs were visible to Adam Smith, and they still pose the basic problem.

So does the fact that many issues in public finance remain inherently controversial. To establish the economic case for the public sector is to delimit the sphere that can be left to the invisible hand and the rules of the market. The scope of existing externalities, the acceptability of a market-determined income distribution, the shape of the social welfare function, maintaining full resource utilisation, the issues of inflation and growth, all these have powerful bearings on the appropriate size and activities of the public sector. So does the capability of public policy to apply appropriate corrections, with the scope of public policy failure matched against that of market failure. Given this array of problems and their linkages, ideological and value issues are never far away. Moreover, the tools of fiscal policy changes with changing fiscal institutions. It is not surprising, therefore, that the history of fiscal doctrine deals with more than the development of economic analysis *per se*. To this writer at least, that adds to rather than detracts from the fascination of our subject.

## NOTES

1. Among histories of fiscal doctrine, see Seligman (1908; 1909), Myrdal (1929), Mann (1937) and Groves (1974). For selected readings, see Musgrave and Peacock (eds) (1958), and Musgrave and Shoup (eds) (1959).

2. See ch. 16 above.
3. For references to these authors and excerpts translated from their major works, see Musgrave and Peacock (eds) (1958), see ch. 14 above.
4. For excerpts see Musgrave and Peacock (1958).
5. See also ch. 20 above.
6. Smith throughout argues that a tax on wages or products would raise prices 'in a higher proportion' than the rate of tax (Smith, 1776, vol. II, p. 349), and thus impose an additional burden on the landlord or rich consumer. One reason is that a tax of 10 per cent imposed on the gross wage must raise the gross wage by 11 per cent to keep the net wage from falling. True enough, but hardly a reason to conclude that the real burden of the tax is increased. Another reason is that the producer will charge a profit on the funds needed to advance the tax, thus resulting in what is later referred to as 'tax spiralling'.
7. For a penetrating discussion of the Ricardian incidence analysis, see Shoup (1960).
8. Ricardo further notes that the overall demand for labour remains unchanged with the introduction of the tax. While demand based on capitalist consumption and investment falls, increased government demand takes its place. Thus the wage bill net of tax remains constant.
9. Ricardo's argument might be interpreted thus: Suppose that before tax wages equal $80 and profits equal $20. Expenditures on necessities equal $80 and investment plus capitalists' consumption equal $20. After a tax of $10 is introduced, gross wages rise to $90, net wages remain at $80, and profits fall to $10. Expenditures on necessities, equal to net wages, remain at $80, outlays on capitalists' consumption and investment fall to $10, and government outlays rise to $10. The total remains at $100 and prices are unchanged.

   One wonders what would happen to Ricardo's argument if government outlays were made for 'productive consumption'. In that case, wages could remain constant, permitting a decline in net wages. There would no longer be a need for the tax to fall on profits! Due to the peculiarity of the Ricardian model (holding the net wage bill fixed in real terms), incidence thus depends directly on how the revenue is used.
10. For a review of this development, see Stigler (1941).
11. It may be noted that this version first appears in the third edition (1889) prior to which the tax was assigned entirely to consumers (Walras, 1874, p. 609).
12. Page references are to the 9th edition.

# REFERENCES

Adams, H.C. (1899) *The Science of Finance* (New York, Holt).

Arrow, K. (1951), *Social Choice and Individual Values* (New York, Wiley).

Auerbach, A.J. and D.W. Jorgenson (1980), 'Inflation-proof depreciation of assets', *Harvard Business Review*, 58.

Barone, E. (1899), About some fundamental theorems on the mathematical theory of taxation', *Giornale degli Economisti*, Serv. 2, 4.

Bastable, C.F. (1892), *Public Finance*, 3rd edn, 1903 (London, Macmillan).

Baumol, W.J. and W. Oates (19175), *The Theory of Environmental Policy* (Englewood Cliffs, N.J., Prentice-Hall).

Bentham, J. (1902), *Principles of the Civil Code*. Reprinted in J. Bentham (1931)

*The Theory of Legislation*, ed. C.K. Odgen, (London, Kegan Paul).

Bergson, A. (1938), 'A reformulation of certain aspects of welfare economics', *Quarterly Journal of Economics*, 52.

Beveridge, W.H. (1945), *Full Employment in a Free Society* (New York, Norton).

Black, D. (1948), 'On the rationale of group decision-making', *Journal of Political Economy*, 56.

Borcherding, T.E. (1977), *Budgets and Bureaucrats* (Durham, N.C., Duke University Press).

Break, G.F. (1957), 'Income taxes and incentives to work: An empirical study', *American Economic Review*, 47.

—— (1974), 'The incidence and economic effects of taxation', in *The Economics of Public Finance* (Washington, D.C., Brookings Institution).

Bowen, H. (1948), *Toward Social Economy* (New York, Rinehart).

Brown, E.C. (1948), 'Business-income taxation and investment incentives', in *Income, Employment, and Public Policy* (New York, Norton).

Brown, H.G. (1924), *The Economics of Taxation* (New York, Henry Holt).

—— (1929), *Economic Science and the Common Welfare* (Columbia, MT, Lucas).

Buchanan, J. (1959), *Public Principles of Public Debt* (Homewood, Ill., Irwin).

—— (1961), 'Fiscal institution and collective outlay', *American Economic Review*, 51.

—— (1965),'An economic theory of clubs', *Economica*, 32.

—— (1975), *The Limits of Liberty* (Chicago, Chicago University Press).

Buchanan, J. and Tullock, G. (1962), *The Calculus of Consent*, (Ann Arbor, University of Michigan Press).

Canard, F. (1801), *Principles d'economie politique* (Paris).

Chamberlin, E.H. (1938), *The Theory of Monopolistic Competition*, 3rd edn (Cambridge, Mass., Harvard University Press).

Clark, J.M. (1935), *Economics of Planning Public Works* (Washington, D.C.), National Resources Committee.

Coase, R.H. (1974), 'The lighthouse in economics', *Journal of Law and Economics*, 17.

Coates, A.M. (1927), 'Incidence of the income tax', Appendices to the Report of the Commission on National Debt and Taxation (London, HMSO).

Cohen, Stuart, A.J. (1889), *Bijdrage tot de Theorie der Progressive Inkomsteuerbelasting* (The Hague); see also Musgrave and Peacock (1958).

Colm, G. (1940), 'Full employment through tax policy', *Social Research*, 7.

Colm, G. and H. Tarasov (1940), *Who Pays the Taxes?* (Washington, D.C., Temporary National Economic Committee).

Committee for Economic Development (1947), *Taxes and the Budget: a program for prosperity in a free society* (New York); see also Smities and Butters (1955).

Corlett, W.J. and D.C. Hague (1953–54), 'Complementarity and the excess burden of taxation', *Review of Economic Studies*, Ser. 1, 2, no. 54.

Cournot, A. (1838), *Recherches sur les principes mathématiques de la théorie des richesses* (Paris, L. Hachette).

Currie, L. and M. Krost (1939), 'Explanation of computing net contribution', Mimeo (Washington, D.C., Board of Governors of the Federal Reserve System).

Demsetz, H. (1970), 'The private production of public goods', *Journal of Law and Economics*, 13.

Diamond, P. and J.A. Mirlees (1971), 'Taxation and public production I: Production and efficiency, and II: Tax rules', *American Economic Review*, 61.

Dietzel, C. (1885), *Das System der Staatsanleihen im Zusammenhang der Volkwirtschaft betrachtet* (Heidelberg).

Domar, E.D. (1954), 'The burden of the debt and the national income', *American Economic Review*, 34.

—— and R.A. Musgrave (1944), 'Proportional income taxation and risk-taking', *Quarterly Journal of Economics*, 58.

Downs, A. (1956), *An Economic Theory of Democracy* (New York, Harper).

Dupuit, J. (1944), *De la mesure de l'utilité des travaux publics*. Reprinted in *De l'utilité et de sa mesure: Écrits choisis et republiés par Mario de Bernardi* (Turin, La Riforma Sociale). English translation in *International Economic Review*, 2 (1952).

Eckstein, O. (1961), 'A survey of the theory of public expenditure criteria', in J. Buchanan (ed.) *Public finances: Needs, sources, and utilization* (Princeton, N.J., Princeton University Press). Economic Report of the President, 1962 (Washington, D.C., Government Printing Office).

Edgeworth, F.Y. (1897), 'The pure theory of taxation', *Economic Journal*, 7. Reprinted in: *Papers Relating to Political Economy*, vol. II (London, Macmillan).

Einaudi, L. (1912), *Intorno al concetto di reddito imponibile e di un sistema d'imposte sul viddita consummato* (Turin).

Fagan, E.D. and R.W. Jastram (1939), 'Tax shifting in the short run'. *Quarterly Journal of Economics*, 53.

Feldstein, M. (1969), 'The effects of taxation on risk-taking', *Journal of Political Economy*, 77.

—— (1974a), 'Financing in the evaluation of public expenditures', in W.L. Smith and J.M. Culbertson (eds), *Public Finance and Stabilization Policy: Essays in the honour of Alvin Hansen* (Amsterdam, North-Holland).

—— (1974b), 'Tax incidence in a growing economy with variable factor supply', *Quarterly Journal of Economics*, 88.

Ferguson, J.M. (ed.) (1964), *Public Debt and Future Generations* (Durham, N.C., University of North Carolina Press).

Fisher, I. (1906), *Nature of Capital and Income* (New York, Macmillan).

—— and H.W. Fisher (1942), *Constructive Income Taxation* (New York, Harper).

Friedman, M. (1948), 'A monetary and fiscal framework for economic stability', *American Economic Review*, 38.

Gelting, J.H. (1941), 'Some observations on the financing of the public activity', reprinted in *History of Political Economy*, 7 (1975).

George, H. (1880), *Progress and Poverty*, 1954 edn (New York, R. Schalkenbach Foundation).

Goldscheid, R. (1917), *Finanzsoziologie* (Wien); see also Musgrave and Peacock (eds) (1958).

Gossen, H. (1854), *Entwicklung der Gesetze des menschlichen Verkehrs*, 1927 edn by F. Hayek (Berlin, Praeger).

Groves, H.M. (1974), *Tax Philosophers*, ed. D.J. Curran (Madison, University of Wisconsin Press).

Haavelmo, T. (1945), 'Effects of a balanced budget', *Econometrica*, 13.

Haig, R.M. (1921), 'The concept of income', in *The Federal Income Tax* (New York, Columbia University Press).

Hansen, A.H. (1927), *Business Cycle Theory* (Boston, Ginn & Co.).

—— (1939), 'Economic progress and declining population growth', *American Economic Review*, 29.

—— (1941), *Fiscal Policy and Business Cycles* (New York, Norton).

—— 1945), 'Three modes of expansion through fiscal policy', *American Economic Review*, 35.

Harberger, A.C. (1962), 'The incidence of the corporation income tax', *Journal of Political Economy*, 70; see also A.C. Harberger, *Taxation and Welfare* (Boston, Little, Brown).

—— (1969), 'The opportunity cost of public investment financed by borrowing, reprinted in R. Layard (ed.) *Cost-benefit Analysis* (Baltimore, Penguin Books).

—— (1974), *Taxation and Welfare* (Boston, Little, Brown).

—— (1980), Tax neutrality in investment incentives in: H.J. Aaron and M. Boskin (eds), *The Economics of Taxation* (Washington, D.C., Brookings Institution).

—— and M.J. Bailey (eds) (1969), *The Taxation of Income from Capital* (Washington, D.C., Brookings Institution).

Hasyanyi, J.C. (1955), 'Cardinal welfare, individualistic ethics and interpersonal comparison of utilities', *Journal of Political Economy*, 63.

Heller, W. (1967), *New Dimensions of Fiscal Policy* (New York, Norton).

Hicks, J.R. (1939), *Value and Capital* (Oxford, Oxford University Press).

Hicks, U. (1947), *Public Finance* (New York, Pitman).

Hobbes, T. (1651), *Leviathan* (Baltimore, Penguin Classics).

Hotelling, H. (1938), 'The general welfare in relation to problems of taxation and utility rates', *Econometrica*, 6.

Hume, D. (1739), *A Treatise on Human Nature*, 1975 edn by L.A. Selby-Bidge (Oxford, Clarendon Press).

—— (1758), 'Of public credit', in *Essays, Moral, Political and Literary*, vol. I, 1882, edn (London).

Inman, R.P. (1978), 'The fiscal performance of local governments. An interpretative review' in P. Mieszkowski and M. Straszhein (eds). *Current Issues in Urban Economics* (Baltimore, Johns Hopkins University Press).

Jenkin, F. (1871–2), 'On the principles which regulate the incidence of taxes', in *Proceedings of the Royal Society of Edinburgh*. Reprinted in Musgrave and Shoup (eds) (1959).

Kaldor, N. (1955), *An Expenditure Tax* (London, Allen & Unwin).

—— et al. (1955), 'Memorandum of Dissent', in *Royal Commission on the Taxation of Profits and Income* (London, HMSO).

Kay, J.A. and M.A. King (1978), *The British Tax System* (Oxford, Oxford University Press).

Keynes, J.M. (1936), *The General Theory of Employment, Interest, and Money* (Harcourt, Brace).

—— (1939), 'Paying for the War', *The Times*, 14 and 15 November. Reprinted in New York, D. Muggridge (ed.) (1978), *The Collected Writing of J.M. Keynes*, vol. 22 (Cambridge, Cambridge University Press).

Klein, L.R. and A.S. Goldberger (1955), *An Econometric Model of the United States, 1929–1952* (Amsterdam, North-Holland).

Krzyaniak, M. (1967), 'The long-run burden of a general tax on profits in a neoclassical world', *Public Finance, Finances Publiques*, no. 4.

Layard, R. (1972), Introduction in *Cost-benefit Analysis* (Baltimore, Penguin Books).

Lerner, A.P. (1944), *The Economics of Control* (New York, Macmillan).

—— (1948), 'The burden of the national debt', in *Income, Employment, and Public Policy: Essays in honour of Alvin Hansen* (New York, W.W. Norton).

Leroy-Beaulieu, P. (1906), *Traité de la science finances*, vol. II, 7th edn (Paris).

Lindahl, E. (1919), *Die Gerechtigkeit der Besteuerung* (Lund, Gleerupska Universitets Bokhandeln).

—— (1928), *Einige strittige Fragen der Steuertheorie*, in Hans Mayer (ed.), *Die Wirtschaftstheorie der Gegenwart*, vol. IV (Vienna); see also Musgrave and Peacock (eds) (1958).

Little, I.M.D. (1951), 'Direct vs. indirect taxes', *Economic Journal*, 61. Reprinted in Musgrave and Shoup (eds) (1959).

Locke, J. (1690), *Two Treatises on Government*, 1960 edn by Peter Lasset (Cambridge, Mentor Book, Cambridge University Press).

Mann, F.K. (1937), *Steuerpolitische Ideale* (Jena, G. Fisher).

Marglin, S. (1963), 'The opportunity costs of public investment', *Quarterly Journal of Economics*, 77.

Malthus, T.R. (1836), 'Principles of political economy', reprinted in *1964 Economic Classics* (New York, A.M. Kelley).

Marshall, A. (1890), *Principles of Economics*, 8th ed. (London, Macmillan).

—— (1917), 'The equitable distribution of taxation', reprinted in A.C. Pigou (ed.) (1925), *Memorials of Alfred Marshall* (London, Macmillan).

McCord Wright, D. (1942), *The Creation of Purchasing Power* (Cambridge, Mass., Harvard University Press).

McCulloch, J.R. (1845), *A Treatise on the Principles and Practical Influence of Taxation and the Funding System* (London, Longman, Brown).

Meade, J.E. (1955), 'The effects of indirect taxation upon the distribution of income', in *Trade and welfare*, vol. II (Oxford, Oxford University Press).

Mazzola, U. (1890), *I dati scientifici della finanza pubblica*, Rome. See also sections on [110].

Mering, O., von (1942), *The Shifting and Incidence of Taxation* (Philadelphia, Blakiston).

Metzler, L.A. (1948), 'Three lags in the circular flow of income, in *Income, Employment and Public Policy: Essays in honour of Alvin Hansen* (New York, W.W. Norton).

Mieszkowski, P. (1969), 'Tax incidence theory: The effects of taxes on the distribution of income', *Journal of Economic Literature*, 7.

—— (1972), 'The property tax: An excise tax or a profits tax', *Journal of Public Economics*, 2.

Mill, J.S. (1848), *Principles of Political Economy*, new edn by W.J. Ashley (London, Longman, Green). Also reprinted in *Reprints of Economic Classics* (New York, A.M. Kelley, 1965).

Mueller, D.C. (1979), *Public Choice* (Cambridge, Cambridge University Press).

Musgrave, R. (1938), 'The voluntary exchange theory of public economy', *Quarterly Journal of Economics*, 53.

—— (1945), 'Alternative budgets for full employment', *American Economic Review*, 35.

—— (1959), *The Theory of Public Finance* (New York, McGraw-Hill).

—— (1969a), 'Cost-benefit analysis in the theory of public finance', *Journal of Economic Literature*, 7.

—— (1969b), 'Provision for social goods', in J. Margolis and A. Guilton (eds), *Public Economics* (London, Macmillan).

—— and P.B. Musgrave (1973), *Public Finance in Theory and Practice* (New York, McGraw-Hill).

—— and A.T. Peacock (eds) (1958), *Classics in the Theory of Public Finance* (London, Macmillan).

——— and C.S. Shoup (eds) (1959), *Readings in the Economics of Taxation* (Homewood, Ill., Irwin).

——— *et al.* (1951), 'Distribution of tax payments by income groups: A case study for 1945', *National Tax Journal*, 4.

———., K.E. Case and H. Leonard, 1974, The distribution of fiscal burdens and benefits, *Public Finance Quarterly*, 2.

Myrdal, G. (1929), *The Political Element in the Development of Economic Theory*, 1953 English translation (London, Routledge).

Neumark, F. (1947), *Theorie und Praxis der modernen Einkommensbesteuerung* (Bern, A. Francke).

Niskanen, W.A. (1974), *Bureaucracy and Representative Government* (Chicago, Aldine).

Nozick, R. (1974), *Anarchy, State and Utopia* (New York, Basic Books).

Oakland, W. (1972), 'Congestion, public goods, and welfare', *Journal of Public Economics*, 1.

Oates, W. (1972), *Fiscal Federalism* (New York, Harcourt, Brace).

Panteleoni, M. (1883), *Contributo alla teoriea del ripurto delli spese pubbliche*, *Rassegna Italiana*. Reprinted in M. Panteleoni, *Scritti varii de economia*, vol. I.

Peacock, A.T. and R.A. Musgrave (eds) (1958), *Classics in the Theory of Public Finance* (London, Macmillan).

Pechman, J. (ed.) (1980), *What Should be Taxed: Income or expenditures? (Washington, D.C., The Brookings Institution)*.

Pechman, J. and B.A. Okner (1974), *Who Bears the Tax Burden?* (Washington, D.C., The Brookings Institution).

Petty, Sir W. (1662), *A Treatise of Taxes and Contributions* in C.H. Hull (ed.) (1899), *The Economic Writings of Sir William Petty* (Cambridge, The University Press).

Pigou, A.C. (1920), *The Economics of Welfare* (London, Macmillan).

——— (1928), *A Study in Public Finance* (London, Macmillan).

Prest, A.R. (1955), 'Statistical calculations of tax burdens', *Economica*, 22.

——— (1975), *Public Finance in Theory and Practice* (London, Weidenfeld Nicholson).

Quesnay, (1760, 1762), *Le tableau Économique*, and *Théorie de l'impôt*. See August Oncken (ed.) (1888), *Oeuvres économiques et philosophiques de François Quesnay* (Frankfurt, J. Bear).

Ramsey, F. (1927), 'A contribution to the theory of taxation', *Economic Journal*, 37.

Ricardo, D. (1817), 'The principles of political economy and taxation, in Pierro Sraffa (ed.) (1962), *The Works and Correspondence of David Ricardo*, vol. I (Cambridge, Cambridge University Press).

——— (1820), 'Funding system', in Pierro Sraffa (ed.) (1962), *The Works and Correspondence of David Ricardo*, vol. IV (Cambridge, Cambridge University Press).

Robbins, L. (1932), *An Essay on the Nature and Significance of Economic Science* (London, Macmillan).

——— (1938), Interperson comparison of utility, *Economic Journal*, 48.

Robinson, J. (1933), *The Economics of Imperfect Competition* (London, Macmillan).

Rolph, E.R. (1957), 'Principles of debt management', *American Economic Review*, 50.

Salant, Walter, W. (1975), Introduction to William A. Salant's *Taxes, the multiplier, and the inflationary gap, History of Political Economy*, 7.

—— (1942), 'Taxes, the multiplier, and the inflationary gap'. Reprinted in *History of Political Economy*, 7 (1975).

Sax, E. (1893), *Grundlegung der Theoretischen Staatswirtschaft* (Wien).

Samuelson, P.A. (1939), 'Interactions between multiplier analysis and the principle of acceleration', *Review of Economics and Statistics*, 21.

—— (1945), *Foundations of Economic Analysis* (Cambridge, Mass., Harvard University Press).

—— (1948), 'The simple mathematics of income determination', in *Income, Employment, and Public Policy: Essays in honour of Alvin Hansen* (New York, W.W. Norton).

—— (1954), 'The pure theory of public expenditures', *Review of Economics and Statistics*, 36.

—— (1955a), 'Principles and rules in modern fiscal policy: A neoclassical reformulation', in *Money, Trade, and Economic Growth: Essays in honour of J.H. Williams* (New York, Macmillan).

—— (1955b), 'Diagrammatic exposition of a theory of public expenditure', *Review of Economics and Statistics*, 32.

—— (1964), 'Tax deductability of economic depreciation to insure invariant valuations', *Journal of Political Economy*, 72.

—— (1969), 'Pure theory of public expenditures and taxation, *Public Economics*, ed. Margolis, J. and Guitton, H. (London, Macmillan).

Schäffle, A. (1867), *Das gesellschaftliche System der menschlichen Wirschaft* (Tübingen).

Schanz, G. (1896), Der Einkommensbegriff und die Einkommensteuergeseteze, Finanzarchiv 13.

Schumpeter, J. (1918), 'Die Krise des Steuerstaates', in *Zeitfragen aus dem Gebiete der Soziologie* (Graz). English translation in *International Economic Papers 5* (London, 1954).

—— (1954), *History of Economic Analysis* (New York, Oxford University Press).

Seligman, E.R. (1908), 'Progressive taxation in theory and practice', *American Economic Association Quarterly* (New York).

—— (1911), *The Income Tax* (New York, Macmillan).

—— (1899), *Incidence of Taxation*, 4th edn, 1921 (New York, Macmillan).

Shepherd, R.W. (1944), 'A mathematical theory of the incidence of taxation', *Econometrica*, 12.

Shoup, C.S. (1960), *Ricardo on Taxation* (New York, Columbia University Press).

—— and R.A. Musgrave (eds) (1959), *Readings in the Economics of Taxation* (Homewood, Ill., Irwin).

Shoven, J. and J. Whalley (1984), 'Applied general equilibrium models of taxation and international trade', *Journal of Economic Literature* 3, XXII.

Sidgwick, H. (1883), *The Principles of Political Economy* (London, Macmillan).

Smith, Adam (1759), *The Theory of Moral Sentiments*. 1969 edn by G. West (Indianapolis, Liberty Classics).

—— (1776), *An Inquiry into the Wealth of Nations*, 1904 edn by E. Cannan (New York, Putnam).

Smith, W.L. (1970), *Macroeconomics*, (Homewood, Ill., Irwin).

Smithies, A. and J.K. Butters (eds) (1955), *Readings in Fiscal Policy* (Homewood Ill., Irwin).

Simons, H. (1948), *Economic Policy for a Free Society* (Chicago, University of Chicago Press).

———— (1953), *Personal Income Taxation* (Chicago, University of Chicago Press).

Solow, R.M. (1956), 'A contribution to the theory of economic growth', *Quarterly Journal of Economics*, 70.

Steuart, Sir James (1776), *An Inquiry into the Principles of Political Economy*, 1966 edn by A.R. Skinner (Chicago, University of Chicago Press).

Tiebout, W. (1956), 'A pure theory of local government expenditures', *Journal of Political Economy*, 64.

Tobin, J. (1958), 'Liquidity preference as behaviour towards risk', *Review of Economic Studies*, 25.

———— (1963), 'An essay in principles of debt management', in Commission on Money and Credit, (ed.), *Fiscal and Debt Management Policies* (Englewood Cliffs, N.J., Prentice-Hall).

Tullock, G. and Buchanan, J. (1962), *The Calculus of Consent* (Ann Arbor, University of Michigan Press).

Vickrey, W. (1947), *Agenda for Progressive Taxation* (New York, The Ronald Press).

# Acknowledgements

I am grateful to the editors and publishers of the following journals and books for permission to reproduce the articles which appear in this volume: McGraw-Hill Book Company for material from *The Theory of Public Finance, The Princeton Symposium on The American System of Social Insurance* and *Paul Samuelson and Modern Economic Theory*; Princeton University Press for material from *Public Finances: Needs, Sources and Utilization*; *Nebraska Journal of Economics and Business*; University of Toronto Press for material from *Modern Fiscal Issues*; *National Tax Journal*; The MIT Press for material from *Social Security Financing*; Nathan Economic Advisory Group; Yale University Press for material from *Fiscal Systems*; Harvard Law School for material from *Fiscal Reform for Columbia*; University of Florida Press for material from *Fiscal Policy for Industrialization and Development in Latin America*; The Brookings Institution for material from *The Economics of Taxation*; The Urban Institute Press for material from *Tax and Expenditure Limitations*; Macmillan Publishing Co. Inc. for material from *Classics in the Theory of Public Finance*; *Quarterly Journal of Economics*; Oxford University Press for material from *The Market and the State, Essays in Honour of Adam Smith*; University of Michigan Press for material from *Economics and the World Around It*; *Public Finance, Finances Publiques*; The University of Wisconsin Press for material from *State and Local Finance: The Pressure of the Eighties*; *Harvard Law Review*; Elsevier Science Publishers B.V. for material from *Handbook of Public Economics*.

# Index of Names

# Index of Subjects